W9-AEV-461

NUMBER THIRTY-SIX

The Centennial Series of the Association of Former Students,
Texas A&M University

SAN ANTONIO, 1929–1941

·

Richard A. Garcia

FOREWORD BY HENRY C. SCHMIDT

·

Texas A&M University Press
College Station

Wingate College Library

Copyright © 1991 by Richard A. Garcia
Manufactured in the United States of America
All rights reserved
First edition

The paper used in this book meets the minimum requirements
of the American National Standard for Permanence
of Paper for Printed Library Materials, Z39.48-1984.
Binding materials have been chosen for durability.

LIBRARY OF CONGRESS
CATALOGING-IN-PUBLICATION DATA

Garcia, Richard A., 1941–
  Rise of the Mexican American middle class :
San Antonio, 1929–1941 / Richard A. Garcia ;
foreword by Henry C. Schmidt. — 1st ed.
      p.   cm. — (The Centennial series of the
Association of Former Students, Texas A&M
University ; no. 36)
    Includes bibliographical references and index.
    ISBN 0-89096-368-1 (alk. paper)
    1. Mexican Americans—Texas—San
Antonio—History—20th century.   2. Middle
classes—Texas—San Antonio—History—20th
century.   3. San Antonio (Tex.)—History.
I. Title.   II. Series.
F394.S2G37   1991
976.4'3510046872073—dc20   90-38788
                                                    CIP

Contents

there was the sensitive voice of folklorist Américo Paredes, explaining the story of a ballad that seemed like a fable, the very way some told it on the Border. During the same period historian Carlos E. Castañeda and educator George I. Sánchez asked questions about Mexican Americans that are still being addressed today. The writers of the sixties and seventies treated Mexican Americans in terms of inequity, racism, worker exploitation, and class conflict vis-à-vis Anglo American society. The eighties generation looks at Mexican Americans more holistically than its predecessors and focuses on consciousness, culture, values, morality, roots, and meaning. Richard A. Garcia's study of Mexican Americans is within this movement.

In the last quarter-century Mexican Americans have risen from the barrio to cabinet positions in Washington. Yet forms of everyday discrimination against them still exist, and the national understanding of them is incomplete. To outsiders the barrio remains isolated and mysterious, visited to eat in a restaurant on a main street, or noticed for its charros and low riders.

The barrio has received serious attention from scholars and creative writers, however, and this book joins that corpus, presenting yet different materials and viewpoints. Diverse themes — including business history, popular culture, and immigrant intellectualism — are interwoven in a dynamic of emergent acculturation and classical Mexicanism. Here we see the workers and middle and upper classes of Mexican San Antonio in the 1920s and 1930s sustaining a conservative, but mobile, order of power and status as a survival of colonial Spanish America. The dual challenge facing the community is to preserve its identity while integrating into the nation.

If there are class distinctions, there is also a shared culture. Image is less crucial to success than in Anglo American society. It is more the soul that counts, the releasing personality. In a Catholic-derived ethos, life is seen as a cosmos of joy and sorrow, which come in perceptible gradations common to all peoples, but always against a model of grace and dignity. An essentially pluralist and universalist value system is lived out in time-easing warmth, irony, and wit. *Alegría*, the sense of community and morality, idealism, and existentialism characterize this Hispanic world, which Garcia captures and interprets.

Following a deep Hispanic tradition, the author's intellectual biography is contingent upon the Mexican Americans he examines. This is not a subjective position but an enhanced relationship between the observer and the observed. In his journey through self-awareness toward fulfillment and meaning, reaching back into memory for the formation of ethnicity, seeking the cultural paradigms, analyzing personal and collective identity, author and work fuse in direct and spiritual experience. Along the way he conveys the abiding values of Mexican Americans that help make ours a richer society.

HENRY C. SCHMIDT

can American, although I did not feel *americano*, either. I answered, however, that I was Mexican American. Yet I felt a space between the Mexican and the American — and a gap between the reality of Mexican American and Chicano.

The woman's question and the turbulence of the decade were forcing me to examine the ontological spaces and gaps of my consciousness and thereby attempt to understand the ambiguities in my identity. I was almost being forced to choose and make a declaration, when I felt very uncomfortable and perplexed about my identity, as well as with the thought that maybe my identity was more complex than the choices allowed. This heightened awareness led me to the second incident, which occurred while I was searching for some commentary on this question of Chicano identity.

I came across an intriguing essay by Eliu Carranza, *Pensamientos on los Chicanos: A Cultural Revolution* (Berkeley: California Book Company, 1969). In his introduction, Carranza stated that these thoughts were offered "as an irritant, a piece of abrasive rhetoric intended not for the settlement of problems, but for the arousal of feelings and the pricking of thought." Carranza basically argued for a new humanism, beginning with Mexican Americans identifying their pluralism, their commonalities, their differences, and ending with the seeking of unity within pluralism. He further urged Mexican Americans to begin the process of "knowing themselves." of finding their own truth and reality and initiating the steps toward, as he said, "decolonization and the liberation of the Mexican-American mind by an examination of our relation to our history, tradition, and culture."

Growing up in El Paso, Texas, I had always had a sense of difference from the U.S. population in general, and from my Anglo friends
in particular, but I had never perceived it in the philosophical, political, and ideological terms that Carranza was advocating. In short,
I had never reflected on my "condition of ethnicity"— I had just lived
it, as a middle-class individual who liked tacos, tortillas, *caldos*, me-
nudo, bullfights, fiestas, and Mexican beer, and had never given any
of it much thought. Ethnicity had never been a thing in itself, it had
just been part of my world in the same manner that speaking Spanish
to my grandmother and aunt and only English to my mother had been.

Mexicans in the United States are not intellectually or culturally
homogeneous. Their history exhibits complexity of ideas and ideologies, multilayered desires and ambitions, multidimensional perceptions, and multiple realities as well as many differences in class, status, and life-style. It is obvious that there is not just one kind of
mexicano, and any attempt to state otherwise distorts personalities
and history. Octavio Romano, the Chicano intellectual and founder
of the influential journal *El Grito* (published in the late sixties and
early seventies), made a similar argument. According to him, pluralism with the retention of individualism was a key part of the Mexican and Mexican American heritage. His thesis was quickly discarded,
however, by the nationalistic and radical Chicano activists who sought
to fit all Mexicans into one identity and a common history and who
denied the U.S. reality of mobility and possibilities.

I fully believe that the study of history allows for a study of one-
self — memories, life, relationships, and personal and societal identity. This book, which concerns a generation prior to my own in a
city other than my own, is nonetheless a search for myself. I am more
aware now, after two decades of intellectual and ideological searching, that the quest for historical identity starts with self-identity.

of the Mexican American generation and who had wanted and hoped to participate in the promise of America without having to give up their ethnicity. I sought their memories, their dreams, and a view of their everyday life. Consequently, during my research in San Antonio I spent hours walking through the Mexican West Side, talking to the *viejitos* and the *viejitas*. I listened, I asked, I remembered with them. I went to the weddings, the Sunday masses, the fiestas, and their cantinas. I sought not only to know, but to understand their "consciousness of collectivity." The records, documents, newspapers, and other sources gave me the information and knowledge, and theory gave me direction and perspective, but the Mexican Americans gave me part of their understanding. Octavio Romano once said that the people in the barrio may not have the knowledge, or total understanding, but they have the memories, the spirit, and the dreams. Therefore, during my research in San Antonio, I spent countless hours in the Mexican West Side and the rest of San Antonio listening to the voices, the silences, the whispers, and the nuances of their different life-worlds: both the Anglo and Mexican voices. I listened in order to understand the Mexican Americans' heart, soul, and mind, especially the traces of their *mexicanidad* and their *americanidad.* In doing this I became aware of the complexities of the Mexican community. I became aware of the multiple temporal, spatial, cultural, social, economic, and ideational dimensions of the Mexican American community. I found a rich historical tapestry of cultural pluralism, political diversity, and a strong sense of individualism within a tradition of community.

I therefore want to thank the numerous people in San Antonio who conversed with me at the bus stops, the *bailes,* the cantinas, the fiestas, and the workplaces. These were not formal interviews. They just shared their memories, personal thoughts, and views. They helped me piece together the strands of the Mexican American thought and culture for the period I was studying and gave me a good sense of the change and continuity. They gave of their time, and some shared their personal papers. The "texts" of their lives were basic to understanding the context of the times. In my study, individuals, groups, and organizations are at the center of change, and ideas, attitudes, and beliefs are the essential indicators of the historical process as they help forge the culture and structures of the community and society. I hope Mexican Americans can read this "biography" and see some semblance of their history and their lives and community.

I especially want to thank Carmen Perry, Mrs. Jacobo Rodriguez, Manuel C. González, and Rubén Mungía for their time, thoughts, and information. They were beacons of light and true representatives of the Mexican American middle class. In addition, I want to thank the staff of the San Antonio Public Library, especially Judy Covell. I also want to thank the Chicano Studies library staff at the University of California, Berkeley, and the University of California at Los Angeles, as well as the staff at the Catholic Archives in San Antonio. My thanks are further extended to the many people who listened to my questions, my lectures, and my comments on this subject, especially students, who helped me in formulating my ideas.

Above all, I want to thank all of the Chicano historians for all their pioneering work that served as a prologue and in some cases for contributing central conceptualizations that helped enrich my work. I especially want to thank two special friends and colleagues, Mario T. Garcia and Alma M. Garcia, for all the discussions on political, intellectual, cultural, and gender questions and theory. These discussions have spanned the last decade. All three of us have shared the promises, perils, and paradoxes of American society, as well as the trial and tribulations of the Chicano discourse. We have not and still do not agree on everything, but we continue to share, I think, many of the same questions in our discourse on ethnicity, community, and society.

My thanks also to John P. Diggins, Mark Poster, Jonathan Weiner, and Spencer Olin, who helped cultivate my interest in history and theory. My special thanks to Henry C. Schmidt for his work on Mexican culture and thought and for agreeing to write the preface of this work.

To my mother and father as well as to "Nama," my special gratitude.

RICHARD A. GARCIA

between 1929 and 1941, because San Antonio was at the crossroads of Texan, Mexican, and U.S. myth, memory, and identity, as well as trade, commerce, and geography. San Antonio, moreover, was the cosmopolitan center of the predominantly Mexican South Texas area. For the Mexicans of South Texas and Mexico, San Antonio was a magnet of employment possibilities, and the city's West Side barrio served as a rich cultural repository that served both as a Mexican womb in the United States and as a central passageway to the West, Midwest, and East. The city, therefore, was both figuratively and symbolically the starting place of the search for a new identity as a Mexican in the United States. With Los Angeles and El Paso, San Antonio was one of the most Mexican cultural centers in this country.

In the 1930s San Antonio was a thriving urban center that needed Mexican workers. City leaders needed to define the city's relationship to the masses of Mexicans who had either been part of the city's nineteenth-century colonialism or had been part of the immigrant generations that had inundated San Antonio, El Paso, and Los Angeles and the rest of the Southwest and the Midwest during the first two decades of the twentieth century.

From 1929 through 1941, San Antonio's West Side was teeming with Mexicans of different social groupings, classes, and political ideas, as well as different levels of acculturation. This Mexican world within the American world of San Antonio represented almost 50 percent of the city's total population in the 1930s and consisted of the minute class of exiled Mexican *ricos* (who had fled the Mexican revolution of 1910 and many of the counterrevolutions that followed), a developing Mexican American middle class (which had risen with the increase of Mexican middle-class immigrants fleeing the revolution and with the city's need for skilled workers and professionals during and after World War I), and, above all, the large working class.

The West Side during the 1920s and 1930s was the Paris of the Southwest urban barrios. The Mexican city within a city was intellectually and politically fueled by the redemptive vision expressed by the exiled Mexican *rico* upper class through its newspaper *La Prensa*, a respected national and international political voice, and through the *ricos'* very extensive social, cultural, and traditional events. The rising middle class also heightened the intellectual and cultural quality of the West Side as it searched for its identity through the sociopolitical activities sponsored by LULAC. LULAC was introducing a new discourse of Mexican Americanism: a *mentalidad* that sought to express the new philosophical and ideological contours of the Mexican American mind. In addition, the large class of Mexican workers enriched the West Side in the 1930s through their struggle to survive and maintain their hopes for the future in a world bombarded by Americanism and Mexicanism.

In broad terms, this is a study of San Antonio's West Side barrio as a microcosm of the Southwest's developing Mexican social groupings, economic classes, and political ideas. Specifically, this study examines the rise of the developing Mexican American generation of the 1930s. Focusing on the minute but viable middle class of Mexican Americans, this book analyzes the process of class differentiation in the community, traces the emergence of a collective Mexican American mentality, and examines the everyday lives of the changing laboring class, the middle class, and the upper class. The central question of this work is quite straightforward: Why and how were the 1930s the period in which consciousness changed from Mexican to Mexican American? This study is an attempt to provide a "biography" of the Mexicans in San Antonio in particular, but also of the Southwest's developing Mexican American population. It analyzes a crucial historical turning point in the development of the Mexicans' consciousness and ideology from Mexican and immigrant to Mexican American and citizen. This Mexican American weltanschauung would continue until challenged by the rising radical discourse of the young Chicano generation of the 1960s.

My underlying argument is that, within the crucible of urbanization and industrialization in the Southwest in general and in San Antonio in particular, there occurred the rise of the middle-class consciousness that was specifically articulated by the organization of the League of United Latin American Citizens in 1929. LULAC sought to shift the consciousness of the Mexicans in the West Side and throughout the Southwest from one of only *lo mexicano*, as the exiled *ricos* wanted, to the incorporation of *lo americano*. LULAC's emphasis on developing a dual consciousness and a program for integrating and functioning in American society coincided with the city's institutional demands (church, education, politics, family) to Americanize the Mexicans, but only to a point.

San Antonio became the focus of this study not only because it was

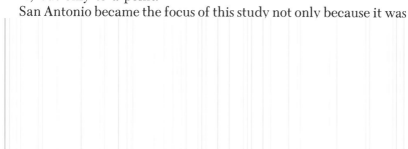

as espoused by the exiled Porfirista and Huertista *ricos* (the followers of the deposed dictator of Mexico, Porfirio Díaz, and of Victoriano Huerto, who overthrew the liberal Madero in 1913). The latter sought to have Mexicans in the United States retain a consciousness of *mexicanos de afuera* and maintain an allegiance to Mexico. The *ricos* sought to stop the change to *lo americano*, as advocated by the Mexican American middle class and LULAC, although in reality they wanted to be Mexicans culturally and Americans politically.

This struggle between the consciousness of collectivity and the consciousness of individuality is examined in light of the historical and institutional forces at play. I fully agree with Felix Gilbert's statement that "whatever one thinks of the forces that underlie the historical process, they are filtered through the human mind and this determines the tempo and the manner in which they work. It is human consciousness which connects the long-range factors and forces all the individual events."[2]

These structural forces have been very well analyzed in innovative studies by Albert Camarillo, Mario Barrera, and Mario T. Garcia. I have also drawn from the excellent work of Richard Griswold del Castillo on the Mexican family and from Manuel Peña's insightful analysis of the relationship between culture, music, and consciousness, as well as from the perceptive work of Arnoldo de León on the beginning development of a dual culture and consciousness in the Mexicans in Texas during the nineteenth century. In addition, I have drawn from the work of Guadalupe San Miguel on the Mexican Americans' drive for educational equality.

Camarillo, Barrera, and Garcia have given me an understanding of the Mexicans' integration into the Southwest; the formation of the barrios; racial, class, and economic subjugation; the relationship to modernization; and the Mexicans' role in the building of the Southwest from the 1840s to the 1930s. Griswold del Castillo, Peña, de León, and San Miguel have given me insights into the family, culture, music, education, and biculturalism of this same period.[3] My study builds on those studies and furthers the story by examining the juncture to which these studies have taken us: the period between the late twenties and early forties, the period during which the native-born and Mexico-born Mexican population in the United States consciously (or not) embraced the American dream of abundance, mobility, possibility, progress, and liberalism, but attempted to maintain a Mexican consciousness of collectivity.

In many ways this study is an interdisciplinary approach to history, since I use different theoretical and conceptual tools to facilitate the sociological, cultural, political, intellectual, and holistic analysis of the story of Mexicans in San Antonio. The narrative in this study moves from one circle of understanding to another: from the Mexicans' structural relationship to the city and the process of economic and class differentiation, to an understanding of the Mexicans' barrio and everyday life (and an examination of the Mexican culture, family, church, and politics), to the level of ideas and ideology.

This analysis is set in the Depression decade of the 1930s, because it was the only period in American history in which the flood of Mexican immigration was almost completely halted. This situation, consequently, allowed me to examine the solidification and consolidation of the Mexican community. Moreover, 1929 was the year in which the exiled Mexican *ricos* of San Antonio turned their attention back to Mexico, because the Mexican government offered them the possibility of returning. The 1930s were the *época de la concordia*, when Mexico attempted to entice the exiles to return and help rebuild the country. Even more important, however, 1929 was the year that different Mexican organizations met in Harlingen, Texas, at a convention reminiscent of the American Constitutional Convention of 1789. The Mexicans established the first major regional Mexican American organization — the League of United Latin American Citizens. LULAC then proceeded, specifically in San Antonio, to try to foster a new consciousness in the Mexican population.

By 1941 it had begun to succeed as a result of organizational and personal activism and communal institutional transmitters of change with continuity. Due specifically to the ideas and activities of LULAC, the Mexican American generation began its struggle with the *ricos* for intellectual and ideological hegemonic control of the minds and hearts of the Mexican communities in San Antonio and the Southwest. Tension was created between Mexican positivism, elitism, high culture, and nationalism, and Mexican American pragmatism, pluralism, liberalism, and patriotism to the United States. The Mexican mind was Porfirista and Huertista; the Mexican American mind was Rooseveltian and Jeffersonian. The Mexican American generation sought an acceptable balance between Americanism and Mexicanism and assumed that by joining the two it could remain Mexican

in American society, not only by the Mexican Americans, but by the *ricos* and the workers. In many ways, this search for identity, educational opportunities, and political efficacy was not very different from the stories of the Irish in Boston, the Italians in Chicago, the blacks in the South, or the Jews in New York.[4] The patterns were the same but the results were different because of the difference in the internal dynamics of the immigrant cultures, ideas, historical time, space, and geography during which they entered the United States, as well as the period in which they began to emerge and define themselves.

Ironically, by 1941 the San Antonio Anglo city leaders believed that they had to integrate the Mexican West Side fully with the rest of the city to push the entire city toward modernization; the urban core could not develop without the periphery. This process is reminiscent of the underdeveloped countries' relationship to the world system and core center. By 1941, as a result of the approaching world war, the continuing conditions in the West Side, and the politics of LULAC, city leaders in San Antonio sought completion of the process of modernization. This meant not only giving recognition to the Mexican Americans but integrating the Mexicans in San Antonio educationally, politically, and ideologically. Yet, they did not want the Mexican to be totally integrated. By 1941 the Mexican Americans' search for identity had begun and the contours were in place: liberal in philosophy, conservative in tradition, and activist in orientation. LULAC, the ethos of the city leaders, the urban institutions, the historical moment, and the *ricos'* return to Mexico dictated the reality of Mexican Americanism: integration, functionalism, and Americanism. They were now *mexicanos de adentro*. It was a major intellectual, ideological, and ontological turning point in San Antonio specifically and throughout the Southwest between 1929 and 1941 for the Mexican American population.

Historian Henry C. Schmidt in *The Roots of Lo Mexicano* states that "the search for identity is characteristic of people bound in some common way and compelled to understand themselves in terms of their history and their relationship to the rest of the world. Tradition transformed from daily events into myth, and a symbolic experience of colony, nation, region, or locale emerges." Schmidt is speaking of the period from 1900 to 1934, when Mexicans in Mexico began to identify what they perceived to be "*lo mexicano*"— an ethos, an identity, a metaphor for being. During approximately this same period, according to Warren Susman, North Americans began to identify their culture and their sense of identity. In both Mexico and the United States, people were in the process of defining self-awareness as a basis for national consciousness.[5]

By 1941 the United States had developed an understanding of the meaning of Americanism as expressed by Franklin D. Roosevelt, and Mexico, of the Mexicanism of Manuel Avila Camacho as metaphors for their unique society. An ideational process had occurred in both instances; the forces of the modernization process had erupted to define fully this consciousness of collectivity, which produced, as Susman calls it, "culture and commitment" on the part of members of society. In the United States it had taken an industrial and urban revolution (1865–1941) to produce this ideational state; in Mexico, a violent revolution (1910–20) had propelled Mexico into a capitalist, modernizing society and produced a new ideational orientation. Ironically, these two ideational processes, which were producing the search for identity in both Mexico and the United States, would converge in the reality of the American Southwest's modernizing process (1900–41), specifically, in the reality of the modernizing city of San Antonio. As a result, Mexican Americanism evolved from two intellectual sources: first, the Mexican consciousness of the exiled Porfirista and Huertista elite and, second, the emerging U.S. consciousness of the Mexican American middle class who propounded the ideas of Jefferson, Wilson, and Franklin D. Roosevelt. This consciousness was specifically expressed in the ideas and ideology of the League of United Latin American Citizens.

San Antonio at this time considered itself the crossroads of Texan, Mexican, and Southwest culture and the hub of industrialization and urbanization. It was a city where Americanism and Mexicanism were forged on the anvil of a modernizing Southwest. For the hundreds of Mexican immigrants fleeing the Mexican revolution, San Antonio was a gateway to the promise of the United States. The winds of liberal change, however, would collide with the winds of conservative continuity in San Antonio, which Carey McWilliams has called the "Fan of Settlement."

But this is not a story of the immigrant seeking refuge from the diaspora in the United States, nor is it a story of urbanization or the urban working-class Mexican. It is a story of the development of a consciousness, of an ideology, of a search for identity and a place in

of Americanism, so did the Mexican population in the United States identify its Mexican Americanism.

In short, it seems that the ideational process for the Mexican American generation began at the turn of the twentieth century, with the beginning of immigration (1900–30). During this period many of the barrios in the Southwest experienced a rejuvenation of Mexican traditions, values, ideas, and behavioral patterns in the close to one million immigrants (rural and urban Mexicans, a small middle class, and a minute exiled *rico* class). In Los Angeles, San Diego, Tucson, Santa Fe, Albuquerque, El Paso, San Antonio, Brownsville, Chicago, and countless rural areas, these classes of immigrants, augmenting the existing Mexican population in the United States, encountered the city, technology, bureaucracy, and pluralism.[7]

U.S. society was caught in the national wave of progressivism, modernism, and secularism, and the Mexican was especially affected by the modernizing forces of urbanization and industrialization in the Southwest. Also of central importance to the rise of a search for identity were the great numbers of Mexicans who joined the U.S. Army in World War I. The war was not only a turning point for the United States' integration into the world community, but was also the catalyst for a shift of consciousness in the returning Mexican war veterans from Mexican to Mexican American. Their consciousness dictated integration into the Southwest with its industrial and urban need for labor; moreover, they observed that the barrios needed to move from underdeveloped to developed.[8]

Thus Mexicans in the United States chose to become activist, especially in the Southwest. They were thrust into the modernizing world of Deweyian education, an Americanized Catholic Church, U.S. culture and thought, and the nascent middle-class movement of the 1930s. Above all, the Mexicans, regardless of whether they were foreign- or native-born, became part of a world where, as sociologist Peter Berger has pointed out, there was a "general though clearly distinguishable split in the social structure of the modern world between the public sphere and the private sphere. The public sphere is dominated by enormous public institutions, the bureaucracies organizing such areas of human activity as government and law, business and commerce, labor, health care, education, communication, the military, and even religion. These megastructures," Berger further explains,

> dominate most of the areas of human activity, but not all of it. There is an area left over — what German scholars have called the private sphere, the sphere of the intimate. This sphere is constituted principally by activities surrounding the family, voluntary association, and the network (of varying sizes) of primary social relationships. The individual in a modern society is usually aware (through varying degrees) of this dichotomization. In the course of daily life, the individual migrates back and forth between these spheres. The split between these spheres is most often recognized as the difference between the world of work and the home.[9]

This study, with some changes, incorporates these dichotomized realities. In short, according to my research, the Mexican immigrants of the 1900–40 period were swept into U.S. society, specifically the modernizing process in the Southwest, a process somewhat mitigated by their entering the world of the Mexican barrios. They entered pluralistic United States with symbolic universes, values, morality, and belief systems engendered by urbanization, mass communications, and public education. They began to emerge into a world where public-sphere rationality and secularization were making inroads into family, organizational, personal, and religious life. For the Mexican population, it was the beginning of change with continuity in their private lives, behavior patterns, child-rearing methods, everyday social relationships, general discourse, and even their leisure habits. Overall, the Mexicans in the United States would need to find new explanatory mechanisms and integrative methods and would need to retain (or accommodate) themselves to, if possible, a changing sense of self and adjust, reformulate, or devise a world view that promised them a new life, new possibilities, and new expectations — if they chose them.

In this historical context the exiled Porfiristas and Huertistas attempted to maintain the homogeneity of their universal values, their

Scholastic temper, their formalism and deference, and their spirit of *lo mexicano*. Moreover, they attempted to impose these sensibilities on the Mexican population as a whole in the world they knew was changing. The *ricos* attempted, for many reasons, to maintain a sense of permanence. The exiled *ricos* in San Antonio and the Southwest attempted, through their newspapers, their intellectuals, and their cultural and social activities, to provide Mexicans with a sense of *lo mexicano* that was rooted in a stable social and cultural

dle class wanted change, but also wanted to maintain some continuity; above all, they wanted to become functional in U.S. life. This study focuses on the hegemonic struggle between the *ricos* and the emerging middle class within the ideational context of the United States' and Mexico's search for identity.

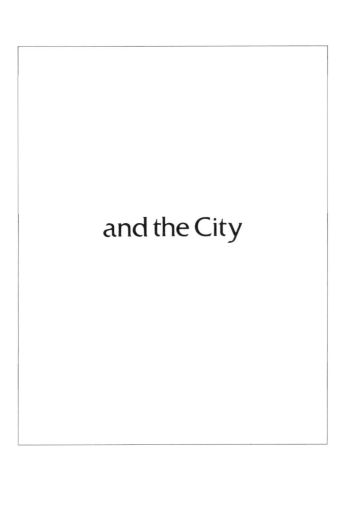

and the City

1

A Town within a City

—Anselm Strauss

San Antonio . . . was distinct . . . a product of its local regions; it clearly exhibited a long past as well as a rapid recent growth. It was the meeting point of two regions and four peoples. All four — Hispano, Anglo, Negro, and German — were colorfully intermingled on the main streets and plazas, but they were rather sharply different in residence and occupation, diet and dress, language and religion.
— D. W. Meinig

INTRODUCTION

Mexicans in San Antonio lived in one of the oldest cities in the United States, situated in Bexar County at the entrance to South Texas. Because of its location and its history, San Antonio was already considered the "capital" of South Texas during the 1930s. It was accepted as the gateway to Mexico and, even as early as 1924, the "Metropolis of the Southwest." Throughout the 1920s and the 1930s, it was also commonly referred to as the "financial, educational, cultural, and recreational capital of South Texas as well as its wholesale distributing and retail trading center."[1]

San Antonio's growth up to 1940 had been "as pronounced in manufacturing as in commerce." In fact, San Antonio's abundant supplies of petroleum and natural gas made it the only industrial center of importance in southwestern Texas.[2] San Antonio also had an extensive agricultural economy within its metropolitan area, an extensive complex of military facilities within its city limits, and an extensive railroad system.

Since San Antonio had been a relatively large and well-known center of commerce and trade for over two centuries, it was also considered a center for labor. Consequently, its metropolitan culture was the most diverse in Texas. By the twentieth century, its racial and ethnic groups were relatively well woven into the fabric of the community, although the extreme diversity of backgrounds, interests, and viewpoints made San Antonio a center of contrasts and conflicts. The Mexican community had always been the largest ethnic group, with most of them residing on the West Side. Since the nineteenth century the "Latin Quarter" or "Mexican Town," as it was called, had been characterized by low income, low education, high unemployment, deteriorating and dilapidated housing, and, on the whole, harsh socioeconomic conditions.[3]

San Antonio and its Mexican population had had a symbiotic relationship since 1835, when Texas established a republic with a provisional government and called for its independence. This ultimately led to the battle at the Alamo where James Bonham, James Bowie, David Crockett, and 780 other Texans, including numerous Mexican Texans, confronted a Mexican army of five thousand troops led by General López de Santa Anna. The battle at the Alamo, although a military defeat, was a moral victory for the Texans. It saw the start of a curious strain of Texas pride and arrogance complemented by a growing hatred of Mexicans, even while the city retained, ironically, a pride in its Spanish heritage.

The intellectual tension between the acceptance of the "Spanish fantasy"—seeing rich Spaniards as contributors to Southwest history while ignoring the role of poor Mexicans—and the rejection of the Mexican reality continued into the twentieth century.

San Antonio became the leading city of the newly formed Republic of Texas. In 1845 the United States annexed Texas and after militarily defeating Mexico, signed the Treaty of Guadalupe Hidalgo, which in essence ceded the whole Southwest to the United States. Mexicans in San Antonio and throughout the Southwest were given a year to decide whether they would return to Mexico or remain and automatically become American citizens. Many stayed; their descendants continued to form the nucleus of the Mexican American community into the twentieth century.

San Antonio retained its cosmopolitan atmosphere and its Spanish appearance. In fact, the Spanish and American influence was so in-grained in the everyday life of the city that Spanish and Mexican mo-tifs have been reflected everywhere in San Antonio from the mid-nineteenth century on: in everyday dress, in music, in dancing, in holiday pageantry, in the intellectual life. Large waves of immigrants bringing their culture during the decades from 1900 to 1930 further consolidated the influence of Mexican culture on the city.[4]

The Mexican population in San Antonio increased from 13,722 in

The Roots of the Mexican Community

Over the San Antonio River bridge in the 1870s the crossing signs read, "Walk your horse over this bridge, or you will be fined" / "Schnelles ruten veber siease bruecke ist verboten" / "Ande despacio con su caballo, o' tome la ley."[6] As this sign indicated, San Antonio was multicultural even in the nineteenth century. Friedrich Zizelman, who founded the First Lutheran Church in San Antonio in 1851, reported that the city was a "Babel on a small scale" with its mixture of ethnic groups, languages, and religions. English, German, and Spanish were the most common languages, which were often all used on public signs, and they reflected the main population makeup dur-ing the late nineteenth century. The city, however, also had a cross section of blacks, Chinese, French, and other ethnic groups; in fact, about 50 percent of the population was foreign-born.[7]

Spanish Mexicans during the early years comprised Canary Island-ers, who had come to San Antonio in 1731, and mestizos, offspring of marriages between the early Spaniards and Indians. The descen-dants of the Canary Islanders were the most prominent members of the San Antonio community; the mestizos were at the lower end of the social ladder. Prominent Spanish Mexican families such as the Urrutías, the Seguíns, the Navarros, the Rodríguezes, the Leals, the Vermandís, the Carvajals, the Galváns, the Menchacas, and the Lo-zanos formed the small layer of wealthy families in nineteenth-century San Antonio.[8]

The second-largest ethnic group in San Antonio, the Germans, came to the city as early as 1812 in an immigration sponsored by foreign associations. The Association of German Princes for the Protection of German Immigrants, for example, brought many German settlers early in the nineteenth century. These immigrants brought their culture and customs to San Antonio and established nearby cities like New Braunfels and Fredericksburg. Some of the more important citizens of twentieth-century San Antonio, such as the Heusingers, the Hertzbergs, the Grosses, and the Mengers, trace their roots to these early German settlers who established their community — Germantown — near the center of downtown San Antonio. By the 1930s many of these German settlers were, for all practical purposes, assimilated into the Anglo community in San Antonio.[9]

The black community was a distant third in population. Most of the blacks arrived from the other southern states during Reconstruction or had worked in the cotton fields of South Texas before they were brought to San Antonio. The city established strict property restrictions to limit the land that was open to them. These restrictions kept them on the east side, while informal arrangements kept the Mexicans on the west side. The blacks suffered, it seems, from de jure segregation and the Mexicans — also considered by many San Antonians as people of color — from de facto segregation. This was not the case for the German population or for the descendants of the Canary Islanders. The Anglo community had always been open to the Canary Islanders because they were considered Spanish, not Mexican or Indian, in the late nineteenth and early twentieth centuries.[10]

Two other relatively large ethnic groups in the city were the French and the Irish. The French came mainly from Louisiana to San Antonio in the late eighteenth century and in a second wave in the 1840s, but their numbers were not substantial and many quickly married into the Anglo American community. The Irish, who also came in the 1840s, came directly from Ireland and established the Irish Flats. The Irish, like their German and French counterparts, slowly became socially and culturally integrated into the Anglo American community by the turn of the century, and by the 1940s, only certain structures, celebrations, and traditions remained of the Irish, German, and French cultures.

A smaller group, the Italians, like the Irish and French, were almost fully assimilated by the end of the 1930s, although they still continued to celebrate certain ethnic holidays, such as Columbus Day. Overall, there were over thirty nationalities in San Antonio in the nineteenth century, but only the Mexican and black communities in the twentieth century remained unassimilated, basically as a result of the considerable immigration of Mexicans in the first three decades of the century.[11]

Until the last decade of the nineteenth century, however, one section of the Mexican population of San Antonio was an integral part of the city's elite. In 1833, for example, a memorandum was sent to the government of Mexico stating that San Antonio, which had been "established one-hundred and forty years ago," was still functioning. This memorandum was signed by the city's social and political elite,

President Mirabeau B. Lamar of the Texas Republic at the home of the Yturri family. The principal guests included Mayor Juan Seguín of San Antonio and his wife.

During the 1840s and 1850s, which included the War of 1848, the Spanish Mexican elite continued to be the social and political leaders of the San Antonio community, and there existed a consciousness of being both Spanish Mexican (but mostly Spanish) and Texan. However, while the Leals, the Urrutias, the Gonzaleses, the Carvajals, and others were upper-class citizens of the city, there were many poor Mexicans who also exhibited this dual consciousness of being *mexicano* and *tejano.*

In this cohesive Mexican society, sense of community and identity was usually expressed through cultural activities, not political power. This was especially evident in Mexican social and religious celebrations rather than in San Antonio's general municipal celebrations. By the 1860s the majority of Mexicans were becoming separated into their own community.[12]

A January 15, 1859, article in *Leslie's Weekly,* a New York newspaper, described this Mexican community in the following manner:

> A large element of the population is Mexican. There are a few respectable, intelligent, and wealthy [Mexican] families, but the majority are of the . . . [working class], with all the vices and none of the virtues belonging to the better situated. The men, whenever they work, are employed as teamsters, herders, or day laborers. The best of their talent is toward livestock.
> The free and easy style of life which is characteristic of the . . .

[working class] of Mexicans is sure to surprise a stranger. He sees children of both sexes from two to six years of age strolling around in the economical and closely-fitting costumes bestowed upon them by nature.

Parties of [Mexican] men, women and children bathe in the San Antonio River just outside the corporate limits without the annoyance of dress. This comfortable fashion was formerly in vogue within the city limits until the authorities concluded it might, with propriety, be dispensed with.

The narrow streets, the stout old walls [of the Mexican Quarter are] determined not to crumble away; [nor] the dark banditto-like figures that gaze at you from low door ways; everything in the Mexican Quarter, bespeaks of a condition widely different from what [non-Mexicans] . . . are accustomed to behold in any other town.[13]

If the Latin Quarter appeared strange to the New York reporter, the holidays that formed the cultural core of the Mexican community would have appeared bizarre. These often appeared curious even to the other citizens of San Antonio. For example, on San Juan's Day (Cinco de Mayo), every Mexican who owned or could borrow a horse would dress it up (the richer classes would use silver saddles) and ride it from plaza to plaza down the main street of the city, often at breakneck speed, from early morning until sunset. On December 12, the feast of Our Lady of Guadalupe, the Mexican population carried a statue of the Virgin of Guadalupe in parade fashion through the streets of the Latin Quarter into the edges of the downtown area. The focal point of the religious and social life of the Mexican community during the nineteenth century (as it still is in the twentieth century) was the celebration of the nativity play: the *pastores*. This celebration was begun in the 1870s and was held every Christmas Eve at the Cathedral of San Fernando. This play was performed through the streets that bordered the *jacalitos* (little huts) on the West Side. These Mexican celebrations often rivaled the Germans' folkfests in popularity.[14]

Celebrations usually took place in the West Side plazas or the downtown plazas. Beginning in the 1850s, the plazas, especially the military plaza on the West Side, were the focal point for the Mexicans. The "Chili Queens," for example, dressed in bright costumes and sold hot chile, chile con carne, tamales, tortillas, enchiladas, frijoles, and sopa de arroz. These women contributed to making these plazas, with their gay illumination and overpowering scent of garlic, onions, and spices, the cultural centers of the Mexican population. The Chili Queens also attracted many from the non-Mexican community and tourists and red-light district patrons. This tradition continued to provide the growing Mexican community with social and cultural joy well into the twentieth century.

If the military plaza was the main center of nocturnal festivities, by day the marketplace (the *mercado*) was the major attraction for both Mexicans and non-Mexicans. It was the city's center of commerce where vegetables, cotton, fruits, and other goods were brought in from the outlying areas and traded or sold (wholesale or retail) to the citizens of San Antonio.[15]

pathies of the people since [it was] largely used by the poorer class of Mexicans." The gravestones had names such as Juan Cortez, Santa María Oca de Cortez that belonged to the Mexican working class. However, many of the Mexicans who had been leading citizens of the city were also buried in the San Fernando Cemetery, as were many early German, French, and Irish settlers. This cemetery was especially important to the Mexicans on All Souls' Day, a day of festivity and celebration for the dead. No matter how poor, each Mexican family went to the cemetery, took something to help decorate it, and brought some "gift of love" for their beloved dead. The Catholic Church played a significant role on this holiday, just as it did on many of the other holidays celebrated by the Mexican poor, by having masses and processions. For the Mexicans, the fiestas, the plazas, the *muertos* (the dead), religion, and the family were the cornerstones of everyday life and culture in the late nineteenth century.[16]

The passing of time did not drastically change the activities of the Mexican workers or of the *tiendita* owners, but it did affect the Spanish Mexican elite. With Reconstruction (1865–77) the non-Mexican community increased in numbers and slowly began to replace the Spanish Mexican upper class as the new elite (especially since immigration did not increase the numbers of the Mexican upper class). People such as the Mavericks and the Callahans began to replace the Seguíns, the Herreras, and the Urrutias as the political leaders of the community. Once the Mexican revolution began, however, exiled Mexican *ricos* began to fill the leadership vacuum in the Mexican community of San Antonio and once again became part of the social and political elite, although not on a par with the Anglo community.[17]

Another important change occurred during the last quarter of the nineteenth century. Inter-marriages which had been socially accept-able from the 1830s to the 1870s, almost ceased. By the last two decades of the nineteenth century, such marriages for the most part had ceased. With this decrease in the intermarriage rate, the increasing non-Mexican emigration into San Antonio, declining Mexican immigra-tion, and increasing industrialization, the Spanish Mexican leader-ship declined.

The downward mobility of the Spanish Mexican elite was thus not based solely on purely psychological or political reasons. It could be traced to increased American population, the industrial progress of the city, Anglo ingenuity, the financial resources of the Anglos, the increase of military bases, and the fact that San Antonio had become a boom town that contracted Eastern monies.[18]

These occurrences correlated with the decrease in emigration from Mexico to the United States during the period from 1861 to the 1890s (from 25,119 between 1820 and 1880 to 2,884 between 1880 and 1900). This meant demographic stagnation for the Spanish Mexican upper class and no growth for the general *tejano* population. The *tiendita* owners continued in their role as the Mexican buffer class, and the *pobres* provided part of the labor force in San Antonio. Not only an ethnic cleavage had developed between Mexicans and non-Mexicans in the city, but a structural and racial boundary appears to have been established between 1848 and 1900. With the turn of the century, the Anglo "new breed" became the dominant class in San Antonio. Ironi-cally, many in this new class had some Spanish or Mexican blood. San Antonio retained its Mexican atmosphere, traditions, and archi-tecture; the Spanish fantasy remained central to the city's spirit.[19]

By 1900 the Canary Islanders, their descendants, and other promi-nent Spanish Mexicans retained only their pride and memories, not their political power or their social standing. They never regained their social or political prominence in the San Antonio community.

It is important to note that by the 1930s many of these old Spanish Mexican families were well assimilated into the Anglo population, rather than into the new *ricos*, who began to arrive during the Mexi-can revolution. It seems that the acculturation process had taken its toll, and although intermarriage was no longer common, it remained a viable option for some old Spanish Mexican families. By the 1930s many of them had intermarried. As a result, the descendants of the Canary Islanders, the early Spanish Mexican families and many of the nineteenth-century laboring Mexican population were prouder of their "Spanish" and "Texas" heritage than of their twentieth-century

"Mexican" one. All of them, especially the Spanish elite, wanted to identify with the San Antonio Americano elite rather than with the Mexican *ricos*, and, of course, never with the over seven hundred thousand Mexicans who arrived in Texas between 1900 and 1930. The Canary Islanders consciously became *tejanos* rather than *mexicanos*, thus by the 1930s abdicating any hope of social or political prominence within the twentieth-century community of the rising Mexican American middle class or the newly arrived comprador class of

of contrasting nationalities, but one in which the "haciendas met the plantations," and a city of extreme social, racial, and economic cleavages. The nineteenth-century Spanish ambiance continued, but the power and knowledge of the old Spanish-Mexican-Texan elite was now just memory in a city that was on the verge of modernization in 1900.[21]

THE CITY AND MODERNIZATION

By 1900 San Antonio was spatially and demographically changing. Although on the periphery of the larger nineteenth-century American Industrial Revolution, it was a developing Southwest metropolis of smaller industrial concerns and was rapidly becoming a magnet for semiskilled and unskilled labor. The city's economic development and spreading fame were closely related to its colorful cultural life, since by the twentieth century distinct intellectual and cultural patterns formed the elan of the city. San Antonio was a city of Spanish and Mexican motifs, of a cosmopolitan population, of ruins and memorials of three centuries, of heroic traditions, and of a distinctive blend of southern charm. Moreover, the Alamo (which was the symbol of Texas independence from Mexico) made it, as far as Texas intellectual thought was concerned, the historical center of the state.

Overall, San Antonio owed its uniqueness to France, Spain, Mexico, the Republic of Texas, the Confederacy, and the United States. Culturally and intellectually, each country had left its mark on the city. Spain and Mexico, however, had left an especially indelible imprint on the city's art, music, customs, language, and architecture. Above all, San Antonio in 1900 was a city of contrasts, a wide open frontier town, a city of southern hospitality and racial deference, a gateway to Mexican culture, a symbol of Texas pride and tradition, a military center, and a booming urbanizing city.

These conditions formed the intellectual and cultural atmosphere that permeated Mexican consciousness in the West Side. The city segregated the Mexicans but employed them, loved their culture but disliked them. In essence, it needed their labor, but rejected their presence. The city praised its Spanish fantasy until 1940, then the city leaders had to recognize the Mexican reality because the city's entrance into modernity necessitated it.[22]

Like the rest of the Southwest, San Antonio, despite its "Mexican problem," was caught up in a wave of urbanization between 1900 and 1930, an urbanization that would allow it to leap from a frontier Victorian town to a modern city in four decades. Discoveries in science, technology, and education helped to change the city's face. In spite of these tremendous collective changes and population growth, however, San Antonio continued to exhibit a peculiar urban developmental pattern that was to become permanent by the 1930s: it contained "separate ethnic towns" and consequently was a city with many "realities."[23]

Aside from the thriving business and political reality that enveloped the city, there were the different ethnic realities. There was also the frontier reality of a city that was a wide open town with saloons, gambling halls, and vaudeville theaters concentrated around the two main downtown plazas and extending westward across San Pedro Creek into the red light district on the outskirts of the West Side. As a result, the Latin Quarter was often seen as being synonymous with San Antonio's nightlife. O. Henry called this the San Antonio of the famous "Jack Harris Saloon," the "White Elephant," and "Cooley's Bar," a city of "frolic and gambling" as well as a city of "high rollers." The evangelist Dixie Williams reportedly called San Antonio "the wickedest city in the Union, except for Washington." This reputation was well earned, since in this town within the city "life was cheap and stakes were high." It coincided with the community of hustlers, street fighters, wild horse riders, and two-fisted whisky guzzlers (who often vowed death before giving up their liquor and guns). But this was only the frontier reality of San Antonio.[24]

There were also the "quaint realities of the exotic Mexican town" and the "lively" German town. By the twentieth century the Mexican town already had a different culture and character from the rest of the city. It was, as one writer said, " a city lifted bodily from one country [Mexico] and set down in another." This segregated, impoverished quarter of the city had its own language, dress, religion, customs, and traditions, and the Mexicans' "sense of community" seemed to have been handed down from generation to generation (as a Catholic priest observed during the 1930s).

In addition to the Mexican Town, there was the other town within

mans. In fact, as early as 1841, Mary Maverick, whose great-grandson Maury Maverick would become mayor in the 1930s, said, "We began to have a society and a great sociability among ourselves. . . . Ethnic clannishness was a trend in San Antonio's population, as were the trends of industrial progress and economic prosperity."[26] However, when the city as a whole began to progress, some of the ethnic sections did not; they remained separate towns within the growing city.

Nevertheless, from 1900 through the 1930s, San Antonians both created and felt the great changes of the Progressive Era, the Roaring Twenties, and the Depression decade. San Antonians welcomed the twentieth century and its "skyline-changing urban mood," as the city became integrated into the rest of the United States. But the old San Antonians still retained their memories and a few traditions from the "wild west days."

The new urban perspective was expressed by the *San Antonio Express*, the morning daily, when it exclaimed that the city was one of varied and substantial resources, a financial center, a large wholesale and retail trade center, a major livestock center, and the home of cattle barons. The newspaper further reported that San Antonio was the richest city in the state because it showed a per capita wealth of $596.88, or $12.02 more per capita than the average of 135 cities in the United States of over thirty thousand population. (Unfortunately, the average was skewed because of the presence of wealthy citizens.) San Antonio, moreover, increased its national prestige to complement its economic and commercial importance when President McKinley came to visit in 1901 and when President Teddy Roosevelt returned and got a rousing welcome from San Antonians as he held a reunion with his Rough Riders.

By the time of Roosevelt's visit, San Antonio was already shifting away from the traditional downtown business area. It was expanding from the Main Plaza, the Military plazas, and from Commerce Street (which went through the downtown area and was adjacent to the Alamo) to the suburbs, which were being opened by streetcars. Coinciding with this geographical expansion, Andrew Carnegie contributed to the intellectual and cultural expansion of life in San Antonio by donating fifty thousand dollars for the construction of a library. Also in the spirit of the Progressive Era, San Antonio's doctors began to investigate means of controlling mosquitoes and disease in the city. The modernization period from 1900 to 1930 not only saw economic development, but also rapid population growth and cultural change. San Antonio was taking in the modernization boom occurring throughout the Southwest coincident with what Frederick Allen calls "the Big Change in American Life," from Victorian America to modern America.[27]

During this period, San Antonio was transformed from a frontier town to a modern city. By 1911 the *San Antonio City Directory*, for example, listed numerous new businesses and industries. Building activity rose 600 percent, assessed valuations rose 130 percent, street improvements rose 900 percent, hotel facilities and office facilities rose by 500 percent. The city directory of 1921–22 reported an 890 percent increase in building activity, 900 percent in street improvements, 730 percent in tourism, and 221 percent in bank deposits. In keeping with the progressivism of the period, the citizens of San Antonio in 1921 voted for a $3,950,000 bond issue for various improvements, including streets, sewers, and a public auditorium. But a definite indicator of San Antonio's growth in the 1920s was property valuation, which had been less than $32 million in 1900, rose to $85 million in 1910, and was $120 million by 1920. During the 1920s, San Antonio found itself Texas' leading city with a population of 161,379, as opposed to Dallas's 158,976, Houston's 138,276, and Fort Worth's 106,482. The first two decades of the twentieth century were without a doubt a booming period for the "Paris" of Texas.[28]

By the late 1920s the technological and industrial changes were propelling San Antonians headlong into a new intellectual and cultural development that would climax in the 1940s, when city leaders had to address the question of whether to incorporate the Mexicans into the city if modernization were to be complete. These changes coincided with new intellectual and cultural currents circulating throughout the United States. Both San Antonio and the United States were beginning in the late twenties, and certainly by the thirties, to accommodate themselves to the intellectual order brought on by the age of technology and industrialization. By the twenties and thirties, people in San Antonio were listening to their radios, going to the movies, heeding national advertising, internalizing the beginning of a new consumer ethic rather than a production one, and being affected by the mobility revolution caused by the automobile. This was

became less provincial and more standardized within the U.S. mold of an urban city. It developed, intellectually and culturally, a new cosmopolitanism that was based on a growing economy of goods and services. San Antonio was literally and figuratively at the crossroads of change in America, and as it established its own identity it had to deal with the increasing Mexican community, which was producing the labor for its development. These changes helped to make San Antonio during the first three decades of the twentieth century the metropolis of the Southwest and a crossroads and mecca for the Mexican population that was steadily drifting north from Mexico.[29]

THE CITY AND THE MEXICAN

San Antonio between 1900 and 1930 needed labor for urbanization and industrialization, and the Mexicans — the existing native population and the emigrating one — were the source that would build San Antonio and the Southwest. By 1900 San Antonio had close to fourteen thousand Mexicans, with most of them living on the West Side. By 1910 the Mexican population of San Antonio was still rural and extremely poor except for the descendants of the Canary Islanders (who not only were better off, but who considered themselves part of the larger San Antonio community, rather than a part of the developing Mexican one).

The poor were conscious of themselves as Mexicans because of everyday experiences as part of a cohesive cultural community. Their awareness of their Mexicanness was heightened not only by their "forced social and economic segregation" on the West Side, but by the parallel sense of ethnic consciousness of the German, Italian, Irish, and other ethnic groups (although these other ethnic groups' sense of ethnicity was already on the decline as they slowly became part of the Americano majority). For the Mexicans geographical and cultural separation contributed to a heightened sense of ethnicity, since they continued to perceive themselves as others constantly identified them — as Mexicans.

The major factor contributing to the existence of this separate Mexican consciousness was the immigration that had begun quietly in the 1890s and had become an avalanche by 1910. It not only continued but strengthened cultural and intellectual ties with Mexico. In fact, during the first decade of the twentieth century, only four cities in the United States had a Mexican population of five thousand or more: San Antonio, Laredo, El Paso, and Los Angeles, with El Paso having the largest concentration. All of these cities had a Mexican quarter with a distinct awareness of itself as a community with a Mexican consciousness. [30]

From 1900 to 1910 the Mexican population of Texas increased by 75 percent; from 1910 to 1920, it increased by eight times the average increase of the 1860–1900 period. Mexican emigration to the United States increased from 49,642 in the 1901–10 period to 459,259 in the 1921–30 period, with many of these immigrants going to Texas. In San Antonio, for example, the Mexican population increased from 13,722 in 1900 to 82,373 in 1930. By 1940 50 percent of the Mexican population in San Antonio was foreign-born, and the city's population as early as the 1920s consisted of 54 percent Americanos, 37 percent Mexicans, 9 percent blacks, and 0.2 percent composed of other racial groups (the German population was included in the Americano percentage). [31]

Table 1 shows the increase of the Mexican population in San Antonio from 1900 to 1940. There were six major reasons for the increase in Mexican population: (1) the city's need for unskilled labor; (2) the need for agricultural workers in the metropolitan area; (3) Mexican workers' need to use San Antonio as a home base from which they could go north to work for five to seven months and then return to live in the Latin Quarter for the remainder of the year; (4) San Antonio's function as a labor center for Texas and the Midwest because of its location; (5) the city's proximity to the border; and (6) the already extensive Mexican West Side.

Many Mexicans, therefore, were first attracted by the work in the Valley's citrus and spinach crops. Many of them then moved through San Antonio's labor funnel to the northern beet fields and the indus-

TABLE 1

San Antonio's Population by Ethnic Group, 1900–40

	Anglo		Mexican		Black		
Year	No.	% of Total	No.	% of Total	No.	% of Total	Total Population
1900	32,000	60.0	13,722	25.7	7,538	14.2	53,321
1910	56,321	58.3	29,480	30.5	10,716	11.1	96,614
1920	86,829	53.8	59,970	37.2	14,341	8.9	161,379
1930	130.737	56.6	82.373	35.7	17,978	7.7	231,542

Therefore, without question, the San Antonio trade and farming area served as a magnet for Mexican immigrants, as a base of population growth for the San Antonio Mexican community, and as a cultural support area for the urban Mexicans in San Antonio who were being acculturated.[32] As a result, the developing Americano intellectual and cultural mind was constantly being tempered by the Mexican immigrant and rural one.

Since the outlying trade area was basically agricultural, the Mexicans had the monopoly on labor in both the urban and the rural areas of the city. Consequently, they could almost always find employment in the agricultural sector in the metropolitan area that extended far beyond the city proper, and within the city there were also jobs available. The city was worker-intensive, since it had never developed a heavy industrial base. Mexicans were needed as a source of cheap labor to work in the city's multiplicity of light industries: railroad yards, packing plants, military bases, garment factories, service establishments, and the retail trade.[33]

San Antonio's principal employer by the 1930s was the government, which had four military bases in the city: Kelly, Fort Sam Houston, Brooks, and Randolph. The city had 310 major manufacturing plants producing goods valued at $40 million in 1939. These factories employed approximately sixty-three thousand persons. The garment industry provided employment for six thousand to seven thousand Mexicans, primarily as piece workers. The pecan shelling industry, consisting of twelve to fifteen shelling and shipping firms, was another major employer for the Mexicans in San Antonio. It hired an additional twelve thousand to fifteen thousand Mexicans during the peak season. There were also bakeries, foundries, machine shops, printing plants, publishing concerns, ice molding plants, Mexican food producers and processors, confectionery and beverage producers, slaughtering plants, and meat packing plants.

In addition to the industrial sector, there were over 1,690 establishments in the service sector: barber shops, beauty parlors, cleaning shops, laundries, automobile repair shops, funeral parlors, and many others. The service sector brought in approximately $9.5 million per year and employed 4,201 persons on the average per year. The variety of jobs divided Mexicans into a working class and a lower middle class.[34]

Because of the many opportunities in industry, the service sector, military installations, and the agricultural sector, the Chamber of Commerce promoted San Antonio as a city of opportunity. It used the existence of a large laboring class of Mexicans as a selling point in trying to induce industry to locate in the city. For example, in 1934, it stated that there was an "abundant supply of efficient and contented skilled and unskilled [Mexican] labor available for manufacturing purposes at reasonable wages."[35]

The capital-intensive sector of the city was dominated by the military-petroleum-cattle complex. Next in capital productivity importance were the large wholesale, service, and retail trade and the tourist trade. Overall, the city's economic pot was "boiling briskly" (to quote Vernon Parrington).

William Knox, a longtime San Antonio resident and educator, wrote that "the earning power of the Mexicans determined their manners of living . . . the wage . . . [was] a deciding social and civic feature."[36] In reality, it seemed that not only was there occurring occupational differentiation, but class and cultural segmentation as well. Nevertheless, the pull of the Horatio Alger myth and the possibilities of mobility in San Antonio were, as for Handlin's Irish, Nelli's Italians, and Howe's Jews, providing a magnet for the developing consciousness of collectivity. Mexicans flocked to the Southwest for the same reasons immigrants from Europe had come to the United States; the differences were only in degree, not in kind, as Herbert Gutman has suggested.[37]

San Antonio needed vast quantities of unskilled and semiskilled labor, and the Mexicans were available. Consequently, industrial and urban development, the employment market, the immigration process, the Depression of the 1930s, and the forces within the Mexican community all began to stratify the nineteenth-century Mexican population and the twentieth-century immigrants economically, cultur-

ally, and ideologically. West Side residents were consciously and struc-
turally being stratified into the laboring and middle classes. The impact of modernization on San Antonio, it seems, had set in motion
not only the need for the communal development of the West Side,
but also the process of Mexican socioeconomic differentiation and,
ultimately, the integration of the Mexicans into the rest of the city
between 1929 and 1941.

With the Americano businessperson's wholehearted support, the

thousand Mexican laborers went through San Antonio each season
on their way to other parts of the country.[38] Table 2 indicates the
number of Mexicans who worked in the San Antonio trade area—
vastly larger than just the city itself—from 1900 to 1940.

Although 28,037 of the Mexican work force within San Antonio
proper in the 1930s were foreign born, they were permanent residents
of the city. The remaining 54,326 Mexicans were either direct descendants of the nineteenth-century Mexican laboring community, of the
Canary Islanders, of the first and second generation of Mexican immigrants who came to the United States and San Antonio in the period from 1900 to 1930, or of the migrants who were seasonal residents. The actual statistical breakdown is difficult to ascertain.

What Irving Howe has said of Jewish immigrants during the early
decades of the twentieth century is also applicable to the Mexicans

TABLE 2

The Labor Force in San Antonio and Its Trade Area, 1910–40

	Anglo		Mexican		Black	
Year	No.	% of Total	No.	% of Total	No.	% of Total
1910	391,458	76.1	80,913	15.7	42,093	8.2
1920	521,786	73.8	140,382	19.9	44,412	6.3
1930	525,119	55.6	370,018	39.1	50,026	5.3
1940	630,103	55.0	458,256	40.0	57,282	5.0

SOURCE: San Antonio Public Service Company, *Economic and Industrial Survey*, 1942,
p. 168.

of San Antonio: "A very few years after the mass migration, there . . . began within the immigrant community that process of external social differentiation which is characteristic of American society as a whole." The class differentiation apparent in the Jewish community in New York at the turn of the century and in the black community in Cleveland in the same period first appeared in San Antonio's Mexican community in the 1920s and became highly visible from 1929 through 1941. It was exacerbated by the number of immigrants and by the Depression, which caused not only economic, political, and social dislocation, but also cultural and intellectual change. Nevertheless, the constant stream of immigrants contributed Mexican culture and thought to the West Side community as well as labor to the city.[39]

This class differentiation and communal development had begun as early as the turn of the century and continued through the 1930s as a result of the economic modernization of the Southwest and the subsequent attraction and encouragement of vast numbers of Mexican immigrants. The Mexican immigrants provided the labor force — the anvil — on which Southwest modernization was forged, just as southern and central Europeans were vital to the development of the rest of the United States in the early twentieth century.[40] Historian Lamar B. Jones has suggested that this influx of Mexicans was the product of two main factors: the rapidly expanding agricultural and industrial development in the Southwest, and the unsettled conditions in Mexico after the beginning of the revolution. Gilberto Cardenas, a sociologist, adding another dimension to these causal factors, emphasizes that growers and industrialists actively encouraged and lobbied Congress for the migration of Mexican nationals. As a result of this push and pull effect, there were three massive waves of Mexican migration: 1900–1909 (24,991), 1910–19 (173,663), and 1920–29 (587,775). In the decade of the 1930s only 27,937 Mexicans entered the United States because of the Depression and deportation and repatriation drives. During this decade there occurred throughout the United States the "voluntary" return of hundreds of thousands of people to Mexico; however, immigration in the thirties was bolstered by the slow but continued flow of illegal Mexican immigration.[41]

Class differentiation and communal development were also accelerated, because the city was often preferred by the exiled rich and middle-class Mexicans due to its already large (and increasing) Mexican population and its proximity to the border. The Mexican population also grew because many immigrant workers who signed labor contracts for the San Antonio area, South Texas, or the Midwest stayed on in San Antonio when their contracts lapsed.

As a result of the three decades of immigration (1900–30), San Antonio gained three types of immigrant: a minute upper class of exiled *ricos*, a middle class of professionals, and an extensive population of laborers. By the late 1920s and 1930s, the Mexican American middle class, a child of the Southwest's industrialization and Mexican immigration, was beginning to be visible in San Antonio, Laredo, El Paso, and Los Angeles, as well as in other developing cities in the West and Midwest. But the *ricos*, through their newspapers — *La Prensa* in San

Between 1900 and 1930, there undoubtedly occurred a process of class differentiation in the West Side. That is, there emerged, as W. Dirk Raat has stated of Mexico during the Porfirio Díaz regime, "groups of people that could be considered as a unit according to economic function, occupation, life style, and social status . . . [although] a conscious identity of interests may or may not characterize the members of such a group." Thus, people came from Mexico to San Antonio and the Southwest and began to develop a consciousness of themselves as individuals, groups, or classes and sometimes even formed different sectors within the classes.[42]

As mentioned earlier, the majority of the immigrants who flooded Los Angeles, El Paso, and San Antonio were from rural or working-class backgrounds, and most of them were uneducated. Many of them were contracted by an *enganchista* (labor contractor) to work on the railroad or to perform any other work not wanted by the Anglo or black population in San Antonio or the outlying areas. American employers drew freely from this labor pool; in many cases, in fact, the industrialist or the agriculturalist paid the cost of transporting the Mexican from the border and even paid agents to go into Mexico and offer jobs as inducements to potential immigrants. Word of mouth and family communication lines also spread the message of jobs and opportunities in the Colossus of the North. Many eventually followed the pattern of Ernesto Galarza, who moved from a peasant boy in Mexico to a barrio boy in the United States.

Unfortunately, when the Great Depression occurred, many of the Mexicans who had been induced to come to the Southwest and Midwest were unable to find jobs and became destitute. With this large labor pool stranded, the greatest deportation and repatriation movement in U.S. history took place. Relief agencies had to provide transportation by train to the border. There the Mexican government undertook to return people to their homes or, in keeping with government policy at the time, placed them in agricultural communities.[43]

Those Mexicans who remained in the Southwest and San Antonio were often enveloped by a dual oppression. Not only were they used as a reserve labor pool and discriminated against in the job market, but they were discriminated against as a cultural and "racial" group. It is important, therefore, to understand that the background of the Mexican immigrants often contrasted sharply with the urban environment they encountered in the United States, because Mexico's more rural states (such as Michoacán, Guanajuato, Jalisco, and Nuevo León) furnished the bulk of immigrants. According to anthropologist Manuel Gamio, these central states, characterized as they were by large landholdings, low wages, and high unemployment, oppressed the peon. Therefore, most emigrated for economic reasons (although some, like the *ricos* and the middle class emigrated for religious or political reasons). But there were also some who came solely for the spirit of adventure and a desire for personal progress. Regardless of their reasons, however, they faced discrimination for being perceived as being part of a distinct cultural or racial group, as part of the work force, or just as rural immigrants.[44]

Many Mexicans who entered the United States went to cities that had an economic need for their unskilled labor. However, in addition to these, there were other occupational categories, as table 3 shows. There were also many who were in professional, technical, or managerial occupations. Many of these quickly moved outside the Mexican Quarter or else found a suitable enclave within the area. These

TABLE 3

Occupations of Mexican Immigrant Aliens Admitted during the Year Ending June 30, 1923

Occupations	No.	% of Total
Professional	331	0.5
Skilled	2,268	3.6
Unskilled	36,642	58.4
Miscellaneous	1,606	2.6
None	21,862	34.9
—Total	62,709	100.0

SOURCE: Edwin Banford, "The Mexican Casual Problem," p. 365.

immigrants augmented the Mexican population already living in San Antonio.

Of the first wave of immigrants who settled in San Antonio (between 1900 and 1910), approximately twenty-five thousand were political refugees of varying political ideologies. Woods reports that some of them, "largely from Mexico's upper classes, looked upon San Antonio more as a refuge than as a permanent home. Some of them left San Antonio as soon as conditions in Mexico permitted, but others

cohesive Mexican community were political and military men such as Juan Sánchez Azcona and Gen. Pablo González. Moreover, some of Mexico's most prominent lawyers and intellectuals sought political refuge in San Antonio: Nemesio García Naranjo, Querido Moheno, Lic. René Capistrán Garza, and even former governors of Nuevo León like Gen. Bernardo Reyes and Gen. José E. Santos. These prominent intellectuals migrated to the United States and San Antonio as political refugees, especially from 1908 to 1914, and returned to Mexico when they were granted amnesty in the late 1930s and early 1940s.[46]

Most of these had been supporters of the Díaz and Huerta regimes. One important intellectual was publisher Ignacio E. Lozano, who fled Mexico in 1908 on the eve of the Mexican revolution. He established *La Prensa* in 1913 in San Antonio and *La Opinión* in 1926 in Los Angeles (both were daily newspapers distributed nationally and internationally). These papers were to be the voice of the exiled *ricos* in the 1920s and 1930s. Lozano hired exiled intellectuals such as José Vasconcelos, Nemesio García Naranjo, and Querido Moheno to be the columnists, writers, and analysts for his newspapers.

Many of the wealthy refugees were also religious refugees, especially those of the 1920s. They were of the same social class as the political refugees. These immigrants came because of the anticlerical campaign launched by Mexican president Plutarco Elías Calles in the late 1920s. The persecution of the clergy started a revolution by Catholics (the Cristero Revolt) and, consequently, hundreds of Mexican citizens fled to the United States. Many of these were either wealthy or middle class and highly educated. They chose San Antonio for the same reasons other Mexican immigrants had, because of the large Mexican community and especially because there was already a developed upper- and middle-class community of Mexicans. A Mexican educator, referring to the political and religious immigrants, observed that both had money, and "[b]oth were cultured and educated." Thus the first and second waves of immigrants to San Antonio were inspired primarily by political and religious oppression, although there were many who came for economic reasons as well.[47]

The last major immigrant wave of the 1920–29 period, however, was composed mostly of laborers and agricultural workers. This group was no different in many respects from the earlier immigrant groups from Europe, which included a large percentage of persons engaged in unskilled or semiskilled occupations. This wave of Mexicans, as one study points out, "cleaned the city's streets, repaired the roads, dug the foundations of buildings, shelled pecans, or worked on the cotton plantations and truck farms that spread out from San Antonio in all directions. Their work was not steady, but those who did find jobs were paid $1.00 to $2.50 a day."[48] According to some reports, these unskilled workers found themselves a little better off than they were in Mexico, even though they were hired only when the supply of unskilled non-Mexican labor was low.

Most of these unskilled Mexicans were on the lower rung of the Mexican as well as the non-Mexican social ladders in San Antonio. Few of the families in the West Side averaged more than five hundred dollars per year, and most earned far less. In fact, families with incomes of three hundred dollars or more per year were considered to be in the upper stratum of the Mexican community and were considered economically well off. Unfortunately, most of the people in the Latin Quarter during the 1930s were not well off. According to observations made by Carlos Castañeda in 1936, the Mexicans' wages during this period were a product of pure exploitation. They were paid "inferior wages for hard work that no one else would do for that or any other wage."[49]

Because of the economic pressures, deportation efforts, and the repatriation drives, more Mexicans left the United States during the Depression than at any other time. Ironically, however, this period witnessed an increase of poor Mexican immigrants to the San Antonio area, because the economic conditions forced migrant workers from the Midwest and South Texas to return to their home base of San Antonio, where they hoped to find jobs or receive financial relief. Specifically, agricultural acreage reduction and new hourly wage laws forced them back to the city, where they also hoped to find an economic and cultural haven in San Antonio's Mexican Quarter.

The high birth rate also helped to increase the Mexican population in the city. Moreover, there were some Mexicans who entered the United States and came to San Antonio as illegal aliens; conditions were bad in the United States, but they were worse in Mexico.[50]

By 1935 the San Antonio business sector was feeling better about the Depression, although workers in the city were not, and business recognized the problem. In San Antonio Mexican cigar workers, garment workers, and pecan shellers were striking; unemployment was

that was strongly dependent on Mexican and black voters, advised the city's social and business elite that plans for the 1936 Texas Centennial celebration should include the idea of employing many of the city's Mexican and black workers.[51]

The city's business and social elite did not control city government, although they agreed with the machine politicians that the centennial festivities could be used to provide relief to the workers. City government was controlled by a political machine that operated in semi-autonomous fashion, although it was heavily influenced by San Antonio's "silk stocking" district. It was not until the late 1930s that businesspeople decided to have more direct control of the city's political machine. By the mid-1930s the city's elite finally began to recognize that San Antonio had developed as a city with various ethnic communities that had never been integrated fully and saw the city's recovery programs as a possible means of strengthening social and cultural life as well as of integrating the city's body politic; modernity, they began to understand, needed order, stability, and consolidation. This understanding was expressed in a statement carried in the *San Antonio Express* as early as May 22, 1935:

> In a material sense, San Antonio unmistakably is entering upon a great building revival [1934–35] . . . with the use of its own resources — capital and manpower — and with [federal] government funds this community and region soon will be building, perhaps on an unprecedented scale. However, the need to build the intangibles — to strengthen and advance San Antonio's civic organization, and social and cultural life — also must be considered. Most important is the reinforcing of confidence in the city's own stability and in its future.

The business and the political sectors of the city (including the machine) knew that the vast Mexican population must be integrated if the city were to continue the process of modernization. In addition, the Mexicans, as they became more Americanized, also wanted to be integrated into the city's politics, culture, and opportunities. It was a major historical juncture for the city and for the development of the Mexican population.

THE LATIN QUARTER

For the most part, the majority of Mexicans were unaware of this juncture of history, modernity, and consciousness; consequently, life in the Latin Quarter of San Antonio remained much the same despite the Depression, poverty, and the repatriations. Poverty and tradition continued to envelop San Antonio's West Side; economic or social change was almost imperceptible to the outside Americano world. The West Side was described in 1939 as one of the most extensive slum areas anywhere in the world. More than one hundred thousand Mexicans accounted for over 40 percent of the population of the city. The majority of these Mexicans had come between 1910 and 1930. Even though many of these native- or foreign-born Mexicans were becoming middle class, one writer was prompted to describe all of them as "hundreds of unclean, impoverished 'paupers' . . . with scores of children." San Antonio received Mexicans by the thousands during the two decades from 1910 to 1930 and poured them out into the Latin Quarter, other southwestern urban barrios, and the Midwest labor markets.[52]

Since the 1850s the city had been divided into ethnic quadrants, and by 1930 the overwhelming majority of the Mexicans were living in the West Side of San Antonio while the East Side was mostly black and the South Side was basically lower- and middle-class Americano. The North Side was the rich and upper-class Americano enclave. The Latin Quarter in the west-central section of the city was characterized by poverty, dilapidated housing, and almost no sanitary facilities. Within this slum area, comparable to El Paso's South Side and to Los Angeles's East Side, there was a cycle of sickness, unemployment, poor living conditions, poor diet, poor education, and poor health. On the whole, the Mexicans were handicapped by menial jobs, burdened by myths and superstitions, weakened by malnutrition, and confronted with a daily struggle for survival in crowded, run-down housing and unsanitary conditions. The area, furthermore, was permeated by what seemed to many Americanos to be an ambience of ignorance and despair. In contrast, the North Side seemed to many Mexicans to exude an aura of knowledge and optimism. It represented about 27 percent of the total assessed valuation of the city and was well supplied with neighborhood centers and parks. In contrast, the West Side in the 1930s had almost no city services, facilities, or construction. From 1930 to 1940 there was a tendency for people to move to the suburbs, especially to the North Side, which was away from the inner city. This situation further isolated the Mexican population

a majority of the twenty thousand families that lived in these conditions were dependent on private charity and whatever they could get from the state or the local government to survive the Depression. Two public health surveys, one taken in 1935 and the other in 1939, confirmed the housing problem: "San Antonio abounded in poor housing conditions, especially for the Mexican population."[54]

In addition to their housing problems, Mexican workers suffered from diseases and debilitating health problems, which were worsened by the general conditions of the West Side. Tuberculosis and intestinal diseases were major causes of death among the Mexican population during the 1930s. In 1937, for example, there were 310 deaths from tuberculosis per 100,000 for the Mexicans in San Antonio as compared with 138 for the black population and 56 for the Anglo community. The two doctors who conducted a public health survey in 1935 stated in their report that they could not treat the problem of tuberculosis in isolation because "the tuberculosis problem in any community . . . [such as San Antonio] was an integral part of the general health problem, which, in turn, [was] part of the entire social and economic problem of the community. This [was] particularly ture of San Antonio where the factors of race, poverty, crowding, and undernourishment have been operative in producing and maintaining the present situation."[55]

Health problems were often compounded by the inefficiency of the city health department, which was used as a political football by the machine. Another survey taken by the health department in 1937 reported that among children under two years of age there was a death rate from intestinal inflammation of 394 persons per 100,000. This was 300 percent higher than the rate among the Anglo population but only 48 percent higher than that of the black population. In addition to the high death rate of children, the death rate for the Mexican population as a whole was so high per 10,000 that "San Antonio had the distinction of being the second ranking city in death rates among the five largest in Texas."[56]

As a direct corollary of these conditions, the West Side had one of the highest crime rates and greatest juvenile delinquency problems in the city. This situation was further exacerbated by the presence of the red light district close to Santa Rosa Street and Produce Row, almost in the heart of the Latin Quarter. This array of prostitution houses attracted soldiers, tourists, area cowboys, as well as Mexicans. The result was increased crime, heightened racial tensions, and continual health problems, namely, venereal disease.[57]

These problems were described very lucidly in a report to the U.S. government by Dr. David M. Gould of San Antonio. The report is worth quoting at length.

> The recital of statistics merely defines the magnitude of the problem; it does not give the answer to the question of why there is so much tuberculosis in San Antonio. Neither does it give an insight into the meaning of the disease to the individual. The misery, the broken homes, the undernourished children, the pauperization of families that stem from this chronic ailment are all implicit in the foregoing figures. It would be futile to give specific examples of what happened to individual families, because they are legion and their tragedies are so varied.
>
> The most obvious reason why one Latin American out of twenty was found to have tuberculosis is poverty. These people have been exploited as a source of cheap labor; they harvest the crops, shell the pecans, wash the clothes, and dig the ditches. For this they receive barely enough to keep body and soul together. In 1939, the housing authorities estimated that 45 percent of Latin Americans earned less than $550.00 a year and that 75 percent earned less than $950 a year.
>
> The natural corollaries of such conditions are cheap, congested, ramshackle houses, narrow, unpaved streets, few toilets, few water faucets, and a minimum of electricity.
>
> Diets are monotonous, high in starch, low in protein, and lacking in milk, meat, fruits, and vegetables.
>
> Under such conditions education is cursory. Many leave school before completing the grammar grades. The majority of young adults do not enter high school. These people are unable to purchase adequate medical care; community facilities and services are likewise inadequate for their enormous needs.
>
> All these factors mean a low standard of living which undermines resistance and makes the Latin American an easy mark for the tuber-

culous bacillus. A vicious circle is established when the tuberculous Latin American becomes poorer and sicker, spreading bacteria to his crowded family and numerous other contacts, and pyramiding the poverty and disease among his people.[58]

The conditions described by Dr. Gould were always present. As a result, the San Antonio elite, like other urban elites with similar ethnic enclaves, had to address the problem from within its own political, urban, and social interests. San Antonio, like the United States

slightly modified by Anglo-American influences."[59]

These conditions cannot be completely explained in terms of a culture of poverty, although, without a doubt, poverty influenced the enclave's intellectual and cultural growth. However, an analogous situation was apparent among the wealthier Mexicans, except that their consciousness was affected by a culture of relative affluence. In both cases factors other than poverty have to be considered to explain conditions: race, class, education, occupation, opportunity, and differences in historical development. The Depression intensified poverty during the 1930s; in particular, the lives of the agricultural migrants were affected, since they were one of the groups hardest hit in San Antonio.[60]

Despite these conditions, however, the West Side, at least in appearance, had a cohesive and homogeneous "flavor," although, in reality, the community's internal class fragmentation had already begun. There was a continuing undercurrent of Mexican spirit and tradition, which to one degree or another had existed since before the 1848 war between the United States and Mexico. It was this cultural cohesion and mask of uniformity that the Americanos generally saw. As early as 1916, Herbert Croly's liberal magazine the *New Republic* not only perceived the cultural and communal cohesion of the Mexican community, the strength of the Mexican spirit and will, the strong sense of intellectuality, and the strong familial ties in San Antonio, but commented on the impact of modernization on the Mexicans and their community. In a condescending but sympathetic article on June 24, 1916, the *New Republic* editorialized that here is a people well endowed intellectually, eager to learn, capable of artistic expression, with an emotional life, intense, but wholesome, with extremely vital family institutions, and apparently with enough co-operative instinct to manage the practical affairs of life [but] without the capacity for individual accumulation necessary for survival in a race like our own [which is] unsocial, unkind. [But, these] people have fallen on evil days; progressive exploitation, followed by general disintegration, [which] has torn apart millions of their intimate family bonds, thrown despair into hundreds of thousands of breasts, made for happiness, demanding so very little for happiness.

In addition to acknowledging the cohesiveness and strengths of the Mexican community in San Antonio, the *New Republic* article stressed the fact that there were rich Mexicans in the city, although the majority were poor. The wealthy Mexicans, the article reported, were, for the most part, not excluded from the social, political, business, or professional life of the city. They were allowed in the social clubs and the civic life of the city, although there was some discrimination.

This commentary by the *New Republic* was not only informational, but ideological. It was a change from the social Darwinian liberalism, which saw ethnics as "beaten races," to a new acceptance of the 1896 *Plessy* v. *Ferguson* view of "separate but equal," and only a step away from FDR's liberal policy of cultural pluralism. San Antonio's Americans and Mexicans were slowly moving through these stages of ethnic and immigrant perception, although from different ends of the ideological continuum.[61]

With the increase of Mexican emigration to San Antonio in 1929 and the 1930s, however, the designation "Mexican" became, as one sociologist relates,

associated with illiteracy, shiftlessness, lack of progressiveness, and a myriad of other uncomplimentary characteristics. Not that this connotation [on the word *Mexican* was] . . . due solely to the sharp increase in Mexican population, for it apparently dates back to the time immediately after [the U.S.] annexation [of the Southwest in 1848] when Anglo-Americans came into contact with Indians, Spanish, and Indo-Spanish. But the presence of large members of indigent Mexicans, undoubtedly . . . intensified "racial prejudice." The old Mexican elite [in 1929 and the 1930s] lost prestige, since the Anglo . . . tended [as a result of this immigration] to place all Mexicans in the same category and to look upon them as intruders and undesirables. Such attitudes roused ethnic consciousness in many of those belonging to old respectable families.[62]

This racial attitude tended to anger the rising Mexican middle class and caused it to separate itself psychologically from the Mexican laboring class and migrants. The middle class now tended to call itself "Latin Americans" or "Americans of Latin American descent." It also tended to emphasize its Americanism to show that members were not Mexicans. For example, Luis Albornoz, a middle-class Mexican born in the United States, felt proud of being an American and deplored the fact that the Mexicans who came to the United States were uncultured immigrants, thus making all Mexicans despised by Americans. This situation made Albornoz ashamed of being of Mexican descent.

it [did not] feel anything in common with the groups of Mexican workmen, [therefore] . . . each [class] ought to be in [its] own environment."[63]

City government was aware of this rift between the "Latin-Americans" and the "Mexicans." A city report contained the statement that the immigrant and migrant groups "lowered the economic status, not only of the city, but its own racial groups." This psychological and cultural separation between Mexicans was increased by the social and the class separation that resulted from the economic and the occupational differentiation that was occurring in the community.[64]

Exacerbating the cultural discrimination among Mexicans and between Americanos and Mexicans was the geographical discrimination in San Antonio. According to stipulations in home and property contracts, blacks were not allowed to buy houses or land outside of their own area; similarly, Mexicans were prohibited from purchasing homes or land in certain areas outside the West Side unless they claimed to be "Spanish" rather than "Mexican." Ironically, this geographical, structural, and spatial pattern of discrimination heightened the sense of ethnicity of the Mexicans already living in San Antonio because it kept them culturally insulated. The new immigrants' culture, however, served as a further catalyst for a constant communal cultural rejuvenation. As a result, many Mexicans were caught in the paradox of an ongoing process of Americanization, but within the structural patterns of Mexicanization.[65]

Many Mexicans, however, never experienced any overt ethnic discrimination because they never left the West Side. They had no need to leave; shopping, church, fiestas, schools, work, merchants, cantinas, and even the red light district were there. It was indeed a town within a city.

In Mexico the most powerful influences on people's lives had been the family, the community, and the church. The majority of Mexicans who emigrated from Mexico to San Antonio and to the rest of the Southwest found different cultural conditions. Their community experience was in keeping with that of the northern and central Mexican states, however, that is, more agrarian than industrial, more oral than written, more homogeneous than heterogeneous, and less technological. Immigrant society also had less of a division of labor, not because the immigrants' culture and sense of community were inferior to the urban Mexicans', but simply because they were, with more group identification and a subsistence economy. The immigrants entering San Antonio's Latin Quarter had many attitudes and values in common with the older Mexican residents. There was continuity in traditions, ideas, and community institutions, but, within the West Side, unlike in their home communities, there were more interactions with Mexicans from other regions (as well as from other class groupings). Moreover, there were encounters with other ethnic groups and Americanos. There was also more written communication, much more specialization in the division of labor and technology, and easier and faster social interactions. More often than not, however, despite some culture shock, the essential elements of the culture brought from Mexico were retained.[66]

Continuity more than discontinuity confronted the Mexican immigrants, although by the 1940s there were definite signs of cultural and ideological change. During the 1930s certain basic elements of the Mexican community were maintained: a strong sense of family solidarity; vocal adherence to Catholicism; the Spanish language; the patriarchal male-female relationship; the concept of early marriage for the women; and the psychology of superstition and fatalism that predominated in their agricultural society. There were cultural, economic, and class differences among the many who came, depending on the sending region, but on the whole, they all had a number of characteristics within the "Spanish Mexican" heritage in common until they were confronted by the American city over a period of time. Robert Park as early as 1912 theorized that over time this movement from initial cultural contact would lead to accommodation to acculturation and possibly to assimilation, although, as he clearly understood (and as John Higham would later point out), there were many factors of ethnicity that could delay this process, although not abort it altogether.

Thus, the developing interrelationship between the urban and the rural culture and the Mexican and the Americano culture was fundamental to the newly emerging consciousness of Mexicans in San Antonio. On the one hand, it helped them to retain their Spanish and Mexican heritage; on the other, neither one nor the other was entirely maintained. Consequently, a synthesis emerged. Thus, the Mexicans who came to San Antonio as immigrants between 1900 and 1940 with a suitcase full of cultural values, traditions, and attitudes

ceptance of a capitalist work ethic introduced changes in everyday life. However, unlike that of many other immigrant groups, their culture was constantly being reinforced by the flow of legal and illegal immigrants and by the fact that they represented not an isolated cultural group, but the northernmost tip of an Indo-Hispanic population. This reality constantly reinforced the memory of their history and traditions, and this, in turn, produced constant reflection (conscious or not), which provided a consciousness of historical collectivity. The consciousness of collectivity and collectivity of consciousness were constantly stressed and propagandized by *La Prensa*, the *ricos'* newspaper, and this *mexicanidad* was also maintained by de facto segregation, which kept them isolated.

Nevertheless, American movies, the radio, the schools, and the American Catholic Church penetrated this social separation and isolation. Ironically, the Latin Quarter of San Antonio, which served to maintain Mexican culture, eventually transformed it. As many of the recent immigrants, migrants, laboring class, and middle class became acculturated, they became the active agents of acculturation for others as well. For example, one Mexican clerk urged his family to become Americanized, that is, to speak English at home and to attend school. They moved away from the *jacales* to a modest home as soon as they could. He wanted, he said, to have his children get the opportunity to succeed and he thought that the "Mexican ways" hampered them in the United States. Others, of course, preferred to retain their Mexican ways and lifestyle. Unfortunately, the economic and commercial structures of the city channeled them into unskilled and semiskilled "Mexican" jobs or into the migrant stream, the city's political machine kept them politically immobilized, and geography kept them in their own town within the city. They did, however, have by the 1930s an internal class structure in their community that enabled them to have persons and goals with whom to identify: the *ricos* and the middle class, the former oriented toward Mexico, the latter toward the United States.[68]

CLASS DIFFERENTIATION

This slow but continual acculturation process was not noticeable in the streets of the Mexican barrio either to the Mexicans or to outsiders. In fact, to many of both groups, the substructure of the community (that is, poverty, unemployment, high death rates, rampant tuberculosis, familial fragmentation, generational conflict, emerging status groups, high crime rates, juvenile delinquency, and alienation) was not changeable. Instead, they focused on the superstructure, which was different and more appealing. For example, they focused on the "streets with typically Latin musical names such as El Dorado (Street of Gold), Angela (Street of Angels), and Dolorosa (Street of Sorrow)." They also noticed the main commercial streets, which were lined with stores that "spilled their wares onto the sidewalks," and had "paper banners" advertising "*gran baratas*" (big sales) and everywhere there were "bright colors" and "gaudy funeral wreaths and . . . paper flowers stuck between beer bottles on the bars." They also noticed the people who were colorfully dressed in clothes ranging from ranch clothes to business suits and the child beggars who filled the streets with their "gay bandanas wrapped around their foreheads." They also were aware of the "radios pouring Spanish music" from the houses and the stores and "small boys, usually ragged, gambling with pennies on the street corners."[69] From a superficial look one got the feeling that the people who lived in the area were untroubled, happy, and culturally intact, regardless of the filth and poverty in which they lived. Max Handman, commenting on the life in the Mexican barrio of San Antonio in the 1930s, wrote,

> The center of Mexican San Antonio is filled every evening and late afternoon and particularly on Saturday and Sunday with men with big sombreros, mellow eyes and gentle expressions and with women with their heads wrapped in dark shawls, gliding along in a soft and shuffling walk. The on-coming generation, however, promenading up and down, presents a different picture. Young dandies put as much glitter in their attire as modern clothes will permit, while Mexican flap-

pers wear the American flappers' garb of independence with more dash and grace than the originator. Here in the Mexican business district are the moving-picture theaters, the Nacional and Zaragosa, the leading and very important Spanish paper (*La Prensa*), restaurants, bookstores of which there are many, grocery stores kept by Chinese merchants for Mexican trade, music stores emanating a constant stream of *jotas* and love songs along with the ever present music of the military band.

In a little park, groups of Mexicans sit on the benches or squat on the ground conversing in soft tones while occasionally a reader, paid

dear to their peasant hearts. The District finally shades off into more dubious types of business — fortune tellers, tattoo artists, shooting galleries and second-hand stores. But after a few more steps we are in the region of skyscrapers and American San Antonio begins.[70]

Julia Kirk Blackwelder also has described the area:

A substantial commercial district stood on the near West Side and served Mexican-Americans of all income levels. West Side businesses acted as a buffer between the Central Business District and the West Side slums. Businesses that printed or sold Spanish-language publications. Spanish-language film theaters; sidewalk cafes serving Mexican dishes; Mexican-American groceries, pharmacies carrying Mexican folk remedies; and the Mexican clinic served the needs of the city's large Mexican community and provided the monies of the Mexican-American middle class. Spreading out west of the business district were the most miserable slums in urban America.[71]

Within these Mexican middle-class enclaves and poorer slum areas of San Antonio, the upper-class Mexicans, through *La Prensa*, were "more concerned with what [was] doing in old Mexico; [the] Mexican middle-class [was] busy making a living in its own way, [while] the majority of [working-class] Mexicans, on the other hand, [were] often indifferent to their community. It [was] an indifference which [was] palpable, almost blatant."[72]

For the working-class Mexicans, life was only work, families, fiestas, drinking, and more work. Life came one day at a time and changes were often imperceptible. Naftali in Richard Vásquez's novel *Chicano* might have been voicing the attitudes and alienation of the majority of these Mexicans in San Antonio when, after having arrived from Mexico and living in a barrio of a large urban area during the 1920s and 1930s, he thought as he "walked and streets of the barrio in his spare time . . . [and] looked at the dirty streets and houses, [and at] the people caught up in this life . . . and . . . he remembered back to the little quiet village where he had roamed free, alone. And . . . he longed to go back." Later, talking to his sister, Naftali says, "it . . . would have been better had we stayed in Mexico." And his sister replies (probably as many often had in San Antonio during the thirties), "Like hell it would, don't you remember, brother, the hunger, the nothing we had, no clothes, beans and corn every day, a big occasion when we had a chicken? Well, now . . . [I] eat chicken whenever . . . [I] want. [I] have a room . . . on the edge of the barrio, where . . . [I] can buy things . . . I like, that we never dreamed we could own in Mexico." Nostalgia was in conflict with reality, but the reality promised a future, the past, only memories.[73]

Naftali's sister was right: conditions were better for the Mexican workers in the United States. They now had choices; they could live beyond a subsistence level. Moreover, they were becoming aware that their labor not only brought a new meaning and a new sense of dignity into their lives, but it heightened their self-perception with a sense of ambition, enterprise, and opportunity. These Mexicans in San Antonio did not fully perceive, although those like Naftali's sister partially did, that they were entering the rhythm and cycle of American history in the pursuit of a dream and like Fitzgerald's Gatsby, they were "wedding their" unutterable visions to San Antonio's and the United States' "perishable breath." And like the moment that Gatsby kisses Daisy—the "incarnation was complete"—the Mexican was wedded to the soul of American life and thought. Immigrants were, as a consequence, quantitatively better off in San Antonio, but only in relationship to their existence in Mexico. It would not be long, however, before they would qualitatively measure the extent of their choices and their material possessions by new standards relative to their existence in the United States. This, together with other cultural changes, would bring a new consciousness to these Mexicans in San Antonio. Naftali's sister would no longer be right: the reality would not only promise a future, it would limit it—especially freedom. And like Gatsby, they would not even know that their moment had passed; equality and materialism would now be pursued by the majority of Mexicans.[74]

In the 1930s Max Handman conducted a study of fifteen hundred Mexicans, who, like Naftali's sister, stayed in San Antonio's West Side. Sixty percent of those studied were laborers; 25 percent were skilled workers; 2 percent were clerks; and over 5 percent were small entrepreneurs. Handman determined that half of those interviewed earned $13.00 a week when they were employed, but only one-fourth of them were employed regularly. Handman also found that the U.S.-born Mexican Americans fared better than the immigrants. They had steadier, more skilled jobs and higher pay. In addition, the study showed that the Mexicans who spoke English did better than those who did not: "the language was worth $5.00 a week to them on the average; and American schooling also increased their earning capacity."[75]

when he stated, "My life is a sad story, especially here in the United States where they drive me crazy from working so much. They squeeze me here until one is left useless, and then one has to go back to Mexico to be a burden to one's country men. But the trouble is that it is true, not only here, but over there [in Mexico] also." Another said, "I don't like the customs of this country anyway. Although my children are already grown-up, I don't want their children to be pochos [culturally half Mexican, half American]."[76]

In spite of the pressure to change, many countervailing forces helped Mexicans maintain their identity. During the 1930s, there were, as one observer pointed out, "all of these [Mexican] agencies, the [Mexican] newspapers, the [Mexican] movies, and [Mexican] culture in varying degrees." Additional influences helping to preserve the culture were the church and family structure; however, even these institutions soon advocated Americanization. Thus, even though Mexicans continued to rely on church, family, and community, just as they had done in Mexico, these institutions were changing them, pushing them toward Americanization. Consequently, there was some economic progress and cultural change for these Mexicans in San Antonio. Even if it was not entirely real, at least it was an improvement when compared to conditions in Mexico. Mexicans often thought that any economic improvement would be accompanied by changes in their social and cultural life. This assumption was only partially correct.[77]

Emory Bogardus, writing in the 1930s about these attitudes and the Mexican immigrant, stated that as "the Mexican immigrant comes into contact with American ways and cultural traits under conditions that are pleasing and favorable to him, his attitudes respond. [As a result] . . . marriage is delayed, the birthrate begins to decline, and the divorce rate, supplementing desertion, increases. American family life had its strengths and its weaknesses, both of which . . . [were] adopted by the Mexican in San Antonio." Moreover, "in the United States the Mexican immigrant family is characterized by increasing social distance between children and parents . . . when there is too sudden [a] change involving a conflict of attitudes, even between members of the same household, family disorganization follows. . . . The parents begin to apply different standards to the [rearing of] the children depending on whether they are boys or girls." The cultural freedom of the American way of life did not alarm Mexican parents in relationship to the upbringing of boys, only as it affected girls.[78]

The Mexicans in San Antonio were often forced, although at times not consciously, to behave in a dualistic fashion. Since they came to San Antonio in stages, and since there were already different Mexican generational ideas, ideology, and lifestyles, there resulted varying degrees of acculturation. The first generation continued to retain its traditional cultural patterns while the second generation had some difficulty functioning in the American community outside the West Side because, as Bogardus indicates, they suffered from tremendous psychic pressures and emotional guilt. They had to accept a duality of roles. "They . . . were stimulated to contradict themselves, to play dual roles, to be hypocrites: at home to act as loyal Mexicans . . . [but] at school and elsewhere to act as loyal Americans. Adding more pressure to this situation . . . were the attitudes displayed by the Anglos who treated them as foreigners regardless of their own identification." "By and large," contributes another writer, Spanish-speaking people were "looked upon as [poor and illiterate] Mexicans and . . . were frequently thought of as aliens." As a result of these pressures, *mexicanos* in San Antonio often left the Latin Quarter as soon as they could afford it, even though the barrio provided a familiar cultural environment. These generational patterns of development have often been apparent in other ethnic communities in U.S. history.[79]

The Mexicans, whether second or third generation, who began to break away from the cultural patterns of their parents exhibited cultural traits and attitudes that closely approximated those of the native-born Americano children. A consciousness was being expressed by the Mexicans that was determined more by Americano cultural traits and values than by Mexican ones. Indirectly, the general process of urbanization was a factor of change; more directly, the family was one of the main catalysts for changing children's consciousness from a Mexican one to an Americano one, since the parents were in a constant state of change and these changes were reflected in child-rearing practices. Also, "the indirect role of [the English] language . . . as a means of communication . . . was significant in changing . . . [their] attitudes." There was a steady and constant process of emotional and intellectual change that was occurring within the Mexican family as well as outside it, but this process was often retarded by the influence of the Catholic Church[80] which may have favored Americanization in the church but opposed American-style secularism.

American custom of using 'bloomers' . . . The children, who are in high school, already speak English, for they have been in the school four years. The family never goes to a celebration of a Mexican national holiday. . . . Nevertheless, their food is Mexican; but on special occasions they eat American food." The family and the church, then, were playing dual roles, as agents of change and as agents of continuity.[81]

It was evident that the workers, the middle class, and the *ricos* in San Antonio now lived in a society that required new responses, emotions, and attitudes. The Mexican middle class was constantly being pulled by the forces of acculturation but rejected by the forces of assimilation, which required conscious acceptance by the Americano community. One Mexican worker described his dilemma:

> I learned a little English here from hearing it so much. I can read and write it, but I don't ever like to deal with those *bolillos* [Anglos] for the truth is that they don't like the Mexicans. Even the pochos [Mexican Americans] don't like us. I have scarcely been able to stand up for my rights with the little English that I have learned, but I would like to know a lot of English so as to tell them what they are and in order to defend my poor [working-class] countrymen.[82]

The acculturation process could be delayed, even modified, but not aborted. The Mexicans in San Antonio, as in El Paso, Los Angeles, Chicago, and Kansas City, were becoming acculturated if not assimilated; that is, they were accepting U.S. values, attitudes, and emotional responses and expressing them through new ideologies commensurate with class position. But they were not accepted. As ethnic historian Manuel Peña has stated, "by moving into new socioeconomic fields they exposed themselves to new sets of social relations that inescapably shut off time-tested cultural strategies. Unforeseen social tensions resulted due to cultural dislocation: the transition from rural to urban modes of life, from Mexican to American cultural environments, and lastly, from proletarian to middle class status was not easy."[83]

The Mexicans' new self-identity came into conflict with the way society identified them, causing them to retreat into and accept some of their parents' culture, at least marginally. Wenceslao Iglesias, a worker from El Paso, expressed this dilemma well for all Mexican workers when he said,

> I have bought a little house near a family of pochos . . . who are very dark and it happened once that [my] children had a quarrel with those of the pocho family. Those kids were calling my children cholos [lower-class Mexicans] and other ugly names. I went to their father and said that I wanted there to be good feelings between us and I wanted him to control his children. The father began to talk English as well as the mother. I talked to them in Spanish and when I was tired of that I also spoke to them in English and they then changed their manner of talking and at once calmed down. I don't like the customs of this country, least of all for my daughters. I want them to be brought up in Mexico.[84]

This psychological conflict was part of everyday life in the West Side. Not everyone experienced it, and the degree varied, but this psychological marginality was present.

Mobility was also a factor in the process of class differentiation and ideological change. In the West Side the "mobility patterns . . . significantly affected the structure and the behavior of . . . [the Mexicans]. A good deal of geographical mobility, property mobility (home ownership), and occupational mobility (skilled status in new industries or in the expanding building trades, small retail enterprise, the professions; and public employment counted as the most important ways to advance occupationally), reshaped" the Latin Quarter. This pattern, as historians and sociologists have shown, parallels the mobility process of the other ethnic communities. Although restricted to the West Side, it did have an effect on the beliefs and the values of San Antonio's Mexicans.[85]

According to one middle-class Mexican's account, the people who began to act and feel like middle-class Americanos started to move to the Prospect Hill area, which was on the north end of the West

Side. The Mexicans who moved to the Prospect Hill enclave or who already lived there were middle-class businesspeople, teachers, and clerks. These Mexicans were the leaders of the community. They began to develop a separate consciousness in the 1920s and 1930s, a consciousness of individualism, mobility, and possibilities, especially of influencing power relationships. This process had slowly developed from two sources: the incipient *tienditas* class that emerged in the nineteenth century, and the arrival of the middle-class Mexican in

and they chose to function only as a comprador class. That is, they wanted to continue to see themselves as Mexican citizens in exile and not as Mexicans accommodating to their new environment. Consequently, they sought to set the cultural tone for the Mexican community in the city through *La Prensa*. As a result, they had no substantial economic or political base in the community nor did they have the desire to integrate themselves into the politics or society of the Americano world in San Antonio. They never fully involved themselves in the everyday activities of the community, although they sometimes helped in the organizational activities of the Americanizing Mexican middle class and at times initiated activities that they felt were culturally important. The *ricos'* class consciousness had no social or political reality: their world of class, tradition, and the possibility of political power had passed with Porfirio Díaz and Victoriano Huerta. Yet they maintained their dreams of a Mexico that was ordered, stable, and cohesive, with themselves as the class in power.

In contrast to these two classes, the laboring class, which was the social base of the West Side, did not exhibit a concise political consciousness. It showed, however, by strikes and other activities during the thirties that, even though it was not concious of its status as a working class in the Marxist sense, it was conscious of its needs as Mexicans, but not yet as Mexican Americans. During the 1934–38 period, however, the laboring class performed the unconscious task of Marxist activity — struggle — but for the non-Marxist goals of better jobs and higher wages. This class suffered the most during the Depression.[87]

2

Mexican Labor and the Depression

A very few years after mass migration, there . . . began within the immigrant community that process of external social differentiation which is characteristic of American society as a whole.

— Irving Howe

The laboring sector of the Mexican community was poor, not only economically but also culturally, since most of them came from the rural villages in the central states of Mexico. Writing in the 1920s, Mexican anthropologist Manuel Gamio detailed their poverty and rurality, but only in passing did he discuss their political background: "It is significant that three states [Michoacán, Jalisco, and Guanajuato] were all located in the central plateau region of Mexico, and that they have been the center of revolutionary and religious disturbances . . . [during] the entire period since the overthrow . . . of Díaz [in 1911]." Thus, while many of these immigrants might have been political, they were, for the most part, "illiterate peasants from a semifeudal agricultural background with a heritage of complacent subservience and dependence on their 'patrons.'" They were unfamiliar, for the most part, with urban customs and the English language.[1]

Most Mexican workers who came to San Antonio, whether they were recent immigrants or not, read very little and often moved about in the migrant agriculture stream. When they did settle, it was in the Latin Quarter. They usually left their families in Mexico, but with the intention of returning to their homeland. Often they sent for their families; if they were not married, they married in the United States and settled down. Depending on their economic situation, they might learn a few words of English and begin to think of educational opportunities and sometimes of citizenship. As historian John Bodnar has stated of other transplanted workers, they did not deny the possibility of opportunity in this country, but they were preoccupied in meeting the more immediate needs of everyday life. Nevertheless, whether real or ideal, the Horatio Alger attitude was often passed on to their children either consciously or subconsciously through the family structure and through the social process of Americanization. A sense of middle classness had begun, and it was both a generational and an environmental process.[2]

Initially, the Mexican worker who settled in San Antonio usually

1936 the Southern Pecan Shelling Company's sales reached $3 million) they paid very low wages on a piecework basis. According to a 1934 labor board hearing, the average piecework wage for a sixty-four–hour week was $1.56. Some of the less skilled earned only $1.16 per week, but other reports documented the salaries at $.05 an hour or $2.50 per week. To make more profits, the larger operators or companies frequently turned the pecans over to contractors who provided their own facilities and subcontracted the pecans to Mexican families. These families shelled the pecans in the unsanitary conditions of the contractor's facilities or in their own shacks. According to one economist,

> home-shelling was a doubly convenient procedure since the pecan industry was concentrated on the West Side of the city . . . where two-thirds of the community's Mexicans resided. [In this life], the only vital substances that ever thrived [and profited] in the area . . . were the germs of tuberculosis and infant diarrhea. Thousands of human beings living in decrepit wooden shacks or in crowded corrals, breathlessly shelled pecans in a race with starvation. In these homes, which lacked toilets and running water and rented for as little as fifty cents a week, pecans were shelled and picked for the fastidious tables of northern and eastern gourmets.

The plight of the pecans shellers of San Antonio was typical of the working conditions of many persons of Mexican background. In spite of the difficulty of the task, the Pecan Shelling Workers' Union of San Antonio and the El Nogal Union attempted to unionize the pecan shellers. El Nogal claimed to have four thousand members in the early thirties. Both of these unions were independent of organized labor.[4]

Agriculture was also an important source of employment for the Mexican working class. Because San Antonio had become in the 1920s and the 1930s a center for marshaling Mexican farm labor to other parts of Texas and the Midwest as well as the outlying agricultural areas, the Mexicans could always find a job in the agricultural sector. The Interstate Commerce Commission often warned truckers about taking Mexicans across state lines, however. It seems that many truckers had been transporting Mexican workers to Northern beet fields without the commission's authority. Although this activity carried a federal penalty, because there was a considerable profit for truckers and others, it continued. The San Antonio farms' placement office supervisor, E. H. Banks, stated that San Antonio played a very important part as a migrant labor center and explained that, although fifteen hundred workers were scheduled to leave San Antonio for fields in South Texas, many migrant workers were being transported outside the state because it was profitable for the truckers and because the Mexicans would receive higher wages outside of Texas. Maury Maverick, who was a dominant force in San Antonio politics during the thirties, stated that Texas was often faced with a labor shortage as a result of this exodus.[5]

The sewing industry also employed many of the Mexican workers, because they could sew in their own homes. The whole family could be employed at low wages, in conditions that were not much better than in the pecan "factories." The San Antonio labor newspaper, the *Weekly Dispatch*, which was affiliated with the American Federation of Labor, deplored these conditions but no attempt was made to organize the workers in the garment industry until the late 1930s, when the Congress of Industrial Organizations (CIO) tried. The editor of the *Weekly Dispatch* stated rather skeptically (after being prodded by some of the Americano women's organizations to take some action against the conditions) in an editorial entitled "Civic Leader to Assist in Homework Clean Up: Deplorable Condition Existing in Bexar County and Surrounding Territory,"

> We are told that an authentic survey has revealed between 15,000 to 20,000 families who eke out a precarious existence from employment in their homes, such as shelling pecans, garment and handkerchief making, which sad to state, are sometimes mere hovels for which words can scarcely be found to portray the squalor existing there. The conditions existing where this home work industry is carried on is [sic], in most cases, unwholesome and unsanitary to say the least, and . . . these conditions resemble the feudal system and the sweatshop which are now mere matters of history to most states and the nations of the civilized world.[6]

The *Dispatch* then proceeded to document conditions within the Mexican community that affected this cottage industry. It emphasized the following points: "large families living in two rooms," "lighting being bad," "women making only $.25 per dozen on baby dresses," "bedridden families working with tuberculosis and some with V.D.," and, "children sick with ringworm and helping their mothers as the latter sewed 'pretty' smocks that would be sold in the Anglo shops." These conditions angered the Americano women of the city because

as the Mexican-born, although some did. On the whole, U.S.-born Mexicans in San Antonio fared better than their counterparts who worked in construction, pecan shelling, or the cigar, sugar, and garment industries. Table 4 details the results of William Knox's study of the occupations of 424 U.S.-born and 777 Mexican-born males.

Knox's study showed that, in general, the U.S.-born Mexican male in San Antonio fared slightly better than his counterpart in the pecan shelling, sewing, or the sugar industries. Knox's research indicated that the U.S.-born Mexican male averaged $17.95 per week while the Mexican-born averaged $15.71 per week (U.S.-born women averaged only $6.70 per week).

Regardless of birthplace, the employment situation was difficult during the thirties. If the Mexicans could not find work in the plants or factories, they could look in *La Prensa*, which had a daily circula-

T A B L E 4

Occupations of Mexican Males, 1927

Occupation	No. Native Born	% of Total	No. Foreign Born	% of Total
Laborers	142	33.5	389	50.1
Unskilled office jobs	125	29.5	115	14.8
Business	36	8.5	58	7.5
Skilled labor	99	23.3	181	23.3
Professional	22	5.2	34	4.3
—Total	424	100	777	100

SOURCE: Knox, *Economic Status of the Mexican*, pp. 21–23.

tion of seventy-two hundred and a Sunday circulation of about sixteen thousand. Here they could find advertised such jobs as "Omaha
Employment Bureau wants vegetable pickers," "Gouger National Bank
wants 50 truckers in Robstown," "Men and women with experience
to sew babies' dresses in your own homes — good pay," "learn to be
a Barber, Lewis Barber College," "Wanted: strawberry pickers,
Highland Farms, $.50 per box — 2 months, Harris County, Texas," and
"Wanted: middle-aged women for housework at the Black and White
Garage." If none of these suited them, they could check another day
and might find "10 dancers wanted — Club Continental, See Jesse
López, dance every night — the new taxi dance — Women dancers $.10
a dance" or "20 men to sell life insurance." For the most part, Mexicans outside of factory work, found jobs in the military establishments,
the wholesale and retail trades, small manufacturing shops, or in the
nondurable goods sector of the economy: foods, apparel, printing,
publishing, transportation equipment companies, electrical equipment companies, bakeries, meat packing plants, cement manufacturing plants, furniture stores, lumber companies, flour mills, cigar
manufacturing, or the breweries. These jobs also served to separate
the Mexican community into laboring class and lower middle class.[7]

According to another study of the Mexican employment situation
prior to World War II, "individual firms established and tended to
maintain patterns of 'Anglo' jobs and 'Mexican' jobs." This distinction
was based primarily on the availability of qualified Anglo workers
at or near the wage acceptable to that of the Mexicans. In the 1930s,
Carlos Castañeda stated that "Mexican wages were, in the final analysis, a product of plain and simple exploitation" and that this "economic discrimination [was] based on the assumption that the Mexican was inferior to the Anglo . . . in ability and physical endurance."
Moreover, he said, "Mexicans . . . [were usually] employed at the
hardest and the filthiest type of work in industry and in agriculture
in spite of the allegation that [they were] too weak to do [a] good
day's work." This, in effect, was almost a practice of "racial dualism."
The situation in San Antonio almost paralleled that found by Mario T.
Garcia in El Paso in the early 1920s:

> Racial dualism . . . meant the second-class subordination of the Mexi-
> can at every level of activity: occupational distribution, residential
> patterns, political representation, participation, and social-cultural re-
> lationship. Such a duality based on the supposed racial and cultural
> under-development of the Mexicans served to maintain the economic
> advantages as well as social privileges which the Anglo-American popu-
> lation derived from a large pool of surplus Mexican labor.[8]

This pattern of economic discrimination was prevalent throughout San Antonio because the Mexican community had a virtual monopoly on the common labor occupational sector. Not only did Mexican workers shell pecans, sew, or make cigars, but they were evident in all the industries in the city as well as in the fields outside the city. They dug trenches, laid railroad tracks, built streets, drove trucks, gardened, and peddled. In fact, they did all the menial work that had been formerly done by other ethnic groups. In addition to the

voir of government funds via its network of military bases, but it had an abundant supply of labor as well.[9]

In 1930 there was a total population of 231,542 people in San Antonio: 130,737 Anglos (56.6%), 82,373 Mexicans (35.7%), and 18,452 others. This last category consisted of blacks, Japanese, Chinese, and Indians, but most were blacks. By 1940 there was some growth in the city's labor market because the population had risen to 254,053. There were now 131,221 Anglos (46.7 percent), 103,000 Mexicans (46.3 percent), and 19,832 others (7.6 percent). The increase in the Mexican population was also due to a high birth rate, even though during this decade deportations and repatriations slightly exceeded the immigration rate in San Antonio.

Therefore during the thirties, the industrial and commercial labor market of the city was composed of approximately 50,000 Anglos, 44,000 Mexicans, 7,500 blacks, and 175 others. The total number of potential workers in San Antonio was over one hundred thousand (one million in the larger trade area) during the Depression decade. The Mexican population, especially the large number of unskilled workers, was vital to the economy of the city and the metropolitan area.[10]

Because of this extensive labor market, there were many unions, but little actual union activity in San Antonio compared with some eastern or western cities. There were the usual unions of the American Federation of Labor (AF of L) (the Brotherhoods of Locomotives, Engineers, Firemen, Conductors, Bus Drivers, Telegraph Operators, and Electrical workers in transportation and utility companies). There were seventy-five unions in San Antonio connected with the American Federation of Labor. In addition, there were the United Cannery, Agricultural Packers and Allied Workers, the International Ladies Garment Workers of America, and the Newspaper Guild, all of which were affiliated with the CIO. The Workers Alliance, a Communist party organization, also had eight unions together with the Communist-oriented Trade Union Unity Leagues. However, the city was relatively free from serious labor disputes during the thirties except in several industries that employed unskilled Mexicans. Mexican strike activity got worse during the 1934–38 period, when San Antonio's population felt the Depression the hardest.[11]

As a result of the devastating socioeconomic conditions, a general wave of strike actions began. In 1933 for example, 350 cigar rollers, strippers, and scrappers (mostly Mexican women) founded a union and began to strike. They demanded recognition of their union, better pay, and better working conditions. After a number of weeks the strike was settled and the employer agreed to adopt the National Recovery Administration's (NRA) cigar industry code. In addition, the employer agreed to pay nine dollars for a forty-hour week; however, the company did not recognize the union.

Although there was no apparent communication among the Mexican unions in the Southwest, 1933 found Mexicans conducting the largest agricultural workers' strike to date in California, where seven thousand Mexican workers went on strike in the southern area of the San Joaquin Valley. In the same year, Mexicans struck for the third time in the Imperial Valley.[12]

In 1934, the independent unions in the pecan shellers' factories struck. They were led by five thousand Mexican workers who wanted an increase per pound of shelled nuts from two cents and three cents to five cents and six cents per pound. They also wanted the nut crackers to get paid fifty cents instead of the usual twenty-five to thirty cents per one hundred pounds of cracked nuts. The nut cleaners also demanded a wage increase. Before the strike developed any further, the NRA settled it and established the shellers' salary at fifteen cents per hour rather than having workers paid by the pound. This settlement did not satisfy everyone, and, as a result, several other union groups were formed: the Cooperativa de Nueceros de San Antonio and the Mandadores de Nuez. These two groups, together with the unions, developed different demands. The uneasiness over the settlement translated itself into further conflict in the ensuing years. But these unions exhibited a consciousness of everyday life and presented strike demands that were like those of Samuel Gompers' American Federation of Labor, that is, oriented toward wages and hours.[13]

The pecan shellers' strike caused much consternation in the San Antonio community. The upper-class Mexicans, in *La Prensa*, called for cooperation and the paper mentioned that the spokesman for the pecan shellers, Magdaleno Rodríguez, was a "fugitive from Mexican law and . . . an agitator who was a traitor to the union." *La Prensa's* point carried weight with the middle sectors of Mexican society, who remained silent about the strike. Labor leader W. B. Arnold, the president of the Federation of Labor in Texas, later called Rodríguez's

Within a month of the pecan shellers' strike, the bakers in San Antonio, headed by the Unión Latino-Americana de Panaderos, struck. They wanted a higher salary in compliance with the NRA regulation. At that time, Zúñiga, the secretary of the union, stated that bakers were getting paid only $1.75 to $2.00 a day. They wanted $2.80 to $3.60 per day. No sooner had the town settled down from these strikes than the cigar workers struck again in the spring of 1935. This time the company, with the aid of the police, continued to operate and broke the strike. Two decades later the head of the cigar company, remembering his father's fight with the union, said he considered his father's "militant victory in the 1935 strike a significant factor in San Antonio remaining a relatively non-union town."[15]

With the victory of the cigar company the strikes seemed to be over. Mexican society returned to its spring festivities. Once again the "soft music and Spanish dances" could be heard from the plush Casino Social where the Mexican intelligentsia and society barons like publisher Ignacio E. Lozano, lawyer Alonzo S. Perales (who was the master of ceremonies for the 1937 annual spring dance), and such businessmen as F. A. Chapa and Carlos Barrera met to talk with and receive praise from the mayor of San Antonio, C. K. Quinn, and Mexican diplomat Elías Colunga. Colunga gave the main speech that spring night praising these upper- and middle-class Mexicans and their club for being very instrumental in "bringing the two countries together." The dance that evening was sponsored by one of the most prominent clubs of the period, the Club Swastika.[16]

On the other side of town, spring was also being welcomed, but not quite so elegantly. This event was sponsored by some of the more active lower-middle-class groups from the Prospect Hill area, groups like the Sociedad Mutualista Medelo, the Latin Booster, the Lucky 13 Masculino, the Lucky 13 Femenino, and the Bohemia. Most of the Mexican workers in San Antonio, it would be safe to say, did not attend either of these fiestas; they could only read, or have read to them, the news about the night's activity when it was reported in *La Prensa*. In spite of these politically calm spring evenings, however, the ripples of conflict had not yet subsided.[17]

The Shirlee Frock Company workers, who were predominantly Mexican women who belonged to the International Ladies Garment Workers Union (ILGWU) Local No. 180, had other interests than spring festivities; they were on the verge of their first strike, which would last three months. That summer of 1937 they won a union shop agreement that lasted three months and also won a wage increase. In summer 1938, after striking again, they won a similar battle with the Texas Infant Company. The ILGWU won similar agreements with three other infant and children's garment companies, including one of the largest, Juvenile Manufacturing Company (which had a separate ILGWU local).[18]

By 1937 the pecan shellers' unions had virtually disappeared, but the problems had not. The remnants of the Pecan Shelling Workers' Union reappeared in 1938. At its helm was a fiery young local woman named Emma Tenayuca—"la Pasionaria"—as the workers called her. Emma Tenayuca was a former college student who, according to rumors, began her career as a "communist revolutionary" because she was angered with the racial attitudes at school, or, as other rumors hinted, she was radicalized by the "leftist" professors at Our Lady of the Lake College in San Antonio. It is more plausible that she was influenced by her family. Julia Kirk Blackwelder has suggested that her grandfather introduced her to socialism, and her radicalism was strengthened by her marriage to a Communist leader of the Workers' Alliance Organization of Texas. But regardless of the origins of her militancy, she ultimately joined the San Antonio chapter of her husband's Communist organization.

With a small cadre of followers, she successfully prodded the Pecan Shellers' union to organize a strike, although she was not an official member. She usually gained the acceptance of the Mexican workers with passionate statements that were indicative of her fervor and militancy, her unrelenting sincerity and compassion. For example, speaking at a rally, she began her speech with the words, "They can stand me up against a wall and fill my body with bullets."

International solidarity for the laboring class was no doubt behind

Tenayuca's actions, but her ideology never fully appealed to the striking workers, although her enthusiasm, passion, and commitment did. A possible additional influence on her, but here we can only speculate, might have been leftist-liberal Lázaro Cárdenas, who was president of Mexico at the time, or socialist Vicente Lombardo Toledano, who was head of the powerful Confederation of Mexican Workers (CTM). It was during this period that some thought that the CTM was making overtures to Mexican workers in the United States as well

Citizens, the Catholic Church, and even organized labor opposed the strike. Bishop Drossaert of the Catholic Church offered assistance to the strikers but only if they rejected the leadership of the CIO, which the *Weekly Dispatch* had been branding as Communist. The strikers refused. The local press, denouncing the strike finally reported that,

> after more than a month, the San Antonio pecan shellers and their employers are submitting their differences to arbitration. As a strike, the dispute was a failure . . . no plant was forced to shut down. Pecan shelling is piece work and can be done by anybody. Paid agents of the CIO and communist agitators before them convinced the pecan shellers that they were being treated unfairly. . . . Chief of Police Kilday, knowing the CIO, did well to take firm action to prevent disorders.[20]

During the strike leadership had been taken from Emma Tenayuca and her small cadre by the CIO affiliate, which had also been organizing the Mexican workers in the garment district and the cigar factories. The affiliate, the United Committee of Agricultural, Packing, and Allied Workers of America (UCAPAWA), moved to settle the strike through arbitration.[21]

Because the CIO was organizing in San Antonio, the AF of L also began to organize the Mexican people and others who had not yet been unionized. H. M. Hoffner of the AF of L said, "This campaign to organize [the Mexicans] is not in line with the method used by the CIO, who take in everybody and his uncle into one union without payment of initiation fees or dues." As early as 1937, Holt Ross, the southern organizer for the AF of L, had spoken out against the role

of the CIO in San Antonio. In the *Dispatch* he said "that the AF of
L [local] should not recognize the CIO and urged San Antonio labor
union members to unite with their fellow unionmen in other cities
to form a united front against the CIO." Ross went on to call John L.
Lewis, the national leader of the CIO, a person who wanted to "be
a glorified Hitler or Mussolini," and he called the CIO an "Autocratic
dictatorship." This tone had helped to lay the framework for the city's
denouncement of the CIO that spring when the pecan shellers accepted their leadership.[22]

The continual strikes during the 1930s in San Antonio certainly
had repercussions in the Mexican community. There was a feeling
of some solidarity among the workers in the striking industries, but,
in effect, the "class struggle" that had occurred served to further polarize the Mexican community ideologically at a time when it was already being polarized socially and economically. In essence, the strikes
increased the cultural and ideological differences in the Mexican community; the *ricos* deplored the strikes and the middle class avoided
them.

The strikes did serve to activate a consciousness of independence
and activism on the part of Mexican women, however. As Blackwelder
has pointed out, "Women were the major actors in San Antonio strikes
from 1933 through 1938. During the Depression strikes were concentrated in the city's lowest paying industries: cigar making, pecan shelling, and garment making. In these three industries Mexican . . .
women predominated, and consequently they were the driving force
behind strikes and the formation of new labor unions."[23]

Regardless of these strikes and union activities, San Antonio was
not becoming a union town, although the *Weekly Dispatch*, the AF
of L newspaper, regularly reported the city's and the state's labor activities. Not the newspaper, the small unions, or Mexican strike activity changed the antiunion sentiment in San Antonio, though. Anti-
unionism continued to be articulated by the Chamber of Commerce
and city government, which often made statements like, "Relations
between the unions and employees are good and strikes the exception, not the rule. Agitators from the outside are frowned upon by
Texas Laws."[24] Consequently, the consciousness and ideology of the
Mexican worker were more closely tied to the ideology of the Mexican American middle class and the *ricos* than to a union or workers'
consciousness. In short, Mexican workers would have an independent
voice, they would reflect the reality of developing Americanization,
and they would seek economic survival and work opportunities for
a better life.

Thus, the large Mexican laboring class, the lack of unionization, and the Depression were factors that drastically affected both the Mexican and the Americano populations of San Antonio during the 1930s, especially with the failure of the city's economy. As has been stated, the strength of the city's economy, besides the military establishments, was the manufacturing and mechanical industries as well as the construction industry, and these industrial groupings suffered the most from the Depression. In addition, San Antonio's other economic pillar — trade, both wholesale and retail — also suffered greatly

suffered more than others. A city government report stated that development during the Depression was confined almost solely to government agencies and government money. Most sectors where Mexicans were employed were greatly affected by the Depression. Because of the economic paralysis, between fifteen thousand and twenty thousand persons were almost permanently unemployed during this decade in San Antonio, and many were on relief.[26]

In 1933, for example, there were 48,575 persons on relief in San Antonio: 18,343 Anglos, 5,919 blacks, and 24,313 Mexicans. Most of the unemployed came from the unskilled and semiskilled groups in the city. In 1935 there were still over 15,000 unemployed workers receiving relief. For laborers, domestics, semiskilled, and skilled workers the decade was devastating: 68.2 percent were on relief in 1935, 68.5 percent were still unemployed in 1937, and 85 percent were still registered with employment services in 1940. In 1937 there were 15,000 totally unemployed; however, there were 6,000 persons employed on public works projects and 8,500 employed part time. According to a report commissioned by the city, "the 1937 census of total and partial unemployment showed that in Bexar County in November of 1937, 6,197 of the 21,234 unemployed were working on emergency projects." Two years later, in November of 1939, there were in Bexar County 10,632 persons certified by the Works Project Administration on the basis of need. Of this total, 6,460 were assigned to work on relief projects and 4,172 were awaiting assignment for employment that was often not available.[27]

During the late 1930s, about 42,600 San Antonio workers were employed by the WPA. Few of these were Mexicans, since many of them were not citizens; nevertheless, about 50 percent of the Mexican people received surplus commodities. Throughout the thirties the industrial and commercial labor market of the city was composed of approximately 44,000 Mexicans, and many of them, if not most, were unemployed, on relief, or receiving some other kind of aid. In spite of the economic conditions, many of the 683,681 Mexicans in Texas — 40 percent born in Mexico — including those in San Antonio, did not want to return to Mexico, although some did return as a result of the deportations and repatriations. This desire to stay in the United States increased unemployment, because many of the Mexicans who had originally passed through San Antonio to northern manufacturing centers and midwestern agricultural areas returned to the city to settle because of the Depression. They felt that they were better off in a city with a large urban Mexican population. Of those who came back, 85 percent were Mexicans, 10 percent Anglos, and 5 percent blacks. These influxes of workers further polarized the Mexican middle class and the workers. The middle class often tried to help its poorer compadres economically, but eventually it retreated more into its own social and ideological enclaves.[28]

The Depression forced the Mexican laboring class, often led by individuals such as Emma Tenayuca and Magdaleno Rodríguez, or organizations like the Nogal Union, the Communist Workers Alliance of America, the Pecan Shelling union, the ILGWU, and the CIO to strike (but of course, not all the Mexicans were striking). These strikes and this militancy outraged the American Chamber of Commerce, the League of United Latin American Citizens, the Catholic Church, and the American Federation of Labor. The strikes and labor agitations had definite repercussions on the Mexican community and served to polarize it ideologically; therefore, even though there seemed to be a homogeneous community in the West Side, this was not the case. They were (as John Bodnar points out about immigrants in general) "not huddled masses sharing a common orientation toward some future, but divided masses debating life goals and strategies."[29]

In short, many factors separated the emerging Mexican middle class from the workers and the *ricos:* the continuing emigration from Mexico, although there was a small exodus of repatriated and departed Mexicans; continuing racial discrimination; the continuing Americanization of the middle class, with its attendant propaganda via the League of United Latin American Citizens; and the daily bombardment by such mediating acculturating structures as the Catholic Church, the educational system, the English language, and the radio. All of these factors were affected directly or indirectly by the Depression. The result was an acceleration of the sociocultural and political fragmentation of the Mexican class structure in San Antonio, the beginning of the rise in the Mexican middle class's consciousness of itself as a class with a predominantly Mexican American psyche rather than a Mexican one, and the beginning of the building of a Mexican American culture that would challenge the cultural hegemony of the *ricos*.

The Depression had a direct effect on the fragmentation and con-

Antonio had formed a town within a city with their own ideological complexities, social tensions, and class divisions. Let us now examine more closely the internal cultural differences, perspectives, and activities of each of these classes.

and Everyday Life

3

tions in the quality of life were becoming evident . . . in the clubs they joined, in the neighborhoods they resided in, in the education they acquired and in the occupations they held . . . [they] were differentiating themselves from their fellows and developing diverse lifestyles.

— Kenneth L. Kusmer

INTRODUCTION

By 1929 racial and cultural divisions were apparent in San Antonio's Mexican community. There was the large impoverished world of the submerged masses of unskilled laborers, the small but developing lower and upper middle class of skilled and professional Mexicans, and the minute but culturally influential group of exiled Porfirian *ricos*. Each group had its own world of thoughts, perceptions, and ideas: the laboring class reflected a world of Scholasticism, fatalism, and realism; the middle class reflected a world of liberalism, optimism, and idealism; the *ricos* reflected a world of Comtianism, elitism, and conservatism. Each class had its separate place in society, yet each had a perception of a common core of community based on a consciousness of historical collectivity and a reality of common everyday problems. Their worlds were pluralistic in development, but communal in sensitivities.

As a result, although the streets were still lined with *jacales* or with rows of shacks made of boxcar wood and covered with tin cans, there were now many "modern three to five room cottages"—some with electric lights, sewers, and gas—which extended to the Prospect Hill and San Pedro Street areas, where the middle class lived. There were even a few palatial homes where the rich lived, like the home of Dr. Urrutia on Broadway Avenue. By the Depression many Mexicans were somewhat aware of each other's lives, although their intellectual ethos, social life, and cultural activities were worlds apart. This chapter will examine these different public worlds and their common problems.

The World of the "Submerged Masses"

Archbishop Drossaert of San Antonio clearly understood the world of the masses when he stated in 1936 that they were "perplexing [and] almost desperate. Extreme poverty, abysmal ignorance [and a constant] . . . moving hither and thither of our peons in search of work and a crust of bread." This description not only fit the laboring class, but the migrants and some of the lower middle class as well. Archbishop Drossaert went on to describe them (in a kind but condescending manner) as the "submerged masses, humble, improvident and childlike. Peons, truly submerged in the most abject poverty, squalor and ignorance. By their numbers . . . they constitute a problem so vast that if left unaided we [the Catholic Church] cannot possibly solve it [ourselves]."[1]

A federal housing survey showed that 14,700 Mexican families were living in substandard homes. Father Carmelo Tranchese, who devoted his life to the housing problems of the Mexicans and was the rector of Our Lady of Guadalupe Church in the center of the West Side, described the housing conditions in 1936 in the following manner:

> There was only one water faucet in the yard [of the wooden structures] which had no handle, and could only be opened by a pair of plyers . . . two toilets served [a] . . . whole community of 60 people, and one of those toilets had [usually] been out of order for a long time. And who were living in those miserable places? the pecan shellers, whom we could term the lowest degree in the labor scale [in San Antonio]; the yard-men, the [other laborers] and those . . . people having a very low income . . . that was unsteady and could not afford better dwellings.[2]

The rent of these tenement dwellings ranged from fifty cents to two dollars per week, and many of these buildings and shacks as well as much of the property in the West Side was owned by middle-class Mexicans who "could become capitalist by putting up a half-dozen shacks at the cost of about one hundred dollars each. In these shacks there was no plumbing to be repaired, no window glass to be replaced, the taxes were very low, and the flow of the rent sure and steady. Because every Sunday morning the landlord would come around at each [home] and claim slum-money." Those Mexicans who did not live in wooden multiple-family dwellings or small shacks lived in "corrals"

businesspeople such as Matilde Elizondo, who was the owner of La Gloria grocery stores and gas stations, had to distribute food packages to the needy. A Federal Housing Authority report in 1939 showed that 25,491 Mexican families (more than 127,000 individuals) living in the West Side earned far less than $950 per year; many earned less than $250. Many did not work continuously, only seasonally; however, they still paid monthly rents of around $3.50. These conditions often drained Tranchese's and Elizondo's resources. The 1939 report further showed that there were 6,558 families paying $14 or more per month for a home without utilities, and sometimes as many as thirty families were forced to obtain their water from a common faucet. Even the one-room *jacales* were overcrowded; seven people, for example, lived in one dwelling at 916 Chihuahua Street. Most of these people, according to a *San Antonio Express* editorial, were "half-fed and rags" in the 1930s. Consequently, the Mexican workers' cultural level was often intertwined with poverty.[4]

Conditions during the 1930s were even noticed by some high-ranking federal officials. Frances Parkinson Keyes, a member of the Roosevelt administration, wrote Eleanor Roosevelt a letter describing these miserable conditions when the latter expressed concern for the San Antonio population after a tour of the Latin Quarter in the 1930s. Keyes wrote that there were "some very shocking figures regarding unemployment among Mexicans [in San Antonio] . . . 14,000 families are living in substandard houses, and . . . of these, 10,000 are very close to the starvation line all of the time." In another letter to Mrs. Roosevelt, Keyes wrote that the Mexican West Side "represents a distinct menace to the surrounding area because the contagious and infectious diseases prevalent there inevitably spread beyond its boundaries."[5]

Conditions were often close to unbearable for the approximately 16,000 Mexican laboring families, especially at times such as in 1937, when 14,000 pecan shellers were out of work. But the Depression decade was as hard, if not worse, for another of the lower sectors of the Mexican working class, the "vast army of migratory agricultural laborers and the thousands of immigrants who gravitated to San Antonio." Accentuating the situation was the fact that most of the pecan shellers, agricultural workers, and migrant workers were unskilled, illiterate, and rural. Consequently, many were willing to work for any wage. These members of the working class were not as fortunate as those who worked at such places as the Apache Meat Packing Company or the eight garment plants.[6]

Mexicans occupationally fanned out into thousands of small manufacturing plants, service industries, and military jobs in the city, and those who had acquired a certain skill or level of education in Mexico or the United States even established their own businesses. However, a common obstacle confronted many of these workers (and the small number of middle-class entrepreneurs): the stereotype of the Mexican as a foreigner that was held by many Americanos, even though the majority of the Mexicans living in the West Side were U.S.-born. Some, in fact, could trace their families back to the nineteenth century. Most, however, by the 1930s, had their genealogical roots in the immigration waves of the twentieth century.[7]

Father Carmelo Tranchese, who was often called the "angel of the slums," very succinctly expressed the misery and plight of all San Antonio Mexicans when he first saw them in the West Side in 1932:

> I had passed through . . . [San Antonio] on my way to Florida and the East. The impression it left on me was simply terrible. Those long rows of miserable huts in the Mexican Quarter, that exhausting heat, that resigned poverty painted on the faces of the Mexicans, all made me give thanks to God I did not live there. Guadalupe District was especially repulsive to me. A huge mass of humanity emerging out of little shacks wrung my heart. Those shacks were built facing dirt roads which became impassable with mud when rain fell. Pale, emaciated faces of the children playing in the dust without laughter in their hearts or on their lips haunted me at night. And the women! They were bent with weariness and their faces were etched with the hopelessness of long years of struggle against sickness and hunger. Their husbands lingered about without jobs and without existence. When I left San Antonio, I was more than glad.

Then in a comparative reflection Tranchese stated, "I am familiar with the slums of San Francisco, New York, London, Paris and Naples, but those of San Antonio are the worst of all."[8]

These conditions could not be ignored by Americano San Antonians, since they affected the cultural, intellectual, and social conditions of the city as a whole. The Mexicans were an integral part of the whole working sector. At a joint Chamber of Commerce and Lions Club meeting on September 3, 1936, Father Tranchese emphatically

he implied. However, many of the remaining 4,000 who could not find any employment, whether Mexican citizens or U.S.-born, had to receive some relief from federal, state, church, or charitable organizations during the 1930s. Therefore, economically or politically, the Mexicans of San Antonio could not be ignored. Tranchese clearly thought that the American political and social elite had to be aware of the Mexicans' cultural presence, their potential political power, and their importance as a labor force, even though most of the Mexican population rarely left the *colonia*.[9]

This residential segmentation contributed to the persistence of the many cultural habits, traditions, and attitudes that had been brought over from Mexico during the immigration waves of the 1900–30 period. But they were also a product of everyday cultural activities and general conditions of poverty in the Latin Quarter. In general, language, dress, religion, superstitions, and customs continued to be Mexican during the 1930s for a number of reasons: first, because the Mexicans lived in de facto segregation; second, because they lived in the midst of the cultural residue of the twentieth-century immigration; and third, because the city, in spite of its modernization, maintained a structural Spanish and Mexican motif. The people of the West Side thus had continuity in their cultural lifestyle and maintained their national distinctions, although they were changing.

Their distinctions varied from one class to another within the Mexican community, however. All were *raza* in their soul, but their sociocultural and intellectual life varied according to occupation, income, status, and acculturation. Often this process of change with continuity was not observable by contemporary observers; even Father Tranchese stated that to him the Mexican community during the 1930s showed "little inclination to change; [the Mexicans'] human nature and sense of community was passed on from generation to genera-tion." Tranchese seems to have been espousing what Oscar Lewis later called the "culture of poverty." For Mexicans in San Antonio extreme poverty helped cement the persistence of ethnic cohesion, and the perceptions others had of the Mexican community's homogeneity helped to condition a sense of self and community.[10]

On the surface, however, Tranchese seemed to be right; the ma-jority of Mexicans in San Antonio had few material comforts, much less luxuries, and most of the large laboring class depended on some form of public assistance. They all seemed to act out of a culture of poverty. But despite its poverty, the working class had a rich everyday life centering on family and church activities. Employed or unem-ployed, tired or not, U.S.- or Mexican-born, the Mexican laborer par-ticipated in many community events after the long workday.

One observer stated that the greatest single influence on the Mexi-cans was their religion, especially the interest in and dedication they had to the lives of the saints. She went on to say that the Mexicans were "doomed to live in poverty and to work hard all of their lives, since their great pleasure and compensation for all their ills was the Church." Salvation for them would come, it seems, not from the fruits of their labor, but from their faith in God and their relationship to the church. The Scholastic mentality of their Spanish heritage seemed to dominate the Calvinistic work ethic of the United States, but the realism of everyday life often confronted their metaphysicial idealism. The little money these workers had was often donated to the church, and most of their moments of joy and of entertainment were con-nected with the church's festival days, saints' days, Mexican national holidays, and Christmas and Easter. If life was alienating, the church was fulfilling; if they were materially poor, they were spiritually rich — or so they thought and felt.[11]

The Catholic Church, which predominated in the West Side, ac-knowledged the terrible conditions of the Mexican poor, but while church officials believed that their extreme poverty interfered with the Mexicans' adherence to religion, they nevertheless believed that the establishment of "Catholic clubs and social centers [was] the remedy." The church felt that, although "the people [were] poor and struggling, . . . the prospects . . . [were] good for the advancement of the 'faith.'" Specifically, the church believed that the "main hope [lay] in the success of our [Catholic] schools. Through the schools we reach the children and through them the parents." Their main objective was religious continuity and conversion and to be the center of religion-oriented activities. In its work with the Mexicans, the blacks, and the Indians of San Antonio, its central role, the church believed, was to function as the cultural core of the community. As a result its goals and activities and the Mexican workers' sense of community coincided; therefore, for the most part, working-class culture emanated from shared religious activities.[12]

by the rational individualistic virtue of the middle class and the civic virtue of the *ricos*. Nevertheless, one writer was correct in stating that,

> to gain an understanding of the Mexicans, of their ancient and unusual social and religious customs, of their manner of thinking, and of their love for everything colorful and dramatic, one might well study their [religious] fiestas, for in them can be seen the reflections of their hearts and souls. Their fiestas and folk customs, portraying the earliest Mexican traditions, have been fostered, nourished and kept alive since the early Spanish period. So significant are [these religious fiestas] in the lives of the [laboring] people that sometimes their daily life suggests a fiesta, and [thus] the expression "the Mexican does not need to stage a fiesta for he lives it."[13]

While this seemed to be true of the *gente pobre*, it was not entirely true of the *gente decente*.[14] It seemed, in an irony of history, that the universality of historical time coincided with the temporality of real time: the workers seemed medieval in temper; the middle class Lockian in time; and the *ricos* Thomist in pronouncements. History was segmenting the collective memory. Macro-history was caught, it seems, in the time warp of San Antonio's Mexican West Side.

Nevertheless, weddings, funerals, saints' days, anniversaries, and national holidays were a constant source of collective cultural activity; in addition, they served as a stimulant to family activities. These church and community fiestas heightened the Mexican workers' sense of community, their sense of Mexicanness, and provided a consciousness of joy in a life of toil, misery, and depression.

If the church provided the external core of cultural activity, the family provided the internal core. For example, the church was the central force in the lives of Quirnio and Benita Gonzales after they immigrated from Nuevo León to San Antonio in 1927. Arriving in economic despair and confused by U.S. customs, Quirnio first found a job as a laborer, then he located the Guadalupe Church on the West Side. The church immediately served as the link with the familiar customs and tradition of Mexico as well as a social and cultural center. It was the cornerstone of the Gonzaleses' new sense of community. On the other hand, Quirnio's home with Benita was not only the haven from the psychological despair of the Depression and from the misery of his job, but a source of hope when he felt frustrated. Thus Quirnio was gratified and felt a sense of stability when Benita, who spoke only Spanish, was making tortillas, cleaning house, and dressing the children, Salvador and Cecilia. The family provided a sense of self-protection for Quirnio, while Benita was, as *La Prensa* advocated, "the essence of the family." This was also in keeping with *La Voz de la Parroquia*'s (a church newspaper in San Antonio's West Side) proclamation that "the happiness of the community is linked with the conservation of the family." Unfortunately, the Depression decade forced many Mexican mothers to leave the home and become not only workers, but the economic head of the family. Richard Griswold del Castillo analyzes the situation accurately when he states that "there has been a persistent tension [in the Mexican family] between the ideals and expectations . . . [and the reality] regarding family life." Economic and daily realities often intruded into what Mexicans valued and expected. In general, however, the church was the core and bulwark of the collective Mexican community while the family was "the haven and the carrier of Mexican culture." But cultural change was slowly occurring because the church and the family in the United States were also serving as conveyor belts for American culture.[15]

In addition to these two cultural cores, the Mexican workers' social and cultural life centered on the plazas, the cantinas, and the movie houses. Hay Market Plaza, Milam Plaza, and even Alamo Plaza (which was outside the barrio) were the night spots of the workers and their families. These plazas provided the working class with the ambience of community: Mexican food, mariachi entertainment, Spanish conversation, and friends. Especially delightful were the chile stands, which were filled with the pungent smell of tacos, tamales, tortillas, enchiladas, and other foods, presided over by the Chili Queens. One commentator described the scene at the plazas as "long tables, illuminated by strings of red, blue or yellow lights, accommodat[ing] an endless line of men, women and children, eating the traditional foods of old Mexico."[16] Music, specifically mariachis or troubadours singing songs of love, hope, despair, gaiety, joy, and the Mexican homeland, accompanied the food and festivities. The mariachis were the voice of the workers, of memory and the ideal of *lo mexicano* being touched by the hand of U.S. reality. But this went unnoticed as the plaza's entertainment enhanced the cultural warmth of Spanish conversation with compatriots and expedited the traditional courtship that was an integral part of this night scene. Mexi-

Spanish variety show before the movie to attract the Mexican clientele. If both the plazas and the movies were boring or unacceptable, the Mexican worker, with friends or family, simply took a walk and "people-watched." One Mexican salesman, remembering 1939, said, "We did not see class differences among us. We just knew that the [upper middle class and the *ricos*] were different, just as we saw ourselves as different from the peons."[18]

For the macho away from the family, the red light district at the edge of the West Side supplemented the neighborhood cantina. Regardless of the location of a social rendezvous — the church, the plaza, the theater, or the cantina — lower-middle-class men such as Juan Costellanos (a carpenter), Porfirio Cuéllar (a barber), John Delgado (a baker), José Esquivel (a shoemaker), Tomás García (a mechanic), or Rodrigo García (a clerk) might be seen together with the pecan shellers, migrants, agricultural workers, and factory workers. Nevertheless, it was primarily at the plazas that the lower middle class and the working class met; there the cultural atmosphere was egalitarian, even though occupational segmentation was not. The fact of segmentation coincides with what John Bodnar has said of immigrant groups in general; that constant occupational distribution "ensured the procreation of class divisions within immigrant communities and among entire groups of immigrants, a process that in turn ensured that divergent perspectives would characterize newcomers in both past and present." It simply was not possible to define the United States in terms of its immigrants without reference to occupation or class. Consequently, the pluralism of ideas, values, and attitudes was a real-

ity because occupational segmentation created differences, in spite
of the sense of community.[19]

The cultural life of the laboring class was closely tied to the level
of jobs and income, but even within the laboring class there were some
differences. Even though many of these Mexican laborers shared a
common cultural past, they came from different geographical areas
in Mexico. Nevertheless, traditions, language, and customs, for the
most part, closely approximated each other; therefore, for all of them,
culture and poverty were the equalizer, and the Latin Quarter's religion and church were their meager salvation. A Catholic Church report
of 1929 stated that many of these laborers, migrants, and agricultural
workers "were born and raised in the isolated haciendas of Mexico
or the boundless ranches of Texas." "It is hardly their fault," the report emphasized, "if they were so terribly ignorant. Are they not vic-
tims of extreme poverty and of circumstances over which they have
no control."[20] For Mexican laboring men and women, whose poverty
was so oppressive, their church and religion, their family, and their
fiestas were the center of their lives and provided a richness to their
individual and communal being.

The 1929 church report specifically emphasized the centrality of
religion when it stated that these laboring people were not only "in-
stinctively religious," but had "an inborn love of the faith," a "reverence [for] the ceremonies of the church," a deep love for the Blessed
Virgin Mary and prayer, and that the rosary appealed to them "with
special force." Religion overlapped culture, and the church equated
Mexicans' piety with heredity, their community with their religion,
and their faith and virtue with their personality. Consequently, the
church reported that "singing the hymns and listening to the instruc-
tions of the faith" was of central importance to them. The "Catholic
faith is rooted . . . deeply in their hearts," exclaimed the report.

Scholasticism seemed to predominate hegemonically. For many of
the workers, the priest was the central figure in the community; in
fact, he was seen not only as a priest, but as the doctor, the under-
taker, and the family counselor. Socially and culturally, the priest was
at the center of the workers' lives. They were poor, but they were rich
with religion; they were culturally impoverished, but they were spiritually cultured — both the church and many Mexicans believed this.
Yet, if the substructure of their lives was rich in faith, religion, and
family, their superstructure was "poverty, stark, brutish and incredible." Even the church commented that "riches are a danger to the
soul of man, but surely extreme poverty too has its fearful drawbacks,
moral, spiritual [and] intellectual."[21]

Thus, for the masses of Mexicans, in spite of their adherence to the church and its importance in their lives, the everyday struggle for survival during the 1930s was predominant. Even the Catholic Church recognized this:"[They are] so engrossed with the struggle for mere existence that any consideration for their soul's salvation is only a secondary consideration with them." Philosophically, the church stated that the Mexican laboring class lived by the idea of "vivere deim philosophari" (a philosophy of living day by day).[22] The "mind" of the working class, especially the lower sectors, was constantly

to make their world view one of axioms and *el ojo malo* (the evil eye). *Dichos* were often passed from generation to generation. They might be treated as a joke by the higher socioeconomic groups, but for the lower classes, were definite guidelines. These *dichos*, like Benjamin Franklin's homilies, served as commonsense sayings to structure their philosophy of life. But, unlike Franklin's optimistic homilies or Alger's self-motivating stories, *dichos* stressed realism, living in the present, and recognition of limits. They structured the population's ambitions and constantly reminded people of the strength of fate, the power of religion, and the reality of outside structures; they also rationalized poverty. *Dichos* and songs many times articulated reflections of self in community and in society, as well as emotions and impressions of the world.[23]

Norteño, or *corrido*, music also reflected sentiments, aspirations, and desires. This music has its roots in the Mexican industrial city of Monterrey, the musical and cultural Paris of Mexico from the nineteenth century to the 1930s. *Norteño* music was often divided into the upper class's *orquesta* music and the lower class's *corrido*. The music of both the upper class and the laboring class was originally linked, but as it flowed through time and space it moved from the salon to the cantina. The ideology of different classes was reflected in it. Although its style was rooted in Mexican elite culture, in its diffusion it had become proletarian.

This *norteño* music was the music of the Mexican working class, and San Antonio became its vital center, because the wealthier Mexicans had the means to record it and the extensive laboring community bought it. As a result, the 1930s in San Antonio saw the development of the *norteño* and Mexican music of such people as Bruno Villareal, Narciso Martínez (el Huracán del Valle — the Hurricane of the Valley), J. Rodríguez, Pedro Rocho, and Lupe Martínez. Pedro Rocho and others often played this music in the Produce Row marketplace near the military plaza, and, on occasion, those musicians who did not like to perform in Produce Row made disparaging comments (Andrés Berlanga, for example, referred to this edge of the West Side as the "Manure District"). Nevertheless, this area was where Americano and Mexican businesspeople as well as the laboring class bought and sold their products. It was a perfect forum for the street singers to sing their *corridos* accompanied by accordions and guitars. Not only did these performers reproduce in their songs the oral traditions of the Mexicans and the Mexican Americans, but the music preserved the collective memory of the important events and heroes of the period and maintained the Mexican consciousness of all the classes in the West Side, via its style, its tone, and its messages.[24]

One of the most popular songs was "La Cucaracha," a ballad sung during the Mexican revolution to poke fun at the forces of General Carranza. Another very popular song among the poor (who often called themselves Chicanos) was the *corrido* entitled "El Chicano," which captured their thinking about going north from Mexico. One of the verses dealt with the almost inevitable theme of acculturation:

Ya me voy mis queridos amigos.	I am going my dear friends.
Vamos todos a darnos la mano.	Let's all shake hands.
Aunque yo esté en	Even though I'll be in
Estados Unidos yo no	the United States, I
niego que soy Mejicano.	won't deny that I am Mexican.

Another *corrido*, "Canción Mixteca," told of the loneliness of being in the United States:

Que lejos estoy del	How far I am from
suelo donde he nacido.	the soil where I was born.
Intensa nostalgia invade	Intense nostalgia invades
mi pensamiento.	my thought.

"El Deportado" (The Deportee) reflected the feelings of the Mexican immigrants toward the treatment of Mexicans in America. Two of the verses went:

Los güeros son muy	The white skinned men are
malorosos	very wicked
Los güeros son muy	The white skinned men
malorosos	are very wicked

se volen de la	They take advantage
ocasión	of the occasion
y a todos los mejicanos	And all the Mexicans
y a todos los mejicanos	And all the Mexicans
Los tratan sin compasión.	Are treated without compassion.
Ahí traen la gran	There comes a large
polvadera	cloud of dust,
Ahí traen la gran	there comes a large

or to commemorate certain events, like "Corrido de Juan Reyna" (who was charged with shooting two policemen) and "La Tragedia de Oklahoma" (two relatives of Mexican president Pascual Ortiz Rubio were killed by policemen in Oklahoma). If the San Antonio Mexicans did not hear these *corridos* at the plazas or at the produce area they could hear them on the radio, on stations KONO, WOAI (Chucho Martínez's program), KMAC ("Mexican Commercial Hour"), WOAL ("Latin Melodies"), or KABC ("La Hora Latina").[26]

Thus, if the workers did not articulate their thoughts, feelings, and attitudes directly, their *corridos* did. It seems that the collective experience reflected in the music and *dichos*, the realism of poverty, the metaphysics of the church, the reality of discrimination, and the memory of Mexico, the "lost land," provided Mexicans throughout the Southwest and the Midwest with a consciousness of collectivity. This collective experience helped to tie the classes together in spite of the individualism and pluralism developing in each. However, the submerged masses of working-class Mexicans lived in the United States without political power, but enveloped in a spiritual community that was in a constant state of tension with a capitalistic, liberal world.

The Acculturation of the Middle Class

Middle-class Mexicans constituted a relatively small percentage of San Antonio's Mexican population; nevertheless, they were by choice, skills, status, possessions, income, and occupation entering the modernization process and the democratic ethos of the Southwest and the United States in the 1920s and 1930s. The class of Mexicans who made up the lower middle class (clerks, government employees, store employees, truck drivers, and the like) and skilled laborers (tinners, bricklayers, barbers, plasterers, shoemakers, plumbers, tailors, painters, mechanics, cement workers, carpenters, and so on) had, for the most part, steady jobs that brought a relatively "modest standard of living . . . a permanency of residence and a possible interest in citizenship."[27] In addition, there was a small layer of upper-middle-class Mexicans: doctors, lawyers, businesspeople. In absolute numbers this middle class was small (approximately five thousand), but its influence went beyond its numbers because of income, status, business holdings, and the ability to articulate ideas.[28]

Of the middle-class Mexicans, one parish priest said, "These Mexicans frequent our schools, speak English with perhaps only a faint trace of foreign accent; . . . [they] are housed in humble, but decent cottages; . . . they are employed in stores, hotels, restaurants, in the city police and fire departments, and . . . for better or worse are more or less Americanized. These [Mexicans] constitute perhaps 1/20th of our Mexican population in the city of San Antonio."[29] Most of these middle-class families still lived in the West Side, but in cottages rather than in *jacales*, tenements, or shacks like the working class, and many had (prior to 1930) bought lots in the ethnic and middle-class enclave of the Prospect Hill area. Even if they remained in the working-class area, they owned their lots. A few had even moved outside the Prospect Hill area. Manuel Gamio points out that those "wealthier" Mexicans who came to live in San Antonio in 1915 moved into the San Pedro Street area, where "the wealthiest class of the Mexican colony [lived], or rather, a number of the wealthier members who made up a sort of 'high society' in the midst of the great majority of the Mexican colony which [was] made up of persons of the working class."[30] Consequently, the middle class was qualitatively better off economically and geographically, for the most part, than the large laboring class; occupation, status, and material possessions (and ideological perceptions) differentiated them even though their *mexicanidad* did not.

This middle sector shared a feeling of the importance of family, church, and religion with the laboring class. However, there were differences. For example, while the laborers were passive benefactors of church activity, the middle class was the active proponent of church organizations. But the Mexican community celebrations were collective activities for all classes. The middle class usually organized the cultural fiestas such as the Cinco de Mayo. As the *San Antonio Express* reported, "the *Cinco de Mayo*, the Mexican National celebration commemorating the 65th Anniversary of the victory of Ignacio Zaragoza over the French troops at the battle of Puebla on May 5, 1862, will be held at San Pedro Park under the auspices of the Mexican W.O.W. [Woodsmen of the World] Comp. No. 2322. The fete will open May 4 and will continue for five days." The program for the evening of the May 5 celebration was the major attraction and included an "overture by the Bloom Chasers Orchestra; followed by a reading of the official historical message by E. Serrano, and Mrs. Ra-

Pedro Park. At this week-long celebration of the Grito de Hidalgo, patriotic speeches and popular Mexican songs abounded. Since San Antonio both mirrored and projected in structure and space this dual atmosphere of Mexicanism and Americanism, non-Mexicans also enjoyed this "Spanish fantasy," which was overlain by and intertwined with the city's historical and temporal character.[32]

Other Mexican holidays were promoted by the middle class in cooperation with the church, but less lavishly. St. John's Day (June 24), for example, commemorating the birth of John the Baptist, was especially important for anyone named John, Juan, or Juanita. On this day, referred to as "*el día del baño*" (day of the bath), everyone was supposed to bathe, but sometimes this took the form of showering a neighbor with a bucket of water. Two other major holidays were November 1 and 2, All Saints' Day and All Souls' Day, respectively. These two holidays brought families together in worship of patron saints the first day and departed relatives' and friends' souls the second day. All Souls' Day was spent at the cemetery and, just as Mexicans did in the 1880s, families took flowers, pictures of the dead, and images of the saints and placed them on the graves at the San Fernando Cemetery.

On December 12, Mexicans of all classes met in their respective families and churches to worship the Virgin of Guadalupe, Mexico's principal religious patron. December 12 differentiated the Mexican church from the American because, to the Mexican church, the Virgin Mary often seemed to take on more importance than Jesus; consequently, the Mexican church had a more feminine tone and character than the American, which was dominated by the figure of Christ. A code of power and knowledge was being established. The imagery of both the Mexican and the American churches accentuated the perception of women as virgins and often served to place them in an idealized position and in constant tension with their reality. Mexican and non-Mexican men sought to accentuate their masculinity.[33]

Following this day of matriarchal orientation, the Mexican community, led by the middle class, especially the women, began to prepare for the Christmas holidays (December 16–25). This period was highlighted by the narrative of the nativity — *las posadas* — and the coming of the shepherds in the traditional *pastores* parade. The *pastores* parade took place throughout the West Side, but unlike the parades at the turn of the century, by the 1930s the main *pastores* presentation and procession was performed at the Chapel of Miracles near the Alamo. This chapel in the 1920s and 1930s was a spiritual and miracle center where Mexicans of all classes and even some non-Mexicans searched for miracles: farmworkers prayed for guidance in finding a seasonal job; laborers asked for advice on their economic needs; and middle-class Mexicans searched for spirituality. Especially during Christmas but throughout the year, this chapel, which was a short distance from the Latin Quarter and close to the German community, was the Lourdes of San Antonio.

The almost constant parade of community and religious holidays, patriotic fiestas, and family and personal holidays (which formed the core of the laboring-class culture) was an important but only peripheral part of the Mexican middle class's changing culture. The Southwest's modernization process was invading the middle-class Mexicans' collective ethnic memory, their oral traditions, and their philosophical and ideological patterns of thought; *lo mexicano* was being shaped by *lo americano* via the process of modernization.[34]

Although many non-Mexican residents of San Antonio considered all Mexicans to be the same, some did notice the changes in the intellectual and cultural life of the middle-class community. For example, William Knox, a high-ranking public school educator, writing about these changes, stated that "the light, cheap, washable clothes brought from Mexico were soon discarded for the American ready-made suits. The shawl and mantilla were replaced by the hat. Beshawled mothers were often walking behind their girls who wore modern head gear. The Mexican traveler came with a bundle in a handkerchief . . . [but] departed with a brand new paper suitcase." Knox also noticed the acculturation process that already had begun in the late 1920s. He observed "the same stress and strain that comes to all foreigners when the children begin to speak English and to change over in manners, customs, and dress to the American type." "[Mexican] parents," he pointed out, "were shocked to see their own children changing ideas as to marriage, religion, or citizenship."[35] Dora Elizondo, the daughter of well-to-do Mexican businessman Matilde Elizondo, remembers a childhood in which both Spanish and English were spoken at home. For her, as probably was the case for other upper-middle-class Mexican children during the late 1930s, *Grimms' Fairy Tales* was read in English and Spanish. By the mid-1930s it had be-

These changes were part of a slow process that began at the turn of the century for many and for some even before that. Certainly by the late thirties, acculturation, class stratification, and ideological differentiation were noticeable in the West Side. By 1930, in fact, many Mexican parents (exhibiting their middle-class consciousness) went to the public schools to consult with the teachers — not in Spanish, but in English. In the barrios many acculturating Mexican business-people were surviving the Depression and even, in some cases, attempting to enlarge their *tienditas* and other business ventures.

In spite of their Americanization, these Mexican middle-class businesspeople continued to exhibit a sense of civic virtue by helping to meet the everyday needs of the Mexican community regardless of class during the Depression. By the 1930s there were enough Mexican businesspeople to aid the poor. As one observer stated, "[Formerly] the businesses, such as the sale of meats, groceries, or clothing, were generally in the hands of the Italians, who later were crowded out by the competition of the Chinese and Syrians. [But,] without them, the Mexican-American, [in the 1930s was] beginning to compete [and succeed in the business world]." These businesspeople became examples, not only of civic virtue, but of success and opportunity. As John Bodnar has written of other ethnic groups, "In nearly every aggregation of immigrants, a group of successful store owners, some bankers, and political lenders emerged to serve as models of individual mobility and to reinforce the notion that personal striving could be rewarded in the United States." This was also the case in San Antonio.[37]

A survey taken in 1928 with a sample of 1,282 Mexicans showed

a cross section of occupational opportunities and possibilities in the Mexican community that helped reinforce the notion that mobility was possible (table 5).

In this small sample, there were no Mexican men who had a college degree and few who had a high school education, but this was generally in keeping with the trends in the United States. It was found that out of the 1,282 persons surveyed, 280 were skilled workers or service employees, and 618 were unskilled laborers. The survey also showed that the socio-economic structure of the West Side was pyramidal, with 90 percent of the workers being skilled and semi-skilled or general clerk-type employees. They were psychologically and ideologically in a middle-class trajectory. Each, in his own way, was entering into a new discourse of Americanism and a new identity of Mexican Americanism.[38]

On the surface these middle-class-oriented Mexicans' lives were similar to the workers', but there was, in fact, a qualitative difference. Regardless of whether it was the lower-middle-class sector of painters, mechanics, tailors, deliverypeople, plumbers, jewelers, or the upper-middle-class one of druggists, store owners, bookkeepers, contractors, painters, newspapermen, doctors, lawyers, and musicians, the middle class had created not only a new social, psychological, and ideological life and mind, but geographic enclaves on the West Side that would allow it protection from the unskilled workers, rural peasants, and radical rabble rousers who were not Americans, legally or ideologically.

A middle-class gestalt formed, as people adopted an attitude of *gente de razón* or *gente decente* as opposed to the *gente corriente* (the high society of reason, manners and culture versus the mass society of emotions, ill manners, and no culture). Of course, this was not always a conscious separation. It was manifested only when they spoke of moving to a better section of town, joining their own clubs, or playing sports only with their friends and others like them. The lower level of the Southwest's (and San Antonio's) Mexican industrial class was attempting to remove itself from the cultural world of the cantinas, the chili queens, the marketplace, and to distance itself from the neighboring world of the pecan shellers and the agricultural workers. It was trying to become part of the "American world" of the service and retail sectors.

On the whole, the upper-class professional and semiprofessional class was almost a world apart from the farmworkers, the pecan shellers, the unskilled laborers, and even from the lower middle class. This was an upper income group that, for the most part, served and ser-

TABLE 5
Representative Occupations, San Antonio's Mexican Community, 1928
(N = 1,282)

Occupation	No.	Occupation	No.
Preacher	1	Tailor	21
Jeweler	1	U.S. government	
Druggist	1	employee	21
Bookkeeper	2	Factory worker	22
~~Butcher~~	~~2~~	~~Painter~~	~~22~~
Newspaper	18	Regular laborer	274

SOURCE: Knox, *Economic Status of the Mexican,* pp. 15–19.

viced its own people (excepting the musicians who played in English-
language theaters) through its network of newspapers, grocery stores,
gas stations, furniture stores, drugstores, construction firms (which
hired only Mexican laborers and built houses only for other Mexicans),
and countless other small service, wholesale, and retail stores.[39]

The professional and business sector of the upper middle class made
up an even smaller part of the Mexican community, but its influence
was overwhelming. This sector consisted of little-known men such as
J. C. Martínez, who was in advertising; Alfred Sánchez, co-owner of
the Sánchez Undertaking Company with M. P. García; Gerónimo
Alvarez, owner of the garage; Pedro Cruz, owner of the automobile
repair shop; Simón González, owner of the Broom and Brush Manufacturing Company; Clemente García, owner of a cabinetmaking business; Rafael Sandoval, who owned a cigar manufacturing firm; Guadalupe Delgado, owner of a contracting firm; and Mr. Escobedo, owner
of a creamery. It also ranged to well-known community leaders such
as Max García, departmental supervisor of Gebhard's Eagle Chile
Powder and Chile con Carne; Dr. R. I. Támez, a dentist; Anacleto
Martínez, a lawyer; Rubén R. Lozano, a lawyer; M. C. González, a
lawyer; Alonzo Perales, a lawyer; Enrique A. Guerra, owner of the
Agencia de Inhumaciones, Servicio de Ambulancia; F. A. Chapa,

owner of the Chapa Drug Store; Miguel Ochoa, president of the Banco Mexicano and Mayo's Money and Exchange; José Rodríguez, a businessman; and Rómulo Mungía, a printer.[40]

On the whole, the life of the lower sectors of the middle class was different from the life of the upper middle class. For example, many of the lower middle class also saw themselves as Texas Mexicans (tejanos) and attended meetings of the Lodge Mexicana-Texana, which had fourteen chapters throughout Texas. The grand master was Alfredo López Prado and the lodge focused on the duality in their lives: being Mexicanos and tejanos (americanos). Jesús Mendizábal underlined this generational and structural process of acculturation when he stated,

> I haven't changed my [Mexican] nationality, and I want to go back to Mexico in order to take my children there to finish their growing up so that they also may be Mexican citizens. They are being Americanized here in the American schools. They speak almost more English than Spanish. I have taught them what little Spanish I know so that they will always remember this country, but it seems to me that they will be American citizens since they were born here in [San Antonio] and [they] don't know anything about Mexico. I am sure that if I can't take them [to Mexico] they wouldn't go [of their own free will].[41]

The lower middle class had its own world of clubs that reflected its growing acculturation and prosperity. These clubs, which often held dances, parties, and other entertainment, were central to their lives not only for social reasons, but also because they were recreational clubs. They had names reflecting the dichotomizing process of acculturation: Gardina, Tuesday Night, What Next, Lucky 13, Casa Loma, and Amado Nervo. These clubs sometimes held dances at exclusive San Antonio hotels. The Lucky Star club, for example, once sponsored a dance at the Hotel Menger in honor of Dora Treviño, Hortensia Ibarra, and Consuelo Garza. Many of this sector's activities also focused on church clubs such as the Association of San Luis Gonzaga de la Parroquia de Imaculada Corazón de María (under the direction of Father A. López), which held occasional benefits, fiestas, and dances.[42]

In many cases, dances, fiestas, or plays were held by these recreational and church clubs not only to benefit the club, but to entertain the community. The club Amado Nervo, for example, sponsored a community dance organized by J. Muñoz, R. Fuertes, and A. Gutiérrez and held at the Labor Temple Terrace. In another instance, a school benefit was held by the recreational club from the Corazón de María School. On February 9, 1930, the recreational club of the Guadalupe School, under the direction of Professor Víctor Almaques, actor Manuel Cotera, and Berta Almaques, organized a festival to get friends of the school and all Mexicans of the barrio to raise funds for the school. This festival was organized to attract all classes; it had Mexican plays, songs, music, and games, and to enlarge its appeal and gain more extensive community support, it was cosponsored by the church group Las Hijas de María. Many events were held to raise

tion of a Mexican constitutional amendment by holding a
dance. Attending this particular function were not only various directors of the Missouri Pacific Railroad, but Mr. Enrique Santibáñez, the consul general of Mexico, as well as Manuel Mora, the president of the Mexican Chamber of Commerce, and others associated with the chamber. Although the Latin Booster Club members were not members of the prestigious and exclusive Casino Social, they did on occasion rent the Casino Social facilities, especially when they wanted to attract the upper classes. Before this dance, as was the custom, there were several speakers. A. G. Zermeño Macías, president of the Latin Boosters Club, spoke on the importance of the constitutional amendment, and Consul General Santibáñez spoke on behalf of the Mexican government. Santibáñez emphasized the importance of the fiesta and commended the "Latin Booster Club for being patriotic and keeping alive the traditions of 'Nuestra Raza.'" Consul Lic. Rafael E. Ruiz, another speaker, directed his remarks to a historical analysis of the constitutional amendment. He spoke of the Mexican traditions, referring to the proclamation of the Plan de Ayutla and to historical figures such as Juárez, Ignacio Comonfort, Guillermo Prieto, and Florencio Villareal. He concluded by emphasizing the importance of the 1857 constitution as a watershed in Mexican history. Lower-middle-class social events attracted the attention of the upper classes only when they revolved around a patriotic theme or political event or when they were a specific type of fund raiser.[44]

Many times, however, events sponsored by the lower middle class were strictly social. The Association of Elevator Operators, for example, organized a dance with a jazz orchestra at Elizondo's La Gloria, an open-roofed dance hall. The event was primarily for its membership but was open to the whole Mexican community.[45]

The Campamento Juárez and the Club Hispano Azteca also cut across Mexican social classes and were part of the association of Leñadores del Mundo (Woodsmen of the World), a U.S. fraternal organization with Mexican chapters throughout Texas. At different times throughout the year, some of the Woodsmen's San Antonio members, such as P. O. López, Dr. Gustavo Martínez, and R. E. Miller, went into South Texas to propagandize, recruit, or attend banquets to initiate new members. Each chapter used a different name: Campamento Juárez in San Antonio, or Campamento Zaragoza in Corpus Christi. In San Antonio, the chapter often held fiestas such as the one held on February 1, 1930, which was a literary and music fiesta to welcome new members. On this occasion, the entertainment began with an overture by Professor Frederico Gonzales followed by Santos Reyes and Filemán Soto singing "Las Golondrinas" and a "Canción Yucatecana." Afterwards, Alicia Morales performed a Cherry Dance, which rivaled a tango by Alicia Mijárez. Numerous other dances, songs, and poems followed in an evening that was oriented more toward the middle class than toward the laboring class. Organizations such as these reflected both Mexican and Anglo themes.[46]

These clubs, in short, not only helped perpetuate the Mexican consciousness of collectivity, but they served to establish mutual understanding and cohesiveness of a common middle-class consciousness as well as a sense of differentiation from the *gente corriente* — the laboring class. The middle class ranged ideologically and culturally on a continuum that touched the laboring class on one end and the upper middle class on the other.

All of the lower-middle-class clubs, regardless of their place on the sociocultural continuum, sponsored social events and benefits, but sports were often a main emphasis, too. These clubs sponsored many athletic leagues and sports activities in the West Side community to attract the plumbers, drivers, salespeople, clerks, cement workers, and so on. In basketball, there was the Liga de la Ciudad (City League) with such teams as the Club Atlas playing the Tuesday Night Club of the opposing Fourside League. The YMCA (a vehicle for Americanization) also sponsored a basketball league and the intense rivalry sometimes promoted ethnic enthusiasm. This sense of ethnicity was evident when the Mexican basketball team Fal beat the Anglo YMCA team in a closely contested game that was filled with excessive fouls. The game was attended by a large Mexican crowd, which consistently supported these athletic professionals.[47]

If the Mexican community, however, wanted more athletic events or if their children were attending high school, they went to see the basketball games at the Sidney Lanier Vocational High School. The school had a long tradition of fielding good teams, especially under such excellent coaches as Nemo Herrera, an idol of Mexican basketball fans in San Antonio and El Paso between the 1930s and the 1950s. In the early thirties, for example, Sidney Lanier made the city basketball finals by beating the Anglo Brackenridge Eagles (38–37)

growing acculturation. Sons de America and Son clubs and businesspeople often sponsored the teams and even formed special teams to tour the outlying areas.

If the Mexican middle class did not like baseball or basketball, they could always play or support soccer teams such as the Carta Blanca, Club Internacional, Lakeview Grocers, Diamond Jewelry Shop, Seminario de San Juan, and the Gonzales Funeral Home, which formed the two main leagues (the San Antonio Soccer Association and the Liga Mexicana de Balompié). Soccer was closely followed by the Mexicans.

Boxing was another favorite pastime of the Mexican lower middle class and, in this case, the working class. They usually went to the Businessmen's Athletic Club at Beethoven Hall to watch their favorite boxers, Frankie Lisson, "Young" Castillo, K. O. Castillo, De Longoria (the Marine Corps champion), Roberto Gómez, "Blackie" Pérez, Carlos Macías, or Bob "Kid" Goldstein.[49]

Sports provided a network that connected middle-class Mexicans to each other and separated them, to some extent, from the upper classes and the lower. Sports also provided a vehicle for channeling frustrations, enjoying success, and establishing a feeling of joy in a basically joyless world. *La Prensa* often reported the results of the sporting events, but usually gave more attention to them when a team from Mexico was in town. One late winter day in 1930, for example, the paper urged everyone in the Mexican community to attend the basketball game between the Mexico City team and the local YMCA Triangles at Woodlawn Gym. *La Prensa* emphasized that the fifty-cent entrance fee went to cover the expenses of the visiting Mexican team, which was playing in San Antonio after touring the West and Midwest. For *La Prensa*, the game was a nationalistic event; for the community (while the attraction was also patriotic and ethnic), it was primarily a sporting event. Sports for the middle class, consequently, were ethnic, socially differentiating, and central to their lifestyle.[50]

The more affluent sectors of the Mexican community, however, lived in a different world. While the laboring class in San Antonio concentrated on daily hardships and needs and weekly social and religious activities and the lower middle class enjoyed clubs and sporting events, the upper middle class and the *ricos* (who lived in an upper-class sociocultural world) observed the Mexican community from a wider focus and perspective. As Ponciano Pérez, the owner of El Poblano Restaurant, said from his comparative perspective, "In no other city of the United States is there more of the Mexican spirit than among the Mexicans of San Antonio."[51]

THE UPPER MIDDLE CLASS AND THE EXILED MEXICAN ELITE

The families of the upper-middle-class professional and business sector of Mexican society in San Antonio were culturally and socially intertwined with the small *rico* class of exiled Mexicans. Many of them attended the same clubs and the same social functions, and their activities were frequently publicized on *La Prensa*'s social page. Both groups attended the main functions at the elite Casino Social, especially the Black and White Ball, as well as the Mexican symphonic performances, but there was a difference: the upper middle class felt Mexican American; the *ricos* felt Mexican. Matilde Elizondo, a well-known merchant, was different from publisher Ignacio E. Lozano; businessman Fortunato de los Santos was different from Dr. Aureliano Urrutia; lawyers M. C. González and Alonzo Perales were different from intellectuals like Lic. Querido Moheno and Lic. René Capistrán de Garza. Their philosophies were different; their ideologies were different. The lower and upper middle class focused their lives in the United States; the *ricos* always focused on Mexico. Watching them in their socio-cultural environment, however, one could not completely tell the difference in the 1930s. The *ricos*, less than one half of one percent of the Mexican population, usually lived outside the Latin Quarter. In fact, no more than sixty families made up this class, although the number was at times increased by the number of notable exiles who came from Mexico, but who often left quickly. The *ricos* included such men as Dr. Joaquín Gonzales, Ignacio E. Lozano,

Lic. Francisco J. Santamaría, Lic. René Capistrán Garza, Jesús Guisa y Azevedo, General Pablo González, Federico Allen Hinojosa, Dr. Aureliano Urrutia, and Nemesio García Naranjo.[52]

These *ricos* were fleeing the changing periods of the revolutions and counterrevolutions in Mexico from the downfall of Porfiro Díaz in 1911 to the end of the Cristero Rebellion in 1926. Some were directly associated with the Porfiriato, others were closer to Victoriano Huerta, and some were emigrés from the struggles of the Callista and

cal Porfirista, Huertista, Felicista, and Orozquista conservatives with a sprinkling of Carrancistas and others of the Right. They had a major common theme: they hated and detested the political fragmentation, the anticlericalism, the cultural liberalization, and the possibility of atheistic Marxism or socialism. By the late 1920s, "el jefe maximo," Plutarco Elías Calles, personified all their horrors. Calles was to them what Stalin would become to Americans in the 1940s and 1950s—the personification of evil.[53]

The *ricos'* ideological and geographical roots in San Antonio, El Paso, and Los Angeles emanated from the end of the Díaz dictatorship in 1911 and from the flight of President Victoriano Huerta from power in 1914. As Michael C. Meyer has written, "Never before had so many prominent Mexicans gone into exile at the same time." Meyer further notes that

> the number of non-prominent exiles from the list of [Carranza's] proscriptions was still greater and, in addition, many persons not on the list [to be tried for treason under the law of 1862], fearing retaliation for Huertista [or Porfirista] sympathies, voluntarily exiled themselves. Uncounted scores sought the shelter of the United States border just to escape the ravages of the continuing war . . . not every one on the exile rolls could be counted as Huertista by any means, but they were all anti-constitutionalists, and none relished the thought of spending the rest of their lives away from home.[54]

These emigres formed the core of the San Antonio ricos.

The *ricos* always looked south. This conglomeration of conservatives, with the temper of Scholasticism, the tone of Porfirismo, but with the conservative realism and arrogance of Huerta and the military eye of Pascual Orozco, once sought in 1915 to lead an armed revolution from San Antonio and El Paso to Chihuahua and on to Mexico City — all financed by German money and weapons. At the time, San Antonio was headquarters of the Mexican Peace Assembly, founded in 1915 by Querido Moheno, Eliseo Ruiz, Miguel Bolaños Cocho, and Ismael Zúñiga, with Federico Gamboa as president. The express purpose of this conservative assembly according to Meyer, "was to bring an end to the civil war which had ravaged the country for four and one-half years." But the Mexican Peace Assembly in San Antonio, regardless of its stand against Carranza's Constitutionalists, the Villistas, and the Zapatistas, was "rampant with division, fear, and mistrust, and divided between Félix Díaz [Porfirio Díaz's nephew] and Huerta."[55]

The dream of restoring the Porfirian "Camelot" ended that same year when Huerta, who was to be the political leader, was arrested by U.S. officials, and Orozco, who was to be the military leader, was shot by a force of Texas Rangers and U.S. military men. As a result, the exiles dispersed to Los Angeles, San Antonio, New York, Europe, Havana, and other Latin American countries. San Antonio was especially attractive as an immediate haven because of its well-established and large Latin Quarter, its proximity to the Mexican border, the beginning importance of *La Prensa*, as well as the city's historical tradition as a site of Mexican political intrigue (Flores Magón's ideological lampoon *Regeneración* was printed there, Madero wrote his plan there, and it had been the center for the Mexican Peace Assembly). Above all, Ignacio Lozano, an emigré from Nuevo León in 1908, and a Díaz and Huerta sympathizer, began to commission and publish the work of leading conservative Huertista intellectuals and activists like Querido Moheno, Nemesio García Naranjo, René Capistrán Garza, Aureliano Urrutia, and José María Lozano. *La Prensa* and its related publication *La Opinión* which was started in 1926 in Los Angeles, served as the ideological vehicle for these intellectuals, and for Lozano's own philosophical, cultural, and religious perspectives. In addition, they gave Mexican conservatives a forum from which to consolidate, revitalize, and focus the thoughts and hearts of the massive waves of peasants, laborers, and middle-class immigrants to the United States.[56]

La Prensa also offered the rising Mexican American intellectuals a forum. Interestingly, for the elite, *La Prensa* and later *La Opinión* served the same propagandistic purpose as the *New Republic* did during the 1920s and 1930s for Malcolm Cowley, John Dewey, and many of the European intellectual emigrés of the 1930s. *La Prensa* would serve as the conservative voice of Ignacio Lozano and publicize his bookstores and his publishing and clearing-house; it would, in fact, become the focal point of Mexican conservatism in the United States. But it was a conservatism that was not reactionary. As Meyer has pointed out, its origins may not have been Revolutionary, but they *were* revolutionary.[57] They did not want the naked "*pan o palo*" (carrot or the stick) of Díaz, but they also did not want liberalism U.S.-

bilities, suited the elite, and they settled into U.S. life, but with the intention of eventually returning to Mexico. In the meantime they felt they could forge the Mexican communities in the United States into a conservative, nationalistic, and hegemonic extension of Mexico, or, if not, they could at least build a fifth column in the Southwest. They were conservative revolutionaries, but not counterrevolutionaries.

The *ricos* and their families, together with others, were by the 1930s, *La Prensa* stated, "the elite of the Mexican community"; they had "splendid houses and handsome incomes." Businessman Ponciano Pérez praised this upper class in general, but specifically, he praised the elite's main symbolic voice in the community, *La Prensa*, and its owner, Ignacio E. Lozano. At a banquet in his restaurant given in honor of this "*gente importante*," Pérez stated that El Poblano Café y Restaurante "prided itself on its Mexicanness" and "congratulated another great Mexican business *La Prensa* . . . [and its owner] for his constant help to the Mexican people and especially for his effort in setting up the Clínica Mexicana." Through his effort, Pérez continued, "Lozano symbolizes both the action and spirit of the Mexican."[58]

The Mexican community's upper middle class recognized the *ricos'* importance and so did San Antonio's non-Mexican "society barons"—although not very much. Mrs. Clara Caffery Pancost, for example, listed several Mexicans in the 1937 *San Antonio Social Directory* of twelve hundred names: Mr. and Mrs. Eusebio Calzado (Mrs. Calzado was the former Jessie Hickey Standish and was a graduate of Incarnate Word College and Our Lady of the Lake College, where she had been a member of a prominent sorority); Mrs. Esther Pérez Carvajal (who was a descendant of the Canary Islanders who had settled San Antonio, a graduate of the University of Chicago, and of the University of Texas, a member of Delta Kappa Gamma, a member of Texas Pioneers and the Pan American Club, and a writer and educator); and Mrs. Adina de Zavala (also a descendant of the Canary Islanders, a member of the Daughters and Sons of the Heroes of the Republic of Texas, president of the Texas Press Women's Association, a fellow of the Texas State Historical Association, president of the Historical Landmarks Association, and a graduate of Sam Houston College). These "Mexicans" who made the social register were listed next to the elite of the San Antonio community: the Mengers, the Mavericks, the Hertzbergs, the Gosses, the Naylors, the Woolfords, the Nixons.

Of the Mexicans listed, one was mentioned because of his American wife, and the other two because they were descendants of the Canary Islanders. Of these, only Mrs. Esther Carvajal was active in the West Side Mexican community. In the directory's introduction Mrs. Pancost stated that "no foreword would be complete without a tribute to the colorful share the Latin Americans have and are still playing in the upbuilding of San Antonio, adding largely to the delightful artistic and cultural life of San Antonio. At fiesta time, [all the Mexicans] . . . mingle in one heterogeneous mass, the [Mexican elite] . . . pass in their glittering motor coach, with the lineage of the ages [of San Antonio] . . . and the fair debutantes of the daughters of the successful [Mexican] businessmen and professional men [evident]." Yet, in spite of this token recognition of the Mexican upper class in the foreword, the names of such men as Lozano (publisher), de Santos (businessman), García Naranjo (writer), Garza (intellectual), M. C. González (lawyer), Perales (lawyer and writer), and Chapa (businessman) failed to appear in the directory. Nevertheless, it did note that "we [the committee in charge] are proud to state that we are unbiased and, indeed unprejudiced in our production of the Social Directory . . . [however] we are only human and therefore subject to errors and omissions."[59]

The Canary Islanders listed in the directory were recognized by the non-Mexicans as being the "worthy" upper class of the Mexican community, but they were not recognized as such by the Mexican ricos. In 1931 some of the descendants of the Canary Islanders organized themselves into the Isleños for the Texas Bicentennial celebrations. Mrs. Esther Carvajal, Mrs. A. R. Spencer, Mrs. F. M. Gillespie, Mrs. Mann, and Mrs. Marguerite Mayers headed this organization of the "direct descendants" of Canary Islanders. But since the few Canary Islanders were not actually representatives of the larger Mexican community, the bicentennial committee finally discarded the idea of erecting a statue to commemorate the arrival of the Canary Islanders to San Antonio. Instead, it authorized Miss Frances Scarborough, one of the descendants, to write a play depicting their arrival, which could be performed at the festivities. The Americano community, it seems, wanted the social link to the nineteenth-century "old" Spanish families, but did not want to recognize the political importance of the twentieth-century exiled *ricos* and the upper-middle-class Mexican

the casino you would have the friendship of "banqueros, comerciantes, industriales, artistas, agricultores, periodistas, profesionistas, and also be in the center of Mexican life in San Antonio." Furthermore, the Casino implied that membership would enhance one's career, social life, and family life. But, above all, men like Fortunato de los Santos, the owner of a furniture store and the 1930 president of the Casino, believed that through Casino membership, Mexicans could "live in a Mexican environment, live in the shadow of our Mexican tradition and enjoy our own [Mexican] customs." The Casino Mexicano was not only the meeting place of the *ricos* and the upper echelons of the middle class, but it was the piviotal point of the Mexican consciousness of collectivity."[61]

The Casino Social was the center of the *ricos*' and the upper middle class's cultural and social world. It was, they believed, the main cultural institution of the Mexican community. For the *ricos*, the professionals, and the businesspeople of the middle class, it represented the institutional core of the community. In 1930, while the Depression was beginning to be felt by the San Antonio community in general and by the Mexicans in particular, the Casino membership, ironically, was planning the installation of a tennis court, the acquisition of a Ping-Pong table, and the purchase of a new pool table. The exclusivity of the Casino was apparent when one of the members of the executive committee told the one hundred new members, "We welcome you to this beautiful center of aristocracy, beauty, and culture that is called the Casino Mexicano." This elitism was also apparent at the Casino's directors' committee meeting when the discussion centered on the question of whether the Casino should allow the community's lower-middle-class recreational clubs the use of its facilities for their dances. The directors finally decided to allow them the privilege "as a demonstration of a fraternal spirit ['*espíritu de acercamiento*'] toward the lower ['*valiosos*'] classes of the Mexican community that have not organized their social and recreational centers very well."[62]

The *ricos*' Comtian philosophy (which emphasized nationalism and society above individual or class allegiances) permeated the Casino and was expressed one winter night at a special banquet in honor of Don Rafael Martínez Carrillo, a legal consultant. Lic. José María Lozano, the lawyer for the Union of the Exiled Family of Mexicans and a former Huertista intellectual, was the master of ceremonies. He spoke at the banquet with a "golden tongue and words of gold" about the need for "peace and harmony" among Mexicans in Mexico. He said that he saw "days of glory and prosperity in Mexico for the great Mexican family," and he urged Mexico to open its doors to all expatriates. Lozano further urged everyone to return to Mexico, especially "all ex-politicians." He used Beethoven to show the plight and suffering of the Mexican people and how they—like Beethoven—could overcome their problems and achieve greatness. In this same vein, Lic. Francisco J. Santamaría eulogized Mexico. The room "vibrated with enthusiasm at the themes being presented." The guests were a *Who's Who* of the San Antonio exiled elites. *La Prensa* reported that Lic. Santamaría's speech "lifted the hearts of the expatriados" when he stated that "even though Mexico was far away it still continued to be near in our hearts." Santamaría also praised the efforts of Lic. Ignacio Lozano as a leader of the younger generation of Mexicans.[63]

The guest of honor at this banquet, Don Rafael Martínez Carrillo, specifically addressed the problem of class divisions among Mexicans in the United States. He stated that the solution would be a strong national government in Mexico to unite the "foreign Mexican community" living in the United States with the home country. The whole theme of the banquet was expressed in Martínez's statement that "Mexico needs the support of all Mexicans to help build Mexico."[64]

It was clear that the *ricos* throughout the thirties would face south, since they would always try consciously to remain *mexicanos*. This attitude contrasted with that of the upper-middle-class Mexicans at the banquet, who saw the struggle of the Mexican community in the United States as one between acculturating U.S. citizens and Mexican citizens. This philosophical and cultural difference was articulated very well by leading middle-class lawyer, Alonzo Perales, who later said that the growth and development of the Mexican Middle class should parallel the growth and development of the Anglo middle class.[65]

The expressed Mexicanist philosophy of the *ricos* was often translated into action by their social activities, especially those sponsored by the Club Mexicano de Bellas Artes, the women's auxiliary of the Casino Social. These women expressed in cultural terms what the men expressed philosophically: "the world of the *ricos*." At one of the meetings, for example, Mrs. Josefina de González, the club's president,

In particular, the Club Mexicano de Bellas Artes sought to translate this philosophy into action by supporting the Orquesta Sinfónica Mexicana, which had been attempting to sustain itself through the efforts of its own members and the help of its leader, Professor Eulalio Sánchez. Mrs. González told the membership quite clearly that

> this is . . . simply [our] patriotic attitude because we must show [the Anglos] in this foreign land the valor and value of the Mexican artist so that people in the United States do not think of Mexico simply as a land of wars and passions, but that there also exists a land of artists that surge forward like the promise of the coming day: we must show . . . everyone [in the United States] the heart of the Mexican . . . through his art; thus, destroying by its brilliance all the ruins of the lower class's [popular culture].

Mrs. González reminded the members of the culturalist philosophy of the club when she said that it was dedicated to promoting the Mexican artist and Mexican art because "the reconstruction of our country [Mexico] was dependent on this base of art."[66]

Upper-class Mexican women through their clubs were the main agents promoting the *ricos'* philosophy. Underlining this theme of cultural reconstruction was a lecture by the famous Mexican artist David Alfaro Siqueiros. (His politics might have been different from theirs, but to the women he was a Mexican and an artist.) The club sponsored a public lecture by Siqueiros, which was publicized by the two well known intellectuals and writers for *La Prensa*, Lic. Nemesio García Naranjo and José Juan Tablado.[67] The women, it seems, were tied to the political ideology of their class, although they had an active feminine world of their own. Overall, however, they (and the men) understood culture to be a "signifying system through which necessarily (though among other means) a social order is communicated, reproduced, experienced and explored." Consequently, for the *ricos* and their wives, culture was not only (as Raymond Williams calls it) a "whole way of life," but "artistic and intellectual activities" that encompassed "all the signifying practices — from language through the arts and philosophy to journalism, fashion and advertising."[68]

The Club Mexicano de Bellas Artes, as a result of its belief in the importance and extensiveness of culture, pursued its objective of promoting the Mexican consciousness by sponsoring a musical contest that would be open to all Mexicans in the Southwest and that would be publicized by *La Prensa*. Individuals were urged to submit plays, musical scores, and poems. The club worked to help build the artistic talent of the Mexican community in order to show non-Mexicans the positive side of the Mexican "heart" and to establish a hegemony of Mexican culture in San Antonio and throughout the Southwest.[69]

COMMUNITY RELATIONS

Community, society, and culture were intertwined but still separated in the West Side of San Antonio: all were Mexican, all were members of la Raza; nevertheless, there were three separate social and intellectual worlds. The large laboring class did not have the time or the money to participate in the lower middle class's social and recreational clubs, and the lower middle class did not have the prestige or money to participate in the upper-class functions at the Casino Social. However, the lower classes read about the elite's functions in *La Prensa* and other local newspapers. On February 4, 1930, for example, *La Prensa*'s social page headlines read, "A social activity without precedent occurred at the last dance of the Casino Mexicano." The paper claimed that, without a doubt, this dance was the best of the many other social events being held that night throughout the *colonia:* "Without question, it can be said that no other function has brought together more Mexican families than this dance for the new Casino members. It demonstrated the Mexican community's sense of self-worth. More than 300 couples attended the beautifully decorated halls of our new *centro social* which was adorned graciously in a multitude of colors." The article further pointed out that, "although dances at the Casino have not always observed proper etiquette in dress, the majority of men and women at this dance were dressed in elegant formal clothing and even correct smoking etiquette was observed by the men." *La Prensa* concluded that "the recent social fiestas [at the Casino] including this one have demonstrated a spirit of democracy, cordiality, and harmony never seen before [in our community] showing that the Casino Mexicano has the best [social] elements of the Mexican society [in San Antonio]."

The events of that February evening were a microcosm of the complex Mexican society. As the Mexican laborers went to sleep in their *jacales* contemplating the next day's work, and as the lower middle

president, Fortunato de los Santos. At 11:00 P.M., the dinner hour was introduced by a violin concerto, and while the rest of the community slept, the dinner and dance continued at the Casino until 2:00 A.M. The three worlds of the West Side were never more separated as classes, yet they were never closer in their sensitivities as Mexicanos — all were la Raza in their "habits of the heart" (to use Tocqueville's phrase), but their mentality was changing.[70]

Upper-middle-class women and the exiled *ricos'* wives moved in tangential circles. They were tied to each other by ideology and class, but they often formed, it seems, a separate, women's world of their own. As a result of their activities and their social standing, these women exhibited a strong sense of self, an independence, and a deep feeling of mission. It was almost a sense of noblesse oblige. Most of these women were members of the Casino Social and the Club Mexicano de Bellas Artes. Other elite women's organizations such as the Club Femenino Orquidia also sponsored lectures and conferences that appealed to the upper middle class and the *ricos*. On October 5, 1931, for example, the Club Femenino Orquidia sponsored Margarita Robles de Mendoza, a noted Mexican authority on women, whose speech was entitled "The Current Condition of Mexican Women." Her lecture was cosponsored by the Mesa Redonda de Relaciones Internacionales under the auspices of the American Association of University Women. The Grupo de Aficionados de Arte organized an art club, Thalia, which sponsored plays by such notable writers as Spain's Muniz Seca. They believed that this allowed the other social classes in the community to enjoy "high culture," which was a key to being *gente decente*."[71]

To try to maintain the high intellectual and cultural level of the community, the upper middle class and the elite sponsored a monthly lecture series. Topics varied from Esther Pérez Caravajal's lecture "Spanish Language and Literature," to Lic. Gustavo C. García's "The Progress of Latin Americans in the Texas Educational System." Moreover, Dr. David Cerna, a well-known Mexican socialite and prominent doctor wrote a regular column in *La Prensa* on Shakespeare to improve the literary knowledge of the Mexican community. (Cerna also helped the laboring class medically, by training midwives.) At times, the upper-class youth engaged in similar intellectual-cultural activities such as literary and musical events sponsored by their own organizations, the Asociación Católica de Jóvenes Mexicanos or the Club Juventud.[72]

La Prensa's Sunday edition, moreover, always carried a supplement with essays on literary and cultural topics. In addition, Ignacio E. Lozano constantly publicized and sold books from his publishing house, Casa Editorial. *El caudillo* by E. Phillips Oppenheim, *El criticón* by Baltazar García, *La guerra de Granada* by Hurtado de Mendoza, and *El alma estrella* by Alfonso Reyes were a few of the titles listed. *La Prensa* sometimes listed over 150 books in seven categories from religion to history to politics to theater.[73] The *ricos* clearly established and promoted a definite intellectual milieu of high culture, a Comtian discourse, a Scholastic tradition, Profirian (Huertista) politics, and a sensitivity to *mexicanidad* (as well as an example of correct diction and language that promoted, within itself, an ideology of formalism and elitism).

The three cultural worlds — of the laborer, the lower middle class, and the *ricos* — were also reflected in the style and organization of community meetings. Business meetings reflected class stratification and the cultural differences in the types and kinds of meetings that were held. The Mexican workers' meetings were usually held at the stark Beneficencia Mexicana Hall by labor organizer Magdaleno Rodríguez, militant Emma Tenayuca, the Communist Workers' Alliance, and the CIO. The lower-middle-class meetings were often held at a drab local tavern or in stuffy church halls. The upper-class Mexicans, however, did their planning over "an exquisite dinner" or a bridge party such as the one held at the home of Enrique Alesio Guerra and his wife, Elivir Pizzini de Guerra. At other times, members of the upper class had an afternoon planning meeting over "punche, pastas secas, and dulces" in the beautiful dining room of Señora Lacadia T. de Teal's house, or over a small downtown luncheon such as the ones held at the Hotel Gunter by Mexican consul general Enríquez Santibáñez. Many times, however, the upper class's meetings were purely social events, such as the elegant New Year's Eve party held by LULAC lawyer and middle-class intellectual M. C. González for the leading Mexican families of San Antonio. Upper-class women often met for tea or supper at the Polly Tea Room in downtown San Antonio to discuss business, but it was a social event as well.[74]

During the 1930s, other members of the upper and middle class had meetings that were for political as well as business purposes. A dinner was held at J. Estrada's El Fénix Restaurant, for example, to

after founding *La Prensa* condemned the preaching of socialism.

San Antonio was not fertile soil for Marxism, socialism, or anarchism, though, as evidenced by its southern élan, conservative history, and modernizing trajectory. Moreover, the Mexican workers themselves were conservative. For example, as early as 1910, the working-class Liga Mexicana (founded in 1909) organized a West Side celebration to "Cheer Díaz," as the *San Antonio Daily Express* reported.[75] The league, in spite (or maybe even because) of the pending revolution in Mexico, joined with a multitude of other Mexican organizations in San Antonio (the Gran Círculo de Obreros, the Sociedad de la Unión, the Sociedad Benito Juárez, the Campamento Bernardo Reyes, the Campamento Servando Canales, and the Club de Trabajadores) to celebrate Porfirio Díaz's re-election.

Other groups, such as Mexican businesspeople, especially those who belonged to the Mexican Chamber of Commerce, held their meetings and reunions at places such as the Carta Blanca Restaurant owned by a Señor Núñez. Chamber members represented their own businesses or the businesses for which they worked when these dinner-business meetings were held. At one such meeting on April 7, 1932, the Mexican business elite, including members of the Mexican Chamber of Commerce, met at Núñez's restaurant to receive a "briefing" by San Antonio banker Jack E. Beretta on the crisis of the Depression. A report of this talk was later heard by many of the Mexican community on Lic. René Capistrán Garza's half-hour program, "La Voz de la Raza" on KACB, one of the Spanish radio stations in San Antonio. Capistrán, a prominent Mexican intellectual and writer, was in exile in the United States and often went on speaking tours to Texas' Mexican communities. He was also a member of the Mexican Chamber of Commerce because he was the director of the radio station. In short, business, politics, intellectualism, and nationalistic commitment were often mixed with pleasure by the upper classes; consequently, they tried to help the lower classes, culturally if not always economically.[76]

Both the upper middle class and the elite, as I have said, often provided cultural entertainment for the lower class. They attempted, in fact, to use culture as a vehicle through which to gain and maintain political and philosophical hegemony. The *ricos* always wanted the intellect, the soul, and the spirit of the Americanizing Mexicans to be colored by a sense of obligation to Mexico. In short, they wanted all Mexicans to maintain a close political and ideological affinity with Mexico. (Jews in the United States after the establishment of Israel would make the same argument.) The middle class, which owned or directed the Mexican radio stations and produced programs such as "La Voz de la Raza" and KONO's "La Estrella" (which was heard from 1933 through 1935), would counter the *ricos'* fifth column arguments with one of Americanism.

The Mexican community could also hear Manuel Dávila's music programs on KEDA, or they could listen to Rubén González's classical music program or his concerts from KGCI, the St. Mary's College station. These stations helped to reach the people who could not read or get the news in any other way. They often broadcast concerts of European music or Mexican songs that helped to provide a sense of cultural and psychological cohesion. In short, the Mexican population could hear not only LULAC's or the *ricos'* political and philosophical propaganda but all types of music as well. The 1929–41 period saw not only a search for identity, but also a search for a coherent view of reality. The radio provided a central instrument for the dispersion of culture if not the message of politics.[77]

To maintain their cultural and philosophical hegemony, the Mexican upper class also sponsored fiestas to benefit cultural organizations, such as the benefit for Rafaela C. de Pajores's Bach Academy of Music. At this communitywide fiesta, the most distinguished Mexican artists of the San Antonio community took part; groups like the Trio Valle sang from the opera *Mignon;* la Orquesta Sinfónica, directed by Prof. Eulalio Sánchez, played, as did the Banda Juvenil, directed by Prof. A. Martínez. Other artists performed classical pieces and danced classical and modern musical numbers.

Sánchez's orchestra not only was the pride of San Antonio Mexican society, it was recognized by the non-Mexican community as well.

The *San Antonio Light* praised it especially after it had performed before three thousand people in a concert at the Municipal Auditorium, but it pointed out that, while the orchestra (which was composed completely of Mexican musicians) demonstrated experience, it would definitely improve even more after its six-month tour outside the San Antonio area. The paper also told its readers, "It is very satisfying to observe the interest shown by San Antonians to good music and the great cultural efforts on the part of the [Mexican] women's

Only pieces by Mozart, Granados, Mascagni, MacDowell, Luigi y Gómez, Beethoven, and Mendelssohn would be played." Those laborers who did not attend could listen to classical music on the radio or at a friend's house or even, at times, at the cantina; the middle class could go to Ignacio M. Valle's music store, el Arte Mexicano, or to the San Antonio Music Company to purchase classical or Mexican records. At these stores they could also buy *corridos*, songs, band music, or recital music. Consequently, even though U.S. ideology and culture were seeping into the West Side from 1926 to 1941, *lo mexicano* was still hegemonic, especially through the efforts of the *ricos*.[79]

Although each class had its own world in the Latin Quarter, they were to some degree intertwined. Consequently, tensions would surface in the post–World War II period concerning questions of community development or individual development; ethnicity or individualism; *lo mexicano*, *lo americano*, or Mexican Americanism. These were only underlying tensions in the 1930s, however.

In spite of these developing philosophical questions, the classes coexisted and knew about the others. The eldest son of Matilde Elizondo told me that he "wasn't aware of the workers' demonstrations or strikes" and that the "workers' strikes often went unnoticed." This is difficult to believe, however, since Rodríguez's Pecan Shellers Union claimed over ten thousand members during the height of the 1934–35 strike. It seems that the middle class did not want to be disturbed. During the 1934–38 period, when different sectors of the Mexican laboring class were striking, the life of the *ricos* and the upper middle class continued as usual. Labor strikes thus did not unify the Mexican community, they separated it. The middle class and the *ricos* did not want to be associated with the rabble rousers, even though the self-proclaimed Communist and labor leader Emma Tenayuca was "listened to" (according to Julia Blackwelder) by *La Prensa* in the strikes of 1938 (probably because she was a Mexican under attack by unionist Rebecca Taylor, Police Chief Kilday, and the English-language press, including the labor newspaper the *Weekly Dispatch*). *La Prensa* sympathized with her but not with her radicalism because, for *La Prensa*, nationalism by 1938 was becoming more important than politics or ideologies.[80]

Health conditions, on the other hand, were overlapping problems that related, not separated, the community. Health-related problems began to affect the whole community in 1932, when the banks began to fail in Texas (three failed in San Antonio in one week). The bank failures affected everyone, but the Mexican poor were especially hurt when the Santa Rosa General Hospital (located close to the West Side) lost its payroll funds as a result of the failure of the Central Bank. Because the hospital had to borrow money to pay its employees, it admitted fewer patients. By 1935 the hospital began to admit more patients, but it could still not yet afford general medical care for the needy. Ignacio E. Lozano decided that the San Antonio Mexican community needed its own health clinic, since the Mexicans' poverty and health conditions were so oppressive and they no longer had a facility with the failure of the Santa Rosa Hospital. This need for a clinic was equally recognized by the middle and upper classes, who were aware of the socio-economic conditions of their "Mexican Town."[81]

Teodoro Torres, a publisher and Ignacio E. Lozano's friend and professional counterpart from Mexico City's *Revista de Revistas* (part of Mexico's prominent *Excélsior* family), decided to publish details of the terrible conditions, cultural activities, and the day-to-day life of the Mexican *colonia* of San Antonio to enlighten his Mexican readers. He hoped that such an exposé would enable Mexicans in Mexico to understand better the conditions of their *patriotistas* in the United States during the Depression. The general conditions during this decade even caused the consul general of Mexico, Enrique Santibáñez, to go to Washington, D.C., to report the "situation" of the Mexicans directly to Manuel C. Téllez, the Mexican ambassador to the United States.[82]

Because of the *ricos*' and the upper middle class's extreme concern for "los mexicanos pobres," and because of their financial influence and potential political power in the San Antonio community, they were given complete access to the findings of the San Antonio Social Welfare Bureau. Mrs. R. C. Hugman, secretary of the bureau, as well as Mrs. Dwight Stone, the director of the Public Health Office, gave *La Prensa* information on the extent of the crisis in the city among the poor, especially statistics concerning the Mexicans. These findings, furthermore, were presented to the Society for the Protection of Children and to the Association of Welfare Organizations of the city in order to find relief for the poor. Thus, the city's non-Mexican and Mexican elite attempted to coordinate efforts to handle the city's health and welfare problems. One proposal was made by the secretary of

can consul general, and others were very alarmed by the nurses' reports, which documented the fact that the worst conditions were in the West Side and that these conditions, combined with the severe winter weather, had produced a high rate of bronchitis, influenza, fever, and coughs (especially among children). The nurses also verified that the high number of tuberculosis cases that had been listed at the Robert B. Green General Hospital were Mexican cases. One nurse noted the pressure she felt from the upper classes of San Antonio to report the poverty cases quickly, rather than the sick ones: "The rich complain more about the poverty than the sickness. As a result there is not one day that we don't have to report cases to the Welfare Association so that they can give help to the emergency cases"[84]

Because of poverty, sickness, severe winters, and hot, humid summers, all exacerbated by the Depression, a *San Antonio Express* editorial of April 1, 1935, suggested that the city investigate the possibility of using the "model village" housing development concept that was being tried by Pueblo, Colorado, for the Mexican population. Colorado officials had organized Mexicans into a community and housed them around a central area that had running water and private gardens. The editorial, emphatically expressing the views of San Antonio city leaders, stated, "It costs . . . a great deal more to keep slums than to eliminate them."[85]

The Mexicans agreed, joined by Father Tranchese, but there was a more immediate problem for many Mexicans — payment of rent or eviction. The rent situation became so acute that in 1935 the consul general went before Mayor C. M. Chambers and the members of the city commission and asked that a city ordinance be passed "declaring a moratorium whereby it would be impossible to evict Mexican tenants who were in arrears of their rent." Santibáñez suggested to the mayor and the city commissioners that with a moratorium of two or three months, the Mexicans in arrears would be able to get seasonal summer employment and pay their rent. Mayor Chambers, however, did not see the rent situation as acute. Besides, he felt that such an action "would be bad publicity . . . [for] San Antonio [which] ranked as [one of the two] American cities holding their own in these strenuous times." He said, "I am willing to offer what cooperation I can to the Mexican government . . . [but] we do not have sufficient funds to employ extra labor [a method] which might be a way of alleviating [these] conditions."[86] The impoverished situation of the Mexicans in the city and throughout the Southwest caused the *ricos* in San Antonio to issue the following statement:

> [All] Mexicans need to know that they are [morally and psychologically] supported by all of us, by [fellow] workers, by our own industrialists, by our businessmen, by our newspapermen, and by our [Mexican] consulates. We have to cooperate to overcome that shame [of our economic condition here in the United States] that overwhelms us. In the meantime if we should permit that one single Mexican individual be unjustly belittled it would also be all of our belittlement. If we can cooperate and if we can better appreciate the grandeur of this country and especially the work of the Mexican agricultural workers, we should have sufficient dignity to respect ourselves. Only [by respecting ourselves] can we respect others.[87]

Continuing to focus on pride, self-respect, and moral support, *La Prensa* during the 1930s also focused its attention on the condition of the most unfortunate of its *compatriotas*, the ones who for many reasons found themselves imprisoned. The *ricos* wanted to initiate a campaign to intervene on behalf of these Mexicans. In one case, Lozano and others, through *La Prensa*, focused public attention on one Mexican prisoner's problems. Although David Bueno was not released as a result of this campaign, he began to draw comic cartoons that were published in *La Prensa;* the *ricos* felt that this in itself was a kind of rehabilitation. They continually called for a united front to survive the Depression decade.[88]

The central focus for the *ricos* and the upper middle class during the early part of the Depression was the elimination of sickness in the Mexican Quarter. They followed Lozano's suggestion to build a medical clinic exclusively supported and run by Mexicans, and Lozano, using his personal (and *La Prensa's*) prestige, spearheaded the

effort. He called on the Mexican communities throughout the United
States to contribute their pennies, nickels, dimes, and dollars to help
the San Antonio Mexican community build and furnish a health clinic.
Mexicans in San Antonio and throughout the United States supported
this effort. From its annual convention in Tucson, Arizona, the Alianza Hispano-Americana, a mutual benefit and fraternal organization, sent $101.00, which was collected at the convention in amounts
of $1.00 to $3.00 per member. The alliance urged all its members to

lines of communication in the United States; (3) the influence of *La
Prensa;* and (4) the strong cultural influence of the exiled comprador
class of *ricos.* Generous contributions were also received from San
Antonio's non-Mexican political and business community because of
the strong influence of the prominent upper- and middle-class Mexicans who were directing the clinic drive. These contributions were
an indication that the Mexican leadership had close political and business ties with non-Mexican merchants and politicians as a result of
their recognition as the buffer zone between the Mexican and the
non-Mexican communities (however, these ties were not social). Moreover, Mérida, Mexico, through the efforts of the newspaper *Diario
de Yucatán*, contributed $50.00. The *ricos'* influence extended even
into Mexico proper.[90]

The Mexicans of San Antonio worked diligently and cooperatively
on the health issue during the early 1930s. Ideology, social status, and
financial standing were not barriers to this cooperation, which saw
the cosponsorship of benefits, dances, and parties to raise funds. Everyone rallied to the cause because the issue was la Raza. The exclusive
Club Femenino Orquidia, headed by Carmen Lozano and Eva Naranjo, donated eighty-six dollars from a fiesta it sponsored and voted
to contribute an undisclosed annual amount for the running of the
maternity and children's wards of the clinic. *La Prensa* editorialized
that this generosity "personifies the attitude that all Mexicans have
had toward the building of the clinic [and] the desire of the women
to donate their money toward the maternity [and children's ward]
is an indication of the latent feelings of motherhood carried by all

women." Other organizations from the upper and middle class also responded: the Club de Jóvenes Católicos de San Fernando voted to donate one hundred dollars to help furnish one of the clinic's rooms and to get a plaque with the club's name posted at the clinic; the Club Artístico Pro-Clínica was specifically organized by all the artists of the community to raise funds.

The lower middle class responded in a similar fashion: the Latin Boosters Club of the Missouri-Pacific Railroad held a dance at the Roof Garden de la Gloria and raised thirty dollars from the entrance fee. The working class also did what it could. The Finck Cigar Factory workers held a meeting and voted to donate one hundred dollars; *La Prensa*, acknowledging this herculean effort by the workers, specifically thanked the cigar workers for their tremendous effort and for their "humanitarianism and their generosity." All of these local efforts, spearheaded by Lozano for the Mexican clinic, were coordinated by the Junta de Beneficencia, a committee of upper-class and middle-class individuals under whose auspices the clinic eventually functioned.[91]

Mexican intellectuals also publicized the need for the clinic. In the *Diario de Yucatán*, an important newspaper run by the noted Mexican "apostle of journalism," Carlos R. Menéndez, an article, "Send Your Donation, Brother," was published by Querido Moheno. In it, Moheno praised the efforts of the entire Mexican community of the United States to help their poor and disabled brethren. This project, Moheno wrote, would help them get a clinic and be taken care of by other Mexicans in a spirit of smiles and cheerfulness, because it was a house of "our poor and our sick." Moheno underlined the necessity for these contributions by using references from the Bible and by pointing out that "those who have [financial means] should help the needy."

The drive for the clinic took great effort by Lozano, but it was successful only because of the full and active support of the Casino Social members and the women of the Club Mexicano de Bellas Artes, the constant participation of the intellectuals of *La Prensa*, the help of the upper-middle-class Mexicans, and the cooperation of Mexicans throughout the Southwest. The national drive for a health clinic was both a pragmatic and a symbolic attempt by the *ricos* and the upper middle class to bring the Mexican communities throughout the United States together through recognition of a common collective consciousness and a sense of civic virtue in regard to their common problems.[92]

Education was another crucial issue. During the 1930s illiteracy was a major problem in the United States. Over twenty million people could not write their names or fill out forms. *La Prensa* and the *gente respectable* recognized this problem not only as a national one, but as a local one as well. Emilia G. Gohmet, a school principal from Marshall, Texas, wrote *La Prensa* asking it to publicize the value of education and to urge Mexican parents to enroll their children in school. *La Prensa* heeded Miss Gohmet's suggestion and publicized the need for education, although with a different focus and in a different manner than the *LULAC News*, the middle-class Mexican American paper, would have done. *La Prensa* viewed education as

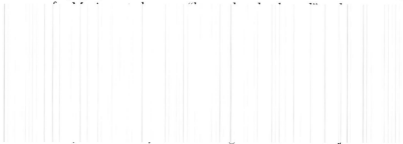

Mexico City.[93]

Alicia was not, by any stretch of the imagination, typical of the Mexican girls in the United States, but to *La Prensa* and the *ricos* she was the ideal. If Mexicans could not be rich and wealthy, they could still be educated and cultured. The *ricos* emphasized a modernist but elitist perspective on art and humanities more than Gabino Barreda's positivist emphasis on science. They were Porfiristas, but not positivists, and they took their intellectual cue from Nemesio García Naranjo, who as minister of education under Huerta in 1913, had accepted Henri Bergson's "philosophical assault" (Meyer and Sherman's phrase), on positivism and had emphasized literature, history, and philosophy, rather than just science. García wanted a balance in the development of the individual, and so did the *ricos* in the 1930s. Wealth was important, but so was culture; civic virtue was preferred to ideology or individualism; and nationalism was more important than separate class visions. For the *ricos*, consequently, art, literature, and humanities were just as important as science.[94]

Middle-class leaders such as Alonzo Perales and M. C. González saw culture, society, and education from a different perspective. Education to them was a vehicle for jobs, not just culture; it was a method for achieving careers, not necessarily status; it was a means of entering the Anglo world, not a way to epitomize the Mexican one. For the middle class, as Dewey had suggested, education was a way to build society, not, as the *ricos* felt, something to be built by society. There was a distinctive ideological difference. The Mexican American middle class took its cue from Dewey and emphasized organic and pragmatic education, not classical. It wanted functionalism, not necessarily an aesthetic balance in the development of the individual. The Mexican middle class, consequently, through the *LULAC News* and LULAC members' activities, urged parents to enroll their children in school to give them a better preparation for the world of work, to give them the opportunity to learn English, and to give them the opportunity to become Americans. "Education rather than political agitation is the essence of progress," said M. C. González, in a statement meant to separate ideologically the middle class from the working-class strikes of the period. Success not models, Americans not Mexicans, were the goals of the middle class.[95]

The Americanizing lower middle class also emphasized and accepted functional pragmatic education but concentrated on the financial side. The athletic club, for example, organized bingo games to raise funds for the Dominican nuns to run the parochial school to which many of the upper middle class and some of the lower middle class sent their children. The American Catholic Church, however, promoted Deweyian education laced with American Catholicism, although it did attempt to maintain the Mexicans' sense of culture. Parents of children attending Catholic schools raised funds by staging theatrical productions to which the entire community was invited. Other clubs affiliated with the church, such as the Hijas de María de la Catedral, held bingo games and fiestas to help the Catholic educational system.

The issue of education preoccupied the Mexican community regardless of class because Mexican enrollment in the San Antonio public school system had doubled between 1924 and 1939, from 28,881 to approximately 57,772. Each social class had its own reasons for placing importance on education, but, all struggled for it.[96]

Deportations and repatriations also touched the Mexican community in San Antonio during the 1930s, just as they touched the rest of the Mexican communities in the Southwest. Representative Martin Dies in 1930 attacked the existing immigration laws, stating that of two million Mexicans in the United States, at least half were illegals and should be deported. Both Dies and Representative John C. Box urged enforcement of the 1917 immigration law that prohibited the poor and illiterate from entering the United States. They urged that this law be applied not only to Mexican illegals, but to illegals from Canada and the Philippines. Box and Albert Johnson, therefore, sponsored a bill calling for the strict enforcement of immigration laws, especially with regard to Mexican nationals.

In response to these actions, middle-class lawyers and prominent LULAC members J. T. Canales of South Texas and Alonzo Perales of San Antonio strongly protested this attack against the Mexican communities before a congressional committee on immigration. Perales especially protested the Box-Johnson attempt to picture the Mexican as a "member of a degenerate race." Canales, using another approach, argued that immigration quotas hurt the agricultural interests of the South Texas Valley, which needed Mexican labor.[97]

The *ricos*, unlike Perales, who worried about racial discrimination, or Canales, who worried about economic discrimination, felt

abuses in the United States as a result of the Box-Johnson attack. An article in *La Prensa* (June 8, 1930) commented that a real terror of persecution, prosecution, and deportation existed among many Mexicans of the lower and laboring class, regardless of whether they lived in urban neighborhoods or rural ranches, or whether they were in the United States legally or were citizens. As a result of racial mistreatment, *La Prensa* pointed out, "these Mexican people hide whenever a North American is seen because of their fear of being deported."[99]

The *ricos* did not confront the immigration-deportation problem directly, since their philosophy coincided with the general thrust of Box and Johnson's initiative, although certainly not their methods. The *ricos* wanted Mexicans in the United States to return to Mexico, but they, as nationalists, sympathized with the plight of their poor compatriots. Therefore, they undertook several actions: first, they asked the Mexican government to grant amnesty to Mexican political exiles; second, they agreed to try to help facilitate President Ortiz Rubio's repatriation plans by attempting to persuade Mexican and U.S. immigration officials not to interfere with the voluntary Mexican exodus; and third, they began to reprint articles from other newspapers in *La Prensa* that argued against the Box-Harris and the Box-Johnson immigration bills.[100]

La Prensa reprinted an article from the *San Antonio Express*, for example, that stated unequivocally that the proposed immigration bills be killed in the House of Representatives because Mexicans were a necessary labor supply in the Southwest and did not take jobs from Americans. This article represented not only the view of San Antonio business and social leaders, but that of the Departments of Labor, Agriculture, and State as well as the office of the president of the United States; none of these governmental offices wanted any restrictions placed on Mexican labor. *La Prensa* also reprinted an article from the *Washington Post* that stated that the congressional committee on immigration, headed by Johnson and Box, should not arbitrarily place quotas on the Mexican or Spanish American population. The *Washington Post* asserted that, although Box had been a proponent of the fight against Mexican immigration for ten years, nothing should be done by Congress unless it was done in consultation with other countries. The *Post*, like the *San Antonio Express*, emphasized very clearly the crucial factor in the whole discussion — the need for cheap surplus labor. The articles reprinted by *La Prensa* underlined the problems that would occur if both the business and the agricultural sectors in the United States were deprived of Mexican labor.

As a consequence of using this technique of reprinting articles that supported their philosophy rather than directly editorializing, the *ricos* had it both ways: they struggled with the other classes against immigration and deportation problems, yet they helped to facilitate the return of Mexicans to the home country. It seemed that the Depression, the conservatives' cry for deportation, the beginning of the end of Mexico's factionalism, and the repatriation mood of the Mexicans in the Southwest were historical and political factors that were coinciding to help bring about a restoration of Mexico's "order, stability, and prosperity." But the process of Americanization for the majority of Mexicans had moved them more from a consciousness of "*mexicanos de afuera*" (outside Mexico) to "*mexicanos de adentro*" (inside the United States). Many Mexicans were becoming Mexican Americans.[101]

Politics and the reform of the barrio were also concerns of the Mexican community. (Politics will be discussed in chapter seven.) In January, 1930, Mayor C. M. Chambers proposed a city bond issue for $5 million. At a meeting of the city commissioners at which the discussion focused on the expenditure of these monies, voters were allowed to make suggestions. City parks and sanitation commissioner Jacobo Rubiola, on whom the hopes of the Mexican community were centered, proposed that $750,000 be given to him to be used on the West Side and that an additional $297,000 be reserved for his office to provide better parks and athletic camps throughout the city. But street commissioner Paul Steffler asked for the bulk of the money, saying that the city needed it for streets and bridges. Steffler's proposal was not necessarily directed toward the improvement of the Mexican West Side. Police and fire chief Phil Wright asked for nothing, but stated that the city needed four new police and fire stations, which would cost $200,000. Frank Bushick, the tax commissioner, suggested that the bond issue be limited to $2 million to reduce the property tax to about $.06 for each $100 of property value (Bushick was protecting the North Side). The mayor ultimately asked that regardless of how the money was allocated, the total bond not exceed his originally proposed $5 million limit. This was the world of city politics, power, and knowledge that the Mexican population had to learn about.[102]

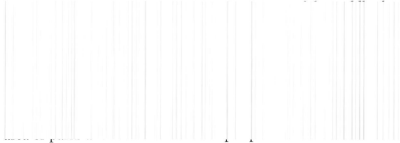

Rubiola. A group headed by businessman Enrique A. Guerra, the president of the San Antonio Lions Club, suggested that the money be used to help change Milam Park to a recreation and exercise center for the West Side. Another group of Mexicans asked that the site of the old market-place be used to establish a modern clinic with rooms for a maternity ward and rooms for a children's ward. A third suggestion came from a group headed by J. O. Loftin, the principal of the predominantly Mexican Sidney Lanier Vocational High School. Loftin's group proposed that a recreation and exercise center be established close to Sidney Lanier. A fourth group proposed the enlargement of the West Side recreational area at the corner of Frio and Matamoros streets and the construction of a new gymnasium at the site to serve not only young children but teenagers of both sexes. This group justified its proposal by pointing out that the West Side was an area in "which resides two-thirds of the school population of San Antonio."[103]

All of the Mexican community's suggestions were considered except for the one that asked for a health clinic (as I have already mentioned). A new gymnasium was proposed and additional recreational equipment was to be placed in the few West Side parks and plazas. More important, the Mexican newspaper reported that "hopes have been elevated that with the passing of the [new] bond more extensive help can be obtained [in the future] to relieve the problems of the West Side."

In addition to the distribution of recreational equipment, the commissioners, as a result of the united effort of the Mexican community, turned in their reports indicating the priorities for the use of the bond money: (1) the allocation of ten thousand dollars for the purchase of two lots adjacent to the swimming pool at the corner of Frio and Matamoros on the West Side to build a new center for recreation and physical exercise; and (2) additional recreation improvements for various areas in the West Side such as Casiano and Milam parks. The passage of the earlier bond issue had been a catalyst for the Mexicans' coordinated efforts in the distribution discussions and provided them with a knowledge of power and the power of knowledge as well as experience in pressure group politics that gave them an additional incentive to work for their share of the larger bond issues to be voted in the future.[104]

Although the Latin Quarter was clearly divided into three social and economic worlds, they intersected on the cultural and ideological issues of health, education, immigration, deportation, and politics. However, the intellectual-cultural hegemony was still held by the *ricos*, although the "counterculture" and ideology of the Mexican American middle class was slowly rearing its head. Nevertheless, through the cultural activities that emanated from the Casino Social, through the sale of Mexican books, through the sale of Mexican records, through the speaking and writing of Mexican intellectuals, and through *La Presna*, the *ricos* of San Antonio continued to maintain the spirit and soul and the Weltanschauung of the community in spite of the shifting and changing tide of acculturation.[105]

Regardless of the differences in culture, society, or class, the Mexicans in San Antonio faced the common problems of racism and discrimination. These were unwanted unifying factors that insidiously wove their way into the fabric of the community. Racism did not respect any class. If the *ricos*' Mexican nationalism was the positive unifying thread in the West Side, the personal and institutional racism of the non-Mexicans was the negative one. However, if acculturation promised relief, racism did not; Mexicans were becoming Americans, but discrimination was keeping them for the most part, second-class citizens.

The Mexicans were also constantly faced with the power of advertisements that subtly emphasized whiteness and not their natural "tan." Rubiva face cream, for example, which was advertised daily in *La Prensa* (February 29, 1930), promised everyone that they could get their skin lighter: "It is not necessary to suffer the humiliation of dark and ugly skin. A new and marvelous invention — Rubiva — whitens the skin in an incredible way in only three days." The company also claimed that "you will have better opportunities in business, love, society, etc., because you will be more 'simpatico'" (January 30, 1930). The comparison was obvious to the San Antonio Mexican: white was better than brown, American better than Mexican. A subjective sense of inferiority and lack of confidence were subtly being introduced.[106]

If this message was too subtle, there were letters to the editor that clearly enunciated the racial code. For example, Walter E. Brown, a resident of El Paso, wrote a letter to the local newspaper that was reprinted in *La Prensa*. Brown accused Mexicans who were living in the United States of just wanting to be housed, fed, and clothed free

Unfortunately, racism was not limited to verbal exchanges. *La Prensa* reminded San Antonio's Mexican community that racial and cultural discrimination affected all Mexicans in the Southwest, regardless of class. As an example, *La Prensa* carried an article concerning Reina Vélez, the sister of popular San Antonio singer Lupe Vélez. The article reported that Reina and a group of friends were denied entrance to an Oceanside, California, night club, simply because they spoke Spanish. The police, the article continued, instead of helping Vélez and her friends, told them it would be better if they left. *La Prensa* stated that "this was not the first time Mexicans had been discriminated against," and the *ricos* of San Antonio filed a formal complaint with the Mexican consul. The *ricos* always viewed the consuls as tools for protecting Mexicans in the United States.[108]

Intellectuals responded to the general stereotypical image of Mexicans held by most non-Mexicans. Well-known intellectual Miguel de Uranga, in an editorial column in *La Prensa*, complained that there was no realistic portrayal of the Mexican in the United States. "The Mexicans were usually characterized" he said, "as human caricatures: long-moustached, sombrero-wearing, fat persons." This was "caused [by] the radio and movie roles . . . [and they] are not a picture of true reality." Uranga continued, "Maybe Mexicans will fare better in the 'talkies.'" Uranga believed that "Mexicans are not just sitting back enjoying this stereotype. Many are protesting and raising their voice in objection. Now with [Hollywood making] Spanish films maybe a new change will take place. This [racial and cultural] caricature is responsible for [the Mexican] peoples' view of themselves and [in turn] of the world around them." Advertising and the communications media were serving to distort the image of the Mexican. Uranga was pointing out what F. Scott Fitzgerald had said of the American in the twenties: the "I" was being lost in the new modern culture.[109]

Overt discrimination, covert racism, and the process and problems of self-identification, consequently, were part of the everyday life of the Mexican throughout the Southwest. The *ricos* did not want Americanized Mexicans or Mexicans who believed and acted out of the U.S. stereotype. They wanted Mexicans to be educated, sophisticated, *gente decente*, and to have a sense of Mexican nationalism. In an article in *La Prensa*, Uranga specifically criticized the *pocho* (Americanized Mexican); he emphasized that the Mexican who was *gente propia* (his or her own Mexican self) spoke two languages — English and Spanish — well and did not "mix his English with his Spanish when he speaks. [This characteristic is] a rare virtue in our own Mexicans in the United States."[110] It seems that Uranga wanted a cosmopolitan Mexican "I" who spoke English, but who did not lose the Mexican "I" via the ideology of the English language and become an "other" — the non-Mexican persona. The *ricos* wanted to have one culture and one society for all Mexicans — one common world of *lo mexicano*. They wanted to hold historical time and the process of acculturation in abeyance; they wanted a synchronic, not a diachronic society. The Mexican middle class, however, participated in and accepted the dynamics of a society that was changing over time. The *ricos*, overall, wanted one view of the world, but, unfortunately, there were three. The middle class also wanted one world — but one of Mexican Americans. Like the ricos, they understood that they were Mexicans, but they also understood that they were becoming Mexican Americans because the consciousness, the culture, the language, and the society of the *mexicano* in San Antonio were slowly being changed by community structures — the family, the church, the educational system, and the political system. Consequently, 1929 through 1941 saw the advent of a new consciousness of living, a new ideology for perceiving, and a new discourse of being, but each differing because of each Mexican's specific economic world, the process of his or her everyday life, and constantly changing gestalt.

4

Also, families did not simply abandon all their traditional traits as they adjusted to industrial demands: ethnic and cultural differences survived.
— Stephen R. Graubard

Introduction

Four institutions were predominant in the West Side: the family, the church, the school, and the political system. Although every Mexican in the Latin Quarter had varying degrees of contact with them, these institutions permeated their everyday life, influenced their daily choices, directed their commonsense thinking, affected their recreational, social, and political life, and generally constructed their *mentalidad*. Variations in this intellectual production differed, however, with each Mexican, depending on class, status, sex, occupation, geocultural background, and ideology. Although the Mexicans' everyday decisions concerning their own lives may have been free, their options often were not; and while the direct impact of all these institutions on everyday life may have varied, the institutions' ideological goals did not.

The basic goal of all of these institutions was paradoxical: how to make Mexicans into Americans while keeping them Mexican. Therefore, these institutions and the Mexicans themselves struggled with the dilemma of duality: balancing Mexican cultural and social pride with American philosophical and political goals and aspirations. The answer was to become Mexican American. Consequently, the family, the church, the schools, and the political system played a dual role. They sought what sociologist Robert Park had said in the 1920s was almost impossible: to Americanize, but yet maintain the Mexicanization of the people in the Latin Quarter.

This objective and institutional dilemma was no different from what other ethnic groups in the 1920s and 1930s were experiencing in the United States: the problem of changing while maintaining the continuity of ethnicity. For the Mexicans in San Antonio, this dilemma of how to retain their ethnicity in a world that (as Park argued) would push them toward assimilation but might still allow them some room for cultural differences became a crucial reality during the 1929–41 period. There were the *ricos* on one side (whose sensibilities were pushing for the retention of a Scholastic Mexican public and private self) and LULAC on the other side (which wanted a functional and liberal American public self, but a private Mexican self), and the institutions in the middle, which unwillingly pushed for dualism. This search for an identity that would balance the Mexican self with the American self carried intellectual contradictions and psychological dilemmas that would plague Mexican Americans until the Chicano generation of the 1960s attempted to negate both and establish a unique self that was more than Mexican or American. Especially influential in the process of forming a new consciousness of duality in the 1929 through 1941 period were the family and the church. This chapter and the next will analyze these two institutions; the following two will focus on education and politics.

The Mexican Family

The Mexican family in San Antonio served as an institution of both change and continuity. It helped to preserve aspects of Mexican culture, but since it did not exist in a vacuum, it also served as a transmitter of U.S. culture. The Mexican family during the 1930s was a fundamental and durable institution, and thus can be seen, as Tamara K. Hareven has suggested, as a "key to an understanding of the interaction between personal development and social change."[1] Every Mexican family was constantly changing according to the impact of the dynamics of American society on each individual in the family. It must be remembered that the Mexican families in the Latin Quarter of San Antonio had a certain cultural homogeneity, but they differed according to class. This would make a difference in the development of ideas, perspectives, and general gestalt. Mexican family structure and non-Mexican were also directly affected by the Depression because often the available work defined the parameters of behavior within the family.

The Depression upset the socioeconomic equilibrium of the Mexican family through the loss of employment, the threat of deportation, the dilemma of repatriation, the declining economy, the conflicts between the second and third generations, and the continuing health problem. Nearly all the Mexican population in the West Side

everyday life.

Above all, industrial conditions and the type of employment available affected the changing consciousness and interrelationships within the family. Mexicans were almost exclusively employed in unskilled and semiskilled jobs and family members often were placed on separate shifts or work crews from their non-Mexican counterparts. Mexican women who were employed outside the home, moreover, were hired to work only with other Mexican women. De facto segregation, then, occurred in the workplace as well. Due to their "reputed manual dexterity," their "capacity for repetitive labor," and their "willingness to work for meager wages," the women worked mostly in the pecan shelling factories, the manufacturing, garment, and food processing sectors, and the domestic and personal service sectors. Although these were basically nonskilled jobs, unemployment was high.

Nevertheless, the class and ethnic identity of the family was affected by the range of occupations, the range of industries, and de facto segregation, since Mexicans were separated, in most instances, from non-Mexican workers. Parents brought their perceptions, images, and feelings home from work. They felt less than American, anger toward blacks, and alienated. A mythology of Americanism and a fragmentation of social perceptions was being developed. Work production, environment, and relationships were affecting consciousness, especially in Mexican women.[3]

According to one historian, the work pattern of Mexican women in San Antonio during the 1930s resembled that of the Italian women in Buffalo, New York. Female occupational patterns tended to remain within Mexican-dominated industries except in the domestic and personal sector, where black women in San Antonio predominated. But family-oriented work was preferred by Mexican women and men. In San Antonio's workplaces, Mexican women suffered more from ethnic than sexual discrimination. Julia Blackwelder, in her study of Mexican women during this period, states that "in San Antonio Mexican women were seen as being the lowest class, more so than Black women." This had a definite impact on their self-perception and ultimately had an impact on family structure and relationships.[4]

In 1930, for example, the Mexican female work force comprised 3,226 women in manufacturing and mechanical industries, 13 in transportation and communication, 670 in trade, 210 in the professions, 2,930 in domestic and personal service and clerical work. The majority, outside of the garment industry, piece work in the home, and pecan shelling, clustered around domestic service, labor, and factory work. In total, however, only 27 percent of Mexican women were employed. From 1929 through 1941 there were approximately 31,180 Mexican women in the West Side, and in 1930 there were 7,316 (23.5 percent) in the work force who were at least ten years old. By 1940 there was a small increase in Mexican women fourteen years of age or older in the work force: 26.9 percent. Over half of the Mexican women employed during the thirties were single (3,784), only 9.6 percent (702) were married, and 41.1 percent (3,029) were widowed or divorced. The majority of married Mexican women, however, were engaged in home production: the needle trade, pecan shelling, hand sewing and embroidering for children's and infants' clothing on a contract basis. This increased the number of women who worked outside the home to 9.6 percent. Of these, 18.8 percent (3,199) were heads of household.[5]

An intellectual pattern of independence was being formed in young single women and in widowed and divorced ones. Moreover, women working at home came under the sway of the Protestant work ethic, since they produced for the marketplace. As a result, a matriarchal sense of power began to develop, although tradition still dictated that the source of power in the family was the male. Consequently, in spite of the number of women in the work force in the 1930s and 1940s, the family remained patriarchal in structure but questions arose concerning authority, power, and hierarchy, depending on who was employed. Two studies, one in 1927 and the other in 1931, indicated the types of household structure. Of 1,481 Mexican families surveyed in 1927 (9,000 persons, or one-eighth of the entire Mexican community), it was found that patriarchy was still very viable, but changing (table 6). This survey found that out of 1,282 families, 532 fathers were laborers, 544 were barbers, bricklayers, clerks, truck drivers,

TABLE 6

Family Wage Earners, San Antonio's Mexican Community, 1927

Wage Earners	No. of Families	%
Family only	835	56.38
Father and mother	76	5.13
Father and children	322	21.74
Mother only	73	4.93
Mother and children	50	3.38
Father, mother, and children	76	5.13

employed as laborers, 27 percent as skilled workers, and 5 percent as store owners or professionals. Their earnings, this study indicated, increased from $13.68 per week for a laborer to $24.90 for professionals. This survey did not include the 15,000 to 20,000 Mexicans who were employed by 110 different pecan shelling plants (10,000 were employed by the Southern Pecan Shelling Company alone) and earned only $1.29 to $2.00 per week and those families that had two wage earners with a total income of $4.83 per week.[6]

In 1933, for example, there were 48,345 Mexican families listed as relief families in the Southwest, while in San Antonio there were only 4,960 families on relief, and a majority of these ranged from four family members to seven. In view of these conditions, the principal of a West Side school stated that "the economic condition of the whole Mexican population forced one-sixth of the women to be wage earners in some way outside of the ordinary family duties. This must be considered a drawback to motherhood, a handicap to the physical and moral being of the offspring, and to the general care of the home."[7]

These studies indicate what Richard Griswold del Castillo in his study of the Mexican family has suggested, that the lower-income family's consciousness, psychology, and perceptions were more affected by the factors of marginality, insecurity, discrimination, and unstability, while the upper classes were more affected by acculturation and biculturalization. Yet the general social reality of the Depression — poverty and, for the upper classes, some mobility — were changing the essence of family structure, if not the form. It seemed that reality was beginning to conflict with the ideal Mexican family model and, as Griswold points out, this was the central historical tension in the Mexican family as it changed over time.[8]

In most cases, however, even though every member of the Mexican family was employed, the family remained patriarchal unless the father had left the family. Max Handman, writing in the 1930s, stated that much of the burden of adjustment to the American way of life and the tremendous pressures brought on by the Depression fell to the Mexican women, because they were perceived as being the center of the family. It must be remembered that Mexican families were modeled on the ideal of Pope Pius XI's encyclical that emphasized that "man is the head, the woman is the heart [in the family] and as he occupies the chief place in ruling, so she claims for herself the chief place in love. The family is more sacred than the state." Mexican women were constantly bombarded by this view (in addition to the traditional Spanish one); in fact, it permeated the gestalt of the Mexican community. *La Voz*, the Guadalupe Church newspaper, pointed out to the community very explicitly that "the happiness of the community is linked with the conservation of the patriarchal family. A ruination of the family will ruin society . . . the stronger the bonds of the family and harmony within the family, the stronger will the society be."[9]

It seemed that modernization was negatively affecting this ideal, even though the Catholic Church, the Mexicans, and even Victorian ideals mitigated the changes in women and in the family. Nevertheless, independence, greater equality of roles, destruction of male authority, and changes in sexuality were all in their nascent stage. In spite of this, there was still a strong family tradition, although the forces of economic production seemed to be slowly changing the relations of reproduction, as Barbara Laslett has suggested. For example even the *ricos'* more liberal view of women did not seek to end the family, marriage, or the "woman's place." An article entitled "Reflecciones acerca de matrimonio" appearing in *La Prensa* in 1930 reflected the *ricos'* view that

> women are not better or inferior to men, nor are men superior or inferior to women. They are complementary. [However], marriage must conform to the laws of the Church and civil law. The woman who has penetrated the heart of the man she is to marry is ahead of the woman who has not. We believe that matrimony is the highest aspiration that a woman should have because within this institution is where a woman can find the happiness of existence.

For the *ricos*, the woman was equal in the family but not in law, but marriage was still her personal "salvation." For the Catholic Church, the woman was the primary key to the preservation of the family and society, but a secondary figure in relationship to the family's power and authority. For the *ricos*, marriage was just one of the higher institutions, but for the church, marriage was the cornerstone of civilization and a supernatural state. Either view defined the woman's role within marriage and the family.

This same view was also held by the lower middle class and the laboring class, which believed that marriage, like birth and death,

wedding was an opportunity to "establish a better household than his father's"; for the woman, it was her opportunity and hope to "reform her husband and be different from her mother, but that is only an ideal dream. She does not stand a shadow of a chance of being different from her mother, since her mother has been the only woman she has ever been closely associated with, and all her knowledge of household matters has been handed down from mother to daughter . . . from her wedding day on, the bride lives to please her husband. She will cook what he wants and keep her household as he thinks best."[11]

The Mexican woman's freedom in marriage did differ in degree depending on her social class, although, in all classes, she was reared emotionally and intellectually to "please, comfort, and know her place." The basic norms and values of the Mexican family in terms of power, authority and roles did not differ substantially from the non-Mexican "cult of womanhood." As a result, the acculturation process, especially in middle-class families, did not change the basic structure of the institution — women were dominated whatever their ethnicity — only the philosophy changed. Consequently, marriage was always celebrated, regardless of class or acculturation. Intermarriage between the classes did not normally occur, although there was some intermarriage between non-Mexicans and Mexicans of corresponding classes. Especially in the laboring class, marriage and the rearing of a large family were the only things the Mexican woman "had to look forward to."[12]

Marriage for the laboring class, however, was not much to look forward to, because within the family structure, for the most part, the man was the sole authority and the woman was confined almost exclusively to the household (even though she might be engaged in sewing or pecan shelling for profit or might participate in strikes). The situation was somewhat different for middle-class women, who regularly participated in church and school affairs, and for the *ricas*, who had an active social life. Women in the two upper classes at least had an outlet and a certain freedom in a world of clubs and social activities separate from the men's. Regardless of class, however, every family member was assigned a ranking in the hierarchy by the mere fact of birth. The eldest son was the most important after the father, the grandfather, or the godfather. The other sons, however, took precedence over the daughters.[13]

La Voz, surprisingly, urged a mediation of this hierarchy through work. In the family, the newspaper stated, "there should be distribution of work among the family members without it being an obstacle [to harmony]. Children [should] learn to help the family and obey the parents." In opposition to the traditional Mexican custom of subservience to the males, specifically the father and the eldest son, the church hoped to redistribute authority and power to both mother and father. This was more in keeping with the U.S. middle-class ideal of equality. For the church, the basic theme was harmony, not change. It did not want to change Mexican family structure too radically. Even Father Tranchese wrote in *La Voz:* "The women who love their homes, work in it, and are tied to it, are the ones who have in their hands the happiness of the whole community. That is the character and role of the Mexican woman. There are [however] those 'modernistas' who dream of changing . . . [the family structure]! It would be like destroying the most precious treasure of Mexico."[14]

It was evident that the church was playing a dual role: it wanted to establish some moderate changes within the Mexican family structure, but still to maintain some of the traditional order and stability. It sought to maintain the stability and control of the Mexican family to counter the freedom of the non-Mexican one, especially in light of the "new woman" wave and changing family of the 1920s. The Catholic Church in America was consequently caught in a paradox of time: serving the traditional Scholastic-oriented philosophy of Rome while existing in the twentieth century United States of egalitarianism, democracy, and modernization.

This tension between traditional "equality" and the new freedoms within the family was also being increased by numerous other factors: the material needs of the family, which were pushing Mexican women to become part of the work force; the ideological impact made on the family by the number of children that were enrolled in the public schools; Americanization programs of the church and LULAC; the constant nationalistic and traditional pressures of the *ricos;* and, above all, the constant bombardment of the English language through the radio, films, and newspapers. Moreover, family traditions and relationships were being affected by the very size and geographical location of houses that varied from the *jacales* of the poor, to the hidden cottages of the middle class, to the luxurious homes of the *ricos.* The

develops tuberculosis it becomes well night [*sic*] impossible to provide proper isolation in the home with the result that the other members of the family are exposed to the infection." In fact, fifteen thousand families lived in small shacks, and ten thousand of these families were close to starvation. By 1937 fourteen thousand pecan shellers were out of work, most of them West Side Mexicans. This class welcomed some economic, political, or social change, regardless of the ideological consequences on the family structure (even though their own personal voice was limited and often unheard in the world of San Antonio society or even, to a large extent, in Mexican society).[16]

Many of these laboring-class families in the late 1930s had members who were U.S. citizens and many were long-time residents: 17 percent were born in San Antonio and approximately 50 percent had come to the city between 1911 and 1931. Of 512 pecan sheller families studied in 1938, 867 children were of school age, 55 percent of those attended school only one term, while 62 percent attended school only through the 1938 school year. Economic survival was more of a priority than the luxury of education. Thus, pecan shelling was a family affair and everyone had to work. Nevertheless, many of these families had to receive welfare from the Guadalupe Church, the CIO, soup kitchens, or from a federal agency to survive the Depression. These impoverished families averaged 4.6 children, and the majority of these children worked. These families, Frances Parkinson Keyes stated in a letter to Eleanor Roosevelt in 1941, "spent their leisure hours picking [the pecans] in the discomfort of their living quarters."[17]

They lived in a community of poverty; consequently, immediate needs, ironically, equalized the family's roles, conflicts, traditions, and aspirations. For most of them, even union dues were a burden; nevertheless, their stark lives left these families no alternative but to strike at various times from 1934 through 1938. Dillusionment with dreams of success left them with only militancy as a means of achieving those dreams. As one pecan sheller stated, "When I was eighteen years old I came from Monterrey, Mexico, to San Antonio, Texas, together with my parents and eight siblings. . . . I dreamed of a clean job and good pay, but I was sadly disillusioned. I had to be satisfied with anything I could find. I remember working in a pecan factory shelling nuts for twelve hours a day for a mere pittance."[18] As a result, their reality tempered their dreams of opportunity. Their consciousness was affected by the "high incidence of overcrowded and unfit housing; lack of sanitary facilities; poor health; lack of school; juvenile delinquency; and social discrimination." Yet, these families of pecan shellers were in status and self-perception better off than the agricultural migrant families.[19]

The migrant families who lived in San Antonio or in the outlying areas often had ten to twelve children. As Archbishop Drossaert reported, "they dwell in shacks and hovels made out of tin, wood, palm leaves or the stuff gathered from the dump piles of a neighboring town or city. Many 'live in tents,' in the 'open' air or in a second hand truck." These conditions affected their family relationships; their hopes continued, but were never really nurtured, since reality allowed little time for dreaming. Only to migrant children were dreams avenues; to adults they were frustration, tension, and fantasy (as the studies of psychologist Robert Coles have suggested).[20]

Another part of the laboring class, however, was somewhat better off. This stratum of families (which considered themselves better than the pecan shellers or the migrant workers) consisted of the common laborers for city government, factories, and businesses. These laborers made up 48 percent of the Mexican population of San Antonio. In a 1927 survey of 1,397 of these families, the average family consisted of 6.9 persons with an income from eight dollars to thirty dollars per week and living in two rooms. Another study, made in 1941, indicated that 64 percent of this segment of the Mexican laboring class had an average of only "one-half room per person, with an average of six rooms per house." Most of these families lived in "corrals" (rows of small houses facing each other), often with no more than one toilet or water faucet and no indoor bathrooms. Most of these families, like the pecan shellers, were U.S. citizens.[21]

In another survey of 1,264 laboring-class families, 518 had only outside and surface toilets and had to go outside for water; 1,141 of these families had to use kerosene lamps because they had no electricity. A letter to the San Antonio trade union paper, the *Weekly Dispatch*, described these workers' homes in the following manner: "The houses are crowded with children, adults, and many dogs. Quite a number of the workers are suffering with communicable diseases which are passed on from them with their work [in sewing clothing for the community at large]. . . . The poor workers are paid a miserable pittance,

During the 1930s the laboring-class families were besieged by problems, as they aspired to better jobs, homes, and lives. They were plagued however, by poverty, the Depression, and changes in family structure. Many of these ten thousand to fifteen thousand laboring-class families were also at the mercy of their landlords. Middle-class Mexicans built three-room houses and then subdivided them into three or four apartments and rented them to six, seven, or eight families. Many of these middle-class Mexican landlords also built and owned rows of shacks on one lot. Each lot would house ten to twelve families, sometimes more. These sins against poor Mexicans were acceptable as they were for profit and, therefore, not judged against the Puritan ideal of ethics.[23]

The families of the common laborers, the pecan shellers, and the migrant workers were organized along patriarchal lines: the father was the personification of authority, and strict child-rearing patterns emphasized submission to male authority. The power and authority the male lacked in general society was given to him by tradition in the private society of the family. In theory, there was also a strict separation of the sexes but, in practice, collective living made this almost impossible. Ironically, egalitarianism and the distribution of authority were being shaped to some extent on this anvil of collective poverty. Members of the laboring class, in their everyday lives, placed primary ideological importance on two things: religion (dominated by a male God) and family (dominated by the father). The middle class also focused on these two areas, with the addition of education, which was seen as basically for males. For all classes of Mexicans, therefore, the world was patriarchal in form and shape.[24]

Regardless of the focus on the general economic struggle for survival, Mexican children's psychological rearing and physical development was a daily preoccupation. Thus, the Mexican family in San Antonio, especially in the laboring class, was being affected by more than just scarce housing, unemployment, exploitation, and the Depression. Its psychological and emotional interiority, its intellectual abilities, and its physical well-being were affected by food shortages, which had an impact on self- and social perception. Many Mexican women had as many as ten children in twelve to fifteen years (the average was five to six). Thus, simply rearing children posed almost insurmountable problems, faced as they were with poverty and malnutrition. The Mexican diet was greatly deficient in calcium, which caused many dental problems, especially during pregnancy and lactation. It was also low in calories, only partially adequate in protein, low in minerals, and low in vitamins, especially vitamin A. The majority of males thus tended to be underweight and thin looking. Their physical appearance was often perceived by non-Mexicans to be an indication of certain manly inabilities and weaknesses. There was also a tendency to digestive disorders, to have children one year of age or under die of diarrhea, to have many stillbirths, and to have a low resistance to disease in general.[25]

In spite of nutritional impoverishment, Mexican mothers, regardless of class, tended to nurse their children somewhat successfully and wean them at a much later age than did non-Mexican mothers. This success in nursing was surprising, because many Mexican mothers, for the most part, did not follow any particular dietary formula before childbirth. Nevertheless, 85 percent of the children were entirely breast-fed, 7.2 percent were only partially breast-fed, and only 7.5 percent were entirely bottle-fed. The common practice (forced by cultural tradition and poverty) was to breast-feed children as long as they would take the breast and as long as the milk lasted. Most children were breast-fed until age one, two and a half, or even three. Eighty-two percent of the Mexican mothers fed their children on demand rather than on a schedule. Decades later, ironically, these methods were to be perceived as being more conducive to child-mother bonding and emotional stability and as generally more nutritionally and psychologically beneficial. Whether this longer period of breast-feeding accounted for more emotional stability and parental bonding (as historian Mark Poster has suggested) is difficult to ascertain, since hunger and poverty continued to plague children as they grew older.[26]

A study of two hundred school-age Mexican children in San Antonio done in 1931 showed that more of them were underweight than were non-Mexican children and that they were considerably below the average height of non-Mexican children. More preschool Mexican children were suffering from malnutrition than were non-Mexican children, especially in calories, calcium, and vitamins A and B.[27]

The lack of proper diet affected not only the children, but the adults as well. For example, the average height for Mexican males in the West Side was five feet, two inches, and their average weight was 147 pounds. Mexican women averaged five feet one inch and averaged

ing class, however, was quite different from that of the poor. Members of one upper-class Mexican family stated that they had no "exclusive preference for any one kind of food." They enjoyed French, Mexican, or American food. Winters's study also showed that, although 50 percent of the laboring-class families as well as some middle-class families lived on diets that were very deficient, the diets of 25 percent were, in fact, adequate.[28]

Thus, the problem during the 1930s was not altogether the quality of the food, but the quantity. Of course, this varied with class. On the whole, however, inadequate diet probably had a direct effect on Mexican children's physical growth, mental processes, attitudes toward work, resistance to sickness, and maybe even educational success — regardless of class. However, the mothers' longer years of breast-feeding and attention to and care of children seem to indicate a tendency toward maternal attachment and emotional stability within family structure. This stability might have helped Mexicans endure the pressures and problems of the Depression decade. Richard Griswold has alluded to this bio-psycho-emotional development as a factor in understanding consciousness, and Mark Poster has suggested the same thing in his theoretical formulations on the family. Many of the Mexican students who registered in the San Antonio schools reflected some of this emotional stability and mirrored all of the problems within the family structure (such as poor diet, male dominance, general poverty, and poor health).[29]

Whereas nutritional impact was important, so was the impact of language, attitudes, and technology found in the home. For example, in 1926 Eunice Parr, a schoolteacher, attempted to document the social and racial differences between Mexicans who attended a predominantly non-Mexican school and those who attended a predominantly Mexican one. She found that close to 9 percent of the Mexican families sending children to both schools had telephones, 29 percent to 36 percent had automobiles, and 59.6 percent to 61.2 percent took *La Prensa* or *El Nacional*. She also found that 80.7 percent of the fathers of the Mexican children who attended a predominantly non-Mexican school spoke English, while only 45 percent of the fathers of the children who attended the mostly Mexican school did. Interestingly, however, the Mexican mothers, regardless of school, spoke more Spanish in the home. Thus, the more middle class the family, the more English was spoken, although the linguistic and cultural influence of Spanish continued through the mother regardless of class. [30]

Parr's findings indicated that, on the whole, within the Mexican middle-class family more English was spoken, but more Spanish newspapers were read, and a good number of these middle-class families had automobiles and telephones. These factors had an impact on children's achievement and success in school, but class, property, and social differences were often mitigated by the children's own intellectual abilities and social activities as well as by the quality of their teachers. Parr did not test for the impact of nutritional and dietary problems.

Parr's findings also inferred that cultural duality existed within the one thousand to twelve hundred middle-class Mexican families in San Antonio, since both non-Mexican and Mexican cultural traditions coexisted in the Mexican upper- and middle-class families that had children at school. This duality had an effect on both the family life and the school life of the children. Fernando Sánchez, a middle-class printer, described his home life in the following manner:

> My wife, my sister, and my sons go to Mass and make confession and receive the sacrament once in a while, but I don't because as I work at night I don't have time to give to practide [sic] my faith, nor even to pray, but as I don't do harm to anyone I don't think that I have any sins. On my Saint's day and on that of my wife, my sisters and my sons, we have little festivals [at home]. We invite our friends and even though it be a little orchestra [that we hire] we make merry these days.
>
> I follow my Mexican customs and I won't change them for anything in the world. I haven't let my sisters cut their hair nor go around like the [non-Mexican] girls here [who go out] with all kinds of boys and I have also accustomed my sons to respect [and] obey [me in every way].
>
> On Sundays when I rest (for I rest on only two Sundays each month),

I stay at home or go to the movies with my wife. Many times friends come with guitars and then we sing and have a good time.

As to my food, since my wife and my sisters cook at home, I eat almost the same as I did in Mexico, with a little change, because the food is cooked here on gas stoves. . . .

I have my own little furniture in my house. I bought it on the installment plan in San Antonio. I also have a phonograph with which I amuse myself when I am not working. I have a great many records

ambition will hurt the others." But there were changes. In the middle-class home there was the "loosening of the paternal hold on the children who show a tendency," as one observer reported, "to get away from such [authoritarian control]." In the middle-class families that had been in San Antonio for a generation or two, many Mexican customs were replaced by non-Mexican ones and, according to a school principal, "gradually in these younger San Antonio children of Mexican parentage there have been built up habitual and conscious controls of conduct that are very unlike those of their ancestors."[32] Over time the work ethic, self-discipline, and self-responsibility, it seems, were replacing the Scholastic and agrarian values of temporality, communalism, and fatalism.

Analyzing this transfer of values and belief systems, Charles Arnold, in a study done during this period, states that for middle-class children authority was being internalized while for the lower class it was still basically external. This was evident, Arnold believed, in upper- and lower-middle-class Mexican children who were becoming Americanized during the 1929–41 period in customs, language, and attitudes (although Mexican culture and customs were still important and of interest to them and, in fact still played an important part in their social and intellectual lives). Consequently, within the middle-class family, children's consciousness changed. As Arnold emphasizes, "superstition and over-credulity are giving place to more rational and independent thinking." The children still spoke Spanish at home, but in school they spoke English even if they went to an all-Mexican school. This situation contributed greatly to the phenomenon that Arnold observed. Moreover, those Mexican students who moved to the suburban areas of the West Side (or outside of it) underwent a more definite acculturation. In some cases, parents who were second-generation Mexicans of foreign-born parents urged their children (the third generation) to make the most of their American educational opportunities. This advice provided more motivation for acculturation.[33]

Although ideological changes accompanied increased acculturation, the dominant Mexican cultural patterns continued within the family. Thus, change (imposed by the new reality of production and everyday life) with continuity (of the ideal and traditional attitudes) was a pattern within the family. Continuities included the hierarchy of ranking, patriarchal authority, and the idea that the mother was the heart of the family. These three patterns persisted because Mexican and non-Mexican cultural patterns were somewhat similar in this regard. For both, the woman was expected to fulfill her role as mother by devoting herself to child rearing, and as wife by attending the needs of her husband and being the heart of the family. In addition, Mexicans girls continued to be closely watched while boys were allowed more freedom. "As a rule," reports Arnold, "all of the boys [in a Mexican family] are preferred to the girls. The Mexican women [therefore continue to] live in a cage of customs. Never, whether married or single, will they appear in public with a man to whom they are not related. The Mexican girl has been trained to discretion and, as a corollary, to extreme skill in flirtation." Furthermore, "within the changing middle class family there still remained, for the most part, generational hierarchies, and during adolescent and early adult years the children continued to be sexually segregated in their separate games, clubs and activities. However, this separation did not occur at dances and other social activities, primarily because sufficient "official" chaperones were always present.[34]

While the general process of acculturation affected everyone, although in varying degrees and regardless of class, the stratified social life within the Mexican community did not. The recreational clubs in the West Side were only for upper- and middle-class boys. This class segregation within the Mexican community made it possible for girls from the upper and middle classes to attend dances knowing that only "respectable" boys would be present. These young women also had their own clubs, but, according to schoolteacher Kathleen González, "the middle-aged women do not belong to any [of their] clubs. They are too busy rearing a family and [then] marrying it off; but the . . . [older] women whose families are well grown have church clubs which meet frequently and [they] take very active part in church activities. Only among the upper class [however] do afternoon gatherings of women exist."[35]

The mothers of young children sometimes joined the PTA while their daughters were preoccupied with recreational clubs, church clubs, or other *clubes sociales*. Mexican middle-class women during the thirties could have fun, socialize, be active in any church or social group, and even be "educated," but all of this was always secondary to their primary role as mothers and wives.[36] It seems that, on the whole,

community, might have looked the same in the 1930s as it did in the 1900s or the 1870s, but it was different. But while the internal family world was glacially changing, the class differences (in relation to status, goods, and occupation) persisted, and Mexicans were aware of them. These differences were manifested in the world of the men as well as the world of the women. All families were ostensibly still Mexican in the West Side, but there were definite patterns of economic and social differences developing as well as in acculturation and ideology throughout the 1930s and 1940s. Oscar Elizondo, for example, the son of businessman Matilde Elizondo, told me that he felt quite a distance between the middle class and the working class as he grew up during the thirties, although he had some contact with the workers because his father owned La Gloria grocery stores. Many of these workers, he remembered, unlike the middle class, called themselves Chicanos, a term of self-reference often used by the laboring Mexicans, but seen as pejorative by the middle class.[37]

But regardless of these class differences, Mexican fathers, especially those of the lower middle class and the laboring class, found their family and their home to be a haven from the outside world. At the same time, however, they believed the home to be a beginning point for Americanizing their children. They wanted their children to become functional in U.S. society, but did not necessarily understand the extent of the social and cultural changes that would be necessary. In most cases, the Mexican father imparted (directly and indirectly) a mixture of important but conflicting feelings and ideas to his family. These included ethnic pride, a love for *la patria* (Mexico), a sense of authoritarianism, a sense of the secondary importance of women, a sense of respect for family, a respect for U.S. education, a sense of ambition for his childhood, and a tolerance or even liking for the non-Mexican ways. But he also imparted a sense of deference and a slight sense of inferiority. According to Kathleen González, the Mexican father

> loved his home in the United States because he finds protection and peace. After a life of anxiety and hardship in Mexico, he is always glad to find a home across the border. He likes the schools and the associations his children form; but he has no love for the flag that flies over his head. He does not take a part in the government, is ignorant of the history of the country, and feels that he is not a part of it.[38]

But this view changed with time, and when the father focused on his children's future, especially after he had personally achieved some occupational mobility. A manager of a West Side furniture store, remembering the thirties, stated that as the years went by he wanted his children to be Americans, to learn English, and to have all the opportunities that he felt could be obtained only through acculturation. This became apparent to him as he changed from a laborer to a lower-middle-class salesman, and as his consciousness changed, he said, from a Mexican to an American one (and consequently, as his goals for his children changed).[39]

The upper-middle-class businessperson and the professional, however, did not seem to accept the simple dichotomy of being "just Americans" or "just Mexicans," as the Mexican salesman did. Manuel C. González, the founder of LULAC and a lawyer, stated that he wanted "to remain Mexican [culturally], but take advantage of the American [political] life—[through] citizenship." Kathleen González, observing the dilemma of the Mexican middle class man wrote in the early 1920s that

> he buys a home, sends his children to school, and yet the [cultural] ideas he gives to each child are Mexican. He teaches them to love, respect, and look up to Mexico. This is due to the fact that . . . he realizes that racially he is not recognized by the Anglo-Saxon races. He is in the same position as the Negro in the North who is considered as an equal in all things; yet socially he does not find himself in the best circles of white people. This is the position in which the Mexican finds himself in San Antonio. To be able to enter into some American gathering, he must at least claim to be a Spaniard.[40]

Consequently, Mexican, Mexican American, or Spaniard—the choices of self-identification were ideologically complex, psychologically debilitating, and socially perplexing for the Mexican family, but the middle-class father did not have to articulate this dilemma to his children. Many times they sensed their father's mixed feelings toward non-Mexicans and his love for Mexico; yet, almost contradictorily, they felt their father's strong desire and ambition for them to succeed in U.S. schools. The sons were caught in a paradoxical vise. Like their fathers, they were not completely aware that with education came not only skills, mobility, and opportunity, but non-Mexican identity and corresponding patriotic sensibilities. As schoolteacher Kathleen

As much as they wanted to retain their old customs, Mexican parents who were laborers, clerks, salespeople, and general workers probably knew that in San Antonio "Mexicans with some schooling," as William Knox, the principal of Sidney Lanier (the all-Mexican high school) pointed out, "have a higher earning capacity than the illiterates." They also probably knew that "native-born Mexicans with some schooling in English have an advantage in earning capacity over those who had schooling in Spanish." In addition, Knox pointed out that "the earnings of the English speaking Mexicans exceed those of non–English speaking Mexicans." But this common-sense perception and general belief was more clearly prevalent among middle-class families, because they could conceptualize beyond the everyday problems of poverty. As a result, the majority of Mexican students who were sent to Washington Irving School, Sidney Lanier High School (and others) were from middle-class families, which were more prone to teach their children to "respect the American flag and all it stands for," even though some of the parents were foreign-born. [42]

The children of the lower middle class also learned to be Americans at school but Mexicans at home. With the passage of time, acculturation became more pronounced for them, since many either could not afford or did not want to return to Mexico. In contrast, the upper-middle-class families many times sent their children to Mexico during the summer to visit and take Spanish classes in order to give them a concrete feeling for their Mexican identity. Many West Side families attempted to have their children learn Spanish and retain their Mexican "habits of the heart" by urging that Spanish classes be taught at public school summer sessions. Once such classes were established, however, not all of the children attended. It seems that the need and desire for Spanish lessons and Mexican culture varied according to the number of years the family had lived in the city. Many parents still felt the "call of the south"; unfortunately, many of the young did not. In 1926–27, Manuel Gamio, a Mexican anthropologist stated, "It is in the second generation that one would look for assimilation [of the Mexicans into U.S. culture] and for conflict between generations." This process of acculturation was becoming noticeable in the thirties; in fact, sometimes even the *ricos* could not fully escape the cultural influences of the time spent in the United States.[43]

The families of the *ricos*, especially the parents, always looked toward Mexico — unlike the other Mexican social strata — and aspired to return there. But even some of them felt the "generational and cultural conflict." Kathleen González, observing this phenomenon, stated that

> the wealthy Mexican in San Antonio, who is here because he is exiled from his country on account of political disturbances and [for] the part he played in them, cares nothing about the government of the United States or what is taking place today. He knows that while he is here he is protected, and that is as far as he is concerned. He buys a home and a business establishment and property or investments, and not because he intends to establish permanently in business here. The money he brings with him [he] does not dare invest here where he can oversee his property, while if he invests in Mexico he cannot oversee them either. He keeps up with the affairs of Mexico [through *La Prensa*]. He may not know even the name of the governor of Texas, but he can surely give authentic information about the latest political movement of Mexico. His radio is tuned for all the Mexican concerts, and the disputes in the Senate in Mexico are heard weekly.[44]

Yet changes within the *ricos* families still occurred. For example, Señor Campos, his wife, his five daughters, and his two sons were wealthy. They were not political exiles, but because of their financial position in Mexico they had to emigrate to San Antonio in 1914 after the fall of Huerta. They settled in the San Pedro Street area where, as Manuel Gamio states, lived "the wealthiest class of the Mexican colony [in San Antonio], or rather, a number of the wealthiest members who made up a sort of 'high society' in the midst of the great majority of the Mexican colony which is made up of persons of the working classes." According to Gamio, the Campos family generationally evolved in the following manner:

The eldest brother of the family left San Antonio for Europe with the purpose of perfecting himself in his music studies which he began in the Conservatory of Mexico. The rest of the children, with the exception of the two eldest girls, entered a private school in San Antonio with the object of studying English. The two oldest sisters studied the language at home and took charge of the domestic duties, for even though they had a colored maid at first, she charged a great deal and didn't do the work satisfactorily. Since times weren't very good for making unnecessary expenditures, they decided that the two sisters, together

Antonio which was now to them, as they say, their place of permanent residence.[45]

Despite trips to Mexico, the Campos children, with the passage of time, became acculturated to the U.S. lifestyle. As Gamio describes it,

> After five years of residence in San Antonio all the members of the family talked English and had conformed to the American customs with the exception of the father and the mother. The eldest of the young women married a young American who was manager of a jewelry shop. Two years later the youngest married a brother of this American who was an employee of the same jewelry store. It seems that these marriages didn't please the father for he constantly declared that these young men didn't "belong to society." The brother who went to Europe returned to San Antonio, Texas, and later moved to Los Angeles, California, where he married a young American girl.
>
> The other male member of the family is much given to the radio and occupies himself with the selling and buying of them, their installation, etc., but he doesn't help the family in any way and he is supported by his father. . . . This family is white, the grandparents of the father were French and those of the mother were Spaniards. Two of the sisters are blondes and the others are brunettes; the brothers are dark. . . . This family believes that it doesn't feel anything in common with the groups of Mexican workmen, for each one ought to live in his own [class] environment. But not for that reason do they deny their "Raza," and the injuries and humiliation of which the Mexican workers are subject hurt them a lot.[46]

Another *rico*, Pablo Puerto Orellano, who was also an exile, described his family life in San Antonio as follows:

> I was mayor of a town in Durango in 1911 and had a good income besides, for I had interests in several mines and had in addition several pieces of land which also produced some money. The revolution broke out and I had to flee from the place together with my family. . . . So with my wife and my children I moved to El Paso, Texas, and from there went to San Antonio, Texas, where I have been since that time.
>
> I passed the first years of my exile rather well, for I received money from the mines and lands which I own still, but things have gone from bad to worse. I don't even know who is administering my holdings, which I have turned over to some relatives of mine there. When my income began to fail I had to go to work. I managed to get a job administering a Mexican weekly. I earned a salary of $18.00 a week at that job. Later I helped to found a daily. Here I earned a little more, for I took charge of the shop where the publication was edited.
>
> In 1916 I took charge of the management of another daily. I was first foreman of the shops and later manager of that paper, reaching a salary of $80.00 a week. I was responsible for the direction of the paper. I saw to it that it came out at definite hours. I also saw to it that all the employees did their work well. I also have to make advertising circulars on my typewriter, answer a great number of letters and even correct the proofs of some of the books which are edited in this same shop.

Then speaking of the education of his children in San Antonio and in the United States, he said,

> I have five children. One of them is now finishing his studies in mining at Denver, and I have all of my hopes pinned on him. All of my children have received their education in the American public schools but I have sent them on trips to Mexico so that they shall always keep within themselves a love for their country. I have sent my eldest son twice to the summer courses in the National University of Mexico so that he loves his Mexican home-land although he is somewhat Americanized, for he has studied here and is finishing engineering and mining in Denver. . . . I wouldn't change my nationality for anything in the world, or rather, my citizenship, for Mexico may be bad now and may get worse, but above everything else it is my country and I am always thinking and hoping the best for it.

Upon reflection, Puerto Orellano summarized his life in the following manner:

> It is clear that I have lived comfortably in this country because I have my family and have gone through all the difficulties with them and enjoyed all kinds of fortune. It has almost been as if I hadn't lived in

the United States, for I have always worked in businesses where almost only Spanish was spoken. At home meals are prepared our style, my friends have always been exiled countrymen, my wife and one of my daughters play the piano and always play Mexican music so that one doesn't feel the change. Nevertheless the sad and humiliating conditions in which our people find themselves in this country always makes me feel a certain ill-will towards those who attack them and I would prefer in every way to live in my country, in my native city where life is peaceful and all the inhabitants are simple and good.[47]

within each social class there were varying acculturational processes occurring within each family. In San Antonio as in El Paso or Los Angeles, these generational changes of consciousness, culture, and ideology often corresponded to changes in class, geography, work, status, and nobility. Moreover, as historian Mario T. García has stated (commenting on the Americanization process occurring in the Southwest), "[b]esides work as a means of acculturation, the public schools represented the principal institution of Americanization utilized by both employers and reformers."[48] However, the central vehicle for ideological change and continuity was the family: at the psychological level, at the level of everyday life, and as a central core of Mexican life in relationship to society.

In spite of this acculturating process, all the Mexican families in San Antonio and throughout the Southwest, regardless of their length of residence in the United States or class background, were still susceptible to Mexican ideas, values, and practices, because these traditions were still hegemonic in the 1930s (although varying in degree within each class). But U.S. ideas, attitudes, and beliefs introduced through work and school often fostered (for the Mexican) a world of shifting and commonly conflicting idealistic and realistic views. Each family and each generation within the family internalized and responded differently to these conflicting ideas, beliefs, attitudes, and values. For example, a pervasive (but not necessarily realistic) view was that the father was the active force in the family and that his views and desires were as powerful and penetrating as the desires of teachers and employers. The mother, on the other hand, was considered the passive agent, for the most part. Regardless of class or work role, she remained in a secondary position; she, as Kathleen González stated, "believes that her husband is right in all things."[49] Furthermore, González observed a pervasive commonsense view:

> When a child is born, the mother hopes and prays that it will be a boy. He is superior to a woman, and the mother wants to bear the best. A son will please the husband far more than a daughter, and she likes to please her husband at any price. Even from the time the boy is young, he is usually favored more by the mother than the girls. He is allowed to play later than the girls, and may mingle more freely with the other children. If a note of praise is sounded by the fond mother, it is always the boy who comes first. She strives to please first the husband, then the son, and lastly the daughter and other relatives. . . . Among the poorer class, the girls always do all the housework, and nursing . . . when the mother is ill. Among the middle and upper classes, the mother strives to teach the girl how to make all kinds of fancy work. [Also] music lessons are given to the daughters, whether she is interested in music or not. The daughters were usually kept in the home more than the sons, and the sons were given more responsibility and independence.[50]

These practices and beliefs were changing, although very slowly, depending on class, education, and the impact of such factors as the church and the personal desire to change, especially as these factors commingled in the matrix of the family.

As a result of these constant changes, authority, power and discipline became an important issue, whether in family or social matters. However, behavioral expectations and patterns varied according to generation. For example, sexual behavior was monitored especially closely. Sexual lessons were not taught to the girls even after they reached adolescence; mothers usually were unable or unwilling to engage in this type of conversation with daughters, even though their first duty was to train daughters to be housewives. On the whole, sex was not a topic for conversation in the Mexican home. The extent of sexual information given out was closely related to the degree that the idea of female passivity was accepted and varied with each class. The upper class, for example, regarded women as more equal to the men than did the lower classes.

Overall behavioral expectations also varied between generations. The more a Mexican family was acculturated (although this never meant full acceptance into the U.S. world — assimilation), the more the attitudes, habits, and emotional responses were determined by U.S. cultural traits. Consequently, there was increased tension within families similar to the tension that arose in other ethnic families acculturating in the United States. However, young men's and women's roles and behavior patterns were still, to a large extent, determined by their traditional ranking within the family hierarchy (and their gender) during the 1930s. The Mexican family, regardless of class and generational composition, thus still had a tremendous impact on the social control of its members, a social control that was on a par with the church's.[51]

Jesús Guzmán, writing in *La Voz* shortly before Mother's Day in

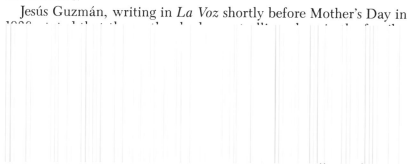

1920s.[52]

In addition to parents' control and protection of their children, the family had another intricate source of extended authority. The godfather and godmother (the persons who baptized the child — the *compadre* and the *comadre*) played a central role in the children's upbringing. They were the sponsors of the child and responsible for the child's baptism, religious training, and care (especially if the parents died). In addition, they could impose certain social and personal responsibilities on the child.

Although the Mexican family was only seminuclear, sometimes, especially among the laboring class, extended family simply meant other families living in the same house or the same room, or a number of families living in one shared tenant building. Collectivity was often an imposed way of life, and these living arrangements also served as a form of social control. The middle class, on the other hand, was more oriented toward nuclear households, often with one set of grandparents living in the house. The children and adults had their own rooms, which tended to place an emphasis, as Poster has suggested, on individuality. For all classes, however, large families were still the rule rather than the exception, and the unity of the family was disturbed by sibling conflicts as well as by the "conflict of culture." These conflicts affected traditional social control.[53]

According to one observer, the daughters also involved the family in conflicts of authority and control. For example, the daughters of the rural or urban poor family that had recently emigrated often developed a "hostile attitude toward . . . [their] parents." According to Kathleen González, "neither the parents nor the girls can analyze the cause of her attitude, so the parents begin to blame the United States for the daughter's [changing] behavior. And the daughter blames the parents for the condition. . . . At this stage, the daughter usually marries because she feels that she cannot bear her family any longer." In another situation where the "daughter is American born and the parents are foreign born, the daughter has a constant conflict between school and home." The parents speak Spanish, the daughter, English; the parents cling to their Mexican ways while the daughter accepts the U.S. ones. Consequently, the daughter's parents, and especially her mother, are surprised and ashamed that an offspring of theirs should be such a social misfit. "The parents secretly blame the schools for the behavior of the child." In a third type of situation, the daughter was more satisfied in her home life because the parents were born, reared, and educated in the United States.

> The problems met at school and elsewhere [for this type of girl] are foreseen by both parents, and many of the causes of dispute are blotted out. Both parents know the problems the child is facing, and they generally discuss them and work them out to their own satisfaction without the daughter's even suspecting that they are interested in her affairs. The only question left for dispute and misunderstanding is the one which parents hope will never appear, that of marriage into another race or religion.[54]

All daughters, as can be seen, had problems. On the whole, however, the upper-middle-class girls experienced more difficulties, since they not only had little sexual training, but almost no freedom outside the home. They were carefully watched by their mothers, protected by brothers, and their roles were strictly defined by family tradition, church teachings, and custom. The girls of the poorer classes, however, did not encounter the full impact of all the problems and pressures engendered by the two cultures that the middle-class or upper-class girls did.[55]

Boys had more freedom regardless of their socioeconomic class. The sons of the lower class were perceived as financial aids to the family, while the sons of the middle and upper class were perpetuators of the family home, business, and tradition. For the upper classes, sons also represented the future. Nevertheless, sons of whatever class had problems, just as daughters did, but the social constraints were fewer and the tensions looser.

But for these young people, of whatever class, the Mexican community at large imposed a general psycho-social network of social control. The ideal of being *gente decente* permeated the everyday life of the entire community. Therefore, culturally, socially and geographically, the family and community served as a form of social control in the relationship among power, authority, and discipline. This was done by emphasizing (and propagandizing) the ideal of civility, decency, and elitism as contained in Mexican tradition and high culture.[56]

As can be noted, there were different levels and kinds of social control to handle any family crisis. Cultural, community, and patriarchal power prevented a complete crisis in traditional family struc-

kind, depending on class. Yet, the power and the authority for social and behavioral control was still tradition and was upheld by the majority of families.

Regardless of family conflicts, the husband's occupational crisis, the children's acculturation, the wife's occupation or social activity, or social problems, the Catholic Church constantly reminded the Mexican community (and the Mexicans believed it) of the dignity of the family. "In our times," *La Voz*, stated,

> the home and the family is in crisis and in danger of new things. We [the church and the Mexican community together] have to rehabilitate the home and the family life . . . the stronger the bonds of the family and harmony within the home, the stronger will society be. There are some that under the pretext of lifting the burden of the parents want to transfer the duties of the family to civil institutions. The Church, however, supports the continuation of the family and the home, as well as the integrity of the family, the maternal role of the mother, and the patriarchal [function] of the father.[57]

The *ricos*, like the church, reminded the various Mexican classes in the West Side of the importance of the mother in the family. "The essence of the Mexican woman is in her motherly virtues." Moreover, "As a mother the Mexican woman has no rival . . . and the Mexican woman's virtues are best when taking care of her children, whom she will never abandon."

Besides the ideological patterns set by the church and the *ricos*, fiestas also served to continue the Mexican system of values and attitudes.[58] Mexican families in San Antonio celebrated many holidays that concretized the three major events in their lives: birth, marriage, and death. They tried to impress on and instill in their children the traditional stability of these events.

Births especially were major family celebrations, although many times they were personal traumas for women, since midwives delivered the majority of the children on the West Side not only because it was less expensive, but because it was the custom. "The Mexicans," wrote Kathleen González, "prefer the midwife because of their false modesty. Often a woman would rather die than go through a medical examination and undergo an operation. Even the men as a general rule would rather their wives were attended during maternity by a midwife than a doctor. This perhaps is because a man does not want any man, not even a doctor, to come in close contact with his wife."[59]

Overall, the community preferred that children be born to married parents. Therefore, church marriages were urged as the only way to have a Christian marriage and, as a result, a proper family. "Only by its [church marriage's] virtue," the church exclaimed, could a husband and wife "pledge eternal love." Outside of Christian matrimony, the phrase "eternal love" had no reality. Because of the fear of secularization, the Catholic Church sought to curb the custom among laboring-class Mexicans of marrying outside the church. Only by Christian marriages did the church feel it could control divorce. In essence, the church wanted to influence the Mexicans' life from birth to death. Father Tranchese reported to the archbishop that many Mexicans in San Antonio married "before the justice of the peace and then wait until the mission time to get married in the church, thus avoiding the marriage fee. So far," Tranchese further reported, "it has not been possible to make them stick to the church rules, with regard to marrying at the proper times and according to the dictates of the Church. This lawlessness is due to the fact that when they are denied something by their own pastor, they get it from another." But not all laboring-class Mexicans were married at all. Some just lived together as man and wife in common law marriages.[60]

Regardless of the type of marriage, Mexicans in the 1930s did not condone divorce, and, because it threatened the unity of the West Side families, the middle class avoided it. "Pride on the one hand and social aspirations on the other hand hold them back." In the middle class, according to Kathleen González, "family honor was more important than 'liberty.'" Although the *ricos* had fewer qualms with divorce, it was in the lower class that there were more divorces. But regardless of class, González reported that "jealousy over sexual matters was usually at the base of many divorces. When it did occur the woman was scorned and the children pitied."[61]

Death, although sad, was seen as a natural part of life. Nevertheless, death, like divorce, affected the whole family. "The women," according to Arnold, wore "deep black clothing during half of . . . [the mourning period] and black and white during the other half. Crepe emblems are worn by the men around their sleeve or as hatbands." The mourning period usually lasted from six months to a year. Before

the impact of Americanization, secularization, and modernity.

As can be noted, the Mexican family on the West Side was enveloped by traditional customs and sentiments and by the ideological and cultural traditions of the *ricos*, while schools introduced the U.S. way of life and the church sought a synthesis of the two. All three institutions — family, church, and education — however, sought to preserve the sanctity, modesty, and virtue of women regardless of changes that were occurring. As *La Prensa* editorialized, "[I]t is alright for women, especially single women, to have their own ideas, but not at the expense of the family otherwise civilization will cease. Women's clubs are fine because they allow women to have an outlet to find outside interests that are helpful to the [Mexican] community. These organizations are helpful for women. But, not all organizations are like this."[64]

In fact, "the unity and preservation of the family began with such things as proper manners and behavior." Young women were also told by the church to learn how to behave first in the family or at the workplace, which would lead to good behavior in public. Felicitas de los Santos, the writer of the *La Voz* column Joys for Women (Encantos para la Joven), wrote that young women should always "give a good impression in public" (April 10, 1938). She urged the young women of the Latin Quarter to follow Emily Post's ten rules for behavior, but stated that they could be reduced to two: "1. love and serve God, and 2. watch the nature of your figure. It should be straight. Be modest in your dress and walk. Moving your arms and neck flauntingly in front of boys is prohibited." De los Santos further urged Mexican girls to get Emily Post's etiquette book.[65] According to the church, to tradition, and to the Mexicans, themselves, the family, especially the woman, was the center of society and culture.

In Mexico the most powerful influences on everyday life had been the family, the community, and the church, and their importance continued in San Antonio during the thirties. This was understood by the upper middle class. Schoolteacher Kathleen González analytically portrayed the ideological change, but with the cultural continuity occurring in the community and the family, when she wrote, "it may be said that as long as immigration from Mexico to the United States is unrestricted, so long will San Antonio have different [classes and] types of Mexicans. [But], [w]ith the educational advantages which the city is offering this race, within the next century there will be a group of Mexicans who will be leaders of their community. The education of the Mexican girl will have a great deal to do with the change, as she will [culturally] influence her children more [in continuing Mexican customs] than the father, who will, in becoming a true American, think more about his business or profession than his family."[66] The Mexican family was clearly an agent of change and continuity.

5

The Catholic Church

Although the family was of primary importance to the Mexican in San Antonio, the Catholic Church and its teachings stood on an equal footing. Without question, religion was a central focus of the Mexicans' life. As was the case with other immigrants, to the Mexicans religion "was intertwined and embedded in the psyche, the folk-life, the very identity of each immigrant. It gave meaning, a system of moral values, self-definition, and community to the immigrants. It ordered their internal, private world and the world outside the family." Just like the Czechs, Poles, Germans, Jews, Irish, and other groups, the Mexicans in "their families and in their religion . . . sought comfort and relief from employers and those who would have them give up their identity."[1] The Catholic Church helped, guided, and molded the Mexicans, as it had done with other Catholic immigrants; moreover, it helped them to "adjust to American conditions, and in the process broke down national and cultural barriers." The Catholic Church, consciously or not, for the most part, operated from within the "politics of assimilation," but, paradoxically, it did not (for the Mexican and other immigrant groups) "eradicate ethnic identity. For better or worse, it [simply] redefined it."[2]

ARCHBISHOP DROSSAERT AND THE INSTITUTIONAL CHURCH

By 1930 there were over 80,000 Mexicans in San Antonio and over 250,000 in the San Antonio Catholic Archdiocese. This was not counting, as Archbishop Drossaert said, "that [middle] class of Mexicans who have frequented our school, speak English with perhaps only a faint trace of foreign accent; who are housed in humble but decent cottages; who are employed in stores, hotels, restaurants, in the city police and fire department and who for better or worse are more or less Americanized. These [middle-class Mexicans] constitute perhaps 1/20th of our Mexican population in the city of San Antonio."[3]

The Catholic Church was not preoccupied with its middle class; it was worried about the souls of the Mexican urban workers and agricultural workers who clustered in the Mexican Quarter around the Immaculate Heart of Mary Church, San Alfonso Church, Sacred Heart Church, Our Lady of Guadalupe Church, San Fernando Cathedral, Immaculate Conception Parish, and other churches. Immaculate Conception Parish was for the Mexican workers who settled near the stockyards and the packinghouses. The church left the middle class to its clubs and organizations and then attempted to involve it to help save the souls of the masses of Mexicans. Archbishop Arthur J. Drossaert also called for help from all Catholics in the United States to help solve the "Mexican problem" of the Southwest and San Antonio.

Without hesitation, Drossaert stated, "Left to ourselves [in San Antonio] we cannot make headway in solving this Mexican problem. [Because in the West Side] you will see . . . more poverty, misery, squalor, incredibly unsanitary housing conditions . . . [and the] huddling together of 2, 3, 4 families in a hovel of 2, 3 rooms." Drossaert further underlined his plea for help at the 1929 National Conference of Catholic Clergy by stating, "Without outside help, no diocese in the Southwest can do for the Mexicans what should be done. This Mexican problem is a national problem; it concerns the entire Church in America."[4]

The problems of the parishes in the Latin Quarter were magnified by the Depression. Our Lady of Guadalupe Parish, for example, which was located in the heart of the West Side and had over eleven thousand parishioners, felt the economic impact more than any other church in San Antonio. Most of the working people in this parish had migrated from Mexico in the early 1900s from Chihuahua, Coahuila, Nuevo León, Querétaro, San Luis Potosí, and Tamaulipas. As a result, there was an overlapping of generations and of aliens and citizens.[5] Due to the social complexity of the West Side and the generally impoverished conditions, Catholic officials felt that there were a number of major problems facing them: the lack of attendance at mass by the Mexican people; Protestant recruiting drives in the Mexican community; the propaganda of the exiled Mexican clergy; the impact of communism; the lack of church-sanctioned marriages; and the lack of adequate education for Mexican children.

In the Guadalupe Church newspaper, *La Voz de la Parroquia*, an article appeared in 1936 urging the people to attend Mass, but, ironically, it complained about the "West Side mud" the parishioners tracked into the church. The church, it seems, reached out to the Mexicans but with an elitist mentality. The Mexicans seemed oblivious to this attitude, because whenever there was an announcement for a reli-

regular novenas (four weekly devotions in May, June, October, and November), daily masses, confessions, and communions.[7]

Because of the church's unwavering belief in the Mexicans' religiosity, the Mexicans were presented a never-ending religious agenda. In spite of this, however, the Guadalupe Church annual report in 1933 showed that for a membership registration of over 8,000 there were only 479 baptisms, 55 marriages (32 were revalidated from a previous civic ceremony), and 182 children registered in Guadalupe Catholic School. However, there were 44,000 communions for the year. Four years later, the parish report showed an increase of registered members to 11,400; an increase in baptisms (512); an increase in marriages (88); an increase in communions (46,700); and an increase in school registration (620).[8] These increases probably occurred because of the continuing severity of the Depression and the increased work of the church. The Mexican laboring class, it seems, attended church and received communion but did not regularly adhere to the principles of the church in regard to marriage and other church doctrine.

Religion unified the workers, but was not a magnet for daily participatory activism, as it was for the middle class. The middle class enjoyed the clubs, planned the fiestas, and saved the souls. The laboring class just enjoyed the milieu of the Sunday services, the atmosphere of the fiestas, and the comfort of the guiding religious principles. For lower-middle-class Mexicans, however, religion was a vehicle to social prominence, since they did not usually have access to the *sociedad de los ricos*. In comparison, it could be said that for the workers the church was just a haven and a comfort. Thus, for many reasons its attempt to get Mexicans to church worked. Even though survival was always foremost in the minds of the Mexicans in the lower stratum, Archbishop Drossaert felt that "deep in their hearts our peons have the Catholic traditions still with them. The seeds of the Catholic faith lie dormant in their souls . . . and with care and work they can be made to sprout and fructify."[9]

The Catholic Church had different approaches to making its Mexican parishioners "sprout and fructify." The church in San Antonio had two approaches that emanated from within what was a standard Christian paradox. It sought, on the one hand, to preserve an emphasis on faith, God, grace, and sacrifice as the basis for the good life in the next world (metaphysical in ideology and institutional in practice). On the other hand, it sought to emphasize praxis, humanity, and material rewards as the basis for the good life in this world (communal in ideology and charismatic in practice). The central tension was how to balance traditional Scholastic theology with liberation theology.

Each of these approaches was personified by a clergyman in San Antonio. Archbishop Drossaert was the voice of the traditional church while Father Carmelo Tranchese was the voice of the human and social church. Drossaert the institutionalist contrasted visibly with Tranchese the humanist. Drossaert, it seems, pursued "souls for heaven," while Tranchese pursued "people for earth." Moreover, the former focused on diocesan policy and the latter on parish activities, especially through La Voz. It was a metaphysical quest for one and a phenomenological one for the other. Yet, in the end, religious stability triumphed over secular activism. Tranchese, the social activist, was, after all, just a soldier of Christ, while Drossaert, the administrator, was a prince of the church. According to church policy, the archbishop was synonymous with the church; his policy was the church's policy. Drossaert and Tranchese personified significant tensions within the church — tradition versus reform, dogmatism versus charisma, institutionalism versus praxis — and both affected the Mexican Quarter. It seemed that the tensions among the archbishop, the priest, and the worker in San Antonio from 1929 through 1941 personified a long-forgotten religious and historical moment of crisis, which was being replayed: the church's (Drossaert's) Scholastic soul but Aquinian mind was in a Hegelian tension with the parish's (Tranchese's) Lutheran Reformational philosophy and the workers' Calvinist and democratic ethic. Drossaert and Tranchese ultimately sought a synthesis (and so did the Mexican population) of identity, modern thought, and traditional religion.

Archbishop Drossaert and the Diocese

In a philosophical manner, Archbishop Drossaert stated that "the Church believed that the [belief in the] Blessed Mother, Maria Santisima," and the belief in the power of the rosary formed the center core of . . . [the Mexican workers'] hidden religion."[10] Thus, the Catholic Church felt it merely had to tap into this hidden well of religiosity. The archbishop of Monterrey, Mexico, was interviewed by

San Antonio.

Archbishop Drossaert was caught in a dilemma on the question of the relationship of religion and nationalism. He sought the institutionalism of religion, but not of nationalism. On the one hand, he argued in an article published in the *Southern Messenger* (the official organ of the Archbishopric of New Orleans and a prominent Catholic newspaper) for the concept of the national church in Mexico; on the other, he argued against a national Mexican church in San Antonio. Either Drossaert, like other Catholic clergy, failed to see the subtle difference between the Mexican Catholic Church and the U.S. Catholic Church, or he believed that the "Mexican internal schism" would affect the Mexicans in San Antonio's West Side if there were a national parish (especially since there were already too many Mexican priests and bishops who were followers of Joachín Pérez, who had sided with Calles in the Cristero Rebellion in Mexico). A national church in San Antonio, thought Drossaert, not only would create a political hotbed, but would delay the Americanization process as well as adherence to the U.S. Catholic Church. Drossaert's head was in conflict with his heart because of his conscious or subconscious acceptance of the U.S. ideal that separated religion and state; yet, at times, he acted as if there were no separation between church and state in converting souls, only in making policy. He wanted the souls of the Mexicans for Catholicism (and their loyalty to Americanism) but he did not want Mexicans' souls to be saved by a Catholic Church tied to Mexican patriotism or to Calles's socialism.[12]

Drossaert identified this danger to the American Bureau of Catholic Missions: "Whole districts [in San Antonio] have thus been infested and have falled prey to the New Schism. They [the West Side Mexicans] notice the difference [between the] . . . Roman Catholic Church and [the] *Mexican* Catholic Church; but the difference is all to their nationalistic likings and often it is [to them] all the same doctrine, the same mass, the same ceremonies, the same sacraments."[13] Drossaert felt that the people saw some differences, but in the end did not care about them.

Unlike Drossaert, the Mexican archbishop was acutely conscious of the difference between the American and the Mexican church (not in fundamental creed, but in the assimilation process into the nation). Because of the large numbers of religious exiles in San Antonio, Drossaert was forced into this controversy headed by Mexican Archbishop Leopoldo Ruiz y Flores and Bishop José de Jesús Marrique Lasarte, who avidly protested the "anarchistic and atheistic" tendencies of Calles's government. Drossaert, like other U.S. clergy, had other religious/philosophical themes (and political tendencies) that affected his policymaking; whether the church in San Antonio should be national or not was not an overwhelming concern, although he knew it was a reality. For example, he supported the New Deal and Rooseveltian reforms, but condemned the Calles-Ortiz socio-political policies. Moreover, his policy for San Antonio and the West Side was clouded with his obsession with communism, which he condemned wherever he thought he saw it (and he thought he saw it in Calles and his "schematics").[14] Drossaert did not seem to want to acknowledge and accept the paradox that in the United States the church was an American Catholic Church just as in Mexico it was a Mexican one (unlike his Boston colleague, Francis Cardinal Spellman, who clearly did). Nationalism and Catholicism did, in essence, hold hands; he just did not want Mexican religious nationalism in San Antonio, especially since he felt it might be tinged with communism.

There was another diocesan problem for Drossaert that was more immediate: the spread of Protestantism among the poor Mexicans in San Antonio. Drossaert and the church had many fronts on which to fight. Although the church had no real regard for the personal integrity or mind of the Mexican poor, the spread of Protestantism worried it because it perceived the Mexican as Drossaert did: a "big child, warm, affectionate, humble, patient, long suffering, charitable and hospitable, but fickle, inconsistent, and a squanderer."[15] In 1929 Drossaert reported this "Protestant problem" to the National Conference of Catholic Clergy on acknowledging that he had begun to see inroads by the Protestant religions as early as 1922:

When first coming to San Antonio some optimistic priests insisted that a Mexican could never be turned away from the Catholic faith. It was a pleasant thing to believe. It eased some of the misgivings and worries. But the awakening came soon enough from this beautiful dream. During some jubilee celebration of the combined Protestant churches of the city some seven years ago, my heart ached sorely when I had to see over one thousand of our Mexicans boldly proclaiming their Protestant allegiance, carrying an enormous open Bible in the parade, and singing hymns as they marched, which surely were not the lovely Span-

tonio were reminiscent of the tremendous Protestant efforts in Ireland.[16]

As a result of the Protestant effort, many Mexicans willingly became affiliated with one or the other Protestant churches. One Mexican woman, for example, who left the Catholic Church during the Depression, said, "The Protestants have nice churches, they give me money for food and clothing; Catholic priests do nothing of the kind; I went over to the religion of charity." Another woman joined because she received fifty cents a month for every member in her family and received clothing as well.[17] Even such prominent citizens as Mr. and Mrs. Jacobo Rodríguez became members of the Church of Christ. Jacobo Rodríguez, an active LULAC member, middle-class Mexican, and Republican, became involved in the West Side membership drives of the Church of Christ.[18]

Mexicans like the Rodríguezes, the Rev. E. Guerra of the Iglesia Metodista, and the Rev. D. C. Acevedo, the pastor of the Iglesia Presbiteriana Mexicana, were constant activists during the 1930s for the Protestant cause. The Reverend Guerra, for example, in speaking to the Protestant-sponsored Club Deportivo Juvenil (Youth Sports Club) at the Methodist Temple of La Trinidad, emphasized the Methodist "right path of life" and urged his listeners to try to follow this path throughout the years.

The Protestant faiths sponsored many sporting events, athletic teams, and recreational clubs to attract and recruit Mexican youth to their churches. In addition, they attempted to appeal to the adults by distributing money and clothing. The Baptists, the Presbyterians, the Methodists, and the Lutherans were also building community centers, kindergartens, schools, seminaries, and churches to attract and convert the Mexicans. The West Side, in particular and the Southwest in general were considered religious missionary frontiers.[19]

Ironically, regardless of who won, Americanism would prevail. And although the struggle seemed to be a reenactment of the Reformation, both the Catholic Church and the Protestant ones were ultimately Christian. The essence of the struggle was not for souls or even against Mexican patriotism, but for power (especially Drossaert's personal power) and religious hegemony.

Drossaert always considered this drive by the Protestant churches to be an extremely critical problem. In fact, as early as 1924 a Catholic report on their own missionary work stated that "the priests and sisters who labor amongst . . . [the Mexicans] all praise their simple, childlike faith and their deep attachment to our Holy Religion. But their poverty and ignorance together with their large numbers and the desperate efforts constitute a vast difficult problem; one indeed which cannot be solved locally. It is in all truth a National Problem." The church particularly asked for the institution of a Catholic Community House for Mexicans in San Antonio to "offset the efforts of the five Protestant centers that were admirably equipped and working day and night to snatch away our people." Immediately, the American Board of Catholic Missions sent five thousand dollars to support the church's missionary effort in San Antonio to hold at bay the "Protestant proselytizers" and the Mexican cismáticos, "the minions of the unspeakable Calles."

Interestingly, the Catholic Church always characterized the Mexican Catholics in San Antonio as "passive, humble, and charitable" in contrast, the Mexican Protestants characterized them as "aggressive, insulting, and spiteful."[20] Both Catholicism and Protestantism held stereotypical views of the Mexicans; for both, in essence, the problem was a vision that lacked knowledge, understanding, and compassion for the Mexicans and their traditions.

The Catholic Church was particularly alarmed at the success of the Baptist Seminary, which had been operating in the heavily Mexican populated Guadalupe District since 1925. The news that a "Communist" school was operating in the same area also alarmed the church: "This plague [of religious and political propaganda] is doing great damage amongst the Mexicans. It is too natural. These people are poor, and they listen very eagerly to the sweet song of the Siren," reported the Guadalupe Church.[21] Due to this rise of Protestantism since the 1920s, Father Tranchese, the pastor of Guadalupe Church, was asked in the late 1930s to assess the situation and compare the predicament of the Mexicans in San Antonio with that of those in other states. He reported to Archbishop Lucy in 1941 that the Mexicans from New Mexico were good Catholics and knew their duty; the Colorado Mexicans were faithful to the church and to the United States; in El Paso they were "enthusiastic" and loved the church; but in San Antonio, the Mexican was different. Religion for the West Sider was a "holy superstition" and, as a result, these Mexicans were "unreli-

sand Catholics, of whom sixty thousand were Mexican) helped provide relief in cash, food, clothing, rent money, and employment rehabilitation programs. The churches, Catholic and Protestant, also worked through parish groups, organizations, clubs, and community centers (such as the Catholic Guadalupe Community Center, the Presbyterian Wesley Community Center, the Inman Christian Institute, the House of Neighborly Service, and the Goodwill Center). All of these centers were located in the Mexican Quarter. Other Catholic institutions, such as the Good Shepherd Home, Santa Rosa Hospital and Clinic, the Catholic Daughters of America, the local Council of Women, the Catholic Women's Association, and the Queen's Daughters of St. Mary's Parish, also provided different forms of assistance to the Mexican poor, especially the pecan shellers.[23]

In spite of this cooperation in the war against the Depression, the Catholic Church established a strong ideological and institutional program to combat Protestantism, communism, and poverty in both the urban and the rural areas. In its urban program, the church in San Antonio focused on four methods: first, the establishment of Catholic athletic clubs, music clubs, and general religious associations; second, the establishment and expansion of educational facilities; third, the formulation of an official policy directing Father Tranchese to continue his social work in the West Side; and fourth, the establishment of an "official" West Side paper, *La Voz de la Parroquia*, to communicate more directly with the laboring class. The church wanted religious hegemony just as the *ricos* sought cultural hegemony among

the Mexican population. The church, however, recognized the difficulty of its endeavor to work in the Mexican community. As Father
Tranchese accurately stated, "It [was] all up-hill."[24]

The rural approach consisted of the formation of a union of Catholic farmers, La Liga de Agricultores Católicos. The regional Catholic newspaper, the *Southern Messenger*, reported that the time had
come to organize all Catholic farmers to better their economic status, because "the farmer, after all, is the back-bone of the common-
wealth and yet, is . . . the 'forgotten man' in all the plans, schemes
and laws of the New Deal" (April 7, 1938). Fortunately, this rural plan
did consider the Mexican Catholic agricultural worker, who was, in
fact, the real "forgotten man." *La Voz*, however, reported that the
purpose of the league was also to give the agricultural worker a voice
in the political system (April 10, 1938). Consequently, when a conference was called by the league, Archbishop Drossaert was invited to
send a representative, since it was known that he was interested in
organizing the Mexican workers and Catholic ranchers in his diocese.[25]

Interestingly, the church's Jeffersonianism was emphasized in the
rural area, whereas its Hamiltonionism and pragmatism were apparent
in the urban area. Drossaert and the church may have been traditional and Scholastic in their heart and soul, but they were American
liberals in their head and possessive and individualistic in nature.

The urban area of the West Side was, of course, the primary focus
of the church's activities. The church understood the importance of
attracting the Mexican poor, even though Drossaert believed the Mexicans were innately religious. Therefore, different activities were held
with the help of the middle class. The prominent historian and leading
Mexican citizen of San Antonio and Austin, Dr. Carlos E. Castañeda,
for example, was made the official historian for the Knights of Columbus Historical Commission and was asked, among other things,
to translate a four hundred–year-old play concerning the church so
that it could be enjoyed by the Mexican community.

Besides plays, theater, and anniversary celebrations, the church
began to sponsor Gran Kermesses (church fairs), bingo games, recrea-
tional and sporting activities, and an extensive array of religious-social
organizations such as the Christian Doctrine Society, the Children
of Mary Society, the Third Order of St. Francis, the Cavadonga Club,
Christ the King Society, the St. Vincent de Paul Society, the Altar
Society, the Nocturnal Adoration Society, the Young Ladies Club, the
Apostleship of Prayer, the St. Ferdinand Ushers, the Holy Childhood
Organization, the Ladies' Altar Society, the Catholic Young Men's
Club, the Holy Name Society, the Mexican Catholic Youth, the Balti-
more Catechism Clubs, and dozens of other organizations. This pro-

liferation of organizations was directed toward increasing and strengthening the link between the growing upper and middle classes and the working class, especially the women and children. The church hoped to attract and retain the Mexicans. Ironically, it was promoting its goals by linking religion, Americanism, and ethnicity and by using the Mexican middle class as a surrogate on the missionary frontier.[26]

In keeping with this strategy of recruiting and retaining church members, the parishes in the West Side directed their attention toward

In the public school the Mexican children learn the tricks of Americans and none of their virtues. And, in the course of the time, these children become almost ashamed of their religion. Thus, hundreds of them are lost to the faith." The parochial schools in the West Side, consequently, taught the Mexican children in English. The church wanted them to be English-speaking Americans, but not secular ones. It wanted ethnicity to be retained because *lo mexicano* was in its essence religious and Catholic. Thus, it pursued a policy of promoting an ideological undercurrent of Mexican Americanism.[27]

Together with its emphasis on organizational activities and education, the Catholic Church discovered that it had to do more charity and health work in the West Side if it were going to attract the West Siders during the Depression. The Catholic Charity Board of the San Antonio Archdiocese therefore launched more specific programs for the Mexican poor in 1931: a care program for the orphans, a home for the aged, a home for working girls, night schools, clinics, and a general welfare program for the Mexican poor. Between 1929 and 1931, the Catholic Charity Board disbursed over $151 million. The church, furthermore, set up welfare centers to provide medical care and general health instruction.

In keeping with this emphasis on ethnicity, Americanism, and Catholicism, Carmen McCormick was hired by Drossaert and the church to teach the Mexican children their "cultural tradition" at these centers. Notices of these parish centers and clinics were posted throughout the community so that Mexicans could come in and be examined for malaria, tuberculosis, and diphtheria. These clinics were supervised by the Damas Católicas. The parishes also organized Latin-American Health Week, which was supervised in May, 1936, by a Mr. Ortega of the Texas State Tuberculosis Society. According to Ortega, "the aim of the week is to educate people on the prevention, detection, and how to combat the T.B. disease." The Mexican-American Boy Scouts of the parishes, which were usually organized by LULAC, were placed in charge of the routine organizing tasks of the week.

Latin-American Health Week, however, was more than simple charity work; it was the middle-class aligned with the church to sponsor a subtle political consciousness-raising week. The division of the week reflected this: May 11, Hygiene for the House: Fix it Day; May 12, Community Day: Work in Our Barrio; May 13, T.B. Day; May 14, Women's Day: Day of Rest for Them; and May 15, Children's Day at School. The church, in all its endeavors, received the help of the *ricos* because Catholicism, family, and community were being emphasized. The Mexican American middle class also supported it for the same reasons but also because the church was promoting a consciousness of Americanism.[28]

The parish priests also appealed to the American population directly from their pulpits. In some cases, they urged the San Antonio business community to hire the unemployed Mexicans who had registered at the Social Workers' Association and at the U.S. Farm Labor Bureau. In other cases, they spoke on specific political issues. For example, although the church appealed for jobs for laborers during the 1930s and conducted charity drives and clean-up campaigns for them, it did not support the pecan shellers' strikes in 1934 or 1938. Archbishop Drossaert, as one of the editors of the *Southern Messenger*, made this very clear in an article in which he focused ostensibly on the Knights of Columbus, the prestigious laymen's organization of the Catholic Church, which had also opposed the pecan strike.[29] Drossaert emphasized that the Knights of Columbus had been fighting communism for the last year and it was their general belief (and Drossaert's personal one as well as the church's) that "communism thrives on labor strikes and is active in the labor movement even though it is disavowed by labor leaders." In spite of Drossaert's position, certain parish priests, such as Father John López, were strong supporters of the pecan shellers during the 1938 strike. In fact, Father López, Father Leo V. Murphy (pastor of the St. Peter Claver Church, the church for blacks), and Father Carmelo Tranchese formed the Catholic Relief Association in 1938 to feed, clothe, and shelter the eight thousand pecan shellers after automation made them superfluous.

The church, at times, was divided between institutional and personal ideology as articulated by Drossaert, and the personal but religious ideological beliefs of the parish priests. The differences, however, were basically in degree and not in kind. Both ultimately wanted religion and reforms (and not revolution or secularism), and both also wanted Mexican Americans and not just Americans. Nevertheless, the difference was in ideological and institutional emphasis (more Scholasticism or more libertarianism), in essence, institutional traditional theology or liberation theology.[30]

cast was directed toward the middle class as well as the workers and continued into the 1940s, although by World War II the church's propaganda assault, which had changed to station KCOR, now emphasized Americanism and urged the Mexican community to buy U.S. war bonds and stamps.[31]

The religious theme changed during the decade of the 1940s to more of an American theme. In fact, the two merged by World War II. The church in San Antonio, it seems, sounded almost the same themes as Henry R. Luce in his "American Century" writings and Francis Cardinal Spellman in his Americanization of the church campaign. Once again, the mission of God coincided with the mission of the state, and the democratic and expansionist thematic echoes of Polk, McKinley, and Wilson resounded through the radios of the San Antonio Latin Quarter. Of course, the themes of the new American discourse were apparent, but not the deep structures of hidden intellectual and ideological meanings that were affecting the Mexican consciousness; it was new religious and political discourse acting as new "loci of power."[32]

Although the Catholic Church in San Antonio (at the archdiocesan level) presented general administrative policies and urged and planned general activities aimed at facilitating Christian education, American citizenship, and the general socioeconomic betterment of the West Side, it was the parish priests who met with the people and attempted to implement Drossaert's policies. They also sometimes initiated policy through a form of activism rather than through the art of preaching. During the 1930s, for example, Father Carmelo Tranchese was called a "pioneer social worker" and the "rumpled angel of the slums," and Fathers Carvajal, Silva, and López were called "social activists" in the Mexican community. Their social activism was based on the two papal encyclicals on social justice: Leo XIII's *Rerum Novarum* and *Quadragisimo Anno*, and Pius XI's *Mater et Magistra*, which stressed the moral basis for social justice.

Tranchese, with this social philosophy in his head, a moral imperative in his soul, and an acute sensitivity to the poor in his heart, almost single-handedly attacked the problems of the West Side. He first pressured the church to establish relief agencies and coorganized the Catholic Relief Association to help the pecan shellers. He established the Guadalupe Community Center, which promoted health programs, and he founded a clinic for vaccinations against diphtheria, typhus, typhoid fever, and smallpox. With the help of the San Antonio Housing Authority Board of Commissioners, the support of Eleanor Roosevelt, and the leadership of San Antonio mayor Maury Maverick, he pressured the U.S. Housing Authority in the late 1930s to expedite the Wagner-Ellendorf bill for a public housing project for the West Side.

As a result of Tranchese's activism, general influence, and political connections, a San Antonio business group protested his housing efforts to the Federal Housing Authority, stating that there "were no slums in San Antonio." Nevertheless, the Apache-Alazán Courts, the Victorian Courts, the Wheatly Courts, and the Lincoln Courts were finally built as a result of his efforts. The majority of the housing was for Mexicans, but blacks and poor Anglos were admitted, although the last two were segregated into housing projects on their side of town.

If during the 1930s the Catholic Church practiced so much Christian charity in the West Side, it was because Tranchese was the catalyst. He was the conscience of the Catholic Church in San Antonio. He was described by his fellow Jesuits as "a person with an unbounded zest for God and all things human." He had, some Jesuits said, "a rich share of what his favorite, Dante, called the love that moves the sun and the other stars."[33]

Tranchese, however, like many of his fellow priests, was antiunion but proworker, anti-Communist but pro-humanitarian, and this was reflected in his activist philosophy. His constant work with and acceptance by the pecan shellers prompted the U.S. government to ask him to give them certain personal information on the striking workers. Labor leader Magdaleno Rodríguez, however, advised the Mexican workers not to fill out the cards given to them by Tranchese, because the government would use the information to close the pecan plants.[34]

One of the main problems Tranchese faced in his work on behalf of the Mexican community was the prejudice and racial discrimination of non-Mexican San Antonians. Tranchese, analyzing his own efforts to obtain better housing for the West Side, stated in a speech, "I have been greatly shocked at the amount of racial prejudice which I have encountered here. The phrase 'Mexican and white people' is a very current one and is always spoken with contempt." Tranchese was also surprised at the resistance of the Mexican middle class to

public housing."[35]

Because of his friendship with the Mexican people, Tranchese saw the importance of the Mexican cultural traditions in the West Side and wanted to preserve them. He felt that ethnic nationalism, and the "spirit of la Raza," would be maintained by designating the West Side Catholic Church parishes (especially Guadalupe Church) as national Mexican parishes rather than as territorial ones. This, he felt, would open up the churches on the West Side to all Mexicans regardless of where they lived in San Antonio, serve to heighten Mexican consciousness of nationalism, and preserve Mexican cultural traditions (and self-identity).[36]

This was in direct conflict with the ideas and policies of Archbishop Drossaert, who was a staunch American and wanted only the persons living in the church's geographical district to attend. He wanted to maintain the territorial concept rather than the national one even though he also wanted Mexicans to retain some sense of their ethnicity. He did not want a Mexican church on the West Side because of the impetus it might give the "Mexican Schismatics."[37]

Tranchese, unlike Drossaert, was the visible clergyman in the everyday work of the church; consequently, he operated as if the church were a Mexican one. The community was grateful for his religious efforts, his political activity, and his general sensitivity toward them. As a result, he was often thanked by the Mexican middle class, praised by the black community, supported by the prominent politico Maury Maverick; given occasional help by the city's political machine; and loved by the majority of the Mexican people in San Antonio.[38] A poem entitled "Alleluyas" presented to him in 1942 captured his importance to the Mexican people:

El ha encendido la Luz	He has lit the
la marcha tras	light in the march
de la Cruz!	toward the Cross!
El nos ha llevado	He has taken us to
al puente para	the bridge to cross
cruzar la corriente.	the flowing river.
Por lo cual, Padre	Therefore, dear father of
querido nuestro pecho	our hearts, our thanks.
agradecido le dice	We say this with great
con efusión Gracias!	emphasis. Thank you!
Gracias! un millon.	Thank you! A million thanks.

If this poem captures the joy he gave to the people as the vehicle of Catholicism, a note from his coactivist and fellow priest Father Leo Murphy captures his significance to the Catholic Church in San Antonio: "I am an eyewitness of your hearty zeal for the . . . Latin Americans. Your faith was not a distant theory . . . for them. It was a dynamic philosophy of life that brought a renewed faith to the Latin American who witnesses Catholicism in action."[39] Tranchese was perceived by the people and by his peers as the leader of a charismatic parish.

Tranchese, in essence, was the instrument for the implementation of the Catholic Church's social philosophy, and *La Voz de la Parroquia* was, in turn, Tranchese's voice. This newspaper began as a mimeographed one-page newsletter initially called *La Estrella del Mar* (Star of the Sea) and compiled from other newspapers by Father Tranchese in 1933. But with the increasing amount of local news, the constant need to reach the Mexicans with the gospel, the increasing crisis of the Depression, the increasing numbers of public school children receiving daily catechism instruction, and the increasing number of unemployed, the need for a larger paper became evident. A decision was made to expand it and begin *La Voz de la Parroquia* to meet the parish's needs. *La Voz* provided the church and Tranchese with a direct voice to the Mexican community. Specifically, it was established to provide the Latin Quarter with the written text of sermons, the message of the week, religious articles and themes, parish news, and any additional special news. Rómulo Mungía, a prominent printer in San Antonio with an affinity for philosophical syndicalism, was to print this newspaper, which had the official imprimatur of Archbishop Drossaert. It was to be written in Spanish initially to facilitate communication with the community.[40]

LA VOZ AND THE WORKER

Between 1935 and 1937, when Father Tranchese was in charge of the newspaper's philosophical orientation and its everyday administration, the paper projected a straightforward Christian philosophy urging the Mexican community to accept and use their suffering in a positive way and not allow their desperate socioeconomic situation to discourage them. The paper urged the Mexicans to use their "trials

dor) to tell the working class that the heart was like a garden that needed to be cultivated. Therefore, the people needed to cultivate their hearts and souls by regularly receiving religious instruction, constantly attending mass and receiving Holy Communion, and always keeping "good" company.

In essence, Tranchese emphasized brotherly love, tolerance, acceptance, goodwill, charity, forgiveness, religion, and having friends with the same ideas and practices (this last point was directly aimed at the Mexican youth). Furthermore, the Mexicans were told to read Christian literature such as *La Voz*. Above all, Tranchese advised the West Side community to avoid a sense of indifference, urging them to become active in their daily lives and in coping with their problems. "Indifference," stated Tranchese, "is the sickness that kills us, the poison that has been inculcated into our own veins. He who 'sleeps,' dies." Most of all, activism, he implied, combated communism, which was immoral.[41] *La Voz* hoped to carry this philosophy of active humility to everyone. With the intellectual arrogance of the Jesuits, Tranchese was emphasizing the humanism of Erasmus, the activism of St. Paul, the humility, love, and strength of Jesus, and the critical sense of confrontation of the Jesuits—the shock troops of the Catholic Church.

Besides carrying Tranchese's philosophical and religious messages, *La Voz* was also a cultural vehicle. There were poems by local poets, some of which attempted to instill personal pride in the residents of the Mexican Quarter. One such poem entitled "A Mi Amiga" dealt with racial pride:

Margarita, Margarita	Margarita, Margarita
eres muy coqueta	You are so vain.
porque tanto	why are you
de Henarieas?	so pretentious?
Eres Blanca?	Are you white?
No lo Creas!	Don't believe it!
Porque así vas a la plaza.	Because that is the way you go
Crees tú que yo creo?	to the plaza.
Ser verdad como veo.	Do you know what I believe?
Si prietita Dios te hizo?	The truth is how I see it.
Así quédate: qué coqueta!	If God made you dark,
Media blanca y media prieta.	stay that way: How pretentious!
	Half white and half dark.[42]

Another poem in parable form tried to instill a sense of community and pride but with a sarcasm directly aimed at the non-Mexican community, although it indicated the developing acculturation process.

El Zoo del West Side	*The Zoo of the West Side*
Viejos, Jóvenes,	Elders, youth,
Chiquillos Vengan todos	Children Come all of you
a este lado; a ver	to see the wonders
las maravillas	of the West Side
Es el hecho más profundo	It is the most profound
una cara no pensada.	accomplishment, a sight
No hay otra	not understood.
en todo el mundo;	there is no other like it
una pulga	in this world;
amaestrada! . . .	A tamed Mexican flea . . .
Esta pulga pica fuerte	This flea stings without
Bebe, come, va	mercy; it drinks, eats,
a la escuela	and goes to school.
curar puede el mal	it understands everything
de muela	even how to cure a toothache.
Joe le dicen los bribones	Joe, the mischievous [American]
de muchachos de cariño;	youth lovingly call him.
Joe contesta a picazones	Joe answers, stinging them,
Y se ríe como un niño.	and he laughs like a child.[43]

In addition to the newspaper's emphasis on the church and on personal pride, *La Voz* urged the community to contain its "fires of the flesh" and to control its emotions by fasting, especially according to Pope Pius X's idea of only eating one meal a day. As a result, the Mexican would be using a "good tonic for the heart": "it will clean and free it restoring spiritual health and facilitating the good Christian life." Many of the Mexican laborers probably tried fasting, not by choice, but because of poverty. However, if any of the Mexican people thought God had deserted them during the Depression, Tranchese reminded them to have faith and believe like Christ at the Garden of Gethsemane because "even at the time of crisis . . . we have not been forsaken by God."[44] Tranchese constantly urged self-reliance, faith, humility, ethnic pride, positive suffering, unwavering faith in God for deliverance, and the gospels as a daily guide.

"if you don't receive [what you want] either you didn't pray right or else you have some personal faults."[45] Central paradoxical tensions were placed within the minds and hearts of the Mexican population: be active but passive; be true to yourself but also true to the church; and be an individual but also communal.

In 1937 *La Voz's* philosophy changed drastically. The change was immediately noticeable in its title, now *La Voz: Periodico de Justicia y Acción Social.* Rómulo Mungía took over administration from Father Tranchese. *La Voz*, consequently, changed from a parish paper to a worker's paper. The reasons for the change were complex, but relatively clear: the agitation of the Mexican workers had become more intensified; the Depression was more severe; Tranchese had become more anti-Communist, especially in his views toward the CIO, which was organizing the Mexicans; and Mungía had become more involved in the writing of the newspaper. As a result, the workers came to use the paper (with Mungía's guidance) as their voice.

An article in *La Voz* on March 1, 1936, had already hinted at this change. The article, *La cuestón social obrera*," stated that, for the church to be in accord with Pius X's social dictum, it had to return to a more active social philosophy that would judiciously deal with both capital and labor. The article, signed only N. N., also commented on communism, stating that there were certain aspects of communism that could be reconciled with Catholicism, even though a Catholic could not also be a socialist. Nevertheless, Catholics had to act, the article emphasized, to restore a better social economy. The article called for a celebration of all persons of goodwill. It forecast the

Christian workers' philosophy that *La Voz* would advocate in 1937.

In accordance with this attempt to become a workers' paper rather than a church paper, *La Voz* was distributed free after all the weekly masses and services, although it still cost ten cents to have it delivered to an individual's home. In addition, *La Voz* began to carry articles on the Spanish Civil War, the CIO, the Mexican Communist party, Lombardo Toledano's Mexican workers, unionism, and local and regional strike information. *La Voz* had entered a new arena of activities, wrote the staff; moreover, they pointed out emphatically that *La Voz* "has never been an organ of the Jesuits but of the writers, who write for our own 'Pueblo Trabajador' to correct social problems."[46]

In 1937 *La Voz* basically attempted to implement the social justice encyclicals mandated by Leo XIII and Pius XI, which focused on the importance of the worker. "As Catholic workers," *La Voz* stated, "we . . . love our religion, our country, our [working-class] brothers; [we have] respect for authority; we [are dedicated] to the honor of work and dedicated to the protection of our rights as workers [but] within a spirit of collaboration with the other classes that form human society." This was the new philosophy. Rómulo Mungía wrote that God wanted the staff of *La Voz* to take certain ideas to the working class, especially the total social doctrine inspired by the holy gospels. "Based upon the Pope's recommendations that we implement social action, we have taken upon ourselves this work located humbly in the Catholic press," he wrote. Although Father Tranchese had helped start the newspaper, Mungía again reminded the Mexican community that *La Voz* had never been the organ of the Jesuits. Its purpose had been "to bring the gospels to the Mexican working class, but now we turn to social action which is the responsibility of the newspaperman."[47]

The philosophy was not Marxist, but neo-Christian. Strategically, its focus was on humanism rather than spiritualism; tactically, *La Voz* emphasized the worker and the importance of labor (rather than the worker's soul or religion) as the focus of the new contemplation. It pointed out to the workers, "We must remember that only the Christian restoration, individual [and] family, and the economic restoration to a material and spiritual prosperity is what we want." Tranchese and Mungía, working for the parish, had turned Christian doctrine inside out, from the institutional to the personal, from the traditional to the charismatic, and from the spiritual to the material. "Honor always the community of workers became the motto, and the natural rights of people, a good material life, and a good spiritual one became the guiding philosophy. If nothing else, Americanism was coming in the back door with the idea that everyone had the right to work for a good life, and that salvation would come from one's labor not just through God's mercy, *La Voz* implied. Calvinism was meeting Marxism on its own vital center, which emphasized labor as the anvil on which the self, the community, and the society were forged.[48]

Class struggle in the Marxist sense was not *La Voz's* aim, but rather a cooperative struggle of classes through unionization. *La Voz*, on October 11, 1937, reprinted an article by the militant *Christian Front* newspaper that advocated the position that Catholics should look

rights] and [to remember that] Christianity was born out of struggle."[49]

This was a direct reference to Leo XIII's encyclical. The Rev. M. Balderama, a writer for the "old" *La Voz*, attempted to counter the "new" *La Voz's* portrayal of Christ as the first socialist and Christianity as a social and radical philosophy. Balderama stated the official position for Drossaert and the church when he wrote that the idea of Christ as the first socialist was "absurd!": "Socialism," stated Balderama, "is the glorification of sin. Socialism is obscurity; Christianity is truth. Socialism is error; Christianity is right, and anyone who uses the rhetoric of Christianity and Socialism as identical before the community is wrong."[50] Balderama, Drossaert, and others did not seem to understand that *La Voz's* new position was within the Christian framework.

La Voz supported the workers and the union but attacked Communist influence, especially during the April, 1938, pecan shellers' strike. By the time of this stike *La Voz's* turn to the Christian Left had been stopped. As early as September, 1937, Archbishop Drossaert had written a letter to Father Tranchese, who was still the official editor of *La Voz*, stating,

> I deem it wwise [*sic*] and prudent to appoint an official censor for your parochial paper, especially in view of . . . *La Voz's* financial backing of the labor leaders in San Antonio.
>
> I hereby appoint the Rev. Joseph B. Carvajal S.J. as the official censor and no issues will be printed without his previous official approval. Let no open C.I.O. propaganda enter into your paper.[51]

Thus, the "radical" period of *La Voz* was over, and the mind of the Mexican worker, consisting of a Christian theology, that had emerged as liberation theology, was submerged. By February 6, 1938, *La Voz* had changed from being the unofficial newspaper of Mexican workers and their activities into, once again, the voice of the Catholic Church and the archbishop. Its role once again was to propagandize the Mexican workers into becoming socially acceptable Catholics who sought their rewards in heaven and not in this world. The church again began to try to improve the workers' lives through an Americanization process while having them maintain their Mexican identity. Yet, on the whole, Americanization via the Catholic Church was a positive move for the Mexican intellectual, cultural, and Scholastic mentality of dependence: the church wanted to provide an American mentality of change, but within religious continuity.

Thus, in 1938, the newspaper that for one year had been under the leadership of Rómulo Mungía and the Mexican workers of San Antonio came under the leadership of the Association of Buena Press and the Catholic Bishops' Association. It now had to obtain the additional approval of the city's Vigilance Committee. What had started as the pastoral voice of Guadalupe Parish and had become the voice of the Mexican workers now became a structure of complete diocesan and municipal domination. Its philosophical orientation once again changed. As the Reverend Balderama had pointed out earlier, "There is a danger in the community [of the West Side] when it doesn't know its religion well; it is exposed to communism and its conquest. A community without a religious culture is like an army disarmed."[52]

Moreover, Father Tranchese now shifted his ideological emphasis by placing the danger on materialism rather than on communism, as he indicated in *La Voz:* "The source of robbery and evil is the societies' emphasis on the material culture — money." Balderama's and Tranchese's criticisms seemed to parallel the lament of southern writer Joseph Wood Krutch, who in 1929 lamented the loss of a culture of religion, feeling, God (and nature) due to the rise of a secularistic and materialistic culture in America. Balderama feared secularism and communism, Tranchese feared materialism. Archbishop Drossaert and the rest of the staff wrote that they had "supported" the previous work of *La Voz* to bring the teachings of Christ to the Mexican working class; however, they did not recommend the return to a philosophy of action, but to a philosophy emphasizing the "word of God."[53]

The "new philosophy" was given in a reprinted speech from Bishop Fulton J. Sheen that attacked communism and Russia. *La Voz*'s new motto was now "justice and love," but fit to a passive metaphysical form rather than an active communal one. By 1938 it seemed that a "balance of tensions and issues" was beginning. Because of the active Mexican labor agitation that was still occurring in 1938, Drossaert and *La Voz* called for the formation of La Confederación Católica del Trabajo. It was a call for a confederation of San Antonio's Catholic workers and it was to be counterposed to the unionization efforts of the CIO and the AF of L. The church sought, as Krutch had wanted for Americans, to give Mexicans a right to a metaphysical moral and

Archbishop Drossaert, who as the head of the Catholic Church in San Antonio dictated the religious and ideological approach the church took toward the more than one hundred thousand Mexicans in the city and the quarter of a million in the surrounding area, felt that the church should emphasize the Catholic clubs and social centers (and the strengthening of the family unit). Family and religious values were to be part of the remedy to keep Mexican workers Catholic and religious. The church's focus was still education, however. Drossaert, paternalistically and with racist overtones, wrote, "The longer I am in the Archdiocese of San Antonio and in daily touch with our immense Mexican population, the clearer I see the absolute need of the Catholic school. It is the only effective means . . . to lift up these poor, simple children from their ignorance, superstition, and slovenly habits. It is the only safeguard of their faith and morals." For Drossaert the Catholic Church and the Catholic school were essential religious and functional institutional imperatives for making Mexicans good Christians and good U.S. citizens as well as the avenue for their personal, intellectual, and social progress. Drossaert felt that Mexicans "[l]eft to themselves . . . can do nothing, build nothing, support nothing. They need the help of their more favored Anglo-American brethren." This help, however, had to be given within the context of Christian training, because the public schools simply made Mexicans, Drossaert believed, "prey to sin" and a "danger to society."[56]

Teaching the Mexican children the English language and Americanizing them was the main goal of the Catholic school, but it carried definite dangers just as the secular world did:

The influence of the Church upon the [Mexican child] is too often only infinitesimal. It may require some knowledge of our English language in the public schools and perhaps even some thin veneer of American ways and manners, but with this comes a large dose of false pride and a superiority complex. The child soon goes to swell that class of "Tejanos" [Mexican Americans reared in Texas] too often cold and indifferent to the faith and an easy mark for masonry and Protestantism.[57]

The Catholic Church in San Antonio during the 1930s exerted a positive influence on the Mexican community in terms of social action, economic relief, and cultural, social, and recreational activities. These activities were usually dominated by the middle class, which subscribed to a philosophy of work, religion, family, and being *gente decente*. Both the middle class and the church agreed on uplifting, socially and religiously, the Mexican masses. Over all, the Catholic Church tried to Americanize the Mexicans, but at the same time to preserve their Mexican culture and identity; the middle class agreed. The Catholic Church also sought to modernize, consciously or subconsciously, the Mexican population into U.S. Catholics and U.S. citizens. As a result, it broke down the cultural barriers, provided the English language skills, and, for better or worse, helped to acculturate the Mexicans. The church, just as the family, was both a haven of cultural continuity and a transmitter of ideological change for the Mexican community. Consequently, both family and church were structures of domination, but, ironically, instilled central tensions in the Mexicans' search for identity, because the family as the heart of the Mexican community and the church as the soul were functioning as both agents of cultural change and retainers of cultural continuity.

6

ued for it.

— Katherine Mequire

EDUCATION AND THE MEXICAN COMMUNITY

Unlike the institutions of the Catholic Church or the family, the educational system in San Antonio was directly related to the industrialization and urbanization process. As early as 1914, the San Antonio School District adopted Dewey's progressive educational theories to be used in relation to Mexican children. The School Board sought to adhere to the central motto of progressive education: "Prepare the citizenry."[1] Schools were to become agencies to help create an orderly, rational, and unified society in San Antonio. The School Board was adhering to Dewey's ideas that schools take "part in the determination of the social order" and that vocational training and Americanization programs were the means by which to make immigrants useful, participating citizens.[2]

This view was adopted by San Antonio when the School Board in 1914 accepted a survey report that stated,

> Most of the 2,200 children of school age in San Antonio will in time be obliged to earn their living. The school should therefore deal with every pupil on the theory that he will be obliged to earn a living. Since one's work is as important as any other function that one will ever perform, [and] if public money is to be expended for education at all, this

should doubtlessly have a share proportionate to its value. A city should expect full returns for this investment through the increased productiveness of labor efficiency.[3]

It was aware that most of its graduates would not enter the professional fields; therefore, it believed that

> while it is the school's duty to help those who are to enter professional and managerial callings as fully as possible, it is nonetheless the duty of the school to provide equally for effective training for those who enter every other useful calling. Since comparatively few students will ever enter the professions, the chief vocational responsibility of the school lies in helping those who are to enter agricultural, manufacture, mechanical trades, commerce, transportation, public service, mining, and clerical occupations.[4]

From 1914 until the 1940s, the San Antonio School District adhered to this progressive educational philosophy, which aimed to socialize youths to live, work, and, as the director of vocational education in Los Angeles stated in 1923, "to do [their] part" as citizens.[5] Many of San Antonio's schools, consequently, offered commercial training, shop, carpentry, furniture making, woodworking, pattern making, mechanical drawing, and other vocational courses. The School Board reported that the city had "taken a very advanced position in comparison with other cities' educational systems." In fact, by the 1930s San Antonio's ranked among the most progressive vocational training programs in the country.[6] The educational leaders of San Antonio understood the important relationship of labor, business, and education as the fulcrum for modernization. They also understood the progressive emphasis on ordering, stabilizing, and standardizing society.

The School Board consequently recognized and acted in accordance with the city's cultural and industrial needs because it recognized the reality of the large Mexican population of the city: "Spanish is a living language in San Antonio. Because of the nearness of the city to Mexico, the language will always be used by a considerable portion of the population for commercial and social purposes." By the second decade of the twentieth century, there were already nine thousand Mexican students in San Antonio, particularly in Navarro, González, Ruiz, Barclay, Johnson, Brackenridge Memorial, and Washington Irving elementary schools. The School Board, therefore, authorized the schools to teach these children Spanish beginning in the first grade in an attempt to overcome their "retardation." All subjects, as a result, were taught in Spanish and English. Spanish, moreover, was considered so important that it was taught throughout the school district, but it was begun in the fifth grade for non–Spanish-speaking children. The School Board appropriated eight thousand dollars a year for the teaching of Spanish in the elementary school and urged the schools to use the local Spanish newspaper, *La Prensa*, because it was a valuable teaching tool. Consequently, the second generation of Mexicans became educated not only in English, but in Spanish as well. Although the School Board pursued an Americanization philosophy, it nevertheless was educating Mexicans in a bicultural manner; the result was an aveune for a Mexican American mentality.[7]

dren in the West Side, leading to not only residential and cultural segregation but educational as well. This "school retardation" was seen as a problem, because many of the children were non–English speaking and only "average" in intelligence. Because of these findings, the School Board declared that "the course of study, we are coming to see quite clearly should be different for different races and classes of people."[8]

Because of this philosophy, schools in the Mexican Quarter were to establish a new curriculum that was different from that of non-Mexican children. School census records included new categories of information to be placed in the students' records: race, nationality, and mental condition. A vocational orientation, not a professional orientation, segregation, not integration, and a retardation category, not a progressive one were established as the philosophical cornerstones for the Mexican student population. This orientation was destined to have a great impact on Mexican children throughout the 1930s. The School Board, with the best intentions in mind, asked the other school districts, as well as the parochial schools, to follow its lead.[9]

All of the ideological attitudes and beliefs that were institutionalized by 1929 in the San Antonio public schools had a tremendous psychological impact on the consciousness of the second and third generations of Mexicans and the immigrants. They were led to believe in the mental retardation and inferiority of their children; the trainability but not educational ability of their children; and that the educational segregation of Mexicans was necessary. In essence, the school district wanted an Americanization and a vocational program for Mexicans because the city needed skilled and semiskilled English-speaking Mexican Americans, not unskilled Spanish-speaking ones. The overall result was the production of skilled and semiskilled middle-class–oriented Mexican Americans by 1941.

The local educational philosophy was supported by numerous studies written between 1900 and 1932 that concluded that the Mexican child was different from the non-Mexican. In fact, these IQ studies did seem to show that Mexican children were inferior. In 1922, for example, Kimball Young, a prominent educator, published a study that had a tremendous impact on the educational system in the Southwest and in San Antonio in particular. Young proposed different teaching approaches for students who were retarded, normal, superior, and foreign. For the foreigners, he proposed Americanization programs with English at the core and vocational programs at the periphery "to train them for occupational efficiency and the proper American habits and attitudes that make for social cooperation."[10]

By the 1930s San Antonio had a wide variety of local colleges, public schools, private schools, parochial and business schools that reflected various educational philosophies. Specifically, there were six colleges (three Catholic), forty-five elementary schools (forty-two for whites — Mexicans included — and three specifically for blacks), six senior high schools and ten junior high schools, five private schools, and over thirty business schools, which offered art to cosmetology to tailoring to secretarial work. Throughout the city there was a policy of de jure segregation for blacks, but only de facto segregation for Mexicans.

This policy, however, did not overtly affect the educational-commercial school system in San Antonio. The system was supported by the public library system, which had several branches throughout the city, including one in the middle-class Mexican area of Prospect Hill and one in the Latin American Center, located closer to the downtown area. In addition, the West Side had a "private" Mexican library, and in the late 1930s the new Bexar County Library was built for the public housing units at the Apache-Alazán Courts.

Because of the wide variety of schools, universities, and libraries, the city boasted by 1941 that "San Antonio [was] the center of intellectual and cultural life in Texas."[11] In spite of this boast, the city, in fact, increased its education and health budget by only 7 percent, from $2,805,000 in 1937 to $2,615,000 in 1938. This was much lower than the education budget had been in 1931: $3,806,209. It was a matter of decreasing interest in education and, most of all, the effect of the Depression. The education and health budgets were the first to be cut.[12]

Nevertheless, all of these educational institutions, as early as 1911 and regardless of their orientation, acknowledged the importance of the city's Mexican heritage and recognized the importance of Mexico's proximity. Consequently, courses in Latin American history and culture were part of the curriculum, and the teaching of Spanish was initiated in most schools, especially after the building of the Pan American Highway connecting the United States and Mexico in 1936. This recognition of the large Mexican population and its importance

population in the senior high schools was Mexican, of a total San Antonio population of 265,000, of which close to 90,000 were Mexicans. By 1930 there was some increase in the junior and senior high school Mexican population; of 5,567 junior high school students, there were 1,351 Mexicans (24.2 percent of the student population). In high school the figures remained low: 330 Spanish-surnamed students out of a student population of 3,582 (9.2 percent).[13] Table 7 shows the junior and senior high school breakdown in 1928.

TABLE 7

Mexican Students in San Antonio's Junior and Senior High Schools, 1928

School	Enrollment	Mexicans	% of Total
Brackenridge High	1,866	120	6.4
Main Avenue High	1,662	210	12.6
Total	3,528	330	9.3
Emerson Junior High	632	86	13.6
Harris Junior High	578	130	22.5
Howth Junior High	673	89	13.2
Irving Junior High	725	290	40.0
Lanier Junior High	602	533	88.5
Page Junior High	883	133	15.0
Poe Junior High	606	46	7.6
Twain Junior High	868	44	5.1
Total	5,567	1,351	24.3

SOURCE: T. H. Shelby and J. O. Marberry, *A Study of the Building Needs of San Antonio Senior High Schools*, p. 11.

There were a number of public schools in the West Side that were almost entirely Mexican, and at the elementary level, five schools were predominantly Mexican: González, 98.7 percent; Ruiz, 98.6 percent; Johnson, 98.5 percent; Navarro, 98.4 percent, and Barclay, 98.4 percent. In addition, Washington Irving, which had been 40.0 percent Mexican in 1928, was by 1941, 81.3 percent Mexican. Also, during the 1930s, Sidney Lanier High School became a combined junior and senior high school, changing the school's enrollment from 88.0 percent Mexican in 1928, to 96.7 percent in 1940.[14]

A comparison of Sidney Lanier with two other senior high schools — Brackenridge (a predominantly Anglo school) and Wheatley (black) — showed that from 1935 through 1939 there were 234 dropouts at Lanier and only 166 graduates; 1,039 left Brackenridge and 2,408 graduated; 322 dropped out of Wheatley and 626 graduated.[15]

The large enrollment of Mexican students in the San Antonio public high schools was due to the city's excellent vocational curriculum in both junior and senior high schools. The vocational orientation of Sidney Lanier High School in the West Side stood out as an example of the opportunities that awaited "foreigners" to help them integrate into the economy of the city. In El Paso, another Texas city with a large Mexican population, there was also an orientation toward providing Mexicans with a predominantly vocational training program. The El Paso Vocational School and the Smelter Vocational School were two of the principal institutions for this training. In Los Angeles similar schools could be found in the Mexican sections of the city.

Regardless of the city, if there were many Mexicans, educational philosophy was oriented toward vocational training, since Mexicans were the principal source of labor for the Southwest's modernization. In San Antonio, Sidney Lanier and the San Antonio Vocational Technical High School served this function. Although these two schools also provided a nonvocational curriculum, their main purpose was to "teach the student to think and to develop in him habits of study, the power of self-help, the capacity to learn habits of work, and attitudes necessary for his future success." The philosophical aim was "to prepare the student to become a good citizen, and a satisfactory worker and a wage earner in industrial or commercial fields." But, as was noted by one school, "this does not, however, exclude him from going to college should he desire to do so" (and some of the Mexicans did, although very few). The curriculum of these vocational schools was divided into academic, commercial, part-time cooperative, and trade and industrial.[16]

This educational separation and emphasis on vocational education helped to develop in the consciousness of both the Mexican and the

non-Mexican population the image and myth of the Mexican as someone who was only suited to be (almost as a result of genetic makeup)
a semiskilled or skilled worker, this in addition to the already-held
view of the Mexican as only a laborer or an agricultural worker. Nevertheless, the vocational programs helped to develop a lower middle
class that had skills, aspirations, a work ethic, and a hunger for success. But above all, they instilled a consciousness of Americanism; an
idealism was engendered in Mexicans who basically lived only in a

of these beliefs, de facto segregation was common in San Antonio
schools and throughout the Southwest for Mexican schoolchildren.

English as a second language was considered imperative, because
often more than 90 percent of the Mexican children in Texas could
not speak English. The San Antonio public schools recognized this
need and, as a result, the city's educational system was noted throughout the decade for its teaching of English as well as for its exceptional
vocational training program. The city's development of the first
English-as-a-second-language program was initiated by Elma N. Neal.
She published the very popular Open Door Series, which emphasized
sentences rather than words and conversation rather than reading.
This teaching method was a pedagogical innovation and focused national attention on San Antonio's public school system. Neal's objective was to immerse the Mexican child in a sea of English, which
would produce not only speech skills, but a consciousness change—
thinking in English.[17]

In spite of this educational orientation toward developing functional skills, the work ethic, and skill in the English language, the
city's separate curricula and its de facto segregation of Mexican children disturbed the rising Mexican middle class, although it saw some
positive aspects. As one teacher observed as early as 1925,

> It is a fact that the better class of Mexicans regard the policy of having
> separate schools for Mexican children as a social discrimination against
> them. Nevertheless, it is true that where there is a large percent of Mexi-
> cans, it is to the advantage of the Mexican children to maintain sepa-
> rate schools for them; because first, teachers, textbooks, and methods

can be selected with a view of meeting the needs of the children, and second, the Mexican children will be freer and happier and will attend during a larger period of years.[18]

Whether these educational advantages overcame ethnic segregation was something the middle class had to consider. By the late 1930s and early 1940s, middle-class Mexican families, however, did object to this segregaton, largely because of the growth between 1936 and 1939 of the Mexican student population. Yet as early as 1931 LULAC, representing the attitudes of some of the middle class, was fighting against segregation not because it did not see the value of its own schools, especially Catholic schools, but because it was an issue that could serve as a vehicle for battling U.S. racial prejudice. As R. de la Garza, a LULAC leader stated, *We must battle [educational] segregation because of race prejudices* [his emphasis]![19]

In spite of the problems, prejudices, and reservations, from 1938 to 1940 the Mexican student population increased by 2 percent at the elementary school level, and by 6 percent at the senior high level (table 8). Consequently, there were more families who had school-age children and were sending them to school. Moreover, there was more "educational consciousness" because of LULAC activity during the 1930s.[20]

The Mexican school-age population doubled between 1924 and 1939. A fifteen-year survey showed that there were 14,796 Mexican students enrolled in 1924; by 1939 the number had increased to 28,881, out of a total school population of 53,428, while all other groups, except blacks, had remained virtually static. In 1924 Mexican students constituted 38.99 percent of the city's total school population; by 1939 the Mexican student population showed a marked increase at the ju-

TABLE 8

Mexican Student Population at Sidney Lanier and Navarro, 1938–40

School	% Mexicans	Total Enrollment	Average Daily Attendance	% of Total
1938–39 school year				
Sidney Lanier Sr.	96.0	407	370.6	91.1
Sidney Lanier Jr.	96.0	1,248	1,092.8	87.6
Navarro Elementary	98.4	1,761	1,468.9	83.4
1939–40 school year				
Sidney Lanier Sr.	96.7	499	448.5	89.9
Sidney Lanier Jr.	96.7	1,214	1,058.4	87.2
Navarro Elementary	98.4	1,774	1,468.9	82.8

SOURCE: Castillo, "Educational Handicaps," p. 29.

nior and senior high school levels. In junior high schools the number of Mexicans increased from 34 percent to 48.4 percent of the total school population; in the senior high schools, it increased from 18 percent to 24.1 percent. There was, for example, a 200 Mexican student increase at Lanier High School. In contrast, the elementary school population increased by only 3.5 percent.

This overall increase was an indication of the success that the Mexican middle class in general, and the League of United Latin Ameri-

There was a pyramidal educational structure in the Mexican community: more children in elementary school than at the junior or senior high school level. This paralleled the Mexican community's class stratification. While there was a certain commitment to education in San Antonio, especially as it benefited the industrial community, this pyramidal structure was no different from that of the United States as a whole, because only elementary school education was being emphasized for all in the 1930s; high school was for relatively few. Overall, a high school diploma was the exception not the rule. A college degree was something beyond most Americans. Nevertheless, because of the Mexican population's size and integral role in the city's economy, there were more educational programs directed toward the West Side community than might have been expected.

With this increase in educational opportunities during the 1930s, Mexican children were constantly bombarded by two lifestyles: a non-Mexican and a Mexican. As a result, whether in the first or second generation, whether foreign- or native-born, some cultural conflict occurred. This problem was exacerbated by the other beliefs and problems that Mexican children often confronted in their everyday life: uneven knowledge of Spanish and English; low socio-economic status; inferior school opportunities; the belief, conscious or subconscious, that inferiority was hereditary; and the common assumption of teachers, principals, and school superintendents that Mexicans were "lacking in ambition not only for improvement in school, but in improving their conditions of life."[22]

In spite of this multiplicity of problems, one Mexican schoolteacher

TABLE 9
Percentage Mexican Students in San Antonio's Elementary
and Secondary Schools, 1939

School	% Mexicans
Elementary schools	
González	98.7
Ruiz	98.6
Johnson	98.5
Navarro	98.4
J. T. Brackenridge	98.4
Barclay	98.4
De Zavala	96.3
Hood	95.7
Margil	93.0
Sam Houston	90.2
Bowie	89.7
Crockett	87.2
Ivanhoe	86.2
Burnett	83.7
Austin	77.6
Nelson	74.5
Brisco	67.8
Ogden	64.5
Collins Garden	53.1
Junior high schools	
Sidney Lanier	96.7
Irving	81.3
Harris	55.9
High schools	
Sidney Lanier	96.7
S.A. Vocational & Technical	42.0

SOURCE: *San Antonio Express*, October 13, 1939, p. 12.

believed that there was only one central problem. Henrietta Castillo stated that the "irregularity of attendance and the drop-out mortality of the Spanish-speaking child are due to economic causes." It was her contention that the economic problem was the greatest single cause of the Mexican child's dropout rate, "retardation," and "lack of ambition" in the U.S. schools. This differed, needless to say, from the schools' assessment.[23]

The situation, of course, was not helped by the fact that San Antonio's 1930 per capita spending on education was lower than all the major cities in the state. San Antonio spent $8.72 per child in comparison with El Paso's $9.46, Houston's $10.75, and Dallas's $11.6. The Boston Public School District spent $19.19.

Education, regardless of city, was not a top priority in Texas. Nevertheless, teachers' salaries were relatively high in San Antonio. In 1932–33 the annual minimum was $600; in 1935–36 salaries ranged from $900 to $1,926, while the average was $1,414 for the fourteen hundred public school teachers in the city.

The salary attracted teachers, but some, especially the young ones who attempted to teach in the Mexican schools, had one main problem. They often simply followed the textbook closely and let the book

aware of both the potential and the possibilities of Mexican children, however, even though they were, for the most part, seen as socially separate and intellectually different from non-Mexicans.[24]

The teachers' perspective (even though well intentioned) and the lack of proper materials contributed to the illiteracy and dropout rate among Mexicans. According to the 1930 census, 7.7 percent of San Antonio's population of ten years of age or over could not read or write; of these, almost nine-tenths were Mexican. But as the 1930s progressed, illiteracy decreased as more Mexicans went to school. However, although more Mexican children attended school, they attended only long enough to learn how to read and write English. Unfortunately, the reduction in illiteracy was more prominent in the middle class than among the laboring class, especially the pecan workers. Nevertheless, their consciousness changed through the acquisition of the English language.[25]

Raymond Brewer, the principal at Sidney Lanier High School, analyzed this problem in 1936. He estimated that 3,000 Mexican children of school age in San Antonio had never entered school, and that only one-half to two-thirds of those entering elementary school finished the fifth grade, despite the increasing number of Mexicans entering school during the 1930s. Many of the pecan shellers' and agricultural workers' children had either no schooling or only a year or two. "The principal reason," stated Brewer, "was poverty and shifting migrant patterns and seasonable work." One school in the West Side showed that the school population varied from 240 in September to 1,499 in February, because of the shifting migrant patterns. In particular, a 1938 case study of pecan shellers' children in San Antonio showed that out of 867 children between seven and eighteen years of age, only 55 percent had attended a full school term and, in fact, only 62 percent had attended school at all that year. This study also showed that 217 children of migrating workers were handicapped to an even greater extent than the 650 children of agricultural families who permanently resided in the West Side. In the migrant group, 22 percent of the children eleven to thirteen years old did not attend school at all during 1938; but in the nonmigrant agricultural group, only 11 percent did not. In addition, almost one-sixth of the pecan shellers' children aged eight to nine had never attended or had never completed the first grade. The average school attainment of ten-year-old children in the pecan shellers' families was only 2.7 grades, of the thirteen year olds, 4.9 grades; for the eighteen-year-old category (total 82), only 5 percent had ever completed even one grade in school. Only 62 percent of these families' children had completed even one to five years of school; 29 percent had completed six to eight years; only 4 percent had completed the first year of senior high school; none had completed the eleventh grade or graduated. In fact, the average grade attainment for the Mexican pecan shellers' eighteen-year-old children was 5.2 grades.[26]

Although there was educational improvement throughout the Mexican community in the 1930s, it was clear that the agricultural workers and pecan shellers did not really benefit. Education, even though it was seen by the city, the *ricos*, and the middle class as positive, was not a democratizing agent; instead, it reinforced the social stratification of the community. The upper and middle classes received more education than the laboring sectors, but the English language did affect the community as a whole and began to serve as a factor in changing the majority of Mexicans to Mexican Americans regardless of class. Only in this sense was education a common denominator. Language and acculturation knew no class boundaries, but the acquisition of knowledge did.

Increased enrollment numbers throughout West Side public schools in the 1930s directly affected the general growth of the public school system, especially in terms of the need for more facilities and programs. However, only by sheer numbers did Mexicans have an impact on the school system. The school district, on the other hand, had a constant ideological impact on both the non-Mexican and the Mexican generations growing up in the 1930s, specifically in the way they viewed each other. Non-Mexicans adhered to a wide range of views. Some, for example, held to the stereotype that Mexicans lacked intelligence, that they fought instead of worked, that they were a nuisance rather than an asset, and that their minds often revealed

great inconsistencies. Many others held a somewhat harsher, but patronizing, attitude, propagandized by a leading writer: "Scratch a
Mexican and you find cruelty; caress him and you encounter senti-
mentality, piety, and generosity." Others, however, especially businesspeople, felt that Mexicans were "America's greatest opportunity."[27]

Still others held a class view rather than a racial one. H. T. Manuel, quoting these statements in his study of Mexicans and their educational and psychological problems, wrote that these Americans felt

gible to better society.

There were still other non-Mexicans in San Antonio, however, as
Manuel wrote, whose "community sentiment frequently is either indifferent or actually antagonistic toward the schooling of Mexican
children. But [who] sometimes, [believe that] special facilities . . .
[should be] provided, i.e. vocational training."[28]

James K. Harris, the principal of Navarro Elementary School, decided to divide the Mexican community and its children into four
groups to conduct an educational and sociological study in 1927 to
test the validity of these same attitudes. The first group was the middle-
class "Spanish" and Mexican families who owned their own homes
and were in business or in the professions. "The children of this middle class are of normal intelligence and normally enter the school
promptly," wrote Harris. The second group was composed of the families that had arrived during the previous twenty-five years, but who
still rented their homes and were, for the most part, manual laborers. "The children of this laboring class show retardation and seldom
go beyond the fourth grade." The third group consisted of the transient agricultural families "whose work residence is wherever work
is to be found." The children of these urban and rural migrants, who
lived part time in San Antonio, "attend school only a few weeks out
of the year and are greatly retarded." The *ricos* made up the fourth
group. These families, Harris believed, were San Antonio's temporary visitors and political refugees. "The children of this group are
few," wrote Harris, "but, nevertheless, they attend school regularly,
learn English rapidly and do good work."[29]

Harris's study showed that Mexicans in San Antonio were not a homogeneous group; consequently, the broadly held views of non-Mexicans were unfounded generalizations, since the Mexican community was ideologically complex, economically separated, and pluralistic in nature. There did appear to be a broad Mexican "consciousness of collectivity" and shared "habits of the heart," however. As a result of this disparity, Harris believed that the educational system in San Antonio should reformulate its teaching, because the laboring-class children tended to suffer the most from these differences in views.

The children of the middle class and the *ricos* suffered very little in school. It was mostly the laboring-class children, according to one teacher, who suffered from the stereotyped image of them, from hunger, nervousness, sickness, who were often "fatigued by the continuous struggle of trying to keep body and soul together." These children were "robbed of [their] childhood by premature work and responsibility."[30]

Almost all of the children, however, regardless of class, experienced a cultural gap between themselves and their parents, because many parents clung "with tenacity to the old cultural ways." This varied not only by generation but by the number of years the family had lived in the United States, its class, and its degree of acculturation. On the one hand, one observer pointed out in the 1930s, "the Mexican child was drawn with almost pathetic reverence and devotion towards the [non-Mexican] teacher" and the non-Mexican culture that the teacher offered. Consequently, "from the outside [it] looks like a shower of fabulous blessings of worldly goods" to the Mexican child. On the other hand, the child was drawn to the culture of his or her parents. This caused a "constant contrast that soon generates a conflict between two cultural patterns and levels between older and younger generations." Furthermore, "in school there was a constant friction between the Mexican and the American student, and in the predominant Mexican schools on the West Side there was a constant conflict between the lower class [Mexican] child and the Americanized Mexican-American child."[31]

As if Mexican children did not experience enough conflict — between classes, between ethnic groups, between cultures, and between languages — they were extremely sensitive to the attitude of the majority of the English speaking who surrounded them and who posed, consciously or not, as a superior race. This caused a sense of inferiority within the Mexican child in San Antonio as well as a sense "of insecurity," of not belonging. "Consequently," wrote Castillo, a schoolteacher in the late thirties, "the Mexican child develops with increasing age an increasingly strong inferiority feeling that adheres to him for life, tormenting him always, regardless of how hard he tries to right himself in the eyes of the [non-Mexican] people who do not even notice his struggle and his effort. Very few survive this process of [self]-inferiority."[32]

Some teachers recognized that Mexicans could get through school, especially to the fifth grade, which was the last elementary school grade in the San Antonio public schools. A report to the assistant superintendent of education in San Antonio on January 21, 1938, in-

sion to [the Mexican students'] yearning for imaginative ideals, crude though their expression may be."[33]

Although Fuller's attitude predetermined what she saw as the Mexican nature, she was sincere and ultimately liberalizing within the view of American progressivism. Another teacher, a Miss Lozano, pointed out the "Horatio Alger" success story of one particular laboring-class child to establish the fact that it was possible for Mexicans to succeed. A Mexican youth whose widowed mother worked at a cigar factory was her example. This boy graduated with honors from high school, although the family was so poor that he had to borrow a suit for the graduation excercises.[34]

Belief in the possibility of educational success for Mexican children was also given impetus by the constant support of a few principals on the West Side, like William Knox. Knox believed in the innate intelligence and capabilities of the Mexican child. He saw no substantive differences between the intellectual characteristics of Mexican and non-Mexican students. "Such differences," he said, "are a mere matter of degree, and a minor degree at that." According to Knox, Mexican children made rapid progress in the elementary grades just as non-Mexican students did. He observed that Mexican children spoke Spanish in the early grades, but in the later grades they spoke English.[35]

Knox, like many other teachers, sought to instill in the Mexican student a pride in U.S. ways without detracting from Mexican culture. On one occasion, Knox recalled, Mexican students refused to salute the U.S. flag, but he pointed out to them that saluting the flag was just a "compliment to a nation, and not a disavowal of the allegiance one might owe to another nation." Overall, Knox sought to impress on the Mexican students the idea that accepting an emphasis on functionalism and equality was only the basis for forming a dual but equal Mexican and U.S. consciousness and ideology, and not a negation of Mexican culture and persona.[36]

In addition to sensitive and helpful local teachers and principals, many others did research in San Antonio to better understand the Mexican children. In fact, the views of the local Mexican and American teachers reflected the changing doctrines and research agendas in the university and college communities throughout the United States. In San Antonio many researchers focused on the intelligence and teachability of Mexican children, and many Master's theses during this period focused on these issues. Willie Brown, for example, in a 1934 study entitled "The Knowledge of Social Standards among Mexican and Non-Mexican Children," concluded that the language handicap was not very important. The main reason for the Mexicans' educational "retardation" was their lower degree of native mental capacity. Nevertheless, Brown believed that the IQ level could be raised by a better economic environment. In contrast, Aurora M. González in a 1932 study had already shown the close relationship between poverty, low IQ, and retarded mental development, but she had not stressed, as Brown would, a lower mental capacity. González stated that if socioeconomic conditions were improved, Mexicans' IQs would not differ from those of their non-Mexican counterparts of the same socioeconomic level.[37] Katherine Mequire, in a study of an elementary school, stated that schools in the West Side should provide a guide to proper health habits, including balanced diets, and adequate rest, and to simple table manners, conversational skills at table, and the idea of "sleep[ing] alone." If all of these cultural changes were introduced to the Mexican children through the educational system, Mequire said, they would "carry over into the homes where usually too many people occupy too little floor space." Mequire further urged San Antonio's schoolteachers to stress various types of houses and lifestyles around the world to show the Mexican children "how homes are kept clean and attractive." Mequire sought to introduce American middle-class mores, customs, and values through the children into the homes. Equality, mobility, and middle class status for the Mexicans in San Antonio was not only a pursuit and goal of LULAC, but, it seems, of some non-Mexican educators as well.[38]

Because of the interest of many schoolteachers in acculturating the Mexican children, their growing numbers in school, and LULAC's activities, a drive began among West Side parents as early as 1934 to improve the educational facilities in their community. They wanted to improve the educational system just as much as the "sensitive" teachers and administrators in the academic community did, but their approach was more concrete. On December 14, 1934, for example, they formed the Liga Pro-Defensa Escolar (the School Defense League). It consisted of more than fifty social, civic, commercial, and religious organizations that united to better the educational facilities and teaching quality in the West Side schools, as well as to combat the racial

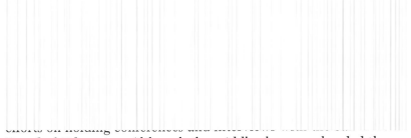

Board of Education. Although the middle class spearheaded the organization, it tried to gain the support of the laboring class as well.

A prominent lawyer and local leader, Gustavo García, a product of the San Antonio Public Schools and the University of Texas, was in the forefront of this drive for educational reforms. Speeches and publicity were intended to indict the school system for its failures: "[In the] West Side the schools are wood and in deplorable condition inside while the rest of the city schools are in good condition. In fact, in many cases they are virtually palaces [compared with the West Side schools]." Garcia also accused the San Antonio School Board of insensitivity to the Mexican plight because members had refused to speak to LULAC on school matters.[39]

The controversy continued between educators and the community. Although there were some improvements, the structural and pedagogical problems remained basically the same in the "Mexican" schools. For example, the key problems the School Defense League would later address were evident as early as 1928, when a comparative study was done between two elementary schools — Margil, an almost all-Mexican school, and W. J. Fannin, a mixed school (80 percent Anglo, 19.2 percent Mexican) — showed many differences in student accomplishment. Margil had a higher dropout rate as students progressed from first to fifth grade and the teachers often passed the Mexican students from one grade to the next because they "understood" that their abilities were hindered by "just being" Mexican. At Margil students progressed at a pace that was uneven and usually dependent on two factors: their ability to learn English, and the stability of their home life. The Mexican students at Fannin, however, progressed steadily from one grade to the next because they came from stable middle-class homes. Many students at Margil became frustrated and left school, unlike those at Fannin. A major problem at Margil, but not at Fannin, was the students' age; at Margil the students were usually two years older in the lower grades than their counterparts at Fannin. Moreover, it was found that, on the whole, Mexican children were handicapped by not knowing English and by not being completely fluent in Spanish. Both languages posed problems, as many teachers agreed. "Language difficulty," a teacher indicated, "does have a bearing on their intelligence scores." Ironically, the Mexicans from Margil tested slightly higher than their middle-class counterparts at Fannin. Overall, however, non-Mexican students seemed to be doing better than the Mexican lower-class and middle-class students. In addition, Mexican customs and close-knit Mexican communities were also considered major obstacles.[40]

Mequire's study, in contrast, looked at different factors. It reported that non-Mexican children tested higher than Mexican children probably because the "American children live in better homes. The fathers do more professional and skilled work. American families take more newspapers, [and] American parents are more literate than Mexicans." The reality, however, was probably a combination, and the School Defense League sought to address these problems through knowledge, criticism, and pressure group politics.[41]

Regardless of all of the political activities and the comparative studies, learning English, having pride, and developing self-confidence continued to be the key factors in the Mexicans' learning, developing, and progressing. Lucy Claire Hoard of the El Paso Public Schools stated that "teachers should make sure they encourage English; the Mexican child in order to feel equal . . . must be able to employ the vital language tool as skillfully [as the non-Mexican child], and in order to do this, he must not be afraid to practice." "Teachers," another said, "must develop the Mexicans' self-confidence and show no social discrimination" toward them. "Above all, teachers were reminded that they must establish [new] habits of thinking and expression in a new language" in the Mexican children.[42] Elma Neal, the director of elementary education in San Antonio and the initiator of the direct immersion method of teaching English, stated the pedagogical method very succinctly: "It cannot be stressed too strongly to teachers of Mexican children that they are primarily teachers of language." Katherine Mequire stated the overall philosophy very bluntly:

> Teachers must develop the Mexicans' admiration for America, as a nation through patriotic exercises, flag salutes, stirring patriotic songs,

and plays. The Mexican will experience a feeling of joy in the thought that they are a part of the great nation and that they can contribute towards its growth. But, [teachers should also] recognize Mexico as a Sister Republic by [displaying] the Mexican flag, [having] Mexican articles in the classrooms, and [recognizing] Mexican holidays as well as American. The Mexicans must be made to see that they are not being urged to lose their social identity, but that they are valued for it. Mexicans keenly resent the thought that they are being forced to desert their race to become American citizens. Show them that their ways though

emphasis on developing the students' personal pride and their industrial abilities. Because of their numbers in San Antonio, their importance to the city's economy, and the city's Spanish and Mexican history and zeitgeist, there had to be a concession, however, a dualistic identity as Mexican Americans.

Mequire's philosophy and Neal's methods of teaching English established the ideological and pedagogical approach to educating the Mexican.[44] The schools in San Antonio thus approached the teaching of Mexican children with these goals in mind: (1) to encourage self-pride and to teach Mexicans about their culture; (2) to instill patriotism toward the United States and the English language and pride in the United States; and (3) to teach industrial skills through vocational education. If these goals were met, Mexicans could better participate in and contribute to the San Antonio economy. The Public School District, in other words, sought to make the Mexicans politically and philosophically Americans, yet simultaneously to retain their Mexican culture and lifestyle.

Of course, time brought cultural changes, but in the meantime there was change within continuity, and stability within adjustment via the educational institution. This was the same task the middle class, through LULAC, wanted to accomplish among the large Mexican laboring class. Both the schools and LULAC, in essence, wanted the Mexican population to be both American and Mexican. The public schools, consequently, played a dual role, as transmitter of American change, and conserver of Mexican tradition. As a result of this approach, many of the Mexican students who graduated from the local high schools knew how to speak English, but they continued to maintain their Mexican consciousness, thereby reflecting the philosophy of the schools. Their social and cultural activities, their families, and their general community activities kept them close to the Mexican tradition.

Regardless of the problems in the schools or in the community, there were, in fact, many Mexican graduates from all social classes, as the following examples show. Isabel Hernández was a 1930 graduate from Main Avenue High School, and belonged to the Club Hispano-Americano and Le Circle Français. Also graduating from Main Avenue High School were José Vargas and Narcisco de la Garza, the president of the Club Hispano-Americano. Among other graduates from this high school were Rogelio Flores, who finished in three years; Mercedes Alcocer, who received a scholarship to Alamo Business College; Ernesto Vargas; Andrés de la Garza; Beatriz Saenz, winner of the literary prize; and Narcisco Castillo, who won high honors.

Throughout the 1930s the number of Mexicans who graduated from the San Antonio schools was small in comparison with the number of non-Mexicans. In 1935, for example, of a total senior graduating class of 1,236 in the public schools, there were 15 (out of 531 seniors) Mexicans graduated from Jefferson High school; 34 at Sidney Lanier; 21 (out of 421 seniors) at Brackenridge; and approximately 250 from San Antonio Vocational and Technical High School, for a total of 320. In addition to the high school graduates, there were a number of college graduates. In 1937 there were also 4 Mexican women out of 53 who graduated from Our Lady of the Lake High School. All 4, María Peña, Gloria Lozano, Josefina Martínez, and Christina Carvajal, belonged to the upper middle class.

For the Mexican students who could not continue school during the day or who just wanted extra lessons, there was the Main Avenue Night School. Its evening classes in English were extremely popular, according to Prof. L. W. Fox. Fox had high praise for the Mexican students because they "love[d] to study" and were very "punctual" and "intellectual"; in fact, he said that "the majority of . . . [Mexicans] are young with great ambition and pay special attention to learning English in order to struggle for better lives in the United States. Mexicans are most appreciative of the night school." Thirty percent of the night students were Mexican in 1930 and attended classes three times a week.[45]

Although the numbers of Mexican students throughout the public school system increased in the mid-thirties, Mexican students usually socialized apart from non-Mexican students. Segregation existed by choice and because of common interests and differences. At Brackenridge High School, for example, Mexican students formed the Hidalgos Club in 1926, which continued into the 1930s. Its purpose was to study Spanish, discuss Cervantes and other Spanish writers, and just to meet together as Mexicans. Students from Main High School also joined the Hidalgos. Other students at Main, however, organized the Club Hispano-Americano, and at Sidney Lanier they had the Leaders Club and the Student Council. In fact, at Sidney Lanier the majority of organizations were for the Mexcian students, since the school

teachers used Latin American rather than Spanish

was tantamount to Mexican American. But regardless of what they called themselves, the Mexican students found a collective consciousness and a sense of social-cultural unity in their school clubs, their church activities, and even in infrequent "political" demonstrations. History was moving them toward acculturation, however.[47]

In December, 1934, Mexican and non-Mexican Catholic school students demonstrated to protest Mexico's new educational plan. Mexican students formed the Unión Espiritual and demanded that Cordell Hull, the secretary of state, J. Daniels, the ambassador to Mexico, Congress and the archbishop of San Antonio lodge formal protests against Mexico's plan to secularize education.[48] The Catholic school system did not usually tolerate political organizations or demonstrations such as this, but secularization of education in Mexico was considered of such importance that the organizations and demonstrations were allowed.

In the 1930s the Catholic schools educated most of the Mexican upper class. It was easier to become *gente decente* with a parochial school education than with a public school education. The Mexican upper class usually sent its children to St. Mark's Elementary School, then to Central Catholic High School, and then to Our Lady of the Lake or St. Mary's University. Sometimes the University of Texas was chosen. Some prosperous Mexicans, however, chose not to send their children to parochial secondary schools; instead they sent them to Jefferson High School in the Prospect Hill area, or to Brackenridge. The general Mexican student population, however, went to Sidney Lanier or to San Antonio Vocational and Technical High School.

Of eighteen thousand Mexican Catholic students, only two thousand were registered in parochial schools in 1930. This worried the Catholic Church and Archbishop Drossaert. He, therefore, announced to those sixteen thousand who went to public schools that "there is not God at home [and] not God at school. My heart bleeds when thinking . . . [of you]. Any wonder so many Mexican homes are amongst the sad daily records of sin and crime." Drossaert then called for more catechism lessons for these children.[49]

Throughout the 1920 and 1930s, the Catholic Church in San Antonio was very disturbed about the impact of U.S. mass culture and secular education on the Mexican and non-Mexican Catholic community. As early as 1928, Archbishop Drossaert agonized over the "family problems, mass moral dangers, the breakdown of all [behavioral] conventions, suggestive movies, high-powered automobiles, elaborate parties, the breakdown of all social conventions that served to guard Christian morals and decency." This situation was even more alarming in San Antonio because Drossaert and the church believed that the "public schools can not control . . . these dangers . . . because of its exclusion of God." "The answer," exclaimed Drossaert, "is in attending Catholic school and [there is] no possible solution . . . [except] this. Religion and morality cannot be picked up somewhere or somehow, it must be taught just like grammar, arithmetic, and taught by a slow and persistent effort."[50]

This attitude toward the "acids of modernity," as Walter Lippman called them, persisted throughout the thirties and "was exacerbated by the crisis and radicalism of the Depression decade." As Joseph J. Quinn, speaking to the Catholic Press Association in 1936, said, "at no time in the history of the United States has there been a greater need for the presentation, absorption, and influence of Catholic teaching. National unrest and social maladjustment are corroding the pillars of our country."[51] The Catholic Church in San Antonio sought to save Americans in general, but Mexicans in particular, from these social and moral "corrosions" of modernity and radicalism.

In San Antonio, then, the Catholic Church advocated that the main hope for the church, the country, and Christ was the success of the parochial schools, because "through the school we reach the children and through them the parents." Overall, the church realized that Mexican children must be enrolled in the Catholic schools because Sunday catechism lessons alone were just not enough. In particular, the church believed that the "Mexicans want a separate education for their children. They do not like [the] promiscuous [public school] education. If this could be accomplished we would need a school for 2,000." "In the public schools," the church believed, "the Mexicans would learn only the sins of the Americans and not the virtues and even lose their religion with time." Moreover, it was the church's belief that, most of all, the Mexican laboring class attending the public schools would acquire only a "thin veneer of American ways and manners," but a "large dose of false pride and a superiority complex." This would propel the Mexican child, the church felt, into "that class of Tejanos [middle-class Mexicans born and reared in Texas] too often cold and indifferent to the [Catholic] faith." Consequently, the main

[Council of Catholic Women], the church taught English classes at] the Catholic Community Center on the West Side to attempt to help the Mexican people "triumph in life," because "they speak English and Spanish, but [are] not masters of either one: English at school; Spanish at home."[53] The church, however, recognized that more was needed than just education and the English language for the Mexicans to succeed in San Antonio, because many non-Mexicans in the city had the perception that every "Mexican . . . is a cut-throat, thief, and bandit." *La Voz* stated that in San Antonio, "Mexican is a term for discrimination and 'desprecio.'" As a result, "the Mexican has been so heavily influenced [by the ideology of his U.S. 'other'] that he now believes that he can't better himself. Thus, we should try to infuse a rational pride of his traditions, his faith and his customs," because the middle class "Mexicans . . . tend to leave the others behind." The church also recognized that its work among the Mexicans was hindered by the social prejudice exhibited by non-Mexican Catholics against Mexican Catholics. The answer, the church hoped, was to end racial prejudice by establishing a system of "free parochial schools." Through this method, Drossaert stated, "our 'Spec Patrae' [Special Family] can get a sound Catholic elementary education and get it free of *All Tuition Charges* [his emphasis]. With this our problem is solved. With this we will renew the face of the earth. With this we will see a fervent Catholic population grow up that will do honor to Mother Church and be a glory to the country."[54] For Archbishop Drossaert and the church, the key to self-pride, civic virtue, Catholic morality, American citizenship, and religious spirituality was a Catholic education, especially for the Mexicans, who could become Americanized but still retain their Mexican traditions. Ironically, the Catholic schools outside of the West Side were segregated during the 1930s and 1940s. Mexican and black children were often refused admission to them outside the West side because of color, race, or poverty.[55]

Elementary-school-age Mexican children thus had the opportunity to attend parochial schools and fulfill Drossaert's aspiration (if they could pay the tuition and were accepted) by attending Our Lady of Guadalupe School and Sacred Heart of Mary School, among others (in spite of Drossaert's wishes, West Side Catholic schools had to charge tuition to exist). If this was impossible, younger schoolchildren, at least, could attend such private institutions as the kindergarten operated by Elías Rodríguez, or the free Saint Anthony Kindergarten. For the extremely poor, who were unable to attend the public, the private, or the parochial schools, there was always Prof. Merced Godiney's private school. Godiney and Sister Carolina offered classes for those Mexican children considered by the regular schools, Catholic or public, to be affected by "incorrigibility, imbecility or . . . from the migratory stream." This school was a two-room shack that required no formal tuition, just a "sack of beans." It had been in operation since 1925 helping the poorer Mexican children.[56]

Throughout the Depression, however, many of the Mexican American middle class and working class sacrificed to pay their children's tuition to the Catholic schools because they understood the value of a Catholic education. The curriculum was often on a par with that of the public schools. In fact, the curriculum of all of the parochial schools met all the requirements prescribed by the Department of Education for elementary instruction, in theory if not completely in practice. In the Mexican Catholic schools, stated a Guadalupe School report in 1938, "English is the language of the school. The Mexican children are learning English rapidly and they speak it in preference to Spanish among themselves. The school children have [also] taken to American sports, and they play baseball, basketball, and football." There was also a troop of Boy Scouts in most of the schools, serving as a transmitter of U.S. and middle-class values and attitudes.

In spite of the emphasis on Americanization, instruction was also given in Spanish, because it was requested by many of the parents. Parents who sent their children to the public schools requested and were granted by the city's Board of Education a summer school for Spanish classes. Therefore, in 1938, Navarro Elementary School held Spanish classes from June through August for all Mexican children from eight to fourteen years of age. The "Castillian language," the school said, would be taught, and in addition vocational training courses would be offered. Many of the upper-middle-class children, however, did not have to attend these summer sessions because they went to summer school or vacationed in Mexico.[57]

Parochial schools, however, were the parents' first choice because they met the state requirements, taught religion, had Spanish summer classes, used English as the main language, and were exclusive and selective. This was exactly what the middle-class desired, especially because it separated them from the Mexican poor.

The Catholic school system's problems, however, were increased

With the Depression, growing acculturation, and LULAC's education drives, parents, especially of the lower middle class, began sending their children to the public schools, where there was no tuition, more classroom space, and "better" educational methods and possible career opportunities. Father Tranchese summarized the problems of the 1930s for the parochial school system in his 1941 Guadalupe Parish Report:

> Our first interest has been the [Catholic] school. But the school [building] was, and is, in bad shape, too small, and dangerous. However, we have tried to carry on the work under the most trying circumstances. There [in the schools] we have tried to take care of the young people, by establishing athletic clubs, music clubs, associations, etc. But, it is all an up-hill work. In fact, big schools for Mexicans are needed, if we expect to get results. The school is the only way of making them good Catholics and good citizens. So far these people are neither Mexicans nor Americans.

The problems of Guadalupe School plagued other Mexican Catholic schools. Nevertheless, some parents, especially the middle-class elite, still favored Catholic school education because it made their children *gente decente*, more "civilized" than the non-Mexican children and certainly more so than the Mexican laboring class.

While the Mexican American generation was being educated throughout the thirties in the San Antonio public and parochial school systems, the adults were not left completely out of the educational process. The *ricos*, through the work of *La Prensa* and the Casa Editorial, constantly advertised a variety of books ranging from boys' books to books on astronomy, geography, botany, and language.[59] If these books were not adequate or interesting, the Mexican laborer, the middle-class clerk, the professional, or the businessperson could go to the Mexican Bookstore on Produce Row, where there was an assortment of Mexican newspapers and periodicals. However, if the Mexican population wanted more detailed information, they went to the Biblioteca Mexicana. This library housed over two thousand volumes, including the *Encyclopedia Universal* (reprinted from the Mexican diplomatic archives), Mexican records, historical documents, and the *Papeles de la Nueva España*. The last were transcripts of manuscripts housed at the National Library in Madrid. The Biblioteca Mexicana also held regular classes for the community on Spanish and Mexican culture and regular lectures and conferences on numerous topics. In addition to these outlets, *La Prensa*'s offices were a place where Mexican adults could ask for information from the newspaper's editor, writers, or simply obtain copies of the paper or of *La Opinión*. Ignacio Lozano stated that while the San Antonio schools— public and parochial—Americanized the Mexican community, the Mexican Bookstore, the Mexican libraries, and the Mexican newspapers all "served to perpetuate the Mexican culture in varying degrees."[60] Lozano understood the importance of a Mexican consciousness of collectivity in a world rapidly becoming Americanized.

The U.S. Department of Education was also interested in the educational level of the entire Mexican community. Therefore, it initiated a Public Affairs Forum series in 1938 to encourage community participation, develop intellectual tolerance and international understanding, as well as to diffuse information. The Mexican and non-Mexican communities were to hold these forums, advertised in the *San Antonio Express*, the *San Antonio Evening News*, *La Prensa*, the *Labor Journal*, and other local publications. Public forums were held throughout the West Side.

Speakers ranged from middle-class LULAC leaders Alonzo Perales and Gustavo García to *rico* Dr. Francisco Urrutia, to historian and folklorist Jovita González, to labor leader Pablo Meza. Topics varied from González's talk on Texas folklore to Meza's lecture on communism in American Labor.[61] All of these lectures were directed at making Mexicans better citizens and focused on U.S. and middle-class values. Interestingly, the lectures in the Mexican and black sections of the city had the best attendance of all. The Forum Committee reported that "in contrast to [the Anglo suburbs] . . . we are pleasurably surprised with the response received from the underprivileged and more or less impoverished [areas]."[62]

During the late 1930s, citizenship classes instead of lectures were held for those Mexicans living in the newly built Apache-Alazán Courts on the West Side. With these lectures and citizenship classes as well as the attention paid them by LULAC and the *ricos*, adults were educationally bombarded throughout the decade — but it was the Mexican youth who profited.[63]

Between 1929 and 1941 the Mexican American student population more than doubled; the English language became more predominant among the children of the laboring class, the middle class, and

the Catholic schools. Of these Mexican students, close to 75 percent averaged daily attendance, and close to 53.7 percent received passing grades. Many of these students (according to one study) were U.S. citizens by 1941, although a number had foreign-born parents.[64]

However, whatever the year, the basic educational and social problems continued for the Mexican community (although there were relative improvements): language; health; non-Mexican attitudes; malnutrition, and arbitrary segregation. As Guadalupe San Miguel has written,

> After the war [World War II], school segregation continued to be viewed as the major factor impeding the educational, racial, and economic mobility of the Mexican-American population. Most Mexican-Americans believed that segregation branded all Spanish-speaking children as inferior and led to their status as second class citizens. Segregation also militated against the learning of English and against the formation of habits conducive to increased participation in the civic affairs of this country."[65]

It was evident by 1941 that, if immigration had been the major issue of the 1900s through the 1920s, and the search for identity was the basic issue of the 1929–41 period, segregation and education would become the major issues of the late 1940s and the 1950s.

Parents continued to be plagued by many other problems: refusal of admission to many public businesses and amusement places after the war; inability to purchase or rent certain real estate in "American residential districts"; discrimination in employment; and prohibition from jury duty.[66] These problems affected the children as well. It seemed that in spite of class complexity, the pluralism of individuals, the matrix of community, the diffusion of educational opportunities, the richness of everyday life, the activism of choice, and the Mexican Horatio Alger models, the struggle toward integration had just begun.

In this light, in the early 1940s, Pauline Kibbe described a continuing problem while H. T. Manuel commented on a specific one. Kibbe, an educator, stated that

> [e]ven among migratory laborers, who are generally speaking, the latest arrivals from Mexico, more than 90% of the children are, by birth, citizens of the United States. They know no other country; yet, they continue to be regarded as "Mexicans" and considered foreigners. On occasion, the word "Mexican" is even applied as a term of opprobrium, and in some cases it is this attitude on the part of the Anglo-American children or teachers that prevents the Latin American child's enrollment in and attendance at school. He is made to feel that he is not wanted, that his presence in the class is distasteful.

Manuel did not dwell on the psychological, but instead focused on the political. He recognized the need to democratize the Mexicans' socio-political situation in the Southwest in 1941 because of the conditions in Europe. He stated, "There is a certain urgency about this problem of the building of democracy in the Southwest [among the Mexican population]. We are now at war with powerful external enemies. We [Americans] shall win the war [if we are unified]."[67]

World War II intensified the effort in San Antonio and throughout the Southwest to educate and Americanize the Mexican population. Without this emphasis on confronting racism, discrimination, and prejudice, and on building a true democracy at home, Manuel, Kibbe, and others felt that the Mexicans would not have supported the war effort. As a consequence of citizens' need to confirm their sense of self, Franklin D. Roosevelt in the late 1930s defined Americanism as being contained within the "four freedoms" and emphasized the ideological and pragmatic theme of "immigrants all, Americans all." America, he announced, was culturally pluralistic, egalitarian, and nonracist. America, it seems, had to define itself in relation to its "other" (fascism and communism) just as the Mexicans in San Antonio had to define themselves in relationship to Mexico, but also within the principles of pluralism, egalitarianism, and a nonracist society. The impending war necessitated that people throughout the United States define their identity. The same situation confronted the Mexican American generation; World War II was the turning point in their search for identity.

Of course, this turning point was reached more quickly because San Antonio's educational system sought to make Mexicans into Americans, although it had to settle for the bifurcation of their consciousness into Mexican and American. In the early 1940s, a San Antonio Welfare report had urged the San Antonio school system to "educationally consider its Latin American History [as an] asset [not a debt] and its [own Mexican American urban] cosmopolitanism as important."[68] This report reflected the politics of FDR's cultural pluralism

Side. The vehicle for this had to be political, not the politics of knowledge, but the politics of power. By 1941 the institution of power would coincide with the institution of knowledge; the pluralism, integration, and acculturation of Mexicans was not only an economic necessity, but a national one.

7

San Antonio Politics and the Mexican Community

[There must be] a growing consciousness of the people in power [in San Antonio] that discrimination against a strong segment of its population is not wise; in fact it is not healthy, either politically, or educationally, or economically or socially, to discriminate . . . against 40 percent of the Latin American population.
— Social Welfare Report, 1941

The city's political elites between the inception of the Great Depression and the beginning of World War II were generally fearful that the Mexicans of the West Side would take Anglo workers' jobs, drive wages down, and exhaust the city's relief funds. They were also disturbed by the strike activities from 1932 through 1938 that were led by the communists and Mexican rabble rousers (i.e., the CIO, Magdaleno Rodríguez, Emma Tenayuca, and the Workers' Alliance).[1] Above all, San Antonio's political and industrial elite felt generally annoyed by the squalor, the poverty, the high rate of tuberculosis, the high death rate, the high juvenile delinquency rate, and the prostitution in the West Side. Many of them realized that these conditions were a hindrance to the city's urban and economic growth.

Four views were held during the 1929 period in the non-Mexican community toward the Mexicans: (1) indifference; (2) a wish for repatriation and deportation; (3) that Mexicans were "criminal"; and (4) the hope for more of an interrelation between the non-Mexican and the Mexican communities. The last two views were the predominant ones. Regardless of the view held, most non-Mexicans had absorbed the political belief that Mexicans were of a lower social class even than blacks. Mexicans were "looked down on . . . because of their race and their foreign language and customs," observed Audrey Granneberg.[2]

In 1939, San Antonio's former chief of police captured the ideological essence of many of San Antonians when, in reference to the West Side, he said, "Crime breeds where there is poverty. Your poverty-stricken class is your criminal class." Another San Antonian remarked, "Oh, well — all they need are a few tortillas and frijoles and they're satisfied." And a public official stated, "If . . . they [Mexicans] earned more than $1 a day, they'd just spend their money on tequila and on worthless trinkets in the dime store."[3] Although views varied in de-

almost as effectively as the Negro. He is not [however], kept apart from the "Anglo-Americans" in lavatories, waiting rooms, and public vehicles by law as is the Negro, but his poverty and low wages segregate him in the poorest sections of the city, in the day coaches of the railroads, in the balconies of the less pretentious theaters, and in the cheapest restaurants. These circumstances tend to perpetuate the racial handicaps under which the Mexicans, and especially the pecan shellers and others of low economic states, are forced to live.[4]

Discrimination and prejudice were not imposed from the top down; they were pervasive in everyday life and activity. In view of the power of de facto segregation, Father Tranchese told the San Antonio Junior Chamber of Commerce and the Lions Club in September, 1936, that the Mexican community "cannot be ignored" because of its "numbers." "They are part of San Antonio," Tranchese said. Moreover, "they are an integral part of our work force and our economy. Above all, out of 90,000 Mexicans in San Antonio, 80,000 [his number] are citizens."[5]

A year later Tranchese appealed to Washington for economic help on the basis that most Mexicans were U.S. citizens and a part of the economic structure of city. The San Antonio business community had always valued the Mexicans' role as the blue-collar "cornerstone" of the city's economy, but in the 1930s, it was forced to realize its own responsibility and obligation to them if San Antonio was to become a modern city. The Depression made business realize that the growth of the Mexican community had to keep pace with the city's growth or it would retard it. Consequently, business people turned to the political arena for guidance, since the political machine had always valued the Mexicans — not as people, but as votes. The machine politicians (the business community felt) knew how to integrate the Mexican community, because the machine had dealt with the Mexicans since the 19th Century.

Since "King Bryan" Callaghan II had ousted the "Mexican" Canary Island upper class from political power in 1885, a political machine had dominated San Antonio politics. In 1928, for example, Mayor John Tobin, who was part Mexican, passed the political mantle to C. M. Chambers; when Chambers died in 1933, his appointed successor, C. K. Quin, became mayor. Quin was the machine's mayor until he was ousted by the freewheeling Rooseveltian liberal Maury Maverick in 1939. Maverick had been the leader of a populist revolt against the machine since the early 1930s. Quin returned to power in 1941.

The machine's existence was a public fact in San Antonio and no one disputed it. The San Antonio political bulletin the *Bexar Facts* on January 24, 1930, for example, stated that "the Bexar county machine can give Tammany Hall of New York lessons when it comes to holding crooked elections and counting candidates out who have been honestly elected. This machine not only pays the poll taxes to its henchmen who vote five to fifteen times in each election, but goes so far as to have the tally sheets made up the night before the election." Many of the Mexicans on the West Side, citizens or not, often voted according to the dictates of the political machine.[6]

The Mexicans' allegiance to the machine was carefully explained before the 1930 hearings of the Committee on Immigration and Naturalization of the U.S. House of Representatives. The committee was told that the Mexicans in San Antonio were "dependent on their jobs as city or county employees. The [Mexicans] follow the commands of bosses at elections. They are so closely watched that they cannot do otherwise. Officials here buy poll taxes for the Mexicans that shows [*sic*] up on election day. Then [the machine] see[s] that he votes their way. Makes it impossible to get a good man in any office, city or county. Makes it hard in enforcing laws."[7] In 1930, however, regardless of the machine, there began a "populist revolt" that culminated in Maverick's election in 1939.

One factor in the democratization of San Antonio politics was John Garrett, a politically conscious San Antonian who published the *Citizens' Revolt*. This populist-oriented newspaper called for responsible citizens to establish more civic organizations to prevent the continuation of "ring politics." Garrett did not want the city's business sector to turn to the machine for advice and consultation on its duties toward the Mexican community; he wanted a separation of the business sector and the political sector, and he advised businesspeople to use such organizations as the Community Chest to exercise their civic responsibility toward the poor. Garrett also urged the business sector to practice political freedom, but with responsibility, with liberty, and with restraint. He further advised the business sector to focus on the coming 1932 election.[8] Garrett, who represented the conservative business wing of San Antonio politics, felt that the machine

relief. "No man from this county" said Maverick, "has ever risen in state politics because of the stench of local [machine] politics." Consequently, Maverick pledged to dedicate himself to the presentation of the rights of freedom of speech, improved health, new housing programs, and a new liberal political climate in the city for all San Antonians in general (and Mexicans in particular).[9]

Labor also had its advocate in San Antonio politics in the American Federation of Labor. The AF of L newspaper, the *Weekly Dispatch* accused the city's machine of playing politics with laborers' health claims, with the correction of sanitation problems in the West Side, and, particularly, with the slum clearance issue.[10] The implications were quite clear: the political machine was just using the laborer. Consequently, conservatives, liberals, and labor, wanted to "push" San Antonio into the modern sociopolitical era, but ring politics and the impoverished half of the population were stumbling blocks.

Left-wing politics brought the turbulent radicalism of the 1930s into the city. The extreme Left in San Antonio was represented by the Workers' Alliance and the Trade Unity League (both Communist party organizations). Stuart Jamieson, a labor historian, states that the Workers' Alliance represented the most militant labor movement in San Antonio. Begun in San Antonio in 1934 by Emma Tenayuca, it soon had a dues-paying membership of thirty-eight hundred workers. Under its leadership, sit-down strikes were staged at WPA headquarters and at City Hall "to enforce demands for [economic] relief and [employment] projects . . . [also] numerous demonstrations and

parades were organized throughout the business areas of the city. . . .
The influence won by the Alliance leaders among the Mexican unemployed and relief clients rapidly placed them in temporary control of the pecan shellers' strikes in 1938."[11]

In addition to the Workers' Alliance, the Communist party also
organized and spearheaded the Trade Unity League. It was headed
by local agitators and Communist party members George Papcun,
Alma Krouse, and T. M. García. Papcun advanced the league's main
political platform in San Antonio when he called for the "overthrow
of the existing city political order, and a Communist political electoral ticket to run in the municipal election," as well as for "bread
and milk and jobs for the workers."[12]

Politics in San Antonio was a microcosm of the national scene in
the 1930s: the business community looking toward itself; the liberals
looking toward the State; the Left wanting to overthrow the government; labor striking; and the general decline of machine politics.
Moreover, there was present in San Antonio the same national mood
that sought a new sense of community, a new political climate, and
felt a need to cope with the Depression.

In San Antonio, consequently, the Depression, the dominance of
the political machine, the extreme plight of the Mexican community,
the business community's newfound social consciousness, and the rise
of the liberal leader Maury Maverick all helped crystallize and shape
the different political groups in San Antonio. These included the
liberals, the businesspeople, the radicals, and labor. Like the national
political groupings, each local group sought a method to achieve
sociocultural modernity in view of the economic-political chaos. All
of these political groups in San Antonio tried to appeal to different
constituents: the Mexicans, the blacks, the middle-class Anglos, the
military, the retired, and business and banking interests. Each political group, however, knew that San Antonio's politics was affected by
the city's peculiar economic base: the military institutions (which spent
thirty-eight million dollars a year in royalties, leases, and payrolls);
the wholesale and retail industry; and the tourist industry (which
brought in ten million dollars a year).[13]

Because of the city's economic constituencies, the political climate
and the ideology of the political elites were always skewed toward
the right. An overall conservative mentality permeated all of San Antonio society, in spite of political label. The new archbishop of San
Antonio, Robert E. Lucy, in July, 1946, wrote to the Rev. Joseph A.
Luther, a Catholic activist who was inquiring about the politics of
the city, "I regret to say that we do not have very many labor unions
here and this is a most conservative or reactionary community."[14]

Change was wanted by all groups in the 1930s, but their quest was tempered by the city's economic reality and its conservative historical tradition. No one forgot that business was still business and that Mexicans were still Mexicans, regardless of the political climate.

In spite of the conservatism in the city's overall political philosophy, the Mexican community represented such a potential political force that it had to be considered. Educator William Knox clearly reminded the business elite of this fact when, in the early 1930s he

Knox, speaking to the Rotary Club in 1930, stressed the city and the Mexican community's interdependence and praised the historical rise of the Mexican in San Antonio from the "peon class" to that of "a man of wealth." In his speech to the city's industrialists, bankers, businessmen and educators (*San Antonio Express* [January 25, 1930]), Knox pointed out the economic importance of the Mexican population to San Antonio's economy. He stated that even the small group of Mexican cotton workers who resided in San Antonio and earned a total of approximately eleven thousand dollars a year spent most of it in the city. This trade, he advised, should be seen in perspective by noticing "that other Texas cities have often passed it up and now were wondering why San Antonio had so much cash trade during the winter and fall," when the migrants were in town. Turning to education, Knox reminded the "city fathers" that "more than 40% of the school children in San Antonio have Mexican names" and "many of these children's parents own property, pay taxes, and invest their money in the city." Moreover, Knox told the Rotary membership, he had studied the Mexican West Side for forty years as a member of the school system and had conducted many surveys to find out the relationship between the Mexican community and the city. Therefore, he said, "those who curse the Mexican do not understand his ways. On the other hand, those who do understand and have worked with them love them."[16]

To prove to the business community that there was a cohesive Mexican community with its own leadership and businesspeople, Knox introduced seven prominent and successful Mexican businessmen:

Henry Guerra, Luis Rodríguez, Francisco Chapa, Raúl Madero, Matilde Elizondo, Emilo R. Lozano, and Ignacio E. Lozano. Knox stressed that these men were making a contribution to the economy of the city. These men, he told the Rotarians, functioned as the intermediaries between the Mexican and the Anglo communities. These men, Knox emphasized, had banked on the honesty and earning ability of the Mexicans on the West Side and had become wealthy as a result. "That is the reason why these West Side merchants seldom have a period of deep business depression." Consequently, Knox pointed out, "the banks in the West Side show increasing deposits, from Mexicans and other foreign-born persons who have saved their money." Knox specifically spoke of the rise of Mexican businessman Matilde Elizondo, who had come to the United States as a poor seventeen year old and now was "independently wealthy." "His money," Knox reminded the Rotarians, "was invested in the city's economy." Knox advised the Rotarians to study the Mexicans and attempt to understand them and their problems. This was the means by which to build a greater economic base, a better interethnic relationship, and, ultimately, a greater city. Knox also eulogized Ignacio E. Lozano as an example of the city's Mexican ricos. Lozano's newspaper *La Prensa*, Knox said, "constitutes a vehicle of culture for all the Mexicans."[17]

Businesspeople understood the power of money and politics and fully recognized that, although the Mexican American middle class's ties with the city were mainly economic, some political influence was inevitable. Organizations like the Mexican Businessmen's Association, headed by Henry Johnson of the West Side Mueblería Johnson (a furniture store), and the Latin American Department, a section of the San Antonio Chamber of Commerce, headed by E. R. Lozano, had a voice, though minor, in the city's political activities. Other organizations, such as the National American Voters' Association, headed by Val Martínez, and the West Side Improvement League, had more direct political influence.

The Mexican community also had some influence through the city's political machine. The machine's direct representative to the West Side was Jacobo Rubiola, the park commissioner. Rubiola, however, represented more the machine in the community than the community in the machine. There were also a few Mexicans who personally exercised some political influence. For example, Lic. Anacleto Martínez gave a check for one thousand dollars to the Subscription Committee for the construction of the R.R. Gulf and West Texas Railroad. But, on the whole, the Mexican American middle class and the *ricos* served as only a minor pressure group in city politics. For the most part, the Mexican vote was controlled by the Chambers political machine prior to 1933, and then by Quin's political machine until 1938.[18]

The Mexican community, unfortunately, had no ethnic political boss like Charlie Bellinger, who bargained the blacks' votes for political favors. Between 1918 and 1935, Bellinger worked through the black churches to get out the vote by promising the clergy and church members to have the machine improve the East Side. He used the *San Antonio Register* as his ideological newspaper. As a result of his

tiation, greater population, and lack of both educational and political knowledge made it difficult to have one political boss or any extensive professional leadership until the 1940s, although the LULAC between 1929 and 1941 were developing this leadership and expertise.[19]

By the 1938 congressional elections, however, there were signs of more Mexican political leadership. It was evident by this time that the Mexican community had become more politically active, although this activism differed according to social class. In 1938 Maury Maverick, who had been in the U.S. Congress since 1935, was defeated by Paul Kilday—24,303 votes to 24,929. By 626 votes, conservative Paul Kilday, representing the silk stocking areas of Alamo Heights and the North Side as well as a portion of the rural Anglo vote, defeated liberal Maury Maverick. Maverick, the "Mexicans' friend," carried the West Side and the poorer areas of Harlandale, Hot Wells, and South San Antonio; the East side was split between them. Maverick, unlike in his previous campaign, did not seek support from the wealthier Anglo areas. In this race, he directed his campaign almost entirely to the Mexican Americans in the West Side and to the low-income Anglos in the suburbs of Harlandale and South San Antonio. Both the Mexicans and the Anglos in these areas supported him and displayed a genuine personal affection for him. The Mexican middle class especially liked Maverick because, unlike other candidates, who tried to speak to the Mexican community in Spanish, he "made it a point to talk to his [Mexican] friends whose ancestors came from below the Rio Grande in English and to treat them in every way as full-fledged American citizens." Some black voters also supported him despite the work of the Quin machine. Of interest in the 1938 election was the fact that the congressional returns showed that the Quin machine could no longer control the West Side. It had supported Kilday over Maverick.[20]

The 1938 congressional election was politically elucidating because it clarified the ideological forces that were active in San Antonio at the time. The Catholic Church campaigned actively against Maverick and his FDR liberalism because it felt Maverick's ideology was one step from communism. The North Side Anglo community campaigned against Maverick because he had supported the pecan shellers' strike and because he was pro-CIO; it therefore viewed him as a "radical." Businesspeople voted against Maverick because of his personal attack on Henry Ford. These views indicated that the predominant ideological currents in San Antonio were anti-Communist, anti-CIO, antiliberal, antistrikes, and generally antilabor and antiradical. The election, moreover, indicated a strong across-the-board feeling against machine politics in the city, since a number of the local candidates the machine had endorsed (except Kilday, because the voters disliked Maverick much more) lost.[21]

The patrician Maverick, who was a Rooseveltian protégé, saw himself as the gadfly of San Antonio politics. Consequently, immediately after his 1938 defeat, he jumped into a three-way mayoral race (Maverick's liberal "Fusion Ticket" opposed Quin's "People's Ticket" and Leroy Jeffers's "Better Government Ticket"). Mayor Quin accused Maverick of using the "issue of race" to advance his career, because he was catering to the ethnic vote. Quin also pointed out to the Mexican community that Maverick had been "born with a silver spoon" in his mouth, but now he was pretending to be the Mexicans' friend. Quin further accused Maverick of being too radical because he supported the CIO and had campaigned at Sidney Lanier High School with César Compa, a Mexican radical labor organizer in San Antonio. Maverick denied the charges and, in turn, accused Quin of putting the Better Government Ticket into the mayor's race "to anger him, and taunt him," as well as to split the liberal vote. Maverick believed that Jeffers' ticket was merely a subterfuge by the "political machine's People's Ticket."[22] Throughout the campaign, the issue of the Mexican vote and the Mexican problem was raised; as a result, urban politics was forced to address the issue of ethnicity. San Antonio politicians wanted Mexicans to help in the modernization of the city but still maintain their "differences."

Maverick continually carried his campaign into the West Side. He reminded the Mexican community that Quin had opposed the pecan shellers' strike and had even put them in jail. Maverick charged that

Mayor Quin was an "enemy of the Latin-Americans," and he repeated his 1938 charge that the health department was part of the Quin political machine, and thus health was often a political issue. Not only did LULAC leaders Joe Chacón and Alonzo Perales support Maverick, but the pecan shellers' union passed out handbills supporting him. However, the AFL, through the *Weekly Dispatch* urged labor to vote for Quin's ticket because "labor never had better friends than these men"; Maverick, as the AFL reminded the worker, was a supporter

be a Mexican American without giving up a personal sense of American self or a collective cultural sense. The quest for identity was producing differences, but also a sense of duality, Mexican and American. LULAC members Philip Mantalbo, Theodore Góngora, Tony Lozano, Gustavo García, and Jesús Ocón not only endorsed Quin and his machine, but campaigned for him. At Sidney Lanier School, Mayor Quin reminded the Mexican audience that they had been given school facilities by his administration. He reminded them that he had brought nine million dollars to the city in federal housing funds for the West Side. James Tafolla, Jr., the master of ceremonies for the evening, told his fellow Mexicans that Maverick's friendship was not sincere.

Leroy Jeffers of the Better Government ticket also campaigned in the West Side and held rallies at Sidney Lanier High School and at Roosevelt Park. Jeffers was supported by LULAC Republican activist Jacobo Rodríguez. In this campaign, both Jeffers and Maverick also used the radio to appeal to San Antonians. Jeffers spoke on WOAI, and Maverick on KTSA: modernity, in the form of the radio, as well as pluralist politics had come to San Antonio and the Mexicans and non-Mexicans listened and learned. Although all three tickets were vying for the Mexicans' vote, none of them had any Mexicans on their slate (although Quin's ticket had Jacobo Rubiola, some questioned whether he was Mexican or Italian).[24]

The New Deal liberal Maury Maverick ultimately was elected mayor in an election that was marked by extremely heavy voting: 18,375 for Maverick, 14,874 for Quin, and 11,503 for Jeffers. Maverick was elected in spite of his liberalism and in spite of his previous congressional loss to Kilday. There were two major reasons for this: first, the Mexican community's heavy turnout for Maverick; and second, the Anglo community's (especially the North Side) anti–political machine and anti-Quin attitude. It had not helped, of course, that Quin had been indicted by the Grand Jury before the race for misapplication of city funds.[25] In addition, many persons in San Antonio, it seems, were tired of Quin and ring politics. The Anglo vote thus was split between Quin and Jeffers. The election, consequently, was an anti-Quin vote by the Anglo community, but a pro-Maverick vote by many in the Mexican community. The Mexican American for the first time had exhibited a knowledge of pressure politics, a consciousness of power, and an awareness of pragmatic (not nationalistic) politics. Education and knowledge were becoming political, and political knowledge was being translated into power.

The importance of this election was clear. First, it made apparent the political interdependence of both the Anglo and the Mexican communities. Second, it revealed the rise of a strong but diversified Mexican middle-class political community. Third, it showed that the middle-class Mexican leadership, which was gaining philosophical hegemony within the West Side, was like the rest of the San Antonio community: anti-CIO, anti-Communist, and, in many ways, anti-liberal. Fourth, it indicated that lower-middle-class Mexicans were fairly liberal. And fifth, it established the fact that the laboring class, especially the pecan shellers, supported both unionism and liberalism and were active. The Mexican laboring class was striking out against the bosses and working for the liberal Maverick. As Richard B. Henderson, Maury Maverick's biographer, has written, "The Mexican-Americans liked Maverick, and with good reason. Sherwood Anderson said that the San Antonio mayor had bought their votes in a 'new and legal way.' In addition to the many pieces of evidence of his great interest in their heritage, Maverick had fought the 'pecan king' to secure better wages for Mexican-American pecan shellers, who were getting as little as $1.75 a week." Mayor Maverick had also brought to the city the "restoring [of] the chili and tamale queens to the plazas of the city, but he had a thoroughly modern concern for the progressive sanitary measures he required of the Mexican-American women who vended the Mexican foods. He also wanted the color of the original Spanish atmosphere to be 'jazzed up' a bit." Henderson has suggested that nostalgia for his boyhood days was Maverick's motivation for the restoration, and his impulse of progressiveness was his motive for the liberal "insurrection."[26]

As a result, Mexican workers not only campaigned in electoral politics, but in July, 1938, for example, the Pecan Shellers' Union, CIO

Local no. 772, sponsored a rally and talk by Vicente Lombardo Toledano, the secretary general of the Confederation of Mexican Workers and Communist party leader. Lombardo Toledano, referring to the Mexicans as "comrades," spoke on the need for Mexican workers to "gain the respect of the world" and to "regulate economic conditions." He also warned the United States against Fascism.[27] However, San Antonio's Mexican workers continued to favor Maverick politics rather than being swayed by Lombardo Toledano's radical unionism.

The San Antonio business community, the religious community, and the political elite recognized all of these changes, and in 1940 they appointed a social welfare and fact-finding commission that was representative of the whole community to evaluate the changes that had taken place during the 1930s. One great change was that by 1940 Maury Maverick, as mayor of San Antonio had, as Henderson points out, "brought about the classification of Mexican-Americans as 'white' on census and other records in San Antonio." Maverick had also emphasized the "Mexican" essence in San Antonio. In 1939, for example, he began the restoration of La Villita (the Old Town) in the center of the city. La Villita was, as Henderson points out, "the civil settlement founded in 1718, that was attached to the Mission San Antonio de Valero, known today simply as the Alamo." Maverick decided, Henderson further states, "that it could be a symbol and monument to those simple people who had made possible the great city which had grown around it." The city of San Antonio, consequently, advertised its dual character with the Anglo Texan Alamo and the Mexican Villita. Mexican Americans acknowledged the restoration's importance and even Maverick's political opponents recognized its importance for the integration of the Mexicans. Mexico was pleased too and invited Maverick to accompany Vice-President Wallace to the inauguration of President Manuel Avila Camacho, which pleased the *ricos*. Even the influential *Dallas News* wrote, "Out of a Texas rubbish heap comes the symbol of peace."[28]

The governing elite of San Antonio wanted to evaluate and establish guidelines to handle the development of the Mexicans' metropolitan and political integration. The fact-finding commission's report

concluded that there was by 1940 "an awakening in San Antonio —
an awakening of the [city's] spirit — the elan vital." It concluded that
this civic "élan" translated itself into the following political purposes:

1. A determination to make San Antonio the modern city it has the
position and the power to be — a city that would hold its own industrially and commercially with other growing metropolitan centers.

2. An awareness that the welfare of its citizens is of basic importance
to its economic health.

3. A growing consciousness of the people in power that discrimination
against a strong segment of its population [the Mexicans] is not wise —
in fact that it is not healthy politically, educationally, economically
or socially to discriminate. Political recognition [must be extended to]
its Latin American population.

4. A belief that San Antonio could preserve its democratic faith.[29]

This commission of prominent citizens had expressed verbally the
"new ideology" of San Antonio's governing elite. This municipal self-
evaluation recognized the existence and extreme importance not only
of the Mexicans but of the Mexican Americans. New self-knowledge
and power on the part of the Mexican Americans was beginning to
bring about integration and some political and social recognition.
The report no longer referred to the Mexican in the West Side as a
"Mexican," but as a "Latin-American" and sought not to alienate the
West Side population. By 1941 the communal structures — the family, the church, the educational system, and politics — had helped to
change many of the Mexicans politically and philosophically into individualistic and pluralistic U.S. citizens. However, they also served,
paradoxically, to preserve the Mexicans' intellectual and cultural consciousness of collectivity, that is, a memory and reflection of a common heritage of ideas, myths, traditions, and events. Each structure
tried to Americanize the Mexicans, but not too much; each structure
valued Mexican culture and traditions because, after all, they were
also part of the city's zeitgeist. San Antonio needed to integrate them
into the community as Americans — politically, economically, and socially — but the city had to keep them Mexicans as well. San Antonio,
after all, was a Mexican and American city, a city cosmopolitan in
history and tradition. Thus, for the Mexicans in San Antonio, by
1941 the intellectual and psychological emphasis was on Mexican and
American and the product was the beginning not only of a new generation's search for identity in San Antonio, but of the emergence in
the Southwest of a Mexican American mentality. This was to be a
generation with its own, not yet visible, paradoxes, contradictions,

and ironies as it continued to engage in the search for collective and individual identity.

San Antonio by 1941 was still a city of southern tradition but American democratic pride; egalitarian in form but hierarchical and elitist in essence; accepting of American individualism, but supportive of a sense of Texas community. San Antonio personified the paradoxical tension of the southern mentality meeting the northern mentality via modernization, and the Mexicans were experiencing these same

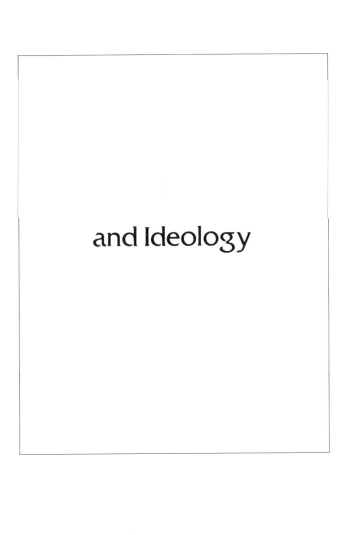

and Ideology

8

only political. We do not simply give information [in our newspapers] on the situation, nor have we just been critical of the men [in government] and the revolutionary proceedings. . . . Our work, which we have always considered primary, has been to study, to purify our [Mexican] tradition to add something new, and to value our [cultural and traditional] qualities.
— Ignacio Lozano

INTRODUCTION

The *ricos* of San Antonio were a comprador class; that is, these exiled Mexicans always "faced south" and were more interested in the politics of Mexico and the rest of the world than in that of San Antonio. These exiled *ricos* were, as Frances Woods describes them, "many of the 25,000 political refugees who settled in San Antonio between 1908 and 1914, as well as many of the religious refugees who came in the 1920s." They were "persons, largely from Mexico's upper classes who looked upon San Antonio more as a refuge than as a permanent home. Some of them left San Antonio as soon as conditions in Mexico permitted, but others remained."[1]

As has already been stated, the *ricos* were part of what historian W. Dirk Raat has called the "revoltosos"— exiled Mexican rebels, moderates, revolutionaries, and conservatives who found sanctuary in the United States between 1900 and 1930 and whose stay depended on the political conditions in Mexico or the U.S. point of view toward them. The *ricos* in San Antonio were part of the conservative wing of these exiles: Porfiristas, Huertistas, Felicistas, *científicos*, Orozquistas, Cristeros, and a host of sympathizers. They were mainly politicians, generals, businesspeople, intellectuals, journalists, lawyers, and government officials. But there were also many of the *burgesía pequeña* (middle class).

These *ricos* and sympathizers came to Los Angeles, El Paso, San Antonio, New Orleans, New York, St. Louis, Chicago, and also settled in Europe and Latin America, especially Havana, between the eve of the Mexican revolution (1908) and the end of the Cristero War (1928). They were part of a diaspora of conservatives comparable to the émigrés from Germany to the United States during the 1930s, except that these people had a number of objectives during their stay: (1) to serve as a government in exile; (2) to be critics of the politics, events, and ideologies in Mexico; (3) to develop and instill in Mexicans in the United States and in Mexico a desire for a sense of order, stability, and unity, which came from accepting a common core of historical thought and traditional culture; (4) to urge Mexicans in the United States to return to Mexico or, if not, to play the role of a fifth column in the United States; and (5) to serve as the intellectual and cultural memory to deter the Americanization of Mexicans in the United States. All of the *ricos* in San Antonio and throughout the United States, regardless of differences, shared an ideological thread: they were, in general, against the development of a post-Porfiriato period that was politically fragmented (liberal or socialistic), economically and socially modernized (mass culture), and philosophically secularized (anti-Catholic). Specifically, they were against the constitutionalist forces in Mexico, and by the 1920s they all began to see Plutarco Elías Calles and the "Maximito" as the personification of the evils in Mexico — not because Calles moved the revolution to the right, but because he emphasized personalism, atheism, secularism, divisiveness, violence, and, above all, was not communal. They also opposed the socialism and leftism of Cárdenas. In essence, the *ricos* in San Antonio were, as Michael Meyer has suggested of the Huertistas, counterrevolutionary, with a small *c*. The *ricos* were Scholastic (a fusion of Christian theology and the philosophies of Plato and Aristotle) in their religious views, Comtian (a fusion of views on humanity, society, family, and intellectuals, and the role of religion) in their social philosophy, and Huertista (an emphasis on continuity) in their politics of realism. Because they lived between 1908 and the early 1940s in a state of exiled purgatory and with their ideological vision as *mexicanos de afuera* (Mexicans outside of Mexico), they were interested in the Mexican population in San Antonio and the Southwest, but only in broad cultural-political terms. Consequently, they used Ignacio E. Lozano's newspapers *La Prensa* (1914–56) and *La Opinión* (1926–present) as the vehicles through which to articulate their ideas, their interests, and their concerns; after all, they felt that they were the Comtian high priests, the caretakers of all Mexicans, inside and outside Mexico.[2]

Consequently, in spite of their elite comprador position, they still supported any improvement of the economic, social, or political con-

inequality of people—but emanated from their own Comtian belief that "reason, feeling and activity" can be harmonized, and thus living and helping others becomes an individual statement in line with the reality that all people are different and unequal, yet part of the same society and culture.

THE *RICOS* AND *LA PRENSA*

This Mexican comprador class was exemplified by Ignacio E. Lozano and his newspapers *La Prensa* (of San Antonio) and *La Opinión* (of Los Angeles). *La Prensa* was referred to as "an intellectual light." At a banquet in 1937, for example, Lozano was referred to as "the highest representative of Mexico" and a person who "ought to be an example for all Mexicans."[4] These eulogies were from both the middle-class Mexicans and other *ricos*, who were trying to have Lozano elected president of the national Alianza Hispano-Americana, which was headquartered in New Mexico. This organization (which had started as a mutual-aid society in the late nineteenth century) rivaled the influence of LULAC in the late 1930s; it was more representative of Mexicans like the *ricos* whose wealthier members identified themselves more as Spanish (*hispanos*) than as Mexicans. There were also some middle-class persons who aligned themselves closer to this sector of the "Spanish" population (especially in New Mexico) than to the developing class of acculturating Mexican Americans in order not to be identified with *lo americano*, the poor immigrant or migrant Mexican. For the "Spanish" *ricos* of New Mexico and the aspiring

"Spanish" middle-class *mexicanos*, Lozano was the "champion of the Mexican people" and the "new Moses." Such praise came from Anglos as well as Mexicans.[5]

Ignacio Lozano was an exile from Nuevo León who arrived in San Antonio in 1908 with his mother and four sisters. Lozano emigrated from a state intellectually dominated by the conservatism of the Reyistas and Porfiristas, rather than the liberalism of Madero. Although he left Mexico in the prerevolutionary period, it seems likely that Lozano was of the middle class. (His early politics and personal ideological attachments are difficult to ascertain, since his personal papers were burned in 1956 and his family declines to comment on his early political and intellectual life.) Apparently, Lozano came to San Antonio armed with journalistic, editorial, and business skills. He also arrived with an elite perspective and a desire to establish an institutional voice for his and the *ricos'* sentiments.

After working in a bookstore and writing for a local Spanish newspaper, Lozano started *La Prensa* in 1913 as a weekly newspaper and established his own bookstore. Within a year, he was publishing *La Prensa* as a daily and his bookstore was functioning as a clearinghouse for Mexican books into the United States as well as an editorial house. In 1926, as a result of increased demand for the newspaper in California, Lozano founded *La Opinión* in Los Angeles and a record- and bookstore. Both newspapers and the bookstores, Libererías Lozano, were run by Lozano from his San Antonio headquarters. By the middle of the 1920s, Lozano's enterprises were not only financially successful, but they were the central focus of the exiled Mexican conservatives' activities.[6]

La Prensa and *La Opinión* reflected not only Lozano's ideas and commentaries, but those of the exiled journalists, intellectuals, and businesspeople. According to Alfredo González, *La Prensa*'s editorial director from 1914 through 1933, there was no question that Lozano saw his newspapers as the repository for Mexican conservative thought and as the central instruments for bringing stable change to revolutionary Mexico. He also saw them as intellectual and cultural means for maintaining the conservative and nationalist philosophy in the consciousness of the Mexican communities in the United States. Francine Medeiros writes that Lozano's newspaper had "a scope and educational tone [that] resembled newspapers in Mexico." "Frequently," Medeiros writes, "*La Opinión* [and *La Prensa*] extolled the Porfiriato as an era of Mexican peace and prosperity that had been shattered by ill-considered insurrections." Moreover, Lozano perceived that Mexico's "revolutionary leaders tended to exacerbate Mexico's afflictions by permitting near anarchy, severely censoring the press, and by suppressing religious freedom to the point of religious destruction." It seems that Lozano, while seeing the evils of the changing revolution also saw the positive continuities of Mexico and felt that he and the exiles were the preservers of the historical and traditional consciousness of collectivity: the Catholic Scholastic perspective; the communalsocietal emphasis of Comte; respect for the centralized state; love of order and stability; the centrality of family; and the need for a culture of universality as well as an emphatic respect for nationalistic

editorials in the 1926–29 period and found that of 1,034 editorials, 73.1 percent dealt primarily with issues in Mexico, 10.6 percent dealt with Mexicans living in the United States, and 16.2 percent dealt with international relations or diplomatic relations between Mexico and the United States or Europe. Without question, Medeiros's findings indicate that, as she writes, "Lozano's newspapers were more interested in the affairs of the patria than those of the colonia." In fact, the existence of Mexican news coverage indicates, she believes, that "Lozano [had] developed a Mexican newspaper in exile, not strictly an immigrant or United States journal." In essence, Lozano's newspapers, with their *rico* philosophy, defended the *mexicanos de afuera* against a "tyranny of injustices and Americanization" in the United States and also simultaneously bombarded them with a "culture of universality," "a sensitivity toward justice," and "the force of Christian humanism," all of which also served constantly to attack the vicissitudes of political, ideological, and temporal changes in Mexico as well. *La Prensa* and *La Opinión* were, as Medeiros accurately notes, "Mexican [conserving] reform organs."[8]

Although Lozano and the *ricos* always philosophically and ideologically faced south toward Mexico, they did have a personal agenda for the Mexicans in the United States. They constantly expounded various central themes: (1) voluntary repatriation; (2) resistance to Americanization (acculturation); (3) the rearing of children with a consciousness of being *mexicanos de afuera;* (4) cultural celebrations to instill *lo mexicano;* (5) a voice for all Mexicans in communal-political decisions; (6) an avoidance of stereotypical behavior; and (7) parental emphasis on virtue and hard work. Lozano also held up successful role models in his newspaper to express the message that Mexican children were not innately stupid (as many Americans and even some Mexicans believed) but were capable of learning and achieving.[9]

As a result, Lozano was the personification of Mexicanism, and *La Prensa* and *La Opinión* were the vehicles for his expression. *La Prensa* had two basic goals: to serve as the voice of the people and the community, and to defend and represent the views of the exiled political refugees who settled in San Antonio and the Southwest.[10]

La Prensa was a paper, Lozano believed, for all the Mexican community, whether in the United States or in Mexico. In fact, Lozano portrayed and advertised *La Prensa* as "the champion of the people." The *ricos*, through *La Prensa*, tried to follow the editorial policy of Mexican journalist Carlos Deambrosis Martíns, who said that the press must write clearly, succinctly, and directly toward the masses, and not toward the elite. The "newspaper," Deambrosis Martíns said, "is like the cloud in the center of the storm."[11] For the *ricos*, the storm was the Mexican revolution and its aftermath, and they were the calm center in San Antonio. The *ricos* did not necessarily see themselves as the elite, but their lifestyle, their interests, their ideas and philosophy certainly did not represent everyday life for most Mexicans. In reality, the *ricos*, through *La Prensa*, were playing the role of a second government, Mexico's government in exile and, consequently, the voice of the Mexican masses. Articles, editorials, and columns constantly criticized, dictated, and proposed policy for the government in Mexico. It was a newspaper for the community, but principally for the community in the homeland. Nevertheless, *La Prensa* did attempt to keep the West Side and the rest of the *colonias* in the Southwest hegemonically Mexican through the writings of its intellectuals.

The articulation of the *ricos*' philosophy was done by Mexican intellectuals who wrote for the paper and were stationed throughout the world because they had been expelled from Mexico: Nemesio García Naranjo, Juan Sánchez Azcona, Luis C. Sepúlveda, Hortensia Elizondo, M. R. Vidal, Jr., Querido Moheno, and others. The philosophy and the ideology of these intellectuals and of *La Prensa* throughout the 1930s clearly represented a social sector that had fled Mexico when Madero came into power in the first stage of the Mexican revolution. This sector was Porfirista in ideology; that is, it adhered to philosophical positivism (or, rather, a scientism, as W. Dirk Raat suggests). They also welcomed foreign economic intervention in Mexico, believed in "strongmen" for political stability, and sought a united nationalist society. They had, for the most part, supported Pres. Porfirio Díaz's regime in Mexico. In the 1930s, however, the exiled *ricos* had no economic or political base either in the United States or in Mexico and, regardless of the time they spent in the United States, they continued to think of themselves as *mexicanos de afuera* rather than *mexicanos de adentro*, like the Mexican Americans. Through the intellegentsia, they urged every Mexican in the United States to return to Mexico to help build it, agriculturally and industrially.[12] In one editorial, for example, *La Prensa* called for an end to the ideological separation of Mexicans and urged ideological homogeneity. The editorial called

unfortunately, was not applicable to the Mexico of the 1930s. Their ideology called for (1) "the allowance of capital investment" by foreigners in Mexico and a change in constitutional articles 27 and 23, which did not allow this type of investment (the articles, they thought, had been inspired by the Bolsheviks); (2) an enlightened and powerful central government; (3) a friendly relationship with the Catholic Church; (4) the cultivation of the Spanish Mexican culture (because "the fine arts do not have any value except in their relation to guarding the social order"); and (5) the development of great men.[14]

The exiled *ricos* believed "that a nation is known by the grandeur of its personalities, its politicos, its artists, its novelists . . . the pride [and progress] of a nation is in having great men, great politicians, first class and second class and . . . great collaborators with them . . . such as great painters, teachers, artists . . . Mexico is great . . . with great men."[15] Progress for the *ricos* did not mean changing the basic social and institutional elements, but refining them and utilizing them to their maximum in a new order, an order of businesspeople, intellectuals, and artists in a harmonious society.

As a consequence of these elitist and personalistic notions, *La Prensa* urged the Mexican government to give amnesty to the exiled Mexican *ricos* in the United States and other places, and called on all of the others, the poor and the middle class, who had fled Mexico to return and lend their muscle to rebuild Mexico.[16] For the *ricos*, all Mexicans were important, although they recognized differences in functions and personas, but the most important of all Mexicans was Porfirio Díaz, the president and dictator who lifted Mexico from disorder to order and from poverty to progress.

Nemesio García Naranjo, who had been minister of education under President Huerta (1912) and who was a well-known Mexican intellectual, wrote in his *Memoirs* that Díaz's remains should be returned to Mexico. The words and ideas he used expressed the feelings of the *ricos:* "The repatriation of your body, more than a patriotic duty, is a vital necessity. Since you left Mexico, this land has suffered all the tortures of a dying nation. The . . . years since you left Mexico in exile have been . . . years of anarchy and distraction . . . the Mexican nation needs you to return to once again be rich and prospering." For García Naranjo and all the exiled *ricos,* Porfirio Díaz, regardless of his excesses, personified "order, stability, and progress"; above all he was "the eagle that dedicated his life to strangle the serpent of our struggles." For the *ricos,* all Mexican immigrants should return as the metaphoric eagle.[17]

Consequently, the *ricos* sought to impose a hegemony of Mexican patriotism and a traditional culture for the hegemony that was, in essence "the spirit of la Raza." As *La Prensa* editorialized:

> We are of this United States, but culturally we are not. We are from Spanish culture and conquistadores. The tendency to become Americanized is nothing new in Mexicans, but it is wrong when there is a beginning of a deep-rooted sense of racial inferiority. Americans do not have this tendency to become part of some other race. Yet Americanism is taken as the standard. This is also the case with Germans, Latins, and others who come to the United States. The Spanish American should admire the United States because it has many things to admire, but they should remember that they are cemented by Spanish culture. The American culture should only complement the Spanish one [and not replace it].[18]

Dr. Joaquín González, speaking on radio for the *ricos,* summarized the philosophy very well: "We [Mexicans] are . . . without a home [in exile]. But, we love Mexico because it is our homeland . . . We must love Mexico . . . Because what does the Mexican have, come what may, [except] that he is Mexican and always remains Mexican! We remain Mexicans always in spite of where we are. In Mexico we are a family, that is, a life of fraternity and love."[19]

Consequently, Mexican Americans or Mexicans in San Antonio, regardless of class, were seen by the *ricos* as always being fundamentally *mexicanos de afuera.* They remained Mexicans who were Christian humanists in their hearts, Comtian in their heads and Porfiristas in their traditions. In short, the *ricos* felt that a Mexican should always begin with Díaz; in 1940, García Naranjo wrote that "no one is entitled to be a Mexican if he passes the city of Paris without visiting the tomb of Porfirio Díaz." It seems that Díaz (in García Naranjo's words) was "the best construction of Mexico" and was not only Comte's "grand-être" (supreme being) but personified Mexican humanity. All Mexicans mirrored this state of extended reality, this feeling that the present was the central point of life and the past and future merely unfolding edges of the present. In viewing historical time, the *ricos* rejected any concept that emphasized a teleological direction.[20]

José Vasconcelos, a prominent Mexican intellectual and educator,

are men of good will. I invite you [Mexicans in the United States] through the foreign press to support me. I also invite you to come to Mexico . . . I invite you to sacrifice [now] if you don't want to cry tomorrow like slaves." Vasconcelos offered all the Mexicans in the United States the home that Dr. González said they did not have in San Antonio and other southwestern cities; this home was in Mexico. Many of those Depression-era "repatriates" who left the United States, after a time returned (disillusioned), however. They had not found their home in Mexico; acculturation had already begun to differentiate them from their compatriots in Mexico.[21]

If many laboring-class Mexicans in time began to recognize the United States as their home, the *ricos*, for the most part, did not. They continued to see themselves as *mexicanos de afuera*. As a result, they applauded president-elect Pascual Ortiz Rubio in 1930 when he announced that very shortly amnesty would be given to all Mexicans who were in exile, even though they once had been considered enemies of the Mexican government. Consequently, the 1929–41 period, according to intellectual José Juan Tablado, was considered the "era of concord." Thus began, Tablado wrote, a period of concord during which the focus in Mexico was to consolidate and accelerate the country's programs for the betterment of the people. The president of Mexico specifically addressed the *ricos* when he stated that all exiles should return to put their intelligence and skills at the service of Mexico, their country. Tablado saw the thirties as the beginning of a new decade for the *mexicanos de afuera*, the "rainbow after the turbulence."[22]

The *ricos* had been against the Mexican revolution and, like their Russian conservative expatriate counterparts of earlier decades, they felt that the revolution and the "socialism" it initiated were destroying the moral fiber of their country. In contrast to Cardenas's "socialism," however, they argued for a new society that emphasized humanist philosophy and economic liberalism. They also wanted strong personal leadeship, but a weak bureaucratic state; foreign investment in Mexico, but a "new" patriotism; overall, they called for "national unity" via a new spirit of class cooperation. Most of all, they wanted an end to Mexico's self-destruction, because the revolution, they said, was a Judas: it destroyed and betrayed its own people. National salvation, they felt, could only be derived from economic production and material growth, not from political robbery, hate, and class murder. Even if some of the *ricos* had disliked Díaz's dictatorship, they longed for his economic programs, which had promoted national growth, his political programs, which engendered order, and his strong control of the state apparatus, which had brought stability. Specifically, the *ricos* believed that, in addition to economic production, the problems of the Mexicans in Mexico and in the United States could be solved by a strong central government and a strong national culture; however, both depended on a highly educated and professional class of citizens.

But their social theory, they believed, was not functional in Mexico in the late 1920s and early 1930s because of the political and social "disrupters" like Calles and the "socialists" like Cárdenas. It pleased the *ricos*, however, when they focused on Franklin D. Roosevelt. This patrician leader, they thought, would protect the American people, keep the central government strong, and, they felt, keep the Bolshevik influence at a distance. This type of man, with his leadership ability and aristocratic background, was what Mexico needed. They saw Díaz in FDR and FDR in Díaz; in effect, they were arguing for themselves as a collective class to function in the role of a Díaz or an FDR to lead Mexico. The Porfiriato was their guide, the revolution was their nemesis, and they were the saviors. They did not necessarily want to return to the Porfiriato, however; they wanted a revolution that maintained continuities, not changed essence.[23]

While the direction and ultimate logic implicit in their overall ideas, goals, perspectives, and expectations did not fully coincide with that of LULAC, there was some compatibility. For example, both acknowledged their Mexican heritage, both were patriotic, both worked for the betterment of the Mexican community, and both opposed the ideology of the radical "Tenayuca-type workers." Moreover, both opposed socialism, class division, and racial prejudice. Above all, there was a similarity in the fact that the Mexican American adhered to the collective state liberalism of FDR and not to the old individualistic liberalism of Jefferson; consequently, the *ricos* and the Mexican Americans both were historically oriented toward a social model of statism, tradition, humanism, and order. However, the *ricos* always remained *mexicanos de afuera*, while the LULAC middle class, who were *mexicanos de adentro*, consciously changed over time to Mexican Americans. The central difference between them lay in their social and ideological base. The *ricos* were consciously rooted in the elitism and nationalism of Mexico, whereas the middle class was con-

tinuities persisted, because their total sphere of experience was in the West Side, and their world was the same. Above all, there was still a historical and intellectual consciousness, but it was being reshaped by multiple temporal realities; for each individual there was established a "paramount reality," as Peter L. Berger calls it.

No class could escape Americanization, yet the socioeconomic class pyramid remained in the West Side. The *ricos* felt that they were the class of people that could return Mexico to normalcy and that they were also the ones who could conserve the spirit of la Raza within the hearts of the Mexicans in the United States. Both the *ricos* and LULAC agreed on the preservation of this spirit, but LULAC and the middle class were adapting to Americanization. For the middle class, change and Americanization shaped their paramount reality; for the *ricos*, it was continuity and Mexicanization. Neither, however, could fully reject their Mexican past or their American present; reflection, choice, and acceptance was the ideological key.[24]

Juan Sánchez Azcona, a Mexican intellectual, wrote an article for *La Prensa* on this theme of change and ethnicity. In "Conservamos el espíritu de la raza," he stated,

> We are of a Spanish tradition that is in our blood. But we can use what is good of the Yankee culture. The tendency to *"ayankarse"* [Americanize] is not new in many Mexicans. We have a lot to learn from the United States, but we have much to teach them too if they expect to be part of the continental confederation and not just a brutal predominance. There is a natural tendency for Americans to consider themselves better than other races — German, Slavic, Latin Americans, etc. The Hispanic American ought to admire the North American because he

has many virtues to be admired, but he should not lose his own [virtues, identity, and culture].[25]

The middle class, specifically LULAC, understood Sánchez Azcona, but its gestalt and spatial relationships were different. It did not see the United States from the outside in, but from the inside out. Consequently, it interpreted the *ricos'* emphasis on Mexican culture and ideology differently. Many embraced the United States philosophically while trying to maintain a Spanish Mexican culture. The intellectuals, like Sánchez Azcona and their business counterparts, on the other hand, always favored Latin culture and were philosophically anti–United States.

By the end of the 1930s, the *ricos* recognized the *Mexicano de adentro* of San Antonio and the Southwest. They referred to the Mexican middle class of San Antonio, especially LULAC members, as Mexican Texans, and even though there were differences in goals, they admired emerging LULAC leader Alonzo Perales. They recognized him as a leader and a "fighter for la Raza," and saw him as an important part of the "Hispano-Mexicano-Texano element" (as the *ricos* called it) in San Antonio. The *ricos*, nevertheless, still considered themselves an important part of this elite element. Dr. Aureliano Urrutia, one of the wealthiest of the *ricos* in San Antonio and the former minister of interior in the Huerta regime, outlined this sense of importance before a banquet for the Anglo, Mexican American, and Mexican leadership in San Antonio in 1930:

> I am very glad to see you especially here in the spirit of harmony; it is an indication of peace in our community. We who are gathered here are the highest talent and money of San Antonio — the banker and commercial element of the city.
>
> All the universe is made up of the same force and energy; it ties us all together [regardless of class or race]. There is a universal confraternity.
>
> The world has shifted in axis during the last number of years with the center being the United States. It is not the machine, the money, the electricity nor the power that moves them [the United States]. It is the dynamics of this American race. There is this dynamics [this personal energy] radiated by these people. It is less in Mexico, but more [of this dynamics is] in the Mexican [American] in the United States. If we in Mexico are to grow we must learn to imitate these new developments especially through characteristics that these people display 1) love of work, 2) a sense of discipline, 3) a love of truth. If we could imitate these three great qualities and inject them in appreciable quantities into our Mexican people, we would be performing a great human act because we would thus be demonstrating — together with our own country [a unique personality and qualities].[26]

Although the *ricos* saw themselves as being very important in San Antonio, they constantly sought to return to Mexico and take with them the United States' great ideological gifts: love of work, self-discipline, and love of truth. These characteristics, they thought, with the Mexicans' innate love of life and patriotism, would bring about the "perfect" world in Mexico. Of course, they understood very well that internal social harmony, national unity, political peace, and a bipartisan effort were essential ingredients for progress in Mexico. The

THE CULTURAL HEGEMONY OF THE *RICOS*

The spirit of la Raza could best be maintained, the *ricos* believed, through everyday cultural activities. Therefore, through activities that ranged from the sale of Mexican books and music to the speaking and writing of intellectuals, the *ricos* of San Antonio continued to maintain the Mexican spirit and soul — culture — despite the pressures of acculturation throughout the 1920s and 1930s. For the *ricos*, in fact, artists were an integral part, indeed the cornerstone, of Mexican culture. Culture and politics produced sophistication, and this was important, the *ricos* thought, to the "better classes."[28]

This merger of culture and politics was also emphasized when "high culture" was promoted in *La Prensa* for the poorer masses of the West Side and the middle-class. For example, *La Prensa* publicized the opera season in San Antonio and urged the entire Mexican community to attend, especially when the Civic Opera Company of Chicago was initiating a new system of bringing operas to the South to acquaint people with opera. Throughout the thirties, the *ricos* reminded the Mexican community that if they could not attend such functions they could listen to station WOAI, which played symphonies from the Capital Theater in New York, or to a daily midday program, "Música Sinfónica," which aired on KTSA. Popular music was also a source of culture; therefore, *La Prensa* urged the community to listen to the "Hora Anáhuac," carried on KTAP every Thursday morning. "La Hora Anáhuac" carried local talent such as Luz González and local pianist Isabel Noriego, as well as saxophone player Amado

Vásquez, Jr., all three very popular with the upper middle class and the *ricos*.[29]

La Prensa also urged everyone in the community to see Mexican films, read its cultural columns, and attend lectures by the intelligentsia. The *ricos* felt that the U.S. film industry did not recognize the fact that it had a Spanish-speaking audience, so made no films in Spanish. The *ricos* believed that this omission was responsible for the uniformity of American culture; diversity was not recognized. The *ricos* sought to preserve the diversity of the United States, at least the Mexican part.[30]

Through *La Prensa* and *La Opinión*, the ricos tried to solidify the Mexican community's sense of cohesion and mutual understanding throughout the Southwest. Every Sunday, for example, *La Prensa* carried an entire page entitled "La Vida Cultural Mexicana de los Estados Unidos," which carried news from the Mexican communities throughout the United States. Moreover, it carried extensive social news from Laredo, Texas—a city with a large Mexican population. For the *ricos*, the Mexicans in the United States were not scattered, isolated Jeffersonian individuals, but viable nationalistic Mexican communities in exile, the keepers of the cultural tradition. They hoped, therefore, not only to have these communities remain culturally Mexican, but to uplift them to a high cultural level.[31]

The intellectuals and writers were sent on speaking tours, especially to other Texas cities. These lectures were usually sponsored by local cultural groups. René Capistrán Garza, for example, was sent to speak on nationalist themes such as "Mexico, Its Traditions and Its People," and "Our Mexican Country and Our Strength." In Dallas, where Garza gave two talks, one at the city auditorium and the other at Santa Ana School, he was sponsored by a local patriotic organization, the Comité Organizador de los Actos Culturales de Dallas. Capistrán Garza always stressed certain themes: Mexican patriotism, cultural unity, and a common historical tradition. He was promoting a consciousness of collectivity.[32]

To augment the work of the speakers and the press, the *ricos* sold books to the Mexican community. Lozano's Casa Editorial Lozano was the main Mexican publishing and wholesale house in San Antonio, and *La Prensa* advertised its holdings and sales and promoted a variety of its books and Mexican record albums. Books on Mexican history, literature, and politics were advertised. The majority were in Spanish, as were the record albums, which usually centered on a "remember the homeland" theme.

To further promote cultural consciousness, but more specifically to promote local unity, *La Prensa* sponsored a yearly beauty contest,

La Reina de la Simpatía (the Queen of Cordiality). It was a contest that the upper classes were more interested in than the lower, because many of the participants were from the Jóvenes Católicos de San Fernando, a middle-class organization. All of these activities helped the *ricos* promote Mexican cultural consciousness, but with no class differentiation; for all of them *mexicanos* were equal in the cultural and social sense, but not in philosophical abstraction or in economic reality.[33]

was the character portrayed by radio and movie roles . . . [and they] are not a picture of true reality," stated Uranga. "Many Mexicans are not just sitting back enjoying this stereotype. Many are protesting and raising their voice in protest. Now with Spanish films maybe a new change will take place." "This caricature," continued Uranga, "is responsible for people's view of themselves and the world around them."[34]

Uranga not only was worried about the discriminatory impact of the stereotype, but he was worried about the impact on the Mexicans' self-image: the *ricos* did not want their countrymen in the United States to become Americanized nor did they want them to learn behavioral patterns from the stereotypes. They wanted Mexicans who were educated, sophisticated, and *gente decente*, not lower-class Mexicans or Americanized Mexicans. Uranga criticized the *pocho* (the acculturated Mexican American) because he "mix[es] his English with his Spanish when he speaks." Uranga concluded that this characteristic of speaking correctly was "a rare virtue in our Mexicans in the United States." He socialized with the upper middle class, and he knew them as *gente decente*, but he did not socialize with the laboring class and knew them only as *gente corriente*.[35]

The *ricos*, as I have said, wanted to have one culture and one society for all the Mexicans in San Antonio. They wanted to hold time and acculturation in abeyance. Unfortunately, time brought change, and the *mexicano de adentro* chose freely to live in the United States (and even, by the 1940s and 1950s to stop reflecting on his or her Mexican heritage altogether). Degrees of acculturation varied, depending on whether someone lived in the barrio or not, and whether he or she chose simply to reflect or actually to participate in Mexican cultural activities.

The *ricos* hoped that their Casino Social Mexicano "would expand and serve as the primary social center of the [entire] Mexican community and bring into membership many of their fellow Mexicans." In this hope they were not being realistic; however, the description of a social event at the Casino was: "[I]t was a dance of elegance and informality. The real union that exists among our [*rico*] families was clearly shown [at the dance]. It was a party of sincerity and friendship . . . [everyone] enjoyed the cordial fiesta that reflected the [cultural] temperament of our society."[36]

Unfortunately, the *ricos* always saw San Antonio through the lens of a nationalist ideology. Whether rich or poor, Mexicans were Mexicans; for the *ricos* classes did not exist. Thus, their wish for homogeneity was idealistic. In direct contrast, LULAC's Americanist ideology was based on most Mexicans' emerging reality during the 1930s.

The *ricos*, however, may have had a sense of their comprador situation in San Antonio whenever they celebrated el Día de la Raza or when they thought of their status as exiles. *La Prensa* writer Juan Sánchez Azcona, for example, lamented the *ricos'* exile during a particular Día de la Raza; Sánchez Azcona wanted to celebrate this "day of Glory" but his spirit did not obey: "My spirit is sad because my body is far from my country. The doors to my country are closed." Azcona and other intellectuals believed that they were exiled from Mexico because they had tried to unveil the truth there about a country that "educates itself in its own lies" and whose "government has a false front under the disguise of democracy." For some businesspeople and intellectuals even the holidays were marred by these political thoughts and reflections; nevertheless, they celebrated. Even during the most difficult days of the Depression they continued their fiestas and parties. The Club Swástica and the Club Femenino were two of their main social organizations and provided "relief" from the isolation and alienation of their comprador status by having dances, teas, lectures, *fiestas patrias*, and banquets, if not for a homogeneous community, at least for themselves.[37]

The *ricos*, in many of these exclusive activities, frequently honored their own or other prominent people at banquets. Dr. Joaquín González, for example, was honored for his work in San Antonio, and Henry Wallace was honored for his political role in the United States (as vice-president to FDR). There were other political banquets, attended by the *ricos*, Mexican Americans, and the Americano political elite, often honoring representatives of the Mexican government passing through San Antonio to New York or Washington. Moreover, the *ricos*, through the Sociedad Cultura Mexicana, promoted banquets such as the one given for Mexican painter David Alfaro Siqueiros. These dinners were not only social events but political statements of a class in exile.[38]

The Alianza Hispano-Americana made more of a political statement. Although it was basically a mutualist organization that provided insurance and death benefits, it was also a strong socio-political organization that represented the interests of the *ricos* and helped

who were of the "clase humilde"; in fact, it had over seventeen thousand members in the United States. The workers were important. One chapter of the alliance in South Texas specifically praised the "virtues of the Mexican working classes," and *La Prensa* applauded the establishment of these chapters because they showed Mexicans in a good light to the Americanos. The alliance helped link the *ricos* and their philosophy to the poor by providing beneficial services to the lower classes. Overall, its existence was also a connection for many lower-middle-class and working-class Mexicans to their historical past. Often, the alliance sought to invest its members' funds in Mexican banks, and thus, it constantly promoted Mexican culture. Throughout the Southwest, it rivaled LULAC in its ultimate goals and general philosophy because it retained its belief in a strong Mexican consciousness and it served as an "investment" organization for the Mexican poor.[40]

Although the *ricos* focused some of their attention on the Mexicans' plight in San Antonio and the Southwest, and even though some of the *ricos* participated actively in the alliance, they were primarily interested in national and international problems, especially as they affected Mexico. In the 1930s these intellectuals, who commuted between San Antonio and other parts of the American continent; were specifically interested in the impact of the Depression worldwide. The Depression decade was seen by the *ricos* and these intellectuals as primarily a "crisis of civilization," a crisis based on the sickness of economic speculation that emanated from the constant growth and the continuing prosperity of a materialistic society. This intellectual,

cultural, and economic period of crisis in society, the *ricos* felt, was
a "purgatory" for the rich, but "hell" for the poor. They always had
a benevolent, although paternalistic, feeling for the poor—*la clase
humilde*—whether in San Antonio or in Mexico, and any sense of
economic or political crisis (such as the Depression or the Mexican
revolution), it seems, had a deep impact on their thinking. This was
true especially as it affected society and the poor as a whole. Both
events had the same impact on them: change. This affected, the *ricos*
felt, their primary philosophical axiom (which was Comte's): "Love
. . . is our principle, order our basis, and progress our end."[41]

Everywhere the *ricos* saw change. This disturbed them because
they wanted tradition, established standards of morality, justice, social classes; ethics and values of universality, continuity, and moderate change (but only if it was within the perception of time as being
elongated; other changes meant breaks and discontinuities). They
looked at Mexico and asked, "The moral forces of the revolution, the
heroes of the revolution, the saints of the revolution, the ideology of
the revolution—what does all this signify? If the Mexican revolution
[and government] should speak a civilized language rather than a
revolutionary one, we could understand . . . [it]." Jesús Guisa y
Azevedo (who wrote under the pseudonym Marco Polo), like other
ricos and intellectuals, could not understand the emotionalism of the
Mexican revolution. The perspective of the *ricos* and the intellectuals
was "rational," "civilized," and within the traditions of the upper class.
As Guisa y Azevedo wrote, all "men should be subject to reason, rationality and discipline." All revolutionary formulas, he emphasized,
were just "formulas of impoverished minds."[42]

Nemesio García Naranjo saw the era of the Porfiriato as similar
to Guisa y Azevedo's analysis of the revolutionary period—a period
of general intellectual impoverishment, emotionalism, and dictatorship. However, he claimed it was also different from the period of
revolution because under Porfirio Díaz there was some economic and
intellectual growth. The Porfiriato had been a time, García Naranjo
believed, when intellectuals like Amado Nervo, Manuel Gutiérrez,
and Justo Sierra could write. Everything, he pointed out, had been
blamed on Díaz by the revolutionaries; yet, it had been a time of civic
virtue, personal honor, cultural, economic, and intellectual progress,
as well as domestic capital investment. García Naranjo also believed
that the Huertista period was a continuation, although a correction,
of the Díaz period. In fact, Michael Meyer has suggested that the
Huerta regime, which was attacked by many in the revolution, was
responsible for many reforms, and those "introduced or proposed be-

tween February 1913 and July 1914 were more far sighted than many of Madero's." The *ricos* seemed to believe this.[43]

For most of the *ricos*, Porfirio Díaz's and Victoriano Huerta's regimes provided the parameters of their social theory and a guide to society's success. Ignacio E. Lozano, like García Naranjo, wanted a stable Mexico, but specifically he wanted peace, freedom to work, a guarantee for foreign investment, facilities for new industries, and suspension of the new agricultural laws. Lozano believed that the

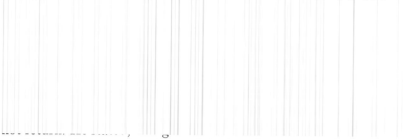

revolution — have moderation, political moderation, a politics of reconciliation. Here lies the solution to our national problems. Have rights for workers, but also have rights for industrialists; [have] protection for poor families . . . but [also] protection for landowners."[44]

For the *ricos*, the catalyst for change to an authentic Mexico was a class of *gente decente*, a cultural and nationalistic elite, but one that was focused and centralized by the leadership of one individual. García Naranjo, for example, in examining this question, placed Porfirio Díaz in the same category with Cromwell, Bismarck, and Bonaparte, because "these men liberated themselves from the collective psychology" and thus could understand how society worked. He and the other *ricos* did not want a dictator; they just wanted a strong leader who was responsible to an educated cultured class.[45]

Lic. Querido Moheno, the secretary of foreign relations under Huerta, analyzing the need for strong leadership, stated that at least "under Díaz we lived in a situation of frankness, [and the] excellence of force of a [great] man. Today [in Mexico] there is a difference between word and deed. [Today] [t]hings happen, but people don't realize it. At least under Díaz we knew how things were." Moheno, in spite of this statement, saw the Porfiriato and the revolution as being basically the same — regimes of force — except that under Díaz theory and practice were united.[46] In the period of the revolution there was a definite division between work and deed. This, Moheno believed, was a step backward for Mexico.

Another *La Prensa* writer, Jesús Guisa y Azevedo, also analyzing the revolution, pointed out that the major problems of the Mexican civil war were predominantly the struggle of classes, the antieconomic feelings of government, and a government that did not know how to intervene in society. "Above all," he continued, "misery was still present [in Mexico]; the poor were still poor; and the assertion [by the Mexican leadership] that the revolution was benefiting the worker is a lie."[47] The *ricos* were quite clear in what they wanted in Mexico: a harmony of spirit, not a crisis of spirit; a unification of classes, not a struggle of classes; absolute universal values, not relative ones; and men of stature and stability, not men of rhetoric and instability. They wanted a society of stability in family, private property, language, and religion (although they would tolerate change and refinements, but all within the consensus of commonly held intellectual and cultural beliefs). Although the 1920s and 1930s were the era of concord, the *ricos* held fast to their ideas. However, when the Mexican government (under Avila Camacho) presented them with an olive branch in 1941, they rushed to take it, but on their own terms, which they believed the president and Mexico were accepting.[48]

Because of their philosophy, the *ricos*, ironically, were respected and worked with Mexican Americans like Perales, González, and other LULAC members because the last, in their own way (the *ricos* felt), also wanted a community of peace, harmony, stability, reason, order, and progress. The philosophical content was different, but the form seemed to be the same. Most of all, both the *ricos* and LULAC wanted a civilized *gente decente* and progress within constitutional boundaries. Both the upper and the middle classes searched for a new order and a new community in the 1930s. Unfortunately, one looked toward the south, and the other toward the north.

The *ricos* emphasized "the Mexican flag and the national anthem" and while the Mexican middle class of San Antonio also placed great emphasis on the flag and the national anthem, for many of them it was the American rather than the Mexican. In the 1930s, however, Mexican nationalism was still of considerable importance in San Antonio, although there were many people already transferring consciousness to U.S. nationalism. In spite of these changing ideological forces, Mexican patriotism remained strong, at least in custom and tradition, through the 1940s, and even beyond, because of the future waves of immigration.

La Prensa writer Cieto González Víquez defined this Mexican patriotism concisely:

> La Patria is not just the land; it is something else. It is the solidarity of those who live and those who have died with those who will come

after us; it is the inheritance of the virtues and faults of our Raza with the willingness to guard in our hearts, like a holy angel, the memory of our fathers, grandfathers, and the traditions, as well as the customs, and "glorias nacionales" and to transmit them to those who will follow us in the constant movement of renovation and evolution.[49]

González Víquez was, in fact, articulating the essence of the consciousness of collectivity that made Mexicans different from Anglos and part of the duality of consciousness that Mexican Americans

although, of course, not all.

Ignacio E. Lozano tried to turn these tides of change by praising the patriotism of the repatriated workers, who were returning to Mexico either to escape the Depression or to help reconstruct the country. But, he stated that patriotism for Mexico was not enough, even though many Mexicans in the United States were willing to return for the national reconstruction; what was needed, Lozano emphatically stated, was a change in the Mexican government. Lozano not only wanted Mexicans to return, but he wanted the Mexican government to change from an emphasis on a political role to an administrative one. More administrators who were intelligent and concerned were needed in Mexico, he said. Lozano, of course, was thinking of the exiled *ricos* as the solution to Mexico's problems.[50]

The *ricos* felt that in Mexico and in San Antonio (and probably everywhere) "there was a need for 'good' men; for men who were examples for all, but there was also needed a [social] class to be seen and emulated. 'La Patria' [country or community] cannot just be talked about, [it must be] made by men of good class, [men] of [a good] upbringing."[51] The *ricos* tried to be these exemplars in San Antonio through their activities and through *La Prensa*, and in Mexico through their pronouncements and critiques as a "governing class" in exile.

As they focused on San Antonio at the end of the 1930s, however, they felt an ambivalence. The cultural hegemony through which they sought to unify the community was being undermined by time, by the efforts of LULAC, by community institutions, and simply by the choice of many Mexicans who just wanted to become Americans. An editorial in *La Prensa*, consequently, warned the West Siders that American culture should only be used to complement their own Mexican culture, not substitute for it. The relationship between the Mexican and the American culture, the *ricos* advocated, should always be equal. Sánchez Azcona, on this point, stated, "I have wanted to recommend to the Hispano-Americanos [of San Antonio] to make the effort to strongly conserve the Mexican culture." By doing this, he believed that the Mexican American could have a better perspective on American culture.[52] Reinaldo Esparza Martínez told the Mexicans on the West Side that "la Patria" was the "supreme sentiment." Mexican nationalism was in "our crib, in our foreheads as children, *la patria* envelops everyone rich [or] poor . . . it is food for our spirits. It permeates everything."

In spite of this constant propaganda to maintain a hegemony of Mexican spirit and culture, the *ricos* recognized that by their very physical existence and everyday life in San Antonio, the West Siders gravitated toward U.S. ways. Therefore, they clearly explained that

> [i]t has been said that patriotism was made by the government to control the people, this is not true. Patriotism is the son of human instinct. . . . It is like the animal instinct. Patriotism well understood, legitimate, is the love of your country; the devotion to its interests and its prosperity; the passion that lets us aspire and serve and maintain its laws and institutions, to defend it and call it magnificent. Patriotism to a country [however] does not exclude love of family, or love of humanity, or [love] of other countries. On the contrary [these patriotic feelings toward the United States] . . . are logical extensions of patriotism for your country [Mexico].[53]

The *ricos*, ironically, considered both Mexico and San Antonio's West Side as homogeneous culturally, socially, and politically. They wanted one class of people, *gente decente*, who were patriotic, civilized, and rational. However, they were worried about San Antonio's Mexicans because of the social, economic, political, and ideological differentiation that was occurring.

Regardless of their wishes, Americanization was a reality. To the *ricos*, American culture was not really equal to Mexican culture. Nemesio García Naranjo articulated the *ricos'* sentiments when he wrote that the United States was becoming "Babbitized," that is that it was becoming culturally mediocre and institutionally routinized. "Americans," he wrote, "do not care, want, or express concern for anything other than mediocrity. Moreover, only mediocre men run the United States."[54] (This feeling, however, changed somewhat when Franklin Roosevelt became president.) As a result of this feeling, the *ricos* felt that the spread of U.S. culture should be controlled. They feared the radio, for example. They felt that it was "the transmitter of [this mediocre] culture." This fear was not a fear of U.S. culture per se, but a fear of popular culture, mass culture. They therefore advised the San Antonio Mexican community to listen to worthwhile programs of "high culture," such as concerts and symphonies on the radio. Like the Lost Generation U.S. intellectuals, the *ricos* criticized mass culture; and like Joseph Wood Krutch, they indicted the "modern tem-

a large proportion of the Mexican laboring population (and Mexico needed their sweat and brawn). This process of emigration, of course, was not as important during the 1930s. Nevertheless, Lozano feared it, especially because he felt that any Mexican immigrant would be exposed to racial prejudice.

José Mario Dávila, another *La Prensa* writer, had other fears. He felt that the Mexican Americans and the Mexican residents of the United States would be the worst enemies of the Mexican immigrants because they favored the Box-Johnson restrictionist bill. Rodolfo Uranga disagreed. Uranga and *La Prensa*'s editorial staff were against the bill. For the most part, the *ricos* (like Box and Johnson) did not want "that kind of poor immigrant Mexican" in their community. Lozano and others did not see the Box-Johnson bill as the solution to immigration; instead, they saw the development of industry in Mexico as the solution. Answering Dávila, Uranga stated that some *mexicanos de adentro* were for restriction of these poor immigrants, but certainly not all of them.[56]

José Pomposa Salazar of *El Imparcial*, the Spanish newspaper in Nogales, Arizona, commenting in *La Prensa* on the immigration problem, wrote that the Mexican revolution should also open its doors the other way—toward Mexico. He urged the Mexican government to open its borders during the thirties for the upper-class Mexican exiles, who were just "wandering about without a country, without citizenship and [who were] souring their lives by being the downtrodden. Salazar emphasized "the tremendous work that has to be done in Mexico," and implied that the exiled *ricos* and intellectuals were the ones to help reconstruct the country. Moreover, "there . . . needs to be a president elected [in Mexico] who will open the border and allow the Mexicans in the United States to cross back standing on their feet rather than [crawling] on their knees to help the country."[57]

Lozano emphatically pointed out that the days of oppression had finally passed in Mexico, and therefore there should not be any Mexican who "is denied his national citizenship — because everyone [regardless of political belief] belongs to the same [Mexican] family."[58] Lozano editorialized that because of the need to reconstruct Mexico, there should be a reconciliation. All Mexicans, he argued, should forget their differences in political or religious matters; the seeking of ideological reconciliation and a new socioeconomic reconstruction of Mexico should be accomplished not only by the order of the government, but by the work of everyone in society. Employment and economic progress should become everyone's main goal. There should be established "a 'new' collective national life, and a 'new' spirituality." "There should especially be," he continued, "a program of equality, truth, and justice for all returning to build a true organic [social] body. We [can then] rid ourselves of our revolutionary convulsions and see the rise of a 'new' Mexican life, rich with work and order. We [in Mexico] are [at present] beaten, we are bloodied, we are poor, and bearers of doubts, and the salvation we seek cries for national fraternity"[59]

In essence, Lozano, Salazar, García Naranjo, Guisa y Azevedo, and others of the San Antonio comprador class were calling for a new order of humanity that stressed the continuities of Mexican history, not the discontinuities. This new order in Mexico would be one of political peace, economic reconstruction, social justice, law and order, spiritual benevolence, ideological moderation, equality, and public liberty. Above all, they wanted the unification of the "Mexican family," but united and led by the *gente decente* — the social and cultural elite. To help this elite, they wanted good administrative leadership and an alliance of the generals, but all within constitutional boundaries and always with the dual goal of national progress and an economic and cultural uplifting of the lower classes.

Specifically, the *ricos* felt that the means to achieve national unity and progress was through education. Unlike LULAC's definition of education, the *ricos* wanted to instill the "spirit of the revolution" in the minds of the Mexican people. This, they felt, was a national feeling "without words and without blood"; it would be a "revolution of actions." The *ricos* borrowed this theme from José Vasconcelos, but it sounded very similar to the cry of Díaz's *científicos* or even Dewey's pragmatists.

This type of revolution, within the political parameters outlined by the *ricos*, would produce a "new morality," a "new honor," and a "new order." Jesús Guisa y Azevedo succinctly outlined the *ricos'* political advice to the Mexican government:

> We want technology, science, reason, justice for all, liberty for the up-
> per classes ["*los buenos*"] and love for the lower classes ["*los deshere-*
> *dados*"] . . . this is neither more nor less, we want *order* [his empha-
> sis]. The order always comes from the top [of society] and never from

national economic progress, social unification, and justice for all were the goals. The *ricos* felt that they had the social theory for the exiled *mexicanos de afuera*, but they were not sure about their theory for the Americanizing *mexicanos de adentro*.[60]

In general, however, the philosophical ideas and the political ideology that the *ricos* held also guided them in their work with Mexicans in San Antonio and throughout the Southwest. Specifically, they did not like the labor strikes in San Antonio during the 1930s because they created divisions in the family, and they did not like poverty because they were humanitarians. They agreed, however, with LULAC's basic goals of uplifting the Mexican community and bringing a "new order" to San Antonio; just as the *ricos* searched for community in Mexico, LULAC searched for community in San Antonio. The *ricos*, consequently, agreed with LULAC on the need for order, community, unity, and progress. They disagreed with LULAC's main emphasis on Americanization, because it oriented Mexicans toward a future in the United States, as Mexican Americans. But, they agreed with LULAC's objective of retaining the West Siders' "Mexicanness." President Rubio of Mexico seems to have captured the reality of the Mexican American situation, and the *ricos* agreed with him, when he stated:

> I don't have to remind you of the need to reconstruct Mexico and
> consolidate the achievements of the revolution and to enhance civil so-
> ciety materially. There need to be a strength of character and virtue
> for this achievement.
> We would want all of the [Mexican] workers to return [from the

United States], but this would be difficult to achieve realistically; [consequently,] there has to be within each [Mexican American] worker a belief in the government of Mexico.

[If this is done], [w]e know that [those] workers living in the United States can promote a better image of Mexico by their every action, but [of course] the most they can do [to help Mexico] is to return and work in Mexico and have faith in the rebuilding of Mexico.[61]

Like Rubio, the *ricos* believed that if Mexicans in the United States could not or would not return to help reconstruct Mexico they could at least promote a better image by their attitudes, behavior, and their belief that, regardless of change, they were still part of a historical consciousness of a Mexican collectivity. For the exiles and for the Mexican government, the Mexicans in the United States were perceived as being only geographically separated from the homeland. They did not seem to grasp that over time the Mexicans in the United States had changed or were changing. They continued to see the Mexicans in the United States simply as a fifth column. The *ricos'* main dilemma during the 1920s and 1930s was how to be in San Antonio and other southwestern cities, but not become a part of U.S. culture and society. They tried to resolve the dilemma by remaining nationalists at heart and internationalists in interests. *La Opinión* and *La Prensa* reflected and articulated this orientation and perspective.

Since Ignacio E. Lozano had begun publishing *La Prensa* and *La Opinión*, the *ricos* never deviated from their dual goal of being critics of the Mexican revolution while trying to maintain a Mexican cultural hegemony in San Antonio, Los Angeles, and other southwestern communities with a large Mexican population. Through their press, their intellectuals, their cultural activities, their charitable promotions, their work in the Alianza Hispano-Americana, and personal example they sought to accomplish their goal of maintaining the "spirit of la Raza" and the nationalist allegiance within the hearts and minds of the Mexican immigrants and the already-resident Mexican Americans. While the revolution raged in Mexico they concentrated on their hegemonic activities in San Antonio, maintaining their lifestyle at the Casino Social. But in 1930, when the Depression began to affect the West Side, when the process of social differentiation began to be accelerated, and when the movement for the era of concord began in Mexico, the *ricos* clearly restated their philosophy, their political themes, and their ideology:

We serve our country [Mexico by] maintaining in this foreign country a Mexican spirit. And we maintain it by putting our compatriots

[living in the United States] in touch with Mexico [through our press].
But, let it not be said that our contact with Mexico is only information
[in our newspapers] on the situation, nor have we just been critical
of the men [in government] and the revolutionary proceedings. . . .

Without a doubt some of the political situations [in Mexico] seem
very important to us and have merited our criticisms; also they have
been important to us because [they] serve to heighten our [personal]
hopes to return. We have not seen or even wanted to see the conditions
of Mexico from just a limited [philosophical or political] point of view.

will is [always] the same: to serve our country. . . .

All the Mexicans of good breeding [*bien nacidos*] want the best for
Mexico: that its authorities preserve its [social and cultural] order.[62]

Lozano's newspapers reflected and promoted this philosophy, and
most of the *ricos* in exile lived by it. As a consequence, Lozano's fame,
in particular, spread throughout San Antonio and the Southwest,
mainly because he was the most visible. His reputation was not necessarily the result of his individual achievements, but of what he
represented — the personification of Mexican culture, tradition, and
gente decente. Lozano's ideas, values, and ideological perspective were
the views espoused by his nationally and internationally distributed
newspapers. He was the epitome of *"los mexicanos."* He was Mexican
in culture, philosophy, and ideology, and he had, above all, a humanistic feeling for his people.

These feelings, these attitudes, and these views were shared by the
rest of the comprador class of San Antonio, although they probably
differed on some points. During the 1930s, many of the *ricos* were
only physically in San Antonio; their hearts and minds were in Mexico. They were concerned, but aloof; they were nationalist, but also
internationalist; they were always *Mexicanos*, but above all they were
gente decente. Lozano once said, "May we never lose our Mexican
nationalism . . . may it fortify itself in the [Mexican] *colonias* in the
United States . . . [this] spirit of our blood of our traditions and our
customs" (April 6, 1937). The *ricos* constantly attempted to instill this
"spirit of our blood" throughout the West Side and throughout the

Southwest, between 1929 and 1941, using *La Prensa, La Opinión*, and other newspapers. As Lozano claimed, their newspapers went beyond frontiers and beyond politics.[63]

Rodolfo Uranga urged that this spirit of "Raza," of "family," of "cultural homogeneity," and of patriotism be translated into concrete action by the exiled comprador class. He urged more direct guidance and consultation and believed that "our *clase humilde*" in the United States, especially in the large cities like San Antonio, always needed personal counsel and orientation from the "cultured and educated Mexicans." They needed, he said, this help even in everyday situations: "to cross the streets in the big cities, to take the trains in the railroad stations, to ride the streetcars, to find the hotels, to eat in the restaurants, [and] in all situations." He added, sincerely but patronizingly "Our *clase 'humilde'* has our help."[64]

The *ricos* were the upper class and, without a doubt, considered themselves as such within the San Antonio community. Their paternalism, ironically, was equal to Archbishop Drossaert's, who was not a *rico*, but, nevertheless, was a prince of the church. The Mexican workers and lower middle class, consequently, labored not only under the oppressiveness of poverty, but under the debilitation of deference and paternalism. Many LULAC members, who were upper middle class and who socialized with the *ricos*, also believed that being Mexican American was tantamount to being *gente decente*. Deference and paternalism were thus pervasive in San Antonio, emanating from the *ricos*, the Catholic Church, the upper-middle-class Mexican Americans, the Anglo elite, the military, and the very southern *élan vital* of the city.

On later reflection, Uranga placed this paternalism and deference on a more philosophical plane when he countered the argument of a California newspaper that stated that "Mexico in the United States is a community without a nationality. It is a 'pueblo sin Patria,' it is neither Mexican nor American." Uranga argued against this by discussing the meaning of "*patria*," ethnicity, and nationalism:

> In spite of the discrimination that we face in the United States, it is not quite accurate to say that we have no *patria* in living in the United States or that we are just separate groups of Mexican individuals [residing in the United States], and it is not true that we are neither *mexicanos* nor Americans. We have something [in the United States] that Mexicans do not have in Mexico, freedom of thought, of expression, of work, [and] of writing. We also have security and peace. We are not subject to the whims of the "little" generals, killers, or caciques, [as are Mexicans in Mexico], and we have more opportunities for education, and [the opportunity] to live in a civilized way. What does

"patria" mean? Just the land we were born on? The concept of *patria* is larger and wider in definition than just native land. "La Patria" is formed by many things: traditions, language, religion, music, art, beliefs, hopes, literature, customs, memories, and other things. We have all of these even though we live in the United States. We thus conserve Mexico here with few exceptions, and each day we value these [Mexican traditions and ideas] . . . without assimilating the good things of the Anglo-Saxon nor returning his hospitality. . . . Mexicans in Mexico

tion [in exile].[65]

Unfortunately, Uranga was speaking of the Mexicans in the United States as if they were all one homogeneous group; ironically, the *ricos*, because of their continued self-perception as exiled Mexicans, were as much agents of the deference and paternalism in the West Side as the Anglos they criticized. The *ricos*' ideological framework was coated with such a nationalistic tinge that even though they did differentiate among middle class and poor Mexicans, they assumed that everyone had something in common: nationalism. They propagandized from this patriotic viewpoint and acted out of it. The *ricos* were an intellectual comprador class that saw the present through the eyes of an extending past, and they saw the historical reality of the 1930s — whether in Mexico or in the United States — as only transitory. The future would be the past, and the past the future.

Ironically, and probably without direct awareness, Uranga's commentary expressed the reality of change: it implied that while he still claimed to be a Mexican in exile and wanted to retain his *Mexicanidad*, he was receptive to the liberties of American life. His Mexican perceptions, reflections, and feelings flowed out of a historical consciousness of collectivity and not out of a reality of collectivity. History, acculturation, and time had caught up with him and many of the *ricos*; U.S. society was beginning to engulf them as well. Only their memories, reflections, and cultural festivities kept them *mexicanos*.

Nevertheless, throughout the 1920s and the 1930s, their philosophy, their ideas, their ideology and lifestyle formed the core of life in the West Side. The perceptions and reflections of people in the West

Side reflected Mexican thought and culture. The *ricos'* cultural super-structure had been hegemonic. Often people who could read (or were read) *La Prensa* became imbued with a sensitivity toward the *ricos'* philosophy. People like Pilar Arranga, who was originally from Coahuila and had come to San Antonio in 1900, faithfully read every issue of *La Prensa* because the newspaper carried national, international, and some community news. *La Prensa*, moreover, always carried advice in a daily column entitled "Thought for the Day." This column recommended what appeared to be simple commonsense advice to the community in the form of simple homilies. In actuality they were very political and ideological statements that were meant to instill intellectual and behavioral changes: "Work is the material of virtue"; "Laziness is the material of vices"; "Language is important; speaking well reflects on our lives"; "Good speech is essential"; and "Moderation is better than an outbreak of temperament." This advice often formed the basis for the community's changing philosophy, which was in turn the basis for changing behavioral patterns; it attempted to make *gente corriente* into *gente decente.* This kind of advice also helped LULAC because it too wanted to be *gente decente,* but Americanized *gente decente.*

The *ricos* were not fully aware of the extent and strength of the process of change and Americanization that was occurring in San Antonio. For them, Mexicans were culturally and ideologically in a constantly expanding and changing present that only had traces of the past and future, and they filled in the ideology and culture of this elongated present. They felt hegemonic in class, culture, and ideology; consequently, they "knew" that the West Side reflected their Mexican ideas, sentiments, feelings, and sensitivities. What Peter Berger has said of culture in general, can be said of the *ricos'* culture and ideology in particular: it was "ubiquitous in presence, complex in detail, and . . . overwhelming and incomprehensible in its totality, and in its intricacy."[66]

Nevertheless, regardless of the *ricos'* desires, thoughts, and activities, a new process of social, cultural, and ideological formation was occurring between 1929 and 1941. The Mexican community of San Antonio continued to be Mexican, but through the process of class fragmentation and differentiation; through the influences of the American Catholic Church; through the acquisition of the English language; through the bombardment of American culture vis à vis education, movies, radio, songs, and politics; and through changing family relations, it was becoming Americanized. The degree differed according to class and time spent living in the United States as well as the extent of rural or urban experience, but nevertheless, the situation was slowly changing. Not everyone was changing in the same way and to the same degree, but change and Americanization were a fact of life. Of particular importance was the fact that the constant immigration had virtually stopped during the Depression, so there were fewer immigrants with their suitcases of Mexican culture to have an ideological and traditional influence on the West Side. During this cultural respite, the Mexican communities in the United States allowed the Americanization process to take root.

to Mexico; the era of concord was over, and what Ignacio E. Lozano had said in 1930 was now, for all practical purposes, true: "The period of isms is dead [in Mexico], Callismo, Profirismo, Maderismo, Carrancismo, and Obregonismo." In fact, even Cardenismo was now over.[67]

As Michael Meyer and William Sherman have written, "Avila Camacho . . . on December 1, 1940 became the 57th president of Mexico. His inaugural address read with United States Vice President Henry Wallace attending the ceremony, suggested the revolution was over, that its tasks had been completed and that Mexico was moving from a period of revolution to a period of evolution." Some years later it seemed apparent to many exiled *ricos* that their vision and dreams of a harmonious Mexico had come true:

> On September 16, 1942 on the 132nd anniversary of the Grito de Dolores, an amazing and unprecedented display of camaraderie occurred on the balcony of the National Palace. Six former presidents — Adolfo de la Huerta; Plutarco Elías Calles (invited to return from the United States); Emilio Portes Gil; Pascual Ortiz Rubio; Abelardo L. Rodríquez; and Lázaro Cárdenas all linked arms with Avila Camacho to indicate that past antagonisms had been forgotten and that Mexico was fully united in time of war.[68]

But, regardless of the impact of World War II on the ensuing unity in Mexico, the *ricos*, many who were returning home, must have felt that the historical, cultural, and intellectual unity and continuities were now a reality in a "new" Mexico.

Those *ricos* who remained could say, as *La Prensa* writer Hortensia Elizondo told her readers in Mexico in 1941, "The United States

is different [now] and not because I have become Americanized . . .
Mexicans should recognize that the United States is more than materialistic . . . Mexicans should not be snobs. In San Antonio there
is now less hostility [than in 1930]. Mexicans here are proud of being
themselves . . . of being bilingual." Elizondo was, of course, referring to the Mexican Americans of the new order, the middle class that
was beginning to build a new community.[69] By 1941 *La Prensa* and
La Opinión (both of which had always been published in Spanish)
were beginning to publish partly in Spanish and partly in English;
bilingualism and biculturalism — Mexican Americanism — had begun.

9

The Emerging Middle Class

...trained, sincere, and earnest leaders can the beautiful ideals of the League of United Latin American Citizens be realized.

— Carlos E. Castañeda

You [Mexican Americans] have been taught in those ideals of liberty and freedom, justice and quality . . . and you have for inspiration, the patriotism, self-sacrifice, and valor of Washington, Lincoln, Roosevelt, as well as Simón Bolívar, Miguel Hidalgo and Benito Juárez . . . You have an opportunity few of your race possess.

— Manuel C. González

INTRODUCTION

The ideas and ideology of the League of United Latin American Citizens were the intellectual wave of the future for the Mexicans in San Antonio's West Side, the expression of a new consciousness: "In 1929, with the great social upheaval of the Depression just ahead, the Texas wind carried a whisper of hope to the most native of all Texas' sons, the Mexican-Americans."[1] Within the extensive Mexican community of San Antonio there was forming a Mexican American mind that was partially a product of the Mexican middle class's search for community and a place in U.S. society during the 1920s and, es-

pecially, the 1930s. In 1939 J. Montiel Olivera, the compiler of the
Latin American Yearbook of San Antonio, described this new mentality as "one isolated from the intellectual roots that nourished it:
the Anglo-American and the Hispano-American minds."[2] This Mexican American mind flourished within the middle class of entrepreneurs — restaurateurs, bakers, barbers, shoestore owners, butchers,
furniture store owners, gasoline station owners, jewelers, tailors, druggists, laundry owners, and over 350 grocery store owners — as well as
the small but significant number of professionals.[3]

It was from these people that a culturally cohesive and intellectually conscious Mexican American middle class developed. Its way
of thinking and feeling, its lifestyle, was different from that of the
ricos and the laborers. This class of Mexicans, wrote political scien-
tist O. Douglas Weeks in 1929, has

> profited from the superior educational and economic advantages thus
> afforded [in San Antonio] as well as from contacts with the new [Ameri-
> cans] . . . who have poured in [to the city] from all parts of the south
> and middle west, in spite of the fact that these new people have often
> not understood them. True enough, many of these city dwellers of Mexi-
> can extraction have remained ignorant and are constantly drawn to
> the newly arrived Mexican immigrants who help fill these Mexican
> Quarters, but the fact remains that there has arisen in their midst a
> class of prosperous, educated citizenry whose living conditions and at-
> titudes compare favorably with American standards.[4]

The consciousness of this small but growing middle class was formulated and articulated by the LULAC members, who sought, in
general, "the promotion of the effective exercise of American citizenship, the cultural advancement of persons of Mexican ancestry, and
the effacement of public school racial distinctions." Commenting on
this new intellectual phenomenon, Paul Taylor in 1934 wrote, "[In]
part the motive of the Mexican-American was simply to assert the
consciousness of American citizenship [and] . . . the Mexican American group recognizes the nature of its self-assumed task of lifting the
cultural level of . . . [all the Mexican] people."[5]

The Mexican American middle class through LULAC attempted
to make all of the Mexican community in San Antonio into Mexican
Americans. This was their formula for success, prosperity, and equality, and of all of the Mexican Americans in San Antonio two leaders
personified the Mexican American mentality: Alonzo S. Perales and
Manuel Carvajal González. These men's goal was intellectual hegemony, their vehicle was LULAC, and their philosophy was liberal and
pragmatic.

The Organization of LULAC

The United States fought World War I to make the world "safe for democracy." It was an attempt to make democracy a reality and reality democratic, and the Mexican population in San Antonio and throughout the Southwest believed in this idea and this ideal. Mexicans attempted to prove their loyalty as U.S. citizens by enlisting by the thousands. Because of patriotism, self-pride, or just poverty they left their home towns, which were worlds of "discrimination, preju-

cording to Lic. M. C. González, returning World War I Mexican veterans, because they were immediately confronted with many social and economic problems, were directly responsible for establishing the Order of the Sons of America, the precursor to LULAC in San Antonio. Given their experience and training in the war, they wanted to fight, not acquiesce, and since, as they believed, they had helped the United States during the war, they now wanted to help themselves.[7]

Some of these returning veterans were doctors, lawyers, artists, musicians, and most were middle class. As part of this cadre, J. Luz Saenz, a schoolteacher and LULAC leader in South Texas during the 1930s, wrote a book reflecting on the Mexican American experience during World War I. In his book he asked,

> Have we saved democracy, these countries' civilization, humanity? I do not know. But I do know that the Mexican American has distinguished and defined himself [because of the war]. The glorious stars and stripes that we have saved with our lives in the fields of war, in Europe, is indisputable. [It is] the flag of our sons in the future. With sacrifices like this, is how we build the country and the flag is honored. Justice is not forgetting to write in the last glorious chapter of the national history of the United States that Mexican Americans have contributed their blood.

Mexican Americans, Saenz emphasized, went to war to fight for this country's national honor and principles and to "guard and protect" the United States. But, as Saenz reminded the emerging Mexican American generation of the 1930s, their war did not stop after World

War I, but "continues against the everyday injustices the Mexican receives daily."[8]

This new pride and sense of mission did not touch the *ricos*. The *Latin American Yearbook* of 1939 served as a somber reminder to the Mexican American middle class that even by the end of the 1920s there was still an upper-class Mexican elite. The directory pointed out that the city still had a "group of hispano-Americans of high culture." J. Montiel Olivera, the directory's editor, also wrote that not only in San Antonio but "in other regions . . . [like] El Paso, [and] Laredo, there is reproduced in a minor way this same [socially stratified] composition and in the [Rio Grande] Valley, Corpus Christi, Houston, [and] Austin, where the density of the Mexican population is also noticeable." Olivera, in spite of the continued intellectual influence of the comprador class of Mexicans residing in San Antonio and throughout the Southwest, saw the rise of the Mexican middle class as positive because of the need for a "new group" and a "new consciousness" to deal with the Mexican communities' geographical segregation and social ostracism and racial discrimination that was worse than the blacks' plight. "It is," he said, "true, and lamentable, [that] the existence of prejudice, directed at the Hispanic American, is vigorously manifest, first in the segregation in the schools, and afterwards in all of the everyday life of the [Mexican] citizen, causing him to be ostracized." Thus there arose in the early 1920s the beginnings of a consciousness whose cry was, as Alonzo Perales would later write, "en defensa de mi raza."[9]

The Order of the Sons of America was founded in San Antonio by a group of veterans and other politically conscious individuals: Frank and Melchor Leyton, Mercy Montes, Pablo Cruz, Jr., Leo Longoria, Antonio Tarín, Abraham Armendaris, Vincent Rocha, M. C. González, and John Solís. All were middle-class Mexicans, and as Solís explained, "we didn't have anything in 1921 [so] we decided to organize our people to try and better the condition of Mexican Americans here in San Antonio and Bexar County." The first year, according to Solís, thirty-seven people joined the organization whose general goal was "to develop better American citizens and urge education." In October of 1921, the Order of the Sons of America, which was the first consciously Mexican American group, was chartered by the State of Texas.[10]

The other goals of the organization were general, but straightforward: the achievement of economic, social, and racial equality with other Americans; the attainment of social and economic opportunity; and the development of political power. The vehicles for achieving these goals were to be the many councils that were established throughout Texas. The main membership requirement, because of the group's integrationist political goals, was U.S. citizenship. A major emphasis was also placed on the members' learning and speaking English to articulate the new discourse.[11] When one of the members was asked why the Order of the Sons was organized, he responded more specifically and more philosophically than Solís:

> There were a number of Mexican men who had served in the war.

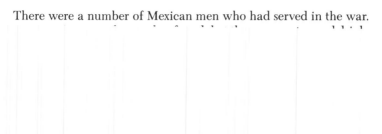

few, they nevertheless managed to establish organizational councils in many towns and cities outside of San Antonio: Somerset, Pearsall, Corpus Christi, Harlingen, Brownsville, Laredo, McAllen, La Gruella, and Encino. Each council, however, differed slightly in its philosophical and personal emphasis from the parent organization and from the other councils. Even the names of the councils reflected this variation from 1921 through 1927: Order of the Sons of America, Knights of America, and the League of Latin American Citizens.[13]

In San Antonio, however, another distinct organization was founded by M. C. González and named Los Caballeros de América, with its own voice, the *Luchador* (the Fighter), to promote the organization's ideals. González and other members traveled throughout Texas establishing their own clubs, giving lectures, distributing manifestos, and constantly calling for the improvement of the Mexican communities. González's group had differences with Perales's League of Latin American Citizens, although the differences were more personal and tactical than philosophical.[14]

Regardless of these differences of "personalisms," all of the organizations agreed with the prominent Mexican American who forcefully, imaginatively, and accurately stated that underlying the principles of these organizations was a concrete vision and desire:

> We want [Mexicans in the United States] to be proud of their race, but to be loyal to the government [of the United States]. First . . . I tell my people that they should be proud of their race. The Latin race has produced the greatest music, art [and] poetry; the Anglo-Saxon, the greatest government and system of dispensing justice. The superiority

of race is not a question of color, but of industry and efficiency, the ability to do more work on less food. The American [for example] eats a big breakfast of eggs and bacon. The Mexican with a cigarette and a cup of coffee goes out and does a morning's work. [It is, therefore, a question of] . . . the ability to save and accumulate—thrift—and to use those accumulations.[15]

The ideology of this "new consciousness" was clear: be proud of being Mexican in culture, but be American in politics, and most of all be industrious, efficient, and productive. The variations in interpretation of this Protestant work ethic reflected the differing councils and organizations in the 1920s. Some stressed American patriotism, some racial pride, some financial equality, and some equal opportunity. This pluralism of differences (but with an overall consensus of purpose) was characteristic of both the U.S. and the Mexican traditions of thought—Americans within a consensus of liberal thought, but Mexicans within a consensus of culture. Nevertheless, the 1920s were the seedbed for the sprouting philosophy of intellectual Mexican Americanism that would begin to flower in the 1930s and 1940s.

With the closing of the Roaring Twenties, when the United States was at the "crossroads of liberalism" (Charles Forcey's phrase), two things became clear to these Mexicans who aspired to be Mexican Americans: they needed a very clear social and political program, and they needed organizational unification. Therefore, early in 1927, a call for a unification meeting of all the major organizations—the Order of the Sons of America, the Knights of America, the League of Latin American citizens, and los Caballeros de América—was issued by prominent Corpus Christi businessman and political leader Ben Garza, the head of Council IV of the Order of the Sons of America (the largest of the organizations). The meeting, which was held at Harlingen, Texas, was the first of a series of meetings aimed at eventual unification, and such prominent San Antonio leaders as diplomat and intellectual Alonzo S. Perales, John Solís, M. C. González, Mauro Machado, and James Tafolla attended. Three other leaders attended from South Texas: Ben Garza, former Texas legislator; J. T. Canales; and J. Luz Saenz. After much discussion, argument, and compromise, on May 19 and 20, 1929, Ben Garza, the president of the session, and M. C. González, the secretary, announced that the League of United Latin American Citizens (LULAC) was now the single representative body of the Mexican American middle class, and Ben Garza would be its first president. The acronym LULAC, it was pointed out, contained the central principles of the organization:

L — for *L*ove of country and fellowman
U — For *U*nity of purpose
L — For *L*oyalty to country and principles
A — For *A*dvancement of a people
C — For *C*itizenship, true and unadulterated.[16]

The LULAC constitution was clear in its ideological commitment: "to develop within the members of our race, the best, purest, and

grate the community into the political and social institutions of American life. The constitution of LULAC illustrates this fundamental transformation from self-help and protective to assimilative activities.[17]

The principles, ideas, and goals of LULAC converged in the middle class, the *ricos*, and the rest of the Mexican population. Alonzo Perales a few months after the convention, on July 5, 1929, wrote, in an almost Kennedyesque temper of optimism and determination, that the essence of this Mexican American program for the unification of the rising middle class was social, political, and intellectual development. The central themes of the article in the middle-class newspaper *El Paladín* (The Champion) were to become the shaping intellectual themes and contours of the Mexican American generation: political unification; American citizenship; economic functionalism; self-responsibility; the pursuit of justice; liberal education; and a redefinition of self and community within a cultural and intellectual redemption of *lo mexicano*. Prophetically, Perales wrote, "The day the Mexican-American betters his own conditions and finds himself in a position to make full use of his rights of citizenship, that day he will be able to aid [all of] the Mexican citizens [in the United States] in securing what is due him and to help him assure himself of his own welfare [justice,] and happiness." Continuing to sound the trumpet, but stressing the stumbling blocks, Perales stated, "Undoubtedly the two greatest obstacles for the Americanization [and integration] of the Mexican Texans are the racial prejudice which the . . . [non-Mexican] harbors against us and certain [cultural] customs which are repugnant to ours, but the Mexican-American has adjusted himself to the latter, adopting only what there is of good in them." Then calling for self-reliance, self-determination, and a new perspective in order to secure a place in U.S. society, he wrote; "Without a doubt we shall have to effect our own *intellectual redemption* [my emphasis]. If we Mexican-Americans and the Mexican citizens raised in the United States are to occupy the honorable place that we merit, it is indispensable to educate ourselves."[18]

This new generation of leaders emerging from the ideological vortex of *lo mexicano* and *lo americano* were, as San Miguel suggests, "conscious of themselves as an emerging middle class," and

> LULAC members assumed the responsibility of educating and protecting the Mexican American population and incorporating it into the institutions of their country. But their integration was not to be achieved at the expense of their cultural background. This group of individuals was not calling for the total assimilation of the Mexican American population into . . . [U.S.] cultural society. . . . Integration into . . . American political and social life was to be a selection process.

In fact, the attitude of the middle class was quite clear about this: even before Perales's unification article, an essay in *El Paladín* on June 14, 1929, entitled "Our Attitude before History" clearly stated that "we solemnly declare once and for all to maintain a sincere and respectful reverence for our social origin of which we are proud." This, the article continued, "ought to be our proof that our efforts to be rightfully recognized as citizens of this country do not imply that we wish to become scattered nor much less abominate our Latin heritage, but rather on the contrary, we will always feel for it the most tender love and the most respectful veneration."[19] This rising middle class sought to maintain a Mexican consciousness of collectivity even though it was accepting the Lockian idealism and Jeffersonian emphasis of individualism and the reality of James Madison's and the New Deal's emphasis on political pluralism.

With the reality of unification, definite political and educational goals, and a common philosophical orientation to make Mexicans into Mexican Americans (while maintaining a Mexican sensibility), LULAC began immediately to spread and attempt to "uplift" cultural pride, to increase the rate of U.S. citizenship, and educationally to advance the Mexican population throughout Texas (especially in the San Antonio area). By 1933 LULAC chapters had spread from Texas to Arizona, New Mexico, Colorado, California, and even the District of Columbia and other eastern states. Wherever there was a Mexican middle-class community, LULAC was embraced.

Because the organization's growth by 1937 was in part due to the work of the women, the Texas LULAC leadership decided to give them equal leadership privileges, but with separate councils. A dual organizational structure was established and Mrs. F. I. Montemayor was elected the first woman to the LULAC general office. LULAC also established the Junior LULAC between 1938 and 1939 — under the sponsorship of the adult councils. LULAC leaders throughout the thirties sought to incorporate the whole family within the organizational

day life.

This Mexican American mind and body sought hegemony in San Antonio's West Side between 1929 and 1941. The peak of LULAC's growth was reached in 1940–41 because of the considerable recruiting and propagandizing work being done in all the states in view of the impending war and the threat to America of fascism. Rapid growth was also due to the organizational tactics put in use in the early 1930s with the formation of the Escuadrón Volante (Flying Squadron). The cadre of San Antonio leaders made sweeps into different areas to organize new clubs and recruit new members as well as take the LULAC philosophy into "all corners of the state and to all hearts." By 1941, however, many LULAC members throughout the Southwest were placed on the organization's inactive rolls because they had enlisted in the military after Pearl Harbor.[20]

Throughout the 1930s, however, LULAC was conscious that it had a historical and ideological mission to accomplish. If the family, the church, the educational system, and the political arena were the institutional transmitters of change for the Mexican American generation, LULAC members were the active bearers of change via their integrationist ideas and liberal ideology. In 1932 LULAC president M. C. González placed LULAC in historical perspective: "We are here on a mission. To make living conditions better for the coming and succeeding generations; not to accomplish that work is to fail in our duties."[21] Then he underlined LULAC's major task as the voice and leadership of the Mexican American generation in the 1930s: the hegemonic confrontation with the *ricos* of San Antonio, because they were only building a Mexican consciousness. "The *ricos* were never part of our [everyday] life," remembers González, "their newspaper, *La Prensa*, kept the image of Mexico alive, but never the welfare of Mexican American citizens of the United States or Texas." The role of the *ricos*, however, was seen as useful by LULAC and González because it helped to preserve the "Spanish Mexican culture."[22]

Using poetic form, González stated LULAC's historical purpose, which would accomplish what he and LULAC felt the *ricos* would not do: "We are builders of a better race [in the United States]. Tho' brief our time and span, there shall be more of happiness than when our age began and tho' we cannot see it now, when all is understood. We shall leave less of wrong behind. And more of what is good."[23] Then, in less poetic language, he, like Perales, formulated the major political, psychological, and philosophical tenets of the Mexican American mind: "The minds of the younger generation of Americans, whatever their racial extraction might be, must be trained to be subservient to no one; to feel and act equal with all others; to grow into manhood upright, with no complexes of any kind, with loyalty to the flag and respect to the constituted authorities, and an abundance of patriotism in their hearts; that is, if we are to have leaders among the Latin citizens of this country."[24]

An editorial in the *LULAC News* underscored the new freedom of the individual and the collective: "We should endeavor to develop aggressiveness of the right sort and be able to pursue our own initiative instead of waiting for someone else to do the things we have thought of doing but never put into execution." Then, in terms of the collective, the editorial continued, "The Latin American people, and only they, can solve the educational [and political] problems that confront us. . . . Only the Latin American people can do this — a united people, firmly resolute, true to the principles of progress and to the betterment of our brothers."[25] The die had been cast; LULAC's leaders had accepted the Enlightenment concept of the progression of time and the concept of the movement of history as being synonymous with progress and optimism. This was dramatically opposed to the *ricos'* perspective and understanding of time and history.

The ideas expressed by González and the *LULAC News* were in part also expressed by *La Prensa*. Although the *ricos* agreed in spirit with the thrust of LULAC's goal to "uplift" the community, they remained anchored to the idea that Mexicans could live in the United States and coexist with American culture, but not become part of it. They always remained convinced that all *mexicanos de afuera* must remain Mexican. However, on January 1, 1930, *La Prensa* realized that many Mexicans wanted to remain in the United States rather than return to Mexico; therefore, it ran an editorial that the editors felt should be the interpretation of the intellectual mood of the emerging middle sector of the Mexican population in San Antonio and throughout the Southwest. The editorial was entitled "Conserve the Spirit of the Raza," and the message was simple and direct: retain the Spanish heritage but learn the American way of life. Remember that the Spanish speaking can contribute "confraternity" to the American spirit of violence.

For many of the lower-middle-class and laboring San Antonio

But, in spite of this, *La Prensa* could still print an editorial such as the above because it did not completely contradict its own basic objective: to maintain a Mexican cultural life-world. (In coming decades continual poverty and immigration as well as personal choice, would maintain this cultural hegemony.)

LULAC's mission was helped by the fact that by the thirties there were numerous towns and cities in the Southwest, including San Antonio, that already contained a population of Mexicans who were second- and even third-generation American citizens; a generational separation that was a drawback to the *ricos'* philosophy. These Mexican Americans in San Antonio and the Southwest were being changed by institutions and their own decisions to change. Yet, these native Mexican Americans often welcomed their Mexican relatives, although by the Depression decade they began to establish some social, intellectual, and cultural distance between themselves and the poor Mexicans. LULAC, as well as the community institutions in the 1930s, also helped them form this feeling of distinctiveness. Douglas Weeks, who had been one of the few non-Mexicans to be invited to the 1929 meeting of LULAC and had observed the phenomenon of this new developing consciousness, wrote that this generationally different Mexican American who had

> recently awakened to a new sense of the potentialities of his race, views which concern not only these [new impoverished] conditions in the towns, but the older conditions which still prevail in the country. He believes in his people; he believes that what he has [socially and materially] accomplished for himself may be realized in part for his less fortunate [working-class] brothers, and he is [also] at present strongly urged

by a desire to organize his own [middle-class] element for the purpose of hastening the development of their people and supplementing what an improved school system in the towns at least has been able somewhat to accomplish [i.e., making Mexicans into Mexican Americans].[27]

The *ricos'* intellectual hold was being weakened, and astute observers like Weeks could see it.

In addition to pursuing this goal of material progress for all and bringing a new sense of dual consciousness, this San Antonio Mexican American middle-class generation led by LULAC sought specifically to eliminate racial prejudice, gain equality before the law, equal educational facilities, and equal political representation in local, state, and national politics. However, LULAC, as the conscious vehicle of the middle-class mind, also acknowledged that, as Weeks had noted, "the greatest stumbling block in the way of accomplishing this end is the Mexican-American himself, who possesses no clear conception of the significance of the privileges and duties of his American citizenship." In other words, LULAC had first to direct its educational and political activities of consciousness raising to the middle class before it could help the rest of the Mexican community. LULAC, therefore, sought to arouse the middle class, as Weeks pointed out, "to consciousness of that citizenship." Thus, it attempted to educate the upper- and middle-class sectors in their political and civil rights and obligations. As a result, Weeks observed that LULAC members were the "intelligent class of Mexican-Americans," but that they were not primarily interested in the Mexican national or the Mexican agricultural transient.[28]

In fact, Weeks pointed out, LULAC saw the Mexican alien and the agricultural class as a deterrent for three reasons: first, they took jobs away from the middle class; second, they also lowered the standard of living; and third, they created racial prejudice by not knowing American customs or American laws. These three factors, according to LULAC and many middle-class Mexicans, were responsible for many of the problems encountered by Mexican Americans. Members of the middle class, nevertheless, were still proud of being Mexican even though they sought the benefits that Americanization would bring them. However, they also realized the irony that "whether citizen or not, the problems of the lowly Mexican in Texas and in the United States are essentially the same [as those of the middle class]." Therefore, as Weeks wrote after having conversations with LULAC members, they fully realized "that an improved status for their [Mexican American] fellow citizens will have as its by-product an improved status for the alien Mexican [as well]."[29]

Although the middle class of Mexican Americans felt drawn to help the poorer aliens and the agricultural workers, it still continued to live in or move to the middle-class Prospect Hill area in the 1920s and the 1930s. And, although members of the middle class lived within the boundaries of the Latin Quarter, they created an enclave that would allow them geographical protection from the workers, peasants, and "rabble rousers" who were not Americans legally or ideologically. Of course, this was not always entirely conscious; it was manifested

[the Mexican American middle class] who work, study, worship, and strive for a better more comfortable life . . . We, who live and work in Prospect Hill, increase our love for this little peice [*sic*] of land daily — our love for our neighborhood increases, so do our obligations and responsibilities increase to make this, our shore in America, a better place to live in total harmony with the rest of our town.[31]

Prospect Hill attracted such middle-class families as Ernesto Garza's (broom factory owner); Severo Gonzales's (importer); Rómulo Mungía's (print shop owner); Sánchez's (funeral business owner); Acuña's (furniture store owner); and Joe Olivares's (real estate and hotels). Also, prominent political activists such as James Tafolla, Charles Barrera, Rudy Peña, and John Peña lived in Prospect Hill. Differences in geography, economics, status, lifestyle, and institutions, thus, often led to a common ideology — not only a new perspective, but new values, desires, and attitudes. These ideas and ideology began to assume a life of their own as early as 1921, when the Order of the Sons of America was established.[32]

The full impact of this developing ideological framework of liberalism in the 1920s did not hit until the 1930s, when LULAC actively began to attempt to remake the Mexican community into a Mexican American one. By the thirties San Antonio institutions had also begun to perform their dialectical function, that is, to make Mexicans into Americans, yet keep them proud of their ethnicity. The Depression, moreover, served first, to force the middle class to retreat from the striking militant ideology of the workers, and second, to help it preserve its fundamental attitude that education and citizenship (instead of "radical" unions or strikes) were the answers to problems. The Depression also forced the middle class to oppose the *ricos'* return-to-Mexico philosophy, although it still supported their cultural orientation.

Several Mexican American leaders articulated this new nonmilitant political and social consciousness. James Tafolla believed that LULAC should "influence all fields of racial, economic, and political action in order to realize the greatest enjoyment possible of all the rights and privileges and prerogatives extended by the American constitution." He felt, as others did, that LULAC should be restricted "exclusively to citizens of the United States of Mexican and Spanish extraction, either native or naturalized."[33]

The middle-class Mexicans of Prospect Hill responded favorably to Tafolla's ideas and to the establishment of LULAC councils. Moreover, other cities and towns in the Lower Rio Grande Valley—Brownsville, Corpus Christi, Robstown, Kingsville, Falfurrias, Alice, and Laredo—that had a Mexican middle class also responded favorably to LULAC. In fact, wherever there were middle-class Mexicans, LULAC chapters were established. As Douglas O. Weeks stated, by the 1930s "there . . . [had] arisen . . . [throughout the Southwest] a class of prosperous, educated [Mexican American] citizens whose living conditions and attitudes compare[d] favorably with American standards."[34] The most active LULAC councils, however, were organized in San Antonio, because of the "vast" middle class and the extensive Mexican working class. As a result, "[the] San Antonio councils established club rooms . . . met regularly and . . . exercised some influence among the Mexican . . . [population] of San Antonio."[35]

In the two main LULAC councils of San Antonio, two men stood above the rest: Alonzo S. Perales, LULAC's national president from 1930 to 1931, and M. C. González, the national president from 1931 to 1932. Each headed a separate council: Perales headed Council XVI, and González headed Council II. Both Perales and González, who were founding members of LULAC, "inspired Mexicans" in the 1930s because they were "articulate, [and had] moving, forceful personalities," stated one council member.[36] Both of these leaders agreed that LULAC should provide an ideological voice for the aspirations and needs of the Mexican community; both also agreed that LULAC was an organizing instrument, although it was not intended to be a political action group per se. Its political ideas were to be carried out by the members, as individuals, and not with the organization's name. LULAC attempted to make Mexican Americans aware of their personal, political, and civil rights so that they could take action as individuals (and to maintain LULAC's ability to operate free of political or racial attack, as, ostensibly, an educational and cultural community organization).

Most members, however, were aware of the broad political impact of the organization and the fact that they were considered to be "organizers and activists" by the non-Mexican community. As one member stated, "[The] purpose of the Latin American League is to make [Mexicans] better citizens and perhaps they may some day [as individuals or as a community] put up candidates for office." Another

munity. The *ricos* objected to the political rise of this middle class organization; one LULAC leader commented on this opposition:

> We have three [kinds of] people to contend with: the American politicians, the Mexican [machine] politicians, who sacrifice their race for their own advantage, and the old Mexicans [the *ricos*]. The Mexican politician controls a few voters for what he can get out of them, and is afraid of our society. . . . The Mexican politicians fight us and knock us and call us renegades, but after a while they join. The American politician has the Mexican politician as his voice. . . . The average non-political American of Latin descent calls us renegades. He says, "you are Mexicans, not Americans." Mexican citizens [the *ricos*] in their press even attack us. We are called [by the *ricos*] "renegades" and "anti-Mexican." We call [the *ricos*] visitors [in San Antonio]. [The *ricos*] . . . ask us, [why] . . . are [you] trying to tell the [Texas Mexicans] to be more loyal to the United States, . . . [since] your forefathers are all of Mexican origin, and you should continue to be Mexicans.[38]

González and Perales both felt, articulated, and actively sought to change the ideological hegemony of the West Side and to confront these three kinds of opposition. LULAC, whether it wanted to or not, was a political organization and Perales and González were its main leaders. LULAC's greatest political opposition was the *ricos*, whose ideas for the most part were hegemonic in the 1920s and 1930s.

As a result, the "Mexican" mind during the 1930s was pitted against the "Mexican American" one, although during this decade the *ricos* also sought to address the era of concord—the time of unification in Mexico. They sought to have the "*Mexicanos de afuera* remember that they were Mexican and that they should return to work for Mexico."

LULAC, on the other hand, sought to commence the search for community (and a cultural and political place in the United States) by reminding the West Siders to remain Mexican, but to remember that they were *mexicanos de adentro*, and thus their loyalties were to their present home—the United States. A LULAC leader forcefully responded to the *ricos'* cry of betrayal: "The Mexicans [the *ricos*] say we're trying to Americanize, and get away from Mexican patriotism. We have to be American citizens [since we live in the United States] whether we want to or not."[39] LULAC faced north and pursued the reality of everyday existence in the United States; it looked toward the present and the future. The *ricos*, however, always faced south and remembered the past and wished to continue it. Regardless of their exile in the United States, they continued to be Mexicans, from Mexico. Paul Taylor, observing this hegemonic confrontation during the 1930s, wrote that "if [community] dissensions were avoided, its [LULAC] program followed, and if its appeal to the working class succeeded, the Mexican-American mind would prevail." Taylor observed this, LULAC believed it, and most of the Mexican community, after a decade, accepted it. But a continuing sense of cultural ethnicity, rather than just a political and philosophical Americanization persisted with "astonishing tenacity" from 1929 through 1941 in the Mexican community.[40]

LULAC's ideals coincided with the Catholic Church's programs, the educational system's goals, and the developmental progress of the family during this decade. These social institutions were in ideological synchronization with the community's activist segment, LULAC. This new middle-class consciousness, sensitivity, and ideology was clearly codified in the LULAC constitution, which expressed the major ideological principles of the Mexican American mind, which I have spelled out following each article:

> 1. To develop within the members of our race the best, purest and most perfect type of a true and loyal citizen of the United States of America. [Americanize.]
>
> 2. To eradicate from our body politic all intents and tendencies to establish discrimination among our fellow citizens on account of race, religion, or social position as being contrary to the true spirit of Democracy, our Constitution and Laws. [Be active against discrimination, racism, and inequality.]
>
> 3. To use all the legal means at our command to the end that all citizens in our country may enjoy equal rights, the equal protection of the laws of the land and equal opportunities and privileges. [Support the principles of the Declaration of Independence and the Constitution.]

4. The acquisition of the English language, which is the official language of our country, being necessary for the enjoyment of our rights and privileges, we declare it to be the official language of this organization, and we pledge ourselves to learn and speak and teach the same to our children. [Learn to speak English as a first language and become functional as a citizen in order to enjoy the fruits of the United States.]

5. To define with absolute and unmistakable clearness our unquestionable loyalty to the ideals, principles, and citizenship of the United

memories.]

8. Secretly and openly, by all lawful means at our command, we shall assist in the education and guidance of Latin Americans and we shall protect and defend their lives and interests whenever necessary. [Have a sense of civic virtue and a commitment to defend, educate, and guide the Mexican community.]

9. We shall destroy any attempt to create racial prejudices against our people, and any infamous stigma which may be cast upon them, and we shall demand for them the respect and prerogatives which the Constitution grants to us all. [Be active against the forces of ethnic oppression and support the freedom, equality, and justice guaranteed by the constitution.]

10. We shall maintain publicity means for the diffusion of these principles and for the expansion and consolidation of this organization. [Build LULAC and its philosophy.]

11. We shall oppose any radical and violent demonstration which may tend to create conflicts and disturb the peace and tranquility of our country. [Oppose any force, idea, or organization that tears the American fabric of democracy.][41]

The ideas expressed in the constitution were not ideas of just an organization; they formed the ideology of an emerging middle-class mentality. This constitution was comparable to the Declaration of Independence: it expressed the middle-class Mexican's imagination, consciousness, principles, and ideology, and it also served as a program for action. These were not the ideas of *La Prensa*, which gave voice to the exiled Mexicans, nor were they the ideas of the working-class sector of the Mexican community, whose ideology, in part, was expressed by their unions, by Emma Tenayuca, and by their demands. Each of these other sectors (in the 1930s) expressed a different consciousness via the ideology that was codified in their organizations and their demands. In general, the workers wanted more money and better working conditions, and the middle sectors — both lower and upper — wanted more equality, less racial discrimination, more influence, and more opportunities. The businesspeople and writers wanted to return to Mexico; they wanted *la patria*. By the late 1930s, the workers were building their everyday lives; the middle sectors were building a liberal Americanized community; the rich were building a Mexican consciousness of collectivity that would engender a feeling, a spirit, a past, and a tradition that they hoped would envelop all of the rest of the community.

That LULAC was creating a community is obvious from the statement made in *La Prensa* by Alonzo S. Perales. He said that the pragmatic aim of the LULAC organization was the development of more lawyers, more doctors, more engineers, and more teachers. Furthermore, he said that the local LULAC councils were at the present time influencing the boys and the girls of the community to pursue their education; in fact, he said, in some cases the councils were even financing the education of these people.[42]

The LULAC councils were busy in other activities besides education throughout the thirties, and these activities were readily reported in the city's newspaper, the *San Antonio Express*. For example, the *Express* reported such activities as "LULACS to stage 'Night in Mexico,'" "LULAC Big Brother Movement to Reduce Crime More" "LULACS Protest over Park Exclusion," or "Church Workers Backing LULAC Activities"[43] The engine of this change was to be knowledge rather than politics. M. C. González of San Antonio Council II stressed this point when he stated that "LULAC supported education rather than political agitation as the essence to progress." However, it was evident that by its very existence and the issues it addressed, it would be engaged in "political activities" in various fields.[44] Also, LULAC's commitment would be individual as well as communal in form. J. Luz Saenz of the Corpus Christi Council put it this way:

> This organization is not a political club, but as citizens we shall participate in all local, state and national political contests. However, in doing so we shall ever bear in mind the general welfare of our people and we disregard and abjure once [and] for all any personal obligation which is not in harmony with these principles. With our vote and influence we shall endeavor to place in public office men who show by their deeds respect and consideration for our people.[45]

The extent of LULAC's planned activities and goals, thus, went beyond culture or politics. This was evident in 1933 when several permanent committees and directorships were added to the organizational structure: an educational committee; women's organizing director; public health director; Boy Scout director; Girl Scout committee; and a legal adviser.[46]

LULAC's basic propaganda ranged from cultural to political; the latter was done individually or through the Club Democrático or the

to the mayor during the pecan shellers' strike, the League of Loyal Americans voted to support the strike, but only if the Communist leadership (Emma Tenayuca and the Workers' Alliance) was ousted. This was the same position taken by Archbishop Drossaert and the Catholic Church, as well as by the San Antonio Mexican Chamber of Commerce. Then in 1939, the League of Loyal Americans focused on the problem of housing and protested the actions taken by the Mexican Consulate and the Mexican landlords who were delaying the construction of a public housing development initiated by Father Carmelo Tranchese. The Consulate was chided for not being adequately informed of the economic potential such a project held for the Mexican community, and the Mexican landlords were attacked for opposing or delaying the project because "they are deriving a good revenue for their [slum] properties — a great number of which consist of unsanitary hovels which they are renting to our less fortunate inhabitants of Mexican extraction." Continuing, a league member said, "[We] wonder if the Mexican Consulate General has stopped to consider that this slum clearance project will provide employment over a long period of time for thousands of San Antonians of Mexican descent who now are on the relief rolls?"[47]

The League of Loyal Americans, under the leadership of Alonzo S. Perales, who was its commissioner on social justice, also asked that the Mexican community give it the names of all commercial firms that did not hire Mexicans. The league also placed an ad in the West Side community newspaper *El Pueblo: El Periódico Hispano Ameri-*

cano de Tejas, hoping to obtain the entire community's help.[48]

In 1940, in addition to these local political activities, many LULAC members worked for Franklin D. Roosevelt's re-election or in state elections. This type of direct personal political work took many members away from LULAC's specific organizational activities. As a result, A. M. Fernández, the national president (1940–41) reminded the membership that,

> [as] has always been the case in election years, many of the members have been busy taking an active part in the recent political campaign[s]. Such activity had necessarily encroached upon the time which the members would normally have given to the LULAC organization and its work. . . . We appeal, then, to the active membership to join us in the re-awakening. A reinstatement of efforts, as it were, that we may shake off the several months accumulation of dust from our shoulders and get back to work [on LULAC's organizational goals]. We have a rightful place among the better citizens of our wonderful United States, but nobody is going to hand it to us on a silver platter. . . . The political campaign is over, but let's get on with our own campaign, for the role of the "LULACKER" and all it stands for.[49]

From the middle of the 1930s through the 1940s, LULAC members (and other middle-class activists) were part of every political, social, or welfare activity in San Antonio, either as individuals or as LULAC members. They were involved in Red Cross drives, Community Chest drives, clothing and food drives, welfare work, Boy and Girl Scout work, Salvation Army work, and city and county health boards.[50] LULAC councils in San Antonio and throughout Texas also lectured and organized around the themes of education, citizenship, the English language, economic opportunities, and civil rights. In particular, LULAC sought educational opportunities and scholarships for Mexican youth as well as adult night schools for the rest of the community. Adult education, LULAC felt, was a method for the entire community to gain self-sufficiency and a higher social standard.

LULAC also tried to Americanize the Mexican masses; this, however, was not always done consciously. For example, all the membership received training in public speaking, debate, parliamentary procedure, citizenship, and general leadership responsibilities.[51] They could speak to the non-LULAC community as well as develop themselves. In fact, LULAC even tried to make its meetings constructive and educational. A typical meeting, for example, was "liberally sprinkled with items of interest to everyone," stated the *LULAC News*. The regular business meeting, according to the organization's newspaper, was complemented by "interesting debates on current, local, and national events. Short talks on personal hobbies, discussions on business, history, and travel." Members also learned about "the latest developments in welfare work, and progress [in other areas]. In addition, various members give discussions about their occupations, and travels."[52] Above all, LULAC meetings were to "breathe the spirit" of the LULAC code into the members so that, in turn, they could articulate it in their work with the community. The organization may have functioned as the voice of the Mexican community in San Antonio, but it also served as a "college of leadership" and a "university of knowledge and

Respect your citizenship and preserve it; honor your country, maintain its traditions in the spirit of its citizens, and embody yourself into its culture and civilization;

Love the men of your race, be proud of your origin and maintain it immaculate, respect your glorious past, and help to defend the rights of your own people;

Learn how to fulfill your duties before you learn how to claim your rights; educate and make yourself worthy, and stand high in the light of your own deeds; you must always be loyal and courageous;

Filled with optimism, make yourself sociable, upright, judicious, and above all things be sober and collected in your habits, cautious in your actions and sparing in your speech.

Study the past of your own, and the country to which you owe your allegiance, learn how to master with parity the two most essential languages — English and Spanish;

Believe in God, love humanity and rely upon the framework of human progress, slow, unequivocal and firm;

Always be honorable and high minded, learn how to be self-reliant upon your own qualification and resources;

In war serve your country, in peace your convictions; discern, investigate, mediate and think, study, at all times be honest and generous.

Let your firmest purpose be that of helping to see that each new generation of your own shall be of a youth more efficient and capable and in this let your own children be included.[53]

Overall the code in many ways was a synthesis of the *ricos'* ideal code of *gente decente* fitted into the realism of America's liberal tradition. In essence, this code called for each Mexican American to (1) integrate intellectually into American culture and into Western civilization; (2) maintain a sense of community with other Mexicans via a consciousness of collectivity; (3) become equal in functional skills and knowledge and responsible in obligations and achievements; (4) develop a restrained, cultured, and "judicious" personal demeanor; (5) understand and accept the dualism of self and consciousness by studying both American and Mexican history and by learning both the Spanish and the English languages; (6) adhere to a religious sensitivity, a humanistic perception, and a vision of progress based more on continuity than on change; (7) develop and maintain a sense of individual freedom, self-reliance, honesty, and honor; (8) be intellectual, critical, and analytical, but in times of war to be guided by patriotism and in times of peace to be guided by conscience and convictions; and (9) work constantly for the progress of one's generation and one's children's generation. If one could include a tenth proposition — join LULAC — one would have ten propositions comparable to the ten commandments. In the spirit of the 1920s' search for identity, this code was comparable in tone, if not in essence, to Wilson's fourteen points or Lenin's twenty-one theses: it sought to fashion a mentality and develop a consciousness of change — to make a new person.

As the code indicated, the Mexican Americans did not want to become assimilated, they wanted duality: a Mexican consciousness of collectivity in culture and social activity, but an American consciousness in philosophy and politics. Within the latter role they tried, specifically, to adhere to democratic ideals such as civic virtue, equality, the right to education, and the right to citizenship. They also favored the acquisition of the English language, but the maintenance of Spanish.

Because of its political activities, ideological forcefulness, and strong advocacy of Americanization, LULAC was often suspect: Was it working in the best interests of the community? This was the question put by Lalo Solís, who hesitated to join LULAC in the thirties because it seemed too radical, but finally joined in the forties, because he finally accepted the "thought of the LULAC movement as a [vehicle for the] betterment for the community [since] they always helped us."[54] Lalo Solís's brother, John, who was a founding member of the Order of the Sons of America and LULAC, felt not only that LULAC was always for the improvement of the community, but that as members, "[we] were always proud of our [Mexican] ancestry and heritage, and we were always proud of being American. We were not trying to be Gringo. Therefore, we could always work with the West Siders."[55]

Regardless of the gestalt of the individual, each member knew that education, whether for the community or for the membership, was the central core of the LULAC philosophy and the guiding theme of its activities. One LULAC leader, attempting to place education in a larger perspective, said it was "the foundation of culture, progress, liberty, equality, and fraternity." This philosophy was always at the center of the ideology emphasized by the LULAC presidents, all of whom from 1930 through 1936 were from San Antonio: Alonzo S. Perales, M. C. González, Mauro Machado, E. R. Lozano, and James Tafolla. Each also understood what LULAC member Sen. Dennis Chá-

culture that they are capable of guiding and directing us properly." By 1941 LULAC leaders, their organization, and their middle-class community were establishing their place in American society and determining, as Perales had advocated, their own "intellectual redemption."[57] In many ways this middle-class movement was providing the impulse for change that the progressive movement had done at the turn of the century (1900–20) for the United States as a whole.

THE LEADERSHIP

By 1941 three academicians from the University of Texas had articulated the concerns, the goals, the ideals, and the aspirations of the middle-class LULAC organization. They, in effect, reflected the differing strands of the Mexican American mind after observing it for a decade. These men, Dr. H. T. Manuel, Dr. Carlos Castañeda, and Dr. George Sánchez, commented, articulated, and sometimes even participated during the 1930s as part of the cutting edge of the Mexican American generation. In addition to these three, two lawyers, Alonzo S. Perales and M. C. González articulated LULAC's philosophy throughout the different sectors of the Mexican community. Of these five men, however, González and Perales were the principal intellectual fathers of the organization as well as the leading forces of the decade. They were intellectuals, activists, national figures, and lawyers. Everyone knew them, respected them, and listened to them.

If the two lawyers, however, actively and ideologically shaped and

molded the Mexican American mind, the university professors helped
to interpret it intellectually. H. T. Manuel, professor of educational
psychology, defined the "new consciousness" by two basic measures:
education and American citizenship. Through the process of education he saw the beginning of each distinctive Mexican American individual, whose mind, Manuel believed, could develop uniquely with
each personality because each person had his or her innate abilities,
personal interests, and emotional needs. Manuel saw the development
of the Mexican American consciousness from an existentialist perspective, rather than a nationalistic one. For him the designation "Mexican American" was weighted on the American side, although individual distinctiveness superseded even the "American" category; in
short, every individual was more than his or her ethnicity or nationalism. Manuel believed that the Mexican American's intellectual and
psychological development, within Americanization parameters, was
interrelated with self-growth.

Manuel perceived Mexicans as unique individuals, but also as
Americans. The U.S. schools, he thought, "helped in the formulation
of reasonable objectives [for the Mexican child], and the school" also
"guided [the child] in his progress toward these objectives." In fact,
Manuel pointed out (in Deweyian terms), "the duty of the school,
then, is clear. It must help the individual child prepare to discharge
his responsibilities with respect to the [Mexican] group, and it must
promote the welfare of each as an individual. In other words, it
must develop in each [child] the qualities of good citizenship, and
it must help each to find the maximum relation of his own [existen-
tial] possibilities."[58]

Existential growth and Americanization went hand-in-hand for
Manuel, who was in the forefront of progressive educational philosophy. Moreover, equality was the essence of Americanization and therefore each Mexican American individual should live by the philosophical tenet, "All men are created equal." Manuel also drew from the
Enlightenment philosophy the precepts of inalienable rights; the right
to liberty, the right to pursue happiness, and the right to life, were,
he felt, the central axioms of the Mexican American philosophy (but
within a mode of everyday life maybe culturally different from that
of the non-Mexicans).

For Manuel, the Mexican American was not only an existential being, but democracy personified, and democracy was American. "Humbly, I thanked God for America and for Democracy!" exclaimed
Manuel, then he asked, "What does this mean?" and his answer was
a partial question: "What is the democratic way of life?—It means
concern for the individual. The democratic way of life stresses two

things: (1) participation of the [Mexican] individual in the affairs of the group, and (2) promotion of individual welfare." Individualism, pluralism, Americanism, and democracy were all intertwined for Manuel. Consequently, the Mexican American philosophy was Americanism, and Americanism was Mexican American; American citizenship for Mexicans in the United States was not, he felt, a status, but a way of life. Education was the vehicle for personal growth, a pluralist perspective, and civic virtue — in essence, the schools were the cata-

in the 1930s, because it was still part of everyday life.

This tension was eased in the Depression by one of the other intellectuals, George I. Sánchez, who was a professor of education. Sánchez, unlike Manuel, did not focus on the individual, but on groups, specifically, the relationships between them. He believed that "the essence of Americanism is tolerance. Respect for the views and rights of others — for their foibles and frailties — is the keystone of the arch of American democracy. Without tolerance, without this mutual respect and sympathetic understanding, there can be no community of interests or action." Therefore tolerance toward others and toward themselves was the central precept of the Mexican American mind, according to Sánchez. This attitude of tolerance eased the psychological tension for some Mexican Americans only as long as they leaned on the American side of the Mexican American combination. When the scale tipped toward the Mexican side, tolerance left and ethnocentric superiority entered. Sánchez felt that this was a danger to the developing Mexican American community, since he did not want ethnic arrogance; Americanism, he implied, was contradictory to Mexican nationalism.

The *ricos* understood this, but the middle class tried psychologically to balance between Mexican and American, an attempt that worked only as long as the former was on the cultural plane of everyday life and the latter only on the ideological-political one. George Sánchez, like H. T. Manuel, also pursued Lockian virtues and Jeffersonian principles, but most of all he sought to avoid Madisonian factionalism. "The right to life, liberty, and the pursuit of happiness," stated

Sánchez, "is a multi-lateral one, and tolerance is its foundation."[60]

Although George Sánchez recognized the explosiveness of the racial or nationalistic issue, he was not against being Mexican nor did he want Mexicans to become culturally assimilated. He just did not want ethnic strife. He recognized and wanted a Tocquevillian world of plurality, but not a society that, as he said, "set class against class, race against race, and sect against sect . . . [because then] they endanger the national creed and undermine the social structure." Too much Americanism, however, was also a danger. Many times, Sánchez felt, people, under the guise of patriotism or Americanism, or because of prejudice, ignorance, or disrespect for cultural differences and language differences, "demean fellow citizens" or "appoint themselves as the 'true Americans' and promulgate their narrow conception of culture as *the* American way." Sánchez believed that this misguided thinking also undermined the spirit of Americanism and "raped" the essence of this country. "Enlightenment and tolerance coupled with firmness in controlling subversive vested interests, is our safeguard," he advised. The principles of tolerance and equality through pluralism were the essence of the Mexican American mind and of American society.[61]

Unlike H. T. Manuel, George Sánchez did not seem to equate equality, liberty, and justice with the American character. Whereas Manuel sought the integration of self and society in a synthesis between the Jamesian "free" existential man and the American character (based on equality), Sánchez focused only on differences between the Mexican American character and the American one. Sánchez interpreted the Mexican American mentality closer to the reality of LULAC's vision: tolerance and differences, pluralism, and only American philosophical integration. "The American way of life," he wrote, "is founded upon much reciprocity — upon the cooperative expression of mutual understanding and tolerance [of groups]." As a result, Sánchez urged the League of United Latin American Citizens in particular, and the Mexican American middle class in general, to review their aims, their purposes, and their programs of action to see if they had not become tinged with "intolerance, narrow [and] undemocratic" thinking. Americanism, he reminded them, tolerated diversity, and, consequently, patriotic civic groups should learn tolerance and respect for others.[62]

He did not want a Mexican American mentality that was narrow and undemocratic. His emphasis on collectivity (of groups) was closer to the *ricos'* emphasis on collectivity of culture and society. For Manuel the basic unit, in spite of his recognition of group pluralism, was the individual and his or her psyche. Ultimately, Manuel reflected nineteenth-century liberalism while Sánchez reflected twentieth-century New Deal liberalism. If Manuel spoke more in terms of certain abstract intellectual political ideals (equality, liberty, and so on), Sánchez spoke in terms of a philosophical-psychological orientation (Americanism), a psychological-emotional flexibility (tolerance), and an understanding of others (pluralism). Both, however, believed in the development of a "Mexican Americanism," a new consciousness for *los mexicanos de adentro.* Manuel's philosophical parameters left no room for cul-

stead on the quality of the leadership for the Mexican American community. Castañeda, the Mexican American archivist and a historian at the University of Texas, believed that "the complexity of modern life, the attainment of universal welfare, the clashing interests of ambitious and unscrupulous men in public life; all this made training leaders imperative today to safeguard personal liberty, insure future welfare, and guarantee to the human race the blessings of the rich heritage bequeathed by countless generations." Castañeda looked toward the quality of people rather than the quality of ideas; he did not seek "natural-born leaders" in the Mexican community. He knew that if they were present, they were a rarity. He therefore urged the immediate training of as many Mexican Americans as possible for leadership positions. This training was imperative for "the Latin-American citizens of this great nation" to incorporate the Mexican people into "the stream of our national life to help us solve our social, political, and economic problems" and to "enable us to develop our innate [intellectual] capacity to the fullest extent." Casteñeda also said that leadership was needed to "make it possible for us to find individual expression." He also firmly believed that education was the means by which to train leaders; specifically, he believed that the "base for the development of a trained leadership" could become a reality only when economic means could be provided for Mexican Americans to obtain "college and university training." Sounding like the black intellectual W. E. B. Du Bois, he urged LULAC to establish endowed scholarships at different colleges and universities in memory of "those patriots of Spanish or Mexican extraction, who fought and bled for Texas independence and for Texas education," and for those Mexicans who died for civil liberties as well as those who died for "democracy and their countries [*sic*] honor" in World War I. Financing education in this way would serve, Castañeda hoped, as a means of providing leadership training, as a memory for ethnic continuity, and as a personal honor for just being Mexican American. "Only through the development of a group of well trained, sincere, and earnest leaders can the beautiful ideals of the League of United Latin-American Citizens be realized."[63]

All three agreed on the need for Americanism, the need for education, the need for LULAC, and the need to develop this "new consciousness." Each, nevertheless, had a slightly different idea of the ontological emphasis in this search for identity. Manuel believed education was the process for existential development; Castañeda felt it was political action; Sánchez believed it was through a process of developing the virtues of tolerance and understanding.

The epistemological bridge between the emphasis on self-development and political leadership was articulated, however, by F. T. Martínez, one of LULAC's national leaders and the regional governor for New Mexico, in the early forties: "Study, positive thinking, proper understanding and intelligence not indolence, together with the understanding of class unity and ethnic harmony will make us [middleclass Mexican Americans] stronger, capable and with equal rights so [that] we may be recognized among the better class of people and get our share of the civilized world." Martínez connected the world of ideas with the everyday world. He also stated that the middleclass Mexican should be educated and united as a class, but responsive and open to the needs of the Mexican lower classes.

Martínez and other LULAC leaders often dichotomized the world into the masses and the elites. This was not usually conscious, but was implied by such statements as "The task of a real LULACKER is not only to educate his children but to educate himself and take an active part in all civic and social enterprise and do his best to educate the masses, especially those of his own origin." LULAC never forgot to attempt to "educate that class that needs the help." Martínez, moreover, voiced the ultimate objective of LULAC's activities, regardless of differences in approach: "We need to unify our forces in a harmonious way and go over the top to struggle to the last man in order that we may, in the near future, raise our standard of living to the level of the average American citizen. That is all we want, once we have all that is necessary to enjoy life, we . . . [can then] consider ourselves fortunate and happy."[64] LULAC, like the *ricos*, carried with its cultural and intellectual ideas the emotions of an elite, but the sensitivity of noblesse oblige. LULAC felt comfortable, therefore, with the patrician and aristocratic tone and the temper exhibited by Franklin D. Roosevelt and his use of Hamiltonian means to achieve Jeffersonian ends.

LULAC in essence had the same basic dreams that other ethnic groups had: self-development, educational success, upward mobility, and, in general, happiness and a good life in the United States. However, circumstances and conditions often added new dreams and new objectives. LULAC also sought to provide a sense of "Mexican self"

during the Depression, when *raza* had to help *raza*, yet this atmosphere of unity was thin — class tensions, labor tensions, and ideological tensions were surfacing. Nevertheless, LULAC in this decade was viable and energetic.

It focused on the upper and lower middle class as the groups in which to propagandize their dreams of "making it" (in Norman Pohondrotz's terms), their program for doing it, and the mentality to accomplish it. U.S. citizenship and education were their immediate objectives, but to achieve functionalism, their long-range goal was to make Mexicans into Mexican Americans. George de la Garza, a LULAC member at the time, remembers that many on the West Side had stong feelings of being Mexican, and people were proud of their culture. LULAC, according to M. C. González, used this nationalism as the vehicle to gain entrance throughout the 1930s. LULAC members led by Alonzo Perales, M. C. González, Rubén Lozano, Jacobo Rodríguez, Alonzo Garza, Gustavo García, John Solís, Joe Oliveras, John Esquivel, and James Tafolla constantly descended on the West Side in a whirlwind of activity that crisscrossed the 1930s. These activities included engaging in civic and political work, helping in school projects, organizing Mexican PTAs, influencing city commissioners, listening to West Siders' complaints, holding rallies, giving lectures, organizing socials, becoming spokesmen for the Latin Quarter, and in general serving as the liaison between the Mexican and the non-Mexican communities. According to de la Garza, LULAC in the thirties "meant quite a bit" to the non-Mexican community; most of all, according to de la Garza, it meant "respect," because they "knew LULAC was civic minded and represented the Mexican community."

Non-Mexicans knew this in 1941 when LULAC confronted non-Mexican and Mexican businesspeople and reminded them of their economic and political obligation to integrate the West Side into the rest of the city.[65]

The LULAC movement often seemed to take on the fervor of a religious movement. In 1940 LULAC council historian Edward Calderón expressed this when he stated, "Each and every one [has] pledged to go forth and proselyte and gather into the fold the best of the noble race that gave them birth, that they might as a united people gain again their place in the sun, that by working for the well-being of the poor and lowly, teaching the high principles of true patriotism as expanded by the League of United Latin-American Citizens, they might lead the way to a better life." By 1941 the fervor and work of LULAC had not subsided. It was not only a conscious organization spreading the word, it was the West Side's consciousness spreading, especially from the Prospect Hill area. In 1943 George de la Garza's eight-year-old son asked, "What is a Mexican?" De la Garza without hesitation answered, "A Mexican is from Mexico." The consciousness of the Mexican American was now answering. The differentiation had been made: Mexicans from Mexico, Mexican Americans from the United States. John Solís captured the zeitgeist of many of the West Siders when he recalled that during the thirties they were "always proud of our ancestry and heritage and always proud of being Americans. We were not trying to be Gringos."[66]

The almost "religious" efforts of LULAC to gain intellectual hegemony, the acute conditions of the Depression, the mediating structures—family, education, church, politics—the very nature of San Antonio's Mexican Spanish élan as well as the city's need to Americanize the Mexican population (because it was almost half of the population) in order to modernize had helped to produce the changing mentality. But there were two Mexican American leaders who above all others personified the LULAC organization as well as the new mentality: Alonzo S. Perales and Manuel C. González. Both held slightly different perspectives on being Mexican American, but their ideas and ideology as well as their activism were central to LULAC's success in the 1930s and 1940s in defining the Mexican American mentality.

ALONZO S. PERALES

Perales was born in 1899 in Alice, Texas. He was graduated from the Alice, Texas, public schools and then was graduated from the Preparatory School in Washington, D.C., the School of Economics and Government (B.A.), and the National University Law School. Perales was from a poor family, but struggled to educate himself. According to Adela Sloss-Vento, a friend and colleague during the 1920s and 1930s, Perales first became committed to his life's struggle against racial injustice in 1919 when he saw an American "commit a cowardly crime to a defenseless Mexican" on a train ride to school in Washington.[67] It seems that Perales never forgot this incident and the racial implications it had for all Mexicans.

nation that existed toward the Mexican communities. Washington, D.C., gave him his education, the diplomatic corps, his perspective and stature, and his humble beginnings, his "social and political consciousness."[68]

Perales attracted people because of his "distinguished appearance," his personality, his great enthusiasm, and his stature as an articulate public speaker." Between diplomatic posts, according to Sloss-Vento, he continued to spend time in Texas and "struggle [for the Mexican community] in public meetings, before the law, and in the newspapers." Perales's commitment continued even when he was on a diplomatic tour. His numerous letters and articles to *La Prensa* in San Antonio, *Diógenes* in McAllen, *El Fronterizo* in Rio Grande City, and other newspapers kept him in touch with the Mexican people. He was driven by the dream "to do away with the problems that prevented . . . [the Mexicans'] advancement and welfare."[69]

He was not even satisfied with his own advancement, although it served as the model for his theory of Mexican American progress through education. In 1937 Carlos Castañeda wrote of him, "With the vision of a prophet, attorney Perales has seen the solution of the problem in the education of its youth."[70] Although Perales saw education as the vehicle for advancement, he also knew, as a lawyer, that racially biased laws first had to be rescinded and then changed to "law[s] [that] . . . would prohibit the [continuing] humiliations of the people of Mexican origin in restaurants, theaters, drug stores, etc., for the simple fact of being of Mexican origin."[71] The struggle for education and racial equality before the law were the cutting edge of Perales's philosophy.

Perales actively campaigned in Texas and in Washington, D.C., for the end of discriminatory laws against Mexican Americans and Mexican citizens. "In my files I have proof," he would say, "of more than one hundred and fifty towns in Texas where there are from one to ten establishments where no service is given to the people of Mexican origin." He finally published this documentation in *Are We Good Neighbors?* in 1948. Throughout the 1930s, Perales, through LULAC, fought to establish a "community of consciousness" while he struggled as the "consciousness of the community" against the poverty, discrimination, and illiteracy in the San Antonio and South Texas Mexican communities. In the 1940s, when more of a sensitivity arose in the Mexican middle class, he fought for the redefinition of laws and the legal termination of the racial falsehoods before the law. Perales, indirectly, indicted all of the Anglos in Texas for the Mexicans' racial and educational problems. "Racial discrimination," he said, "is practiced in Texas against the people of Mexican origin by a minority of Anglo-Americans it is true, but they have the approval of a majority of the Anglo-American people in Texas, and the proof is that they [the majority] have never done anything to prevent the minority from continuing to humiliate the people of Mexican origin for the simple fact of being of said origin." Perales implied that there was a clear ethnic and racial separation between Mexicans and Anglos, and all Anglos were accomplices in this discrimination against the Mexicans and Mexican Americans, whether overtly or covertly.[72]

In spite of ethnic differences, Perales sought to remind Anglos that Mexican Americans were also citizens and that this status meant equality. For Perales, Mexican Americans, without question, had all the rights and privileges of citizenship just because they were Americans. The law, the Constitution, and citizenship gave the Mexican Americans de facto and de jure equality, regardless of race, creed, or color. For Perales, the rights of humankind were within the law not nature: "being" was legally defined, not ontologically established.[73]

Perales, it seems, believed in Blackstonian legal formalism; this emanated from his Mexican emphasis on tradition. Yet, given his activism and his political emphasis on justice, equality, and opportunity of education, he also stayed arm in arm with the Holmesian emphasis that law was an empirical and experimental endeavor and that "law is the witness, as Holmes stated in his *Path of the Law*, an external deposit of our moral life. Its history is the history of the moral development of the race."[74] Perales's philosophy was also indicative of the Mexican American paradox of being a realist and pragmatist (American) while still having formalist (Mexican) tendencies. The tension he felt between moralism and realism, and between formalism and pragmatism also was to be felt by many Mexican Americans.

Moreover, for Perales, while ethnicity was a given, Americanization was both a right and a goal. When LULAC was formed in 1929, Perales wrote Adela Sloss-Vento, "My only purpose in forming said organization is to bring about the rapid, intellectual, social, and political evolution of Americans of Mexican descent and people residing in Texas and to promote the general welfare of all Latin people residing in Texas and to produce the highest type of American citi-

was especially apparent in his strong

bership should include only Mexican American citizens and not citizens of Mexico. Perales felt that the inclusion of the latter would split the organization, because the Mexican citizen would still have allegiance to Mexico. Mexican Americans, however, would see themselves and their future in the United States, although they would still respect Mexico.

This harmony in legal status within LULAC created a commonality of goals, citizenship, and dreams that would be conducive to success and achievement. Above all, it allowed Anglos to see Mexican Americans (Perales felt, and LULAC concurred) as seriously wanting to be part of the United States.[76] According to Perales, once Mexican Americans gained their "rights and privileges," they could aid their Mexican brethren in the United States. Thus, he focused on changing state and federal laws, but he knew that Mexican Americans would eventually have to be their own catalysts for change by becoming citizens and exercising their legal rights and by voting. Inevitably, this new consciousness as Mexican Americans would be translated into political power.

Perales also felt that LULAC should not be a specific vehicle for any political candidate. The LULAC Constitution therefore specified that it was a nonpolitical organization. Perales, nevertheless, realized that "the political field, contrary to general belief, includes more than the simple function of voting, for it means loyalty to country, the fulfilment [*sic*] of the duties and obligations of citizenship, the enjoyment of constitutional rights and prerogatives, administration of justice, etc.; all this must be included in the political phase of our evolution."[77] The LULAC organization also accepted this premise of a sub-rosa style of politics.

Perales in early 1931 analyzed the San Antonio West Side's social differentiation, "political consciousness," and political possibilities in view of his own and the LULAC philosophy. The Mexican American middle class, he observed, had a distinct lifestyle, its own businesses, and its own residences, which separated them from the rest of the Mexican community and paralleled those of the Anglo middle class. This Mexican middle class, noted Perales, had a profound respect for its cultural origins, but, in addition, was gaining more of a respect for its U.S. citizenship. In contrast, Perales wrote, the lower class, even though many were born in the United States, was not aware of its rights as U.S. citizens because its primary language was Spanish. Moreover, since most of them were extremely poor and illiterate, they submitted to prejudice and discrimination. Because of these conditions, Perales felt, the Mexican people were often used by the urban political machines, and, worst of all, he thought, the Mexican American middle class many times served as the lieutenants and the intermediaries between the political bosses and the Mexican community. Perales believed that in the future the "rising" Mexican American middle class, with the help of its Anglo counterparts, could and should end the political bossism of the machine in the West Side. Perales also hoped that the middle class would raise the Mexican laboring class's consciousness to this new concept of politics: an alliance with the city's Anglo middle class and an antimachine position.[78]

The vehicle to bridge the gap between the Mexican American and the Anglo communities in San Antonio, according to Perales, was LULAC. For him LULAC was both a social and a political activist organization, as well as the voice and mind of the Mexican middle class. He warned the membership, however, that they should remember that LULAC was "not a mere political club . . . should it at anytime pursue such a course, you may rest assured that I shall have nothing to do with it." Nevertheless, Perales clearly pointed out that "LULAC should encourage people to vote, but it should not tell them whom it should vote for. . . . By voting in mass and without thinking, simply because some ambitious politician says 'vote for so and so' . . . [would] . . . not improve our condition one iota, although it might improve the condition of one or more members of our race . . . [and help] further the ends of ambitious welfare politicians."

John Solís and other secondary leaders followed Perales's dictum: raise the political consciousness of the whole Mexican community, but do not control it. They too did not want LULAC to become simply another political machine. "We must play an independent role in politics without allegiance to a single party or faction," Perales further outlined.[79]

In some ways LULAC's and Perales's ideas paralleled Lozano's and the *ricos*': to establish a class as an instrument of power, but to retain a pluralism of ideas, lifestyles, and dreams held together by a core of historical, traditional, and cultural memories and reflections, a consciousness of collectivity. Serving the collective interests of the West

in city or county government positions.[80] In other words, Perales always wanted a political quid pro quo with Mexican American political candidates.

As a result of the pluralism of ideas and groupings, Perales recognized the possibility of factionalism within the Mexican community, but accepted these political differences. Above all, he sought to place Mexican Americans in office without scrutinizing their political ideas. But he did have one criterion and he urged LULAC members to follow it: place only Mexican Americans in office who were responsible, sincere, competent, and, above all, who "were interested more in the well-being of the whole community than their own."[81]

In addition to setting the general intellectual tone and working principles for LULAC's political and legal action, Perales wrote for and lectured to the San Antonio and South Texas Mexican middle class throughout the 1930s. He saw the middle class as the active leaders of their communities and recognized their rapid rise from the 1920s to the 1930s. He believed that the Depression decade was the time to "double our efforts to accelerate our general [social and political] evolution in San Antonio." Perales especially urged the middle class to use its cultural activities to help educate, uplift, and help the Raza. Collective activities, he told the middle class, were the method to promote Mexican American consciousness and the goal was hegemony. In his lectures and writings Perales specifically urged Mexican Americans to have racial pride and to help such community organizations as the Clínica Mexicana, Cruz Azul Mexicana, Bexar County Health

Association, the American Red Cross, San Antonio Child Protective and Humane Society, Associated Charities, and the Salvation Army "to avoid any Mexicans being or becoming wards of the city or county." Appealing to the community's spirit of "la Raza," he stated, "For no reason should we let it be said, that we descendents of Hidalgo y Cuauhtemoc are public charges of the communities in which we live in the United States." Perales, it is clear, believed in a Mexican American cultural and social sense of responsibility that emanated from a nationalist feeling of unity and responsibility, but that expressed itself from within an American political consciousness and ideology of justice, liberty, individualism, and the freedom to vote. Education, self-initiative, and self-responsibility were the other central themes of Perales's philosophy of Mexican Americanism.[82]

Regardless of Perales's diplomatic interests and positions, he never avoided his responsibility to the Raza. From 1925 through the 1940s Perales never left the San Antonio community in thought or sentiment, nor did he ever lose faith in la Raza. In 1938, when the Depression was still going strong, when fascism and nazism were on the rise in Europe, and when in San Antonio the pecan shellers were striking and the CIO and the Workers' Alliance (under Tenayuca and Rodríguez) were propagandizing in the West Side, Perales wrote a series of articles on the "correct" philosophy of Mexican politics in Rómulo Mungía's *El Pueblo*. Perales urged the Mexican community, regardless of class, to continue its struggle for racial justice, but to avoid, at all costs, any Communist, Nazi, or Fascist leadership in its strikes. He urged it never to support or to be a member of any organization that had Communist affiliations. Mexican Americans should not embrace, he pointed out, any government or idea that was not a democratic one. In difficult times, such as in 1938, he wrote that Mexican Americans had the opportunity to show their loyalty to the United States and its democratic institutions; however, they should still continue to fight for social justice. The Mexican American struggle, Perales emphasized, must be "well defined," but "unequivocally" within the American political framework. "Republican representative government" was best for the "American nation," Perales emphasized, "and should be supported by the Mexican-American vote." In spite of the support for Democratic principles, ideology, and organizations, Perales stated that Mexicans should continue their struggle for racial justice, adequate education, proper housing, a middle-class lifestyle, and justice before the courts. In short, Perales urged the middle class and the laboring class to struggle for their rights as Americans, but always within the democratic framework.[83]

This was the creed of the Mexican American mind: struggle, but democratically; demand the rights of a U.S. citizen, but remain proud of the Mexican heritage, in other words, equality not privilege, cultural pluralism not assimilation, justice not discrimination, pride not inferiority, literacy not illiteracy, and economic self-responsibility not welfare. These were the central features of Perales's Mexican American mind. From 1929 through 1941 he never changed his ideas. They worked for him and therefore, he felt they should work for the com-

he wanted to protest the testimony before the committee that had characterized Mexicans as "an inferior and degenerate race." Perales then stated,

> I have heard that the people who want to restrict the immigration of Mexicans into the United States have said that Mexicans are inferior and degenerate and are incapable of being assimilated and becoming good American citizens. These charges are false and constitute a grave injustice on our dignity. The truth is, gentlemen, that it is a charge hurled against the [entire] Mexican community [and] has been inspired by prejudice, a profound racial prejudice that is deep [in the United States]. Racial prejudice has existed since the world began. Consequently I am not surprised that those who support the protagonist [Congressman] Box [of Texas] want to restrict the entrance of Mexicans into this country.[84]

As examples of "Americanized Mexicans," Perales presented himself and other LULAC leaders to the committee.

This had been the start of a new era, and the *ricos* were proud of Perales's defense of the Mexican Raza while LULAC members were proud of his defense of the Mexican American Raza. Perales, from 1929 through the end of the Depression decade, bridged all classes with his ideas, his drive, and his accomplishments. The *ricos* liked his emphasis on cultural dignity; the Mexican Americans responded to his emphasis on Americanism; and the laboring class acknowledged his emphasis on justice and struggle. He was the ideal type: culturally and racially Mexican, but politically and philosophically American. He felt *mexicano* but acted *americano*.

Manuel Carvajal "M. C." González

Perales was a strong, personable, forceful, and articulate man; his very persona seemed to engulf people. His "Mexicanness" visibly enraptured some, but his Americanism permeated all his actions. In contrast stood M. C. González, a handsome, scholarly, aristocratic-looking man whose urbanity, fragility, gentleness, and intellectual ability affected everyone. While his Americanism was quickly detected, his Mexicanness never left him. Where Perales was passionately articulate, González was gracefully intellectual, but both were personifications of the Mexican American mind: two sides of the same coin. Drugstore owner Chapa once remarked about González, "on his large, intelligent forehead there are many wrinkles, which indicate his mental prowess."[85]

M. C. González, unlike Perales, was a man whose presence you might miss, but not his intelligence. Perales, it seems, was a pragmatic but formalistic man who took history by the hand and led it; González waited for the historical moment and caught it by the wings. Nevertheless, both were voices of the Mexican American consciousness.

M. C. González was born on October 22, 1900, in Hidalgo County, Texas. At age ten, he moved with his mother to San Antonio, where he attended public schools. Although his mother worked, they were poor. González tried to do everything he could to help lighten the load of economic and intellectual poverty, especially the latter. He was a precocious youth and a voracious reader; "he always had a book or a newspaper in his hand," reported one account.[86] González later commented on his intellectual qualities: "I guess I was inspired by Lincoln, because I began to read and read and read."[87] Lincoln's appetite for reading, leadership, and justice seemed to have affected González, and later events channeled him into his leadership role. By the age of twelve, he already knew the value and reality of work. He had been employed at Western Union while he attended school, then he worked as a delivery boy at the very popular Mexican middle-class soda bar and pharmacy, Chapa's Drugstore. It was at this job, at age thirteen, that González began to think about his future. He was undecided, but he was ambitious; moreover, work and education were almost endemic to his personality. He was not afraid of the former and thirsted for the latter. While at Chapa's, he confidently remarked, "I will become famous in the world of letters, politics, or the military, or in some career of public life."[88]

González attended San Gerard High School in San Antonio and Nixon-Clay Business College in Austin. Both were private schools. At

Nixon-Clay College González learned secretarial skills in addition to his other studies, but financial pressures forced him to leave. After working for the district court in Hidalgo County for a short time, González returned to Austin to work as a secretary for the law firm of Patterson and Love. It was here that the law began to appeal to him, and he began to study it at the firm. He maintained his interest in the Mexican community by being the secretary and treasurer of the Liga Protectora Mexicana. Because of his diligence, the Mexican

and to gain cultural and social experience, González joined the U.S. Army when he left Austin in 1918 and was assigned as a secretary to the military attaché at the American embassy in Madrid. In 1919 he continued to serve the U.S. government by working as secretary to Sen. Harry B. Howes of St. Louis, rather than staying in the military and working at an embassy in Latin America. In St. Louis González was interviewed because of his tremendous drive and because of his continual interest in and consciousness of the plight of the Mexican community. When asked what factors were responsible for his "state of mind," he answered,

> I was born poor, reared poor and for the most part my childhood was spent with poor people of my Mexican race, and I became acutely aware of the exploitation that [Mexicans] were constantly victims of; of the millions of discriminatory acts they constantly were the objects of; of the suffering they underwent because of the constant humiliations and sufferings they underwent simply because there was no man of my race to defend them, who would fight for them, who would gain respect for them before the law and [therefore], in short, I always felt the desire to have an occupation that would allow me to channel my energies, my aspirations, my whole life to the defense of those [people] who changed countries [and became Americans].[90]

González attended law school at St. Louis University; however, he did not finish his studies in St. Louis but instead returned to Austin, where he finished his legal studies at the University of Texas. He entered law practice in San Antonio in 1924.[91]

González returned to San Antonio, leaving a possible career in diplomatic work, because he wanted to continue to "struggle for his ideals" and to practice law and fight for justice in behalf of the Mexican community in San Antonio.[92] This, he believed, was his personal and political struggle, and he sought to infuse these goals and ideals in others. He immediately was appointed assistant district attorney for the city.

Fluent in French, Spanish, and English, González jumped into local politics on his return to San Antonio. In 1924 a local newspaper reported, "Mexican Voters Being Stirred to Support 'Better Governmenters' by Former Interpreter at Embassy." The newspaper reported that González "has developed into one of the 'wheel horses' of the campaign and accompanies 'Better Government' candidates each night in their visits to the precincts. . . . He urges the Mexican voters [in the West Side] of the city to 'sever their political alliance with the Court House Gang' [the machine] and to vote for all the 'better governmenters.'"[93]

Unfortunately, in 1924 González still did not have the LULAC organization behind him, and the Mexican community had not yet begun clearly to crystallize into "conscious" classes. Nevertheless, González, who had been given moral and educational support by middle-class businessman Chapa ten years earlier, was by the late 1920s and early 1930s engraving his name as a leader in the San Antonio community. Remembering those days, González would state, "When I was a young man, Texas had many thousands of Mexican aliens. They were illiterate and exploited, and racial prejudice was rampant. Mexicans couldn't even go into certain places to eat. There were even signs that said so. . . . There was no leadership, no [organized] professional men [who were Mexican Americans] when I passed the bar exam in [1924]. I was the only one."[94]

In 1924, a San Antonio Mexican newspaper reported González's one-man crusade and his activism: "Armed with his degree and backed by law [he] marched a straight and direct line to battle the injustices perpetuated against the Mexican-Americans whom he loved. With his capabilities and law degree González has turned down diplomatic posts and magnificent [occupational] opportunities to dedicate himself to the completion of his dream [to uplift the Mexican community]."[95]

González, however, was not satisfied to campaign for just a better government. He published the newspaper *El Luchador*, in which he wrote articles in Spanish and English. His theme was always the same: Mexican Americans should fight for their rights, in spite of the fact that poverty, ignorance, and timidity were major problems. Besides urging them to "fight back," he sought to bring unity to the community with his newspaper and his community work.

Moreover, with John Solís and others, he organized Hijos de Texas, an activist organization. González, like Perales, was also a member of many social, cultural, and recreational clubs, and these clubs, González felt (as did Perales), could help bring a "new political sensitivity" and unity to the middle class. González also believed in approaching the middle class through cultural themes that would help in their search for identity and their struggle for a better life.[96]

In 1939, with LULAC already organized, González—as Perales did

out tension or any equivocation. However, he differed slightly from Perales. Perales, even though he announced that he was also proud of being an American, saw himself as a dual man: a Mexican and an American, in an equal partnership of consciousness. However, he did lean to the Mexican side. González, although a Mexican culturally and socially, tended toward a clear emphasis on the American side. On the basis of appearance, Perales's public persona seemed Mexican while González's seemed American; yet, the inner core, the central commitment, and the memories and reflections of both were Mexican. González married an Anglo woman and moved out of the West Side and had to defend vehemently his right to marry an Anglo and to live outside of the Mexican community. Nevertheless, his work continued, undisturbed, for his Mexican brethren, regardless of the criticism.[98]

The impact of González's marriage and his change in residence cannot be measured fully, but it can be said that there was a resentment on the part of many Mexican Americans toward anyone who moved out of the barrio to an Anglo suburb. The impact on González, however, was negligible, as he clearly pointed out in an article entitled "What Is LULAC?" written in 1932: "I know of no organization . . . as uplifting and patriotic [as] . . . LULAC. It matters not what race you descend from, when you have gathered in the spirit of LULAC, you are cleansed in both body and soul, and you are happy at the opportunity of having been in [the] midst of 'LULACKERS,' a truly American organization, which stands for America's glorious ideals."[99]

González was always more open toward Anglos, Perales less. Perales saw a democratic America with separate ethnic groupings; González saw a socially integrated America, but with individual cultural rights. These differences of ideology and personality would also be manifested in later generations by many others; however, in the Depression decade González would still say,

> We [LULAC] are builders of a better [Mexican] race . . . that the League is flourishing speaks with eloquence . . . it is powerful enough to supply the needs of its members, and the love and respect that the Latin race has for it, as well as the admiration, deference, and high estimation in which the anglo-Americans have placed on this extraordinary patriotic and civil institution bespeaks of and proves that LULAC will be a dominant factor in the governmental structure of the affairs of our state and nation.[100]

In the early thirties the different intellectual strands of the Mexican American mind were still being intertwined and most attention was still on combating racial prejudice and discrimination. As González pointed out, the "effects of World War I were still fresh on the minds of this segment of our population [the Mexican American middle class] . . . the unanimous voice of all [Mexican Americans was directed to making] . . . plans to bring about [conscious] understanding and equality of opportunities for all Latin Americans."[101] As a result, according to González, LULAC activities of the thirties focused "on a five point program: (1) to end the segregation of children in the public schools, which prevented the facile use of the English language; (2) to fight the denial of participation in the administration of justice [no jury service for Mexican-Americans]; (3) to stop the statewide policies of no admittance to restaurants, picture shows, swimming pools, etc.; (4) to end the inability of Mexicans to purchase land in restricted residential areas designed for 'white only'; and (5) to struggle against the denial of the right of suffrage."[102]

This was the program González advocated. He believed that if Mexicans were good enough to fight for America's rights abroad they were good enough to fight for civil rights at home, especially to obtain more education and to fight school segregation. Above all, González believed that "the clarion call to arms in the great adventure" of bringing to "consciousness" the Mexican American middle class in 1929 at the LULAC convention was comparable to the Mexican cry for independence in 1810 and America's declaration of independence in 1776.[103] González felt that 1929 was the beginning of a "new consciousness," "new activities," and "a clear expression of independence" to search for a "new identity," and that LULAC was taking this new "mentality" to all of the South Texas counties and particularly Bexar

County. Above all, González thought, LULAC would arm the people with the right to vote and provide them with an impetus and an instrument to develop the "economic, civic, political, patriotic, and intellectual spheres of the Mexican people." LULAC, therefore, had a mission "to make living conditions better for coming and succeeding generations."[104]

During the 1930s González was in LULAC's Council II and Perales was in Council XVI because of their differences. González devoted

vate suits.--- He also fought for separate Mexican F...

In business affairs, he was a leading member and, for a time, president of the Mexican Chamber of Commerce. The Mexican chamber during the late twenties had primarily been a business organization to "encourage and promote business relations between American concerns in Mexico and in San Antonio, Texas." But in the 1930s the constitution was changed to make it into a civic organization that dealt with "sanitation, streets, recreation, illiteracy, and education." This change of role was motivated by the LULAC members who belonged to it. As a result of this change, the leading members of the organization became the Mexican American businesspeople instead of the Mexican *ricos*, and the Mexican Chamber of Commerce began to promote Mexican Americanism rather than Mexican nationalism. González was a principal motivator in these changes.[106]

The decade of the thirties had been difficult for the Mexican population of San Antonio, in spite of LULAC, because of the tremendous economic, ideological, and cultural changes. Individuals like Father Tranchese, Magdaleno Rodríguez, Emma Tenayuca, and Rómulo Mungía had worked to improve the conditions of the Mexican workers, while others such as Alonzo S. Perales, Manuel C. González, George Garza, Gustavo García, and Jacobo Rodríguez, through the League of United Latin American Citizens, had sought to organize the middle class and improve the whole West Side. This latter group was replacing the *ricos*. The new ideology of the *"mexicano americano"* was sweeping San Antonio and the Southwest, and as González observed in 1940, the middle class's search for identity "was becoming sharply defined as Mexican-American. By the late 1930s a change in the Mexican community [of San Antonio] had become apparent. Even the Church by the 1940s with [new archbishop] Lucy [had] helped to make [us] Mexican American."[107]

Consequently, by the early 1940s, LULAC's original ideals had begun to become a concrete reality, although they would not become completely visible until the 1950s, with the end of the segregation of Mexican children in public schools in San Antonio and throughout Texas; the abolishing of discrimination that restricted Mexican Americans from buying property outside the West Side; the increasing enrollment of Mexican children in public schools; and the growth of LULAC councils. Through the fervor of the 1920s and 1930s had stood M. C. González, the "American Mexican" who was the mirror image of Alonzo S. Perales, the ideal type for Mexican Americans. Both had provided the *elan vital* for a generation in search of its identity.

PERALES, GONZÁLEZ, AND LULAC

M. C. González's and Alonzo S. Perales's philosophies were the central ideology of LULAC in particular, and the Mexican American mind in general. For both, being in LULAC, fighting for the poorer Mexican community, fighting against discrimination, changing Mexicans into U.S. citizens, and developing a love for the United States was being a Mexican American. For González, specifically, nationalism was just a means, not an end. "We used nationalism to organize them [Texas Mexicans] for civil rights and Americanism." They did this, he said, for them to have a "share of [American] life, accomplish something [for themselves, and] achieve something. [The] people were hungry for education, for a better life." They wanted to "teach them to be Americans and stress[ed] education since 90% of our people were illiterate." LULAC, according to González, wanted to be classified as an American not a Mexican organization in San Antonio, and "we wanted to speak English to show [that] we were not Mexicans [aliens] because to work as a Mexican organization would [have been] . . . a barrier. [However,] [w]e wanted to remain Mexican [culturally], but take advantage of American life, citizenship."[108]

LULAC was, as a result of this philosophy, the only voice in the 1930s calling for self-identity, seeking to maintain a Mexican American lifestyle, and working against the Mexican Americans' problems in education, health, politics, and discrimination. The organization consisted of middle-class men and women with a "new consciousness." The LULAC Constitution and Code reflected their desires, their aspirations, their dreams, and their goals. The LULAC program, in

fact, reflected the ideas and ideology of a rising class — a class searching for a new identity, a new order, and a new community. Alonzo S.
Perales, M. C. González, H. T. Manuel, Carlos E. Castañeda, and
George I. Sánchez were a few of the articulators of the embryonic
Mexican middle class. Reflecting on his personal change of consciousness from Mexican to Mexican American, M. C. González stated, "I
liked Mexican food and culture, but no matter what, I became part
of the American philosophy." Then, speaking of the central problem

Mexican aliens. They also sought to be viewed as *gente decente*, not
as *gente corriente*, and philosophically, they wanted civil liberties,
equal justice, equality of opportunity, freedom from discrimination,
and cultural rights. These were the core tenets of a developing Mexican American mind that accepted the United States, the flag, service, and honor as the main political symbols. In addition, they accepted cultural pluralism and voting as the main political pillars of
their Americanization, and education, above all, was the key to progress, achievement, and prosperity. Mexican Americans believed in the
virtues of struggle and work. Accordingly, LULAC during the 1950s
fought and worked for more education and for integration — in swimming pools, real estate, hotels, dance halls and bars, schools, and all
other spheres of everyday life. Above all it fought for education as
the means to better homes, upward mobility, and better jobs. LULAC
and the middle class wanted doctors, lawyers, teachers, not necessarily an intelligentsia, but a managerial class. Not that they were
anti-intellectual, they were just pragmatic: basic needs first. From
the seedbeds of the 1920s had sprouted the seedlings of the Mexican
American mind, and the events of the 1930s had fertilized them while
LULAC cultivated and reaped them.

In the early 1940s, M. C. González, at the culmination of more
than a decade of LULAC work, spoke to the graduating class of San
Felipe and Sidney Lanier schools. His words, it seems were directed not
only at the students, but at the rising Mexican American generation:

> You have concluded your school career, and you are commencing
> a new life. You have been given a diploma as evidence of your gradua-

tion from this institution of learning. However, you are faced with a more adventurous, more exciting, more significant future than other [Mexican] students who passed through these portals on their way to face life. They tread[ed] an avenue leading into a world of peace prepared to battle life on an economic basis alone, where as you face a world engulfed in a struggle to determine whether we [as Americans] are to be ruled by the forces of tyranny and oppression, or whether democracy and the American way of life shall in the end prevail.

You have been taught in those ideals of liberty and freedom, justice and equality which founded this continent, and you have for inspiration, the patriotism, self-sacrifice and valor of Washington, Lincoln, Roosevelt, Simón Bolívar, Miguel Hidalgo and Benito Juárez. You spring from a valiant race of men possessed of indomitable courage and were taught and reared in a country where the dignity of man and the freedom of God-loving people stated as the only goal for which to work, fight and die, forsaking all other isms and totalitarian forms of government. You have an opportunity few people of your race possess. . . .

Such a country, your country, is calling you to help defend it, to help destroy those who would tear down the sacred principles of the Bill of Rights; our country and our flag are offering you the greatest opportunity in your life to prove the metal which you and your ancestors are made of, and that challenge, I know, will be readily accepted by you; as Christian believers, you are reminded of Miguel Hidalgo, who using the image of the Virgin of Guadalupe for a flag, led the people in revolt against the yoke of Spain. From the viewpoints of courage you are reminded of the last Emperor of Mexico, Cuauhtemoc, who endured the pains of hell as his feet were burned in order that he would reveal hidden treasures to the Spaniards. And as to those of our race who have already distinguished themselves, you will find Joe P. Martínez, 23, of Colorado, who was awarded the Medal of Honor and recognized as the Hero of Attu; and you will find that today there are more than 250,000 Latin Americans glorifying the heroic deeds of their ancestors and fighting shoulder to shoulder with their Anglo-American fellowmen under the sea, on the sea and above the sea, in the Mediterranean, in Guadalcanal, in the South Pacific, in all parts of the world.[110]

González stressed the essence of the Mexican American mentality: pride in education, individual achievement, heritage, patriotism; religious grounding; youthful enthusiasm; political principles; obligations of citizenship; struggle for democracy; racial and cultural pride; and the promise of "a more adventurous, more exciting, more significant future" than any other Mexican generation. This was, after all, the new order of Mexican Americans. Many Mexicans in San Antonio's West Side, as well as throughout the Southwest, were now, for the most part, Mexican Americans, and those who were not would soon be exposed to the patriotic outburst of World War II — a new catalyst for change — and when the new veterans returned, LULAC would be waiting to help them fight for equality, justice, and the right to vote. But, unlike after World War I, Mexican American intellectual tenets would already be in place. The Depression decade had indeed been the period of the making of the Mexican American mind, especially in San Antonio. It had been a decade of criticism, social change, and a search for identity.

Epilogue: From Search for Identity to Formation of Ideology, Leadership, and Organization

1929 TO 1941

Between the great Depression and America's entrance into World War II, Mexicans in the United States were in a "crucial historical juncture," but it was also a crucial juncture worldwide. Jack Roth has argued that both the United States and Europe during the period between World War I and World War II were at a critical "turning point" in world history. The United States, for example, confronted itself in the ideological split between the idea of progress and the force of nostalgia, in the political split between the liberalism of pluralism and the liberalism of the individual, and in the societal impact of what Walter Lippman called the "acids of modernity" (technology, automobiles, mass production, mass consumption, radios, movies, mass media, science, and the modernism of religion) on a communal, organic, and "simple" culture and society. Europe, according to Roth, also confronted the conflicting forces of liberal democracy, cultural modernity, rising fascism, ebbing traditionalism, and state socialism. All of these countries were, essentially, in an ideational confrontation with the meanings and implications of modernity. It was a situation that Emerson had very aptly characterized as early as the nineteenth century as a "fundamental split in society between the Party of the Past and the Party of the Future, the Party of Memory, and the Party of Hope." As has been shown, the Mexican American middle class in San Antonio and throughout the Southwest was also caught in this ideational conflict, but, of course, in a smaller, although significant, way.[1]

Essentially the 1929–41 crisis for the Mexican American was a philosophical and ontological turning point that was characterized by a search for self. There was a need to define a new intellectual and political relationship to the modernizing and changing conditions in Mexico and the United States, especially the Southwest. Consequently, as has been shown, by World War II, the Mexican Americans in San

Antonio under the leadership of the League of United Latin American Citizens had chosen the Emersonian "Party of the Future" and the "Party of Hope," the Lockian and Jeffersonian philosophy of liberalism, but with a sensitivity and an affinity to the Rooseveltian New Deal conservative revolution (1932–44) of pragmatic liberalism with its emphasis on pluralism, statism, centralization, and its sense of humanism. Above all, they favored the general perspective that Franklin D. Roosevelt had outlined as the definitional theme for an

American weltanschauung that still allowed for balancing gional, and individual perspectives. González, in essence, was calling for an end to the Balkanized nature of the Mexican communities in the Southwest with their separate identities and ideals, by binding them to the Mexican American identity, the "American Promise," and the "liberal tradition." This idealist vision of Americanism coincided with the modernizing urban reality that many Mexicans were beginning to experience by 1941: more mobility, abundance, equality, and a feeling of hope and possibilities.

This urban structural reality was ideologically enhanced by Franklin D. Roosevelt's national and international interpretation of an Americanism that also called for the extension of the basic four freedoms to everyone: freedom of speech, freedom of worship, freedom from want, and freedom from fear in order to establish a pluralist America and a pluralist world. Many urban Mexicans listened to this emphasis on Americanism and accepted it because it coincided with their rising expectations. They began to accept the themes of citizenship, Americanization, and integration advocated by LULAC. This message, which was repeated throughout the period from 1929 to 1941, emphasized the development of a strong Mexican American identity and the acceptance of the "promise of America."

LULAC's social and political organizing activities and its emphasis on developing a dual Mexican and American mentality thus gave rise to two eras of Mexican Americanism (1929–68 and 1978–present) and to the development of a movement that focused on the issues of education, integration, civil rights, politics, housing, and racial inequality, and also attempted to mitigate, to some extent, the tidal

wave of Americanism that inundated the Mexican American communities in the late 1940s and especially the 1950s. LULAC had been,
from 1929 through 1941, the central organizational vehicle in the
Mexican immigrants' search for an American identity in a world that
was beginning to become pluralist.[3]

THE 1940s

The early 1940s, consequently, were crucial years because the Mexican Americans were entering an era of "new consciousness" of identity and assertiveness, as Pauline Kibbe acknowledged in her assessment of the Mexican population in Texas during the 1940s. This new
consciousness of Mexican Americanism was not only an individual
perspective of self-identity, but, as Kibbe further pointed out, a group's
consciousness for communal action that indicated that Mexican Americans in Texas "have acquired a new courage [and] have become more
vocal in protesting the restrictions and inequalities with which they
are confronted." World War II not only served as a catalyst for more
urbanization and industrialization in Texas and throughout the Southwest, but it increased employment opportunities for Mexicans and
Mexican Americans and, thereby, increased their sense of rising expectations. In addition, World War II accelerated Mexican flight to
the urban areas.[4]

Observing this increasing urbanization, Carlos Castañeda, the San
Antonio intellectual whom FDR appointed the regional director for
the Fair Employment Practices Committee (FEPC), stated in 1943
that "throughout Texas, New Mexico, and Louisiana the shipyard, the
airship factories, the oil industry, the mines, the munition factories,
and the numerous military and naval installations slowly, reluctantly,
and with much misgivings, began to give the Mexican-American a
trial in semiskilled positions, and eventually in some skilled jobs." As
a result, Mexicans, like many non-Mexican women throughout the
United States, experienced the exhilaration of a new sense of economic
and social possibility, personal hope, and self-development.

In spite of this, racism, sexism, and discrimination continued and
in some cases were even more severe, according to the published documentation by intellectuals such as Alonzo Perales and Carlos Castañeda. In fact, Castañeda in 1948 vehemently announced in an article
entitled "The Second-Rate Citizen and Democracy" that

> "the time has come for frank dealing, for the examination of the facts
> in the case, for the presentation of ungarbled truth [concerning the

racism and discrimination against the Mexican Americans in Texas]. Failure to reveal the true facts in regard to our second-rate citizenship can lead only to the ultimate destruction of the basic principles of democracy. If we admit the damning theory of racial superiority implied in such a condition we are no better than the Nazis.[5]

The four hundred thousand to five hundred thousand Mexican Americans who returned from the war agreed with Castañeda as they quickly perceived the contradictions and tensions between their self-

according to historian Feliciano Rivera, "The Mexican-Americans pressed for social acceptance, civil and political rights, decent education, and expanded economic opportunities. In other words, [they] . . . began to desire, and to demand, citizenship in the fullest sense." Within this climate of ideas, historian Rodolfo Acuña has correctly observed that, "as in the case of World War I, the returning Mexican-American veterans formed their own organizations. Participation widened as new veterans' groups such as the American G.I. Forum competed with LULAC for hegemony." It was, however, for organizational, not ideological, hegemony.[6]

Examining this phenomenon, Ricardo Romo points out that after World War II Americanization accelerated because "nationwide, Mexican-Americans returned as the most decorated ethnic group in the armed services, winning seventeen Medals of Honor. Those who did not receive Medals of Honor often gained in other ways from their experiences in the service. Many soon applied the skills that they learned while in uniform to civilian life." Moreover, "the postwar years were also marked by increased political activism aimed at obtaining local political representation, metropolitan services and improvements, and equity in the judicial system."[7]

In forming one organization after another, the Mexican Americans of the 1929–41 period, pushed by the returning veterans and both armed with the new identity of Mexican Americanism and still marching to the patriotism and spirit of the war effort, did not ask, "Who am I?"; they were now asking, "What do we do?" They began, as a result, two decades of political activism, and "unlike the mutual

aid or voluntary associations of the previous [immigrant] generation,"
writes Romo, the new political organizations of the 1940s, for example, the Community Service Organization in Los Angeles, "claimed
no allegiance to Mexico, nor did its members assign a leadership role
to the local Mexican consul. One of its early leaders was Edward Roybal, a college graduate and veteran of World War II." Romo further
points out that "in East Los Angeles some of the veterans formed a
chapter of the American G.I. Forum, a Mexican-American organization founded in Texas by World War II veterans. [And] in the League
of United Latin American Citizens (LULAC), the barrio residents
of Los Angeles and surrounding communities found an ally in chal-
lenging the segregation of children in the public schools." It seemed
that the mentality of Mexican Americanism was not "searching," as
in the 1920s, it was "doing" in the 1940s. By the end of the 1940s the
search for self had spread throughout the Southwest, and Mexican
Americanism as an identity was becoming hegemonous. With this
new ontological perspective a host of Mexican American middle-class
organizations arose to push their new identity to the level of a viable
ideology and used it as a vehicle for the acquisition of knowledge and
the development of power.[8]

Intellectually, it was evident that there was the gestalt of a new
identity, a new consciousness, and a new ideology that formed in the
minds of the rising middle class of the 1930s and the returning veterans of the 1940s. In structural terms, David Montejano has written
that

> the returning veterans, via the G.I. Bill of Rights and college degrees,
> formed the base for the expanding middle and skilled working classes
> among Texas Mexicans. The G.I. Bill of Rights, the compensation of
> World War II and Korean service proved to be a most significant avenue
> for upward mobility for Mexicans and Blacks. . . . Although no figures
> are readily available, enrollment in state and private colleges [also] in-
> creased substantially. Home ownership by Mexican-Americans was fa-
> cilitated by V.A. loans in the late forties and early fifties. [In addition,]
> the military industrial complex, . . . provided well paying employment,
> thus laying a foundation for stable middle and working classes.[9]

In San Antonio this developing Mexican American civil and political rights era coincided with the Anglo elite's desire to maintain "an
environment free of political and social conflict." Consequently, as
in national politics, consensus took precedence over conflict, and
throughout the forties and fifties the Americano urban city fathers
throughout the Southwest (in order to continue the modernization
process) integrated Mexican Americans politically, socially, and, to
some extent, racially.[10]

Mexican Americans, consequently, were elected to the House of Representatives, to the Senate, to the lieutenant-governorship of New Mexico, to school boards, to city councils, and in 1957 in El Paso, to the office of mayor. David Montejano, in analyzing the structural implications of the rise of this middle-class movement with its viable weltanschauung, writes that,

> in the [Southwestern] urban areas, these changed political conditions
> steadily eroded the Jim Crow structure within a decade after the war.

ideology and the development of pragmatic organizations. The decade began a new era of politics under the ideological reality of Mexican Americanism; an identity and ideology that were within the U.S. liberal consensus of the New Deal and Fair Deal politics of statism, centralism, McCarthyism, and Keynesianism. There still remained, though, the underlying Mexican American conservatism that emphasized the importance of the family, community, religion, and traditionalism. This generation, without being fully cognizant, was ideologically in line with Eisenhower's liberal conservatism, because its philosophical and political roots emanated from a heritage of both a Scholastic realism and a liberal idealism.[12]

The development of these organizations caused a corresponding development of middle-class leadership and Mexican American mentality; therefore, in addition to Perales, González, Castañeda, Manuel, and Sánchez (the powerful leaders of the 1930s), there were now new names added to the pantheon of Mexican American leaders: Manuel Ruiz, Jr., of California; Dr. Héctor García of Texas; Henry B. González of Texas; Dennis Chávez of New Mexico; and Edward R. Roybal of California. All of these leaders and organizations knew that they were functioning Americans, but they were also aware and readily acknowledged and cherished their Mexicanness. Identity was not a question of ontology for them, it was just a reality of experience. They were pragmatists who functioned with a balanced Mexican and American consciousness, as well as a private and public sense of security. Their own success and personal sense of security in their Mexican American identity coincided with a strong belief that the conditions of the majority of the Mexican American population in the United States could be improved by political and educational means, because 80 percent of the Mexican Americans now lived in the urban centers (which helped to instill the Anglo faith in hope and progress), especially in San Antonio, Los Angeles, El Paso, and Chicago.[13]

The Mexican American leadership and developing generation perceived the world from within the Mexican American mind, which emphasized community, civic virtue, and individualism, but within a world of equality. This Mexican American mind also emphasized and accepted the pluralism of ideas, the reality of different classes, and the viability of constantly changing occupations, roles, and life worlds. This pluralism established the multiplicity of realities and gestalts within the different Mexican American communities; social, cultural, and intellectual heterogeneity was the reality, not homogeneity. Moreover, this mentality recognized the family as the central part of the community, the cornerstone of society, and as the main institution for developing individual consciousness, identity, values, and perceptions. In addition, the Mexican American mentality accepted and espoused a centralized government that established harmony, order, and stability, but not one that imposed its authority or its dictums. Patriotism was also of central importance to the Mexican American perspective, and great value was placed on a sense of justice, brotherhood, morality, and religion.

Paradoxically, the Mexican American mind and self-identity were both politically liberal and conservative, without question, because of the emphasis on family, traditional values, religion, community, and the individual (with his or her self-interests), but with a sense of the collective consciousness. It must be remembered that the Mexican American mind had its intellectual roots in the exiled *ricos*' Scholastic and Comtian conservatism as well as the middle class's Lockian liberal tradition.

Philosophically, the Hamiltonian rather than the Jeffersonian liberal tradition of individualism within the structure of society and a centralized government fitted the new Mexican American mentality like a glove. Both the *ricos* and the middle class, therefore, accepted the Rooseveltian version of Comtian liberalism "from above." As a result, in the 1940s the Mexican American mentality exhibited a liberal-conservative tendency toward self-help, free enterprise, liberty, hard work, religion, and patriotism. At the same time, there was a tendency toward accepting a conservative centralized government (which, ironically, was emphasized by New Deal liberalism) but opposition to any socialism or radicalism. Mexican Americans would have found it easy to identify with Theodore Roosevelt's Hamiltonian liberalism, which emphasized a Comtian society of order, stability, state management, and the centralization of authority and power via a strong leader, but with an emphasis on Jeffersonian individualism.[14]

In essence, the Mexican American identity and mentality was one of conservative-liberalism, or as it is currently called, neoconservatism, but within the intellectual, rational, and Catholic conservative orientation of people such as William F. Buckley, Jr. This conservative-liberal Mexican American perspective was not, however, exhibited as

World radicals, as some of the Chicanos of the 1960s wanted them to become. In short, the Mexican American philosophy that evolved after 1941 emphasized rationality tempered with intuition, civic virtue in the use of political power, a strong family that also allowed for individualism, an organic community as the basis for society, a collective memory of Mexican tradition within the American cultural reality, and a society of political order, stability, and a centralized government — but one that allowed for political pluralism and emphasized change within continuity.

During the 1940s most Mexican Americans still retained their collective memory of immigration and Mexican cultural traditions and their impressions of the Mexican revolution. But during the 1950s, Americanism began to erase this memory and seemed to short-circuit the evolving Mexican American philosophy. Interestingly, it was this sense of collective memory that Octavio Romano tried to rejuvenate through his writings in the 1960s and 1970s in *El Grito*. Romano's articles called for a redeeming of the historical and personal collective consciousness of *lo mexicano*.

Clearly, the Mexican American generation of the 1930s and 1940s still lived within the historical memory that Romano tried to redeem, but it was somewhat different for the middle-class generation of the 1950s, which was more prone to Americanism, relativism, secularism, and possessive individualism, especially as it moved away from its *Mexicanidad*. This middle-class ideational dilemma was evident at a conference held at Occidental College in 1963 on the question of self-definition, where it was concluded that Mexican Americans were too "individualistic" and without any "sense of obligation" to their community. The conference further underscored the fact that there was a multiplicity of cultural and ideological realities. Consequently, *lo mexicano* for many was not an everyday reality.[15]

The first generation of Mexican Americans in the 1930s and 1940s had wanted a balance of Mexican (*rico*) perspectives and American (liberal and modernist) views. The second and third generations of Mexican Americans throughout the Southwest and in San Antonio in the 1950s had become more Americanized, as the conference recognized. Therefore, they had forgotten the original philosophical goals and cultural sentiments of LULAC and the ideas of Perales, González, Castañeda, Manuel, and Sánchez; that is, of a generation that essentially wanted to remain Mexican in culture and be American only in politics. With the coming of the fifties and the sixties, many of the Mexican American middle class would either move away from the barrio into an Anglo neighborhood, or if they remained in the barrio, they would become more Americanized in spirit and temper (although somewhat more aware of *lo mexicano*).

In San Antonio, however, Mexican Americans, regardless of generation or class or status, remained in the West Side; the "lid" of Mexican tradition and *lo mexicano* continued to maintain and provide a collective memory and to hold the line of the original LULAC philosophy, unlike in Los Angeles and other cities. In San Antonio, given the city's acceptance of the duality of structure and urban philosophy and given that the city remained the tip of the South Texas Mexican "iceberg," there was a retention of *lo mexicano* as an everyday reality and as part of a collective historical memory. Nevertheless, Americanization had become more of a reality.

The situation in San Antonio was somewhat similar to that of the Mexican Americans in El Paso, who were able to observe, participate in, and accept the reality of their neighboring city of Juárez, Mexico, which provided a constant enforcement of their Mexicanness. Unlike the other major urban "cities within a city," San Antonio and El Paso continued to be ethnically bonded by the constant emergence and re-emergence of the "collective intersubjectivity" of la Raza and the evolving Mexican American liberal-conservative philosophy. Therefore, regardless of the impact of the Americanization process (as Robert Park had outlined in the 1920s) from acculturation to assimilation, San Antonio and El Paso had mitigating factors to shape, although not fully to abort, the process of Americanization and modernization.[16]

George I. Sánchez, who had been the national LULAC president in 1942, in the early 1960s pointed out (in relation to these changes in citizenship, Americanization, and Mexican culture from World War I to the early 1960s) that "in a way, World War I [had] served a good purpose. Full employment, good wages, and the educative results of military service stimulated acculturation in the Southwest. However, the issues were much too large and complex to be met adequately by the by-products of war." In addition, "World War II had [also had] its good effects. . . . As in World War I." Sánchez believed that World War II with its "military service and improved economic

can immigration were the keys to the integration and functionalism of the Mexican population in the United States.[17]

As an educational psychologist, Sánchez also argued through the 1940s and 1950s, just as he had done in the 1930s, that positive self-esteem leads to feelings of self-confidence, self-worth, strength, ability, and an adequacy of being that is useful and necessary in the world. The key to this positive self-esteem was, Sánchez felt, the retention and promotion of the Spanish language in the everyday lives of the Mexican Americans. Sánchez did not oppose acculturation, but he saw in bilingualism the key to providing the essential positive psychological fulcrum for maintaining the balance between the positive memory of the Mexican self and the functioning American "I." For Sánchez a Mexican American who had the linguistic capability of Spanish acquired a sense of history, culture, and positive sense of self that could serve as the psychological and emotional basis for a strong feeling of self-esteem and motivation. This feeling, in turn, could lead to the self-confidence that was necessary to succeed in the reality of American society. In the 1940s Sánchez had recognized that Mexican Americans could still maintain a balance between the Mexican self and the American, and therefore maintain a strong sense of self-esteem, even if the national zeitgeist, as emphasized by Roosevelt, Henry Luce, Wendell Willkie, and others, was on Americanism.

But by 1951, given the impact of the war and the economic gains, there was a slight shift by the middle class toward the American end of Mexican American. This was not only a matter of personal choice, or of a pragmatic (organizational) political choice, but because of, especially in Texas, extreme racism and discrimination. According to Sánchez, these conditions led to the assumption that *lo mexicano* in a Mexican American was tantamount to being inferior. Thus, Sánchez felt, the acceptance and recognition of bilingualism in the 1960s would provide the basis for a functioning and successful American of Mexican descent.[18]

THE 1950s

In retrospect, one can see that by 1951 a shift in the Mexican American identity had begun to take place, although it was still well within the parameters outlined by M. C. González's "city on the hill" speech. On May 18 and 19, 1951, the American Council of Spanish-speaking People was established at a meeting in El Paso. The meeting was called by George I. Sánchez, one of the leading Mexican American intellectuals of the 1930s and the 1940s, and signaled an ideological shift in the search for identity. The emphasis was now on Americanism rather than on Mexicanism. Ironically, it was this shift in consciousness that would begin the tilt that a decade later would help activate the sons and daughters of the Chicano generation to attempt to redeem that sensitivity to and emphasis on *lo mexicano*.

The shift in 1951 was suggested by Sánchez to keep within the temper of the decade; that is, anyone who was not a 100 percent loyal American was thought to be a Communist. Sánchez also saw this shift toward Americanism as a pragmatic way to continue to implement his Tocquevillian version of pluralism without having the Communist hysteria in the United States indict or accuse the organization's ethnic militancy. This shift of personal and organizational identity facilitated political organizing and the development of a civil rights movement in a society that suspected any political action of being leftist. All the Mexican American organizations that attended that 1951 meeting — the Community Service Organization of California, the League of United Latin American Citizens of Texas, the American G.I. Forum of Texas, and the Alianza Hispano-Americana of New Mexico — endorsed this turn to the right. The organizations and members participating in this meeting were endorsing not only pragmatic politics, but also the Mexican American consciousness, but now in light of the U.S. political climate.

This meeting was also significant because there was present a new generation of Mexican American leaders: Gus C. García, Tony Ríos, Ignacio López, José Estrada, Sen. Dennis Chávez, Jr., of New Mexico, and Tibo J. Chávez, the lieutenant governor of New Mexico, who

was elected president of the council. George Sánchez was appointed
to serve as the council's executive director. Remaining active until the
mid-fifties, the American Council of Spanish-speaking People served
as a major umbrella organization to coordinate the Mexican American middle class's advancement in the issues of education and civil
rights. This shift of ontological and organizational emphasis to
Americanism in the face of McCarthyism was also, it can be construed,
a visible sign of a strong sense of underlying personal and social

offers. These social securities are inseparable from the web of a culture. To identify with them is to participate in them with a sense of
security, trust, and reliance. If the original process of acculturation —
and it happens only once, as I have said — provides, even as it imposes
the bonds, restrictions, and prohibitions of the particular culture, [and]
a sense of enjoyment of those securities, then the foundations of [a positive ethnic] identity are also laid. Thereafter the individual who is thus
happily equipped is able to cope.[20]

Galarza was emphasizing the fact that many of the Mexican Americans of the 1940s and early 1950s were still rooted deeply in their Mexicanness, but the later Mexican American generations would not have
the security of this initial bonding. Consequently, in 1951 an identity
as an American posed no threat to the self-identity of many of the
Mexican American leaders.

Galarza also perceived these increasing political and cultural Americanist activities as a move from the issue of self-identity to the issue
of community building, which is what the Mexican American civil
rights movement was doing in 1951: providing for individual success
and development, but with corresponding community development.
As Galarza stated, "The significance of cultural [and political] activities — speech, thoughts, techniques, and the like — is that they represent the individual search for security and identity in a network
of human relations." Thus, the turn to Americanism in 1951 can be
seen as a shift from a preoccupation with developing only a self-identity
to a wish to develop more of a group identity. Galarza particularly
warned, however, that "history [is what] tells us the origin of those
cultural forms [of the life world] and the common [historical-tradi-

tional] experience that lies behind . . . [everyone's daily life]. It helps us [however] not to confuse [culture] with ethnicity, which merely insulates it; or with society, which embodies it; or with the state, which likely as not will prevent it; or with government, which polices it." In essence, Galarza, in a discourse that extended forward and backward in time, warned that culture or ethnicity should not be accepted as a thing in itself, but as an organically developing process that should not be mistaken for identity, society, a state, or even a government.[21]

Galarza suggests that one's everyday culture is only an indication of one's everyday reality — by choice or not — and should not be seen as being the same as ethnicity. For Galarza, being a Mexican American was based on a relationship between his ties to the Spanish language and his historical memory (which was a product of study, everyday barrio reality, or an initial Mexican or Mexican American bonding process). According to Galarza, if the initial bonding is filled with emotional security, ethnic culture, and a positive group identity, the result will be a strong sense of self without any major psychological insecurity or feelings of inferiority. Without these conditions, one can still be Mexican American, but possibly with a consciousness of self that is filled with ambiguity, doubt, and a lack of clarity within the historical memory.[22]

The Mexican American leadership in the 1950s seemed to be quite conscious of these different developments in group and individual culture as well as the shifting currents of identity. They were pragmatists within an American Mexican mentality; they were not ideologues seeking homogeneity of identity or everyday reality. What was noticeable in the early 1950s was that the Mexican American leaders who were born in Mexico (as was Ernesto Galarza) or reared in the strength of a Mexican family and community (like Henry B. González) had a strong sense of self; they were secure even when a shift of emphasis in identity occurred. They seemed to be aware that there was still Mexican continuity within the American ideational change. The identity of Mexican Americanism was secure in the private persona of the 1930s, 1940s, and early 1950s and, as a result, so was the Mexican American weltanschauung of that period. However, with the 1950s and the erosion of *lo mexicano*, there began to exist a doubt and an ambiguity as to the real validity and truth of the status of Americanism (and even the truth of Mexicanism) within the self-identity of the American generation of Mexican descent. This question of the real self would, consequently, rise again in the youth of the 1960s.[23]

It seems, however, that with the prosperity of the 1950s the hunger and militancy of the middle class's civil rights movement had also become somewhat diluted on (to use Werner Sombart's phrase) "a sea of roast beef"; in fact, although the Mexican American communities in the Southwest were still laced by a "string of racism," Mexican Americans were becoming, to some degree, more a part of David Potter's "people of plenty." They shared, although less than other Americans, in the abundance, mobility, and prosperity of the United States in the Golden Fifties. Demographically, for example, Mexican Americans in California, Texas, New Mexico, Colorado, and Arizona had increased by 51.3 percent (compared to 36.5 percent for Anglos

in California, and 62.1 percent in Arizona).

Between 1950 and 1960 the number of years of education also had increased in every state, including Texas. Moreover, throughout the five southwestern states the Mexican American middle class had grown, regardless of whether members were Mexican-born or second- or third-generation native-born (with the last having a sharper rise in the professional employment categories). The median salaries of the Mexican American population had also increased by 1960, although they were still substantially lower than those of the Anglos, but still higher than those of nonwhites. For example, 51.6 percent of the Mexican American population in Texas earned less than $3,000, but 45.7 percent earned between $3,000 and $10,000 and 2.7 percent earned over $10,000. Of political significance were the facts that as early as 1950, 83 percent of the Mexican Americans were U.S. citizens; between 1950 and 1960 the Mexican American population in the Southwest increased by 51.3 percent; and all incomes rose from 1950 to 1960 in absolute as well as relative terms.[24]

In 1963, as a result of all these changes, Julián Samora with a grant from the Rosenberg Foundation called a conference of Mexican American intellectuals and Anglo scholars to analyze the Mexican American era. As a whole, they found that the Mexican American organizations and individuals were "demonstrating a growing sophistication and ability to cooperate and work toward common goals in action programs, ranging from conferences and meetings to power-producing community organization efforts, non-partisan political activity, and, . . . picketing and racial protest efforts. . . . [However, these efforts were local] and unable to attack problems on a regional or national basis." Overall, Samora wrote, "there is some evidence of some improvement, but the rapid change by non-whites and [Anglos] . . . makes it most difficult for the Spanish-speaking to catch up."[25]

SAN ANTONIO: THE CENTER OF MEXICAN AMERICANISM

The differences and difficulties were not as apparent in San Antonio, because during the 1950s it remained not only the cradle of Texas and Mexican American identity and liberty, but a major trade and economic center in the Southwest that needed Mexican and Mexican American labor. It was also the cultural and intellectual center of Mexican American social and political activities. Unlike other urban centers, San Antonio remained tied to the South Texas area, and Anglos in San Antonio continued to view and accept *lo mexicano* and *lo americano* as the ethos of the city. The city continues to accept its bicultural reality, its American-Texan-Mexican cosmopolitanism, and its rich and varied history, although to some Anglos the Mexicans continue to be just "Meskins."

While there continued to exist the reality of segregation, impoverishment, and discrimination for many of the lower classes of Mexican American workers in the West Side's "town within a city," there were definite qualitative political and social differences in the 1950s and 1960s. Overall, the overt discrimination of the 1930s and the 1940s became the institutional racism of the late 1950s and early 1960s, but even this type of discrimination lessened with the necessities of modernization, the Mexican American middle class's power politics, new federal and state legislation, as well as the impact of the general temper of the 1960s. All of these factors helped minimize racism and discrimination. San Antonio, however, unlike Los Angeles or El Paso, remained a city of deference and racial differences; it was still a southern center.

Since the 1940s the Mexican American zeitgeist in the barrio had promoted a climate of hope, optimism, and the possibility of mobility via education, politics, and new leadership. As a result of World War II, more Mexican Americans had found civilian jobs in the city's military bases, and by the 1950s many of these Mexican Americans had moved to supervisory and technical positions. In addition, many Mexican American organizations constantly pressured the city in the 1950s to open up the job market and provide more opportunities for the Mexican American population.

With the developing professional, service, and blue-collar job market, the Mexican American population in San Antonio increased from

160,420 in 1950 to 243,627 (about 45 percent of the total population of the city) in 1969. Salaries also increased in relative and absolute terms, although the overall wages for everybody in Texas were considerably lower than in most southwestern states. Political activity, citizenship, and voting increased throughout the fifties in San Antonio as a result of LULAC and other organizations' activities. As Rodolfo Acuña has written; "Definitely, the San Antonio Mexican community was more politically active during the postwar period. Voter

a book entitled *Mexican Ethnic Leadership in San Antonio, Texas*. Woods argued that the success of the LULAC organization in San Antonio and regionally was visible and apparent within the politics of the time. LULAC by the late 1940s, she said, "spread throughout the Southwest, until at present there are over 151 LULAC councils." The organization was "flourishing" in its activities, such as filing successful lawsuits against four California school districts in 1945 and against several Texas schools in 1948. Moreover, as a result of LULAC activities and the spread of its "new consciousness," as Pauline Kibbe called it, additional organizations arose in San Antonio and throughout the Southwest. Kibbe in her 1946 book on the Mexican Americans in Texas also praised the efforts of LULAC, stating that "during the seventeen years of its existence, LULAC has continued to gain strength and to contribute to the betterment of United States citizens of Mexican descent in the fields of education, citizenship, and civil rights." She acknowledged the spread of LULAC into every corner of the Mexican communities in Arizona, Colorado, New Mexico, California, and, of course, Texas.[27]

In 1947 the Pan American Progressive Association (PAPA), following LULAC's example, was formed in San Antonio to, wrote Woods, "relieve want and suffering among the inhabitants of Latin-American descent in the county of Bexar and elsewhere and to educate inhabitants in the rights and duties of American citizenship." This organization, according to Woods, was to be "directed by Americans of Mexican descent who are leaders in the fields of education, business, social work, and other types of professional work." Within five months of its inception, PAPA had over one thousand noncontributing members and fifty contributing members who pledged thirty-five thousand dollars. Throughout the Southwest it was apparent that the middle class continued to be on the rise politically, ideologically and organizationally during the 1940s.[28]

It should be noted that the term that Woods used was "Americans of Mexican descent"; this was indicative of continuing Americanization, but with the security of the Mexican identity and positive self-assertiveness that Galarza believed existed. PAPA, like the Coordinating Council for Latin American Youth, which was founded by Manuel Ruiz, Jr., in 1941 in Los Angeles, was integrating the Mexican community, together with LULAC and other organizations, into the mainstream. New organizations such as PAPA sought to continue and expand the work of LULAC. These new organizations, which were part of the massive Mexican American movement of the 1940s and the 1950s, were also led by the middle class, wielding an assertive identity and a "radical" ideology of Mexican Americanism that sought to help all the Mexicans in the Southwest attain a better education, social equality, voting rights, a higher standard of living, economic security, as well as secure a functional identity of Americanism.

This middle-class movement in San Antonio and throughout the Southwest was ideologically pragmatic, Americanist in its patriotism, and acutely conscious of its civic obligations to all Mexican Americans regardless of class or status. The middle class specifically focused on developing a mass political power base to facilitate more educational, legal, and economic opportunities for Mexican American individuals and communities. The Pan American Progressive Association could have been speaking for most of the Mexican American middle class leadership of the 1940s through the 1980s when it stated that, "like many other 'new' Americans, Mexican-American people have been undergoing a turbulent process of acculturation to the American social system. Our people are faced with the 'acid test' of social adjustment and they are therefore in great need of the assistance that can be furnished by experienced leadership. Their abilities and potentialities are great — they must be [however] guided and trained."[29] This statement was indicative of the renewal of the pledge taken in 1929 by the LULAC leaders at their constitutional convention at Harlingen, Texas, except that in 1947, as PAPA emphasized, the movement now had "experienced leadership" and, by implication, it had a coherent Mexican American world view and an understanding of U.S. society and politics.

This was LULAC's legacy, because in the period between 1929 and 1941 it had changed the "homeless mind" of the immigrant generation into a "Mexican American mind" and began to instill the security of a positive self-image, regardless of which side of the equation the individual stressed, or whether he or she chose to be "liberal" or "conservative." LULAC had also established the cultural guidelines for maintaining the historical memory of Mexicanness, the psychological guidelines for making the transition from Mexicans to Mexican Americans to Americans of Mexican descent, the ideological guidelines for integrating the *ricos'* Scholastic-Comtian perspective into the American liberal-conservative (Jeffersonian-Hamiltonian-Madisonian)

It must be remembered that the Mexican American middle class, its numerous organizations (although sharing general experiences and a sense of mission, as M. C. González had stated in the early 1940s), was segmented and fractured by regional, generational, communal, ideological, and individual differences, as well as by levels of acculturation. It was not a unified or monolithic movement; there existed diversity within the unity. However, these middle-class Mexican American reformers, like the rest of the American middle class, shared commonalities. They all feared any political radicalization from labor or the Communist party, and, like other Americans of the 1950s, Mexican Americans accepted the liberal consensus with its fear of communism and its adherence to MaCarthyism. To the Mexican American generation, as it had been for the *ricos* of the 1930s, communism personified the anti-Christ, and regardless of regional, local, organizational, or individual differences, this generation had taken an oath to be "loyal and progressive citizens of the United States of America; to uphold and defend . . . [the] American form of government and . . . [its] institutions; to take an active interest in the civic, social, and moral welfare of the community, [and] to unite the members in the bonds of friendship."[31] This was a basic theme of the LULAC Mexican Americanist philosophy, and it was a hegemonic ideological and psychological bond: the acceptance of Americanism, liberalism, and patriotism.

In spite of this acceptance and the emphasis on Americanism by all the organizations and leaders in the 1940s and 1950s, Mexican Americans continued to emphasize the consciousness of collectivity in organizing as ethnic Americans. This method of organizing was originally proposed by M. C. González in the 1930s as well as by the exiled *ricos* in *La Prensa*. They used the concept of "la Raza" as a rallying cry to obtain a "unity within the diversity." Woods also noted that the Mexican leadership in San Antonio during the 1940s always "recall[ed] the glory of the past in order to awaken race pride and encourage race loyalty." This practice continued during the ensuing decades. Mexican American leaders always operated during these decades with the conservative "soul and heart" of the *ricos*. In a twist of historical irony, although the Mexicans in the United States had become Americans, they still retained a strong affinity with the soul of Mexico, as the *ricos* had wanted; in their hearts and minds the Mexican American generation retained a sensibility to the *mexicano de afuera*.

It is this collective memory that continues to distinguish Mexican Americans from Anglos in their political perceptions and organizing. As Virginia Woolf said, "if life has a base it is a memory." For the Mexican Americans of the 1940s or the 1950s, the memory that provided a base for their lives, regardless of differences, was the communal, traditional, and historical memory and change within this continuity. The *ricos'* ideas and philosophy had remained the gate-keepers of the Mexican Americans' consciousness of collectivity via the memory of the Mexican revolution (the Mexican holocaust), immigrant experience (which continues), the Scholastic and Spanish tradition, and the mestizo heritage (although it became diluted with the intermarriages beginning in the 1950s). These factors constituted, as Octavio Romano argued in the late 1960s, the true essence of the "consciousness of collectivity." These past experiences and realities formed the "cultural core of historical folkways," the basic memories of the Mexican American identity, especially in San Antonio.[32]

San Antonio, according to Rodolfo Acuña, "in 1960 was unquestionably the most important [ideological, cultural, and political] Texas city for Mexican-Americans because by 1960 there were 217,688 Mexican-Americans in the city that were second and third generation, and only 30,299 that were first generation. In fact, San Antonio with its West Side contained 17.2% of the 1,417,810 Mexican-Americans in the state of Texas." And while there still remained considerable economic and social inequities for the majority of the acculturating Mexican Americans, many felt middle class in aspiration, hopes, and feelings, although they might be classified formally simply as workers. The majority of West Side Mexican Americans from the 1950s through the 1980s exhibited a Mexican American identity, functioned with a consciousness of liberalism that had conservative underpinnings, acted as individuals with a sense of hope and possibility, and had a proclivity for pluralistic everyday realities. From the 1950s through the 1970s they also exhibited a desire for political activity, which resulted in their having constant direct representation in city government from 1951 through 1971. LULAC and the G.I. Forum remained the basic political and educational organizations throughout these years, although the Mexican American generation was also active in the Spanish-Speaking Congress, the Unity Leagues, the Community Service Organization (CSO), La Asociación Nacional Mexico-

than John Locke's individualistic one. Above all, the Chicano youth accepted the idealistic mythology of the Aztecs, Villa, and Zapata, more than the realistic memory of Díaz, Huerta, and Madero, to shape their historical continuities. The Mexican American identity and mind, consequently, confronted the Chicano identity and mind between 1968 and 1978 in a struggle similar to that of the 1930s, except that the Chicano youth, ironically, also wanted the fruits of American liberalism (education, opportunity, and success) but not the nominalization of Americanism. The Chicano youth, in a state of intellectual myopia, yearned for equality, not freedom. The Mexican American generation had always wanted freedom, but with equality. Overall, however, what the Chicano youth wanted was not completely clear within the perspective of the New Left, the "counterculture," and the Third World. But with time it became evident that they wanted a balance between Mexican and American once again, Mexican Americanism, but with more freedom of self. In essence, they wanted *lo mexicano*, which the Mexican American generation had begun to shed in 1951.[34]

For example, José Angel Gutiérrez, one of the major Chicano youth leaders in the Southwest, was from South Texas and educated in San Antonio. Gutiérrez was a middle-class product of San Antonio and the South Texas Valley. He did his undergraduate and graduate work at St. Mary's University, which has been the center for the liberal-conservative, humanistic, and Catholic education of aspiring middle-class Mexican youth since the 1930s. He wrote an MA thesis on the possibility of revolution in South Texas, but, in retrospect, it was more an analysis of a condition for a revolution of opportunity (led by César Chávez) that the *mexicano* population wanted in the rural areas and a revolution for goods and services that the Mexican Americans wanted in the urban areas. It was apparent that neither the urban nor the rural workers in Texas or elsewhere wanted a revolution as envisioned by the radical Chicano theorists of colonialism or socialism. Gutiérrez, even though his radicalism was well known, never moved beyond the boundaries of left-wing liberalism. What was ultimately radical about him was his charisma and his uncanny ability to personify the Chicano need to redeem *lo mexicano* and the desire for political power via a Raza Unida movement in order to intimidate the Texas elite. His populist *mexicano* rhetoric also served to activate the consciousness of the "forgotten Americans," as Julián Samora called the Mexican American population in 1963. Gutiérrez, in the long run, simply redeemed the *ricos*' philosophy from the 1930s and cemented it to the power politics of the Mexican American generation to attack the barriers in Texas: institutional racism and personal discrimination.

After the passions of the sixties subsided, Gutiérrez settled in Crystal City in South Texas with his newly earned PhD, a judgeship, and a predilection toward establishing exchange programs with Mexican universities to allow students to regain the psychological and intellectual balance of *lo americano* and *lo mexicano*. For Gutiérrez, as for many of the middle-class Chicano youth, the discontinuity of the radical ideology and militant identity of the 1960s was over. The historical continuity of the Mexican American ideology and identity in the United States picked up again by the late 1970s, but qualitatively better; there was more political understanding and self-understanding.[35]

By 1978 LULAC had recaptured the ideological and organizational leadership of the Mexican American communities that had always been disturbed by the Chicano movement's political radicalism, although they respected the ethnic commitment and spirit of their sons and daughters. By 1980 the organizational and political efforts of the San Antonio Mexican American generation, especially through LULAC, had borne fruit: the middle class, by means of different coalitions such as the Coalition of Mexican-American Communities (COPS), and with the blessing of the city's elite and armed with the renewed vigor of the Chicano movement, elected Henry Cisneros as the first Hispanic mayor of San Antonio since the election of Juan Seguín in 1841.

Cisneros has roots sunk deep in the history of San Antonio's West Side. He is the son of Elvira Mungía, who was part of the exiled *politicos* of the city and who married a middle-class Mexican American. Moreover, Cisneros's maternal grandfather, Rómulo Mungía, was the printer-intellectual who took control of the Catholic workers' paper *La Voz* in the 1930s and pushed toward the left in support of the working-class Mexicans. Henry Cisneros in 1981 not only embodied the goals and dreams, historically and personally, of the exiled *ricos*, the Mexican American middle class, and the working class, but he personified the Horatio Alger story: he was middle class; he was an American of Mexican descent; he had an MBA from Harvard and

Cisneros could now answer the question asked by an early 1920s after returning from World War I: "What are we, Mexicans or Americans?" He could also answer Solís's frustrated observation that "to the average American, we are just Mexicans." Cisneros could now respond, "We are Americans, but distinct individuals as well who can choose to maintain a memory of Mexican collectivity, or simply, as in San Antonio, to exist in the reality of *lo mexicano*." Cisneros's education, his economic and political success, and his Americanization represented the climax to the struggle to accept not only Emerson's "Party of Hope," but also the philosophy of conservative-liberalism represented by Emerson's "Party of the Future." Cisneros, above all, exemplified the rise of the Mexican American generation and its search for the ultimate discovery of its identity. With Cisneros's election, forty years after the successful rise of the Mexican American middle class and the choice of Emerson's Parties of Hope and of the Future, the historical pendulum has swung back and now Mexican Americans are once again, to one degree or another, using Emerson's "Party of the Past" and "Party of Memory" to fashion a synthesis of *lo mexicano* and *lo americano*. In many ways, this is what the United States' Anglo population has been doing as it seeks to reconcile Rooseveltian liberalism with Jeffersonianism.

The rise of the discourse of the League of United Latin American Citizens and the Mexican American generation that occurred in Harlingen, Texas, in 1929, is still heard today. In fact, in 1988 I still heard, as I watched Henry Cisneros as mayor, and being mentioned as a possible presidential candidate, the words of Alonzo S. Perales: "The day the Mexican betters his own conditions and finds himself in the position to make full use of his rights of citizenship, that day he will be able to aid . . . [all] Mexican citizen[s] in securing what is due . . . [to them] and help . . . [them] assure . . . [their] own welfare and happiness." I can also hear Manuel C. González's lyrics: "We are builders of a better race, tho' brief our time and span, there shall be more of happiness than when our age began and tho' we cannot see it now, when all is understood. We shall leave less of wrong behind and more of what is good."[37]

Although Cisneros has had problems stemming from his private life which may cost him his political future, he remains to many Mexican Americans the fulfillment of the American promise: "making it," while still retaining a sense of community, a sense of ethnic roots, and a vision of Americanism that contains ethnicity. In many ways Cisneros personifies the Mexican American generation that from 1929 through the 1980s forged a new identity and ideology that are still visible today.

As a consequence of my study, I now have, in Lewis Simpson's words, a better sense that my own essential nature lies in the "possession of the moral community of memory and history." If the Anglo woman were to question me again about my identity, I would now say "American," but with a stronger sensitivity and understanding of *lo mexicano* — the consciousness of collectivity. There would still be a space between the memory of *lo mexicano* and the reality of *lo americano*, but this time it would be by choice and understanding, because that ontological "space" would be me, *Richard*, enriched by both the American and the Mexican historical, intellectual, and cultural traditions that explained my friends and family. As for the break in continuity introduced by the Chicano Renaissance, that remains for another book to explore.

3. Alberto Camarillo, *Chicanos in a Changing Society: From Mexican Pueblos to American Barrios in Santa Barbara and Southern California, 1848–1930;* Mario Barrera, *Race and Class in the Southwest: A Theory of Racial Inequality;* Mario T. Garcia, *Desert Immigrants: The Mexicans of El Paso, 1880–1920;* Richard Griswold del Castillo, *La Familia: Chicano Families in the Urban Southwest, 1848 to the Present;* Guadalupe San Miguel, Jr. *"Let All of Them Take Heed": Mexican Americans and the Campaign for Educational Equality in Texas, 1910–1981;* Arnoldo de León, *The Tejano Community, 1836–1900.*

4. See Oscar Handlin, *The Uprooted;* Humbert S. Nelli, *The Italians in Chicago, 1880–1930;* Herbert G. Gutman, *Work, Culture, and Society in Industrializing America;* Kenneth L. Kusmer, *A Ghetto Takes Shape: Black Cleveland, 1870–1930;* Lawrence Levine, *Black Culture and Black Consciousness: Afro-American Folk Thought from Slavery to Freedom;* Thomas Kessner, *The Golden Door: Italian and Jewish Immigrant Mobility in New York City, 1880–1915;* Irving Howe, *World of Our Fathers: The Journey of the East European Jews;* Eugene Genovese, *Roll Jordan Roll: The World the Slaves Made.* Herbert Gutman in addressing the different ethnic histories says that "the articularities are different; the tensions different. Ethnic experience may be similar in kind, but different in degree." He also quotes E. P. Thompson (*The Making of the English Working Class*) as saying, "There has never been any single type of transition" (*Work, Culture, and Society,* p. 74).

5. Henry C. Schmidt, *The Roots of Lo Mexicano: Self and Society in Mexican Thought, 1900–1934,* p. 18; Warren L. Susman, *Culture as History: The Transformation of American Society in the Twentieth Century,* pp. xix–xxx.

6. Carey McWilliams, *North from Mexico: The Spanish-Speaking People of the United States,* p. 13.

7. Manuel Gamio, *Mexican Immigration to the United States: A Study of Human Migration and Adaptation.*

8. For the "turning point" concept, see Jack J. Roth, ed., *World War I: A Turning Point in Modern History.*

9. As quoted in Robert Wuthnow et al., *Cultural Analysis: The Work of Peter L. Berger, Mary Douglas, Michel Foucault, and Jürgen Habermas,* pp. 58–59.

1. A TOWN WITHIN A CITY

1. William T. Chambers, "San Antonio, Texas," *Economic Geography* 16, no. 3 (1940): 293; Edwin Larry Dickens, "The Political Role of the Mexican-Americans in San Antonio, Texas," diss., Texas Technological College, 1969, p. 92.

2. Chambers, "San Antonio," p. 294.

3. Robert Garland Landolt, "The Mexican-American Workers of San Antonio, Texas," diss., University of Texas, Austin, 1965, pp. 44–45; Chambers, "San Antonio," pp. 294–96.

4. Edward W. Heusinger, *San Antonio: A Chronology of Events,* pp. 1–12; Donald E. Everett, *San Antonio: The Flavor of Its Past, 1845–1898,* pp. 5–10; Harvey D. Smith, *The Charm of Old San Antonio: A Spanish Settlement of the Southwest,* pp. 20–30; Frederick Charles Chabot, *San Antonio and Its Beginnings,* pp. 20–25.

5. Meinig, *Imperial Texas,* pp. 64–65.

6. Marjorie Paulus, "Fifteen Years in Old San Antonio, 1850–1865," Master's thesis, St. Mary's University, 1939, p. 9.

7. Sam Woolford, *San Antonio: A History of Tomorrow,* p. 9; San Antonio Public Service Company, *Economic and Industrial Survey,* 1942, p. 167.

8. Paulus, "Fifteen Years in Old San Antonio," p. 23; Frederick Charles Chabot, *Genealogies of the Early Latin, Anglo-American, and German Families,* p. 15.

9. Chabot, *Genealogies,* p. 104.

10. Federal Writers Project, *San Antonio,* p. 4; Peyton Green, *San Antonio: City in the Sun,* pp. 10–30; interview with Rubén Mungía, June 8, 1978.

11. Federal Writers Project, *San Antonio,* p. 4; Green, *San Antonio,* pp. 10–30; interview with Rubén Mungía, June 8, 1978; Paulus, "Fifteen Years in Old San Antonio," pp. 23–25.

12. Ibid., pp. 15, 239; S. J. Wright, *San Antonio de Bexar: Historical, Traditional, Legendary,* p. 37; Paulus, "Fifteen Years in Old San Antonio," p. 82.

13. Quoted in Paulus, "Fifteen Years in Old San Antonio," pp. 22–23.

14. Wright, *San Antonio,* pp. 98, 100, 139.

15. Ibid., pp. 107–108, 113–14.

16. Ibid., pp. 113–35; Paulus, "Fifteen Years in Old San Antonio," p. 37. See Octavio Paz, *The Labyrinth of Solitude,* for a discussion of the death ritual in Mexican life.

17. Frances Jerome Woods, *Mexican Ethnic Leadership in San Antonio, Texas,* p. 18.

18. Woods, *Mexican Ethnic Leadership,* p. 17; William J. Knox, *The Economic Status of the Mexican Immigrant in San Antonio, Texas,* pp. 7–8; San Antonio Public Service Company, *Economic and Industrial Survey,* 1942, pp. 17–18.

19. See Barrera, *Race and Class;* Mario T. Garcia, *Desert Immigrants;* David Montejano, *Anglos and Mexicans in the Making of Texas, 1836–1986;* Richard B. Henderson, *Maury Maverick: A Political Biography.*

20. Woods, *Mexican Ethnic Leadership,* p. 17

21. Meinig, *Imperial Texas,* pp. 55–57; Landolt, "The Mexican-American Workers," p. 14.

22. Wright, *San Antonio,* pp. 87–89; Claude B. Aniol, *San Antonio: City of Missions,* p. 5; San Antonio Express, *San Antonio Express: 100 Years of Progress*

25. Carmelo Tranchese, "Los Pastores, T.S.," in Tranchese Papers, Special Collections, St. Mary's University, San Antonio; Samuel H. Lowrie, *Cultural Conflict in Texas, 1821–1835,* p. 52.

26. Woods, *Mexican Ethnic Leadership,* p. 17.

27. San Antonio Express, *San Antonio Express,* pp. 8, 9; Frederick Lewis Allen, *The Big Change: America Transforms Itself, 1900–1950.*

28. *San Antonio City Directory,* 1911, pp. 1–2; 1921–22, pp. 1–4.

29. San Antonio Municipal Government, *San Antonio: Where Life Is Different,* p. 10; San Antonio Express, *San Antonio Express,* pp. 8–9. For a discussion of the 1930s as a period of transition from Victorian America to a modern America and a period in which the country "searched for community," see Warren Susman, ed., *Culture and Commitment: 1929–1945;* idem, *Culture as History;* and Richard H. Pells, *Radical Visions and American Dreams.* San Antonio was especially attractive to citizens of Monterrey, Mexico: Manuel Peña, *The Texas-Mexican Conjunto: History of a Working-Class Music,* pp. 19, 24, 25, 26, 42–43; Alex M. Saragoza, "The Formation of a Mexican Elite: The Industrialization of Monterrey, Nuevo León, 1880–1920."

30. The phenomenon of seeing ourselves in light of how others see us is a Hegelian concept discussed in relationship to minorities, specifically Jews. See Jean Paul Sartre, *Anti-Semite and Jew.* For a discussion of the development of these cities' barrios, see Ricardo Romo, "The Urbanization of Southwestern Chicanos in the Early 20th Century," in *New Directions in Chicano Scholarship,* ed. Ricardo Romo and Raymund Paredes; idem, *East Los Angeles: History of a Barrio;* Mario T. Garcia, *Desert Immigrants.*

31. Texas State Employment Service Division, *Origins and Problems of Texas Migratory Farm Labor,* pp. 8–9; San Antonio Public Service Company, *Economic and Industrial Survey,* 1942, p. 167.

32. San Antonio Public Service Company, *Economic and Industrial Survey,* 1942, pp. 169–70.

33. Ibid., pp. 6, 31, 32; *San Antonio Light*, January 4, 1931, p. 1; San Antonio Chamber of Commerce, *Manufacturing for Less in San Antonio*, p. 11; Landolt, "The Mexican-American Workers," pp. 153–215.

34. Harry Hansen, ed., *Texas: A Guide to the Lone Star State*, pp. 318–19; San Antonio Municipal Government, *San Antonio, Texas, through a Cameraman's Club*, pp. 2, 4; *San Antonio Express*, January 7, 1930, p. 1, January 8, 1930, p. 12; San Antonio Public Service Company, *Economic and Industrial Survey*, 1942, pp. 34, 41, 66, 314; *San Antonio Chamber of Commerce, Chamber of Commerce Report*; idem, *You Can Manufacture for Less*, pp. 3–5; Federal Writers Project, *San Antonio*, p. 43.

35. San Antonio Chamber of Commerce, *You Can Manufacture for Less*, p. 3.

36. Knox, *Economic Status of the Mexican*, p. 12.

37. For a comparative view, see Handlin, *The Uprooted*, and Gutman, *Work, Culture and Society*.

38. American Corporation, "Our Minority Groups: Two Spanish-speaking People," *Building America Bulletin* 8 (1943): 146; Landolt, "The Mexican-American Workers," pp. 337–38; Audrey Granneberg, "Maury Maverick's San Antonio," *Survey Graphic* 1, no. 28 (1939): 423.

39. Howe, *World of Our Fathers*, p. 117; Lawrence W. Levine, "Progress and Nostalgia: The Self-Image of the 1920's," in *The American Novel and the 1920's*, ed. Malcolm Bradbury; Geoffrey Perrett, *America in the Twenties: A History*.

40. But see Mario T. Garcia, *Desert Immigrants*, for development of the modernization interpretation; McWilliams, *North from Mexico*, for the basic arguments in the development of the Southwest's Mexican culture and economic imprint. Also see D. W. Meinig, *Southwest: Three Peoples in Geographical Change, 1600–1970*, for a key geographical and demographic interpretation.

41. *United States Presidential Report of the Commission on Migratory Labor: Migratory Labor in American Agriculture*, p. 37; Lamar B. Jones, *Mexican-American Labor Problems in Texas*, p. 3; Gilbert Cardenas, "United States Immigration Policy toward Mexico: An Historical Perspective," *Chicano Law Review* 2 (1975): 66–80; Abraham Hoffman, *Unwanted Mexican-Americans in the Great Depression: Repatriation Pressures, 1929–1939*, pp. 24–116.

42. San Antonio Express, *San Antonio Express*, pp. 8–9; Woods, *Mexican Ethnic Leadership*, pp. 18–20. Ignacio E. Lozano started *La Prensa* in 1914 and *La Opinión* in 1926. For a discussion of Mexican labor strikes in the 1920s and 1930s, see *Aztlán* 6, no. 2 (Summer, 1975). This issue is devoted to Mexican labor in the United States. Also see Judith F. Laird, "Argentine, Kansas: The Evolution of a Mexican-American Community: 1905–1940," diss., University of Texas at Austin, 1983; American Corporation, "Our Minority Groups," p. 145; U.S. Bureau of the Census, *15th Census of the United States, 1930*, p. 20; W. Dirk Raat, "Ideas and Society in Don Porfirio's Mexico," *The Americas* 30, July, 1973, p. 32.

43. *San Antonio Express*, February 2, 1935, p. 11; Hoffman, *Unwanted Mexican-Americans*, pp. 24–116. Also see Galarza, *Barrio Boy*, for an understanding of one person's immigration to the United States and his life and development there.

44. Gamio, *Mexican Immigration*, pp. 13–51; Woods, *Mexican Leadership*, p. 21. For a good case study of the oppression in a Mexican community, see

Mario T. Garcia, "Racial Dualism in the El Paso Labor Market, 1880–1920," *Aztlán* 6 (Summer, 1975).

45. Woods, *Mexican Ethnic Leadership*, pp. 20–21.
46. San Antonio Express, *San Antonio Express*, pp. 8–9.
47. Woods, *Mexican Ethnic Leadership*, pp. 20–21.
48. American Corporation, "Our Minority Groups," p. 146.
49. Ibid., p. 146; Landolt, "The Mexican-American Workers," pp. 337–38; Granneberg, "Maury Maverick's San Antonio," p. 423; Castañeda quoted in Landolt, "The Mexican-American Workers," p. 61.

53. Landolt, "The Mexican-American Workers," pp. 44–45, 337–38; Granneberg, "Maury Maverick's San Antonio," p. 423; P. I. Nixon, *A Century of Medicine in San Antonio*, p. 308; H. T. Manuel, "The Mexican Population of Texas," p. 48; San Antonio Public Service Company, *Economic and Industrial Survey*, 1942, pp. 349–50.

54. San Antonio Public Service Company, *Economic and Industrial Survey*, 1942, pp. 301–306; Granneberg, "Maury Maverick's San Antonio," p. 423; Nixon, *A Century of Medicine*, p. 308; Manuel, "Mexican Population," p. 48; Green, *San Antonio*, pp. 5–53; American Public Welfare Association, *Public Welfare Survey of San Antonio, Texas: A Study of a Local Community, 1940*, p. 30; U.S. Public Health Service, *Public Health Survey of San Antonio*, pp. 50–51.

55. Nixon, *A Century of Medicine*, p. 308; Manuel, "Mexican Population," p. 48; Green, *San Antonio*, pp. 51–53; American Public Welfare Association, *Public Welfare Survey*, p. 30; U.S. Public Health Service, *Public Health Survey*, pp. 50–51.

56. Henderson, *Maury Maverick*, p. 178; Nixon, *A Century of Medicine*, p. 308; Manuel, "Mexican Population," p. 48; Green, *San Antonio*, pp. 51–53; American Public Welfare Association, *Public Welfare Survey*, p. 30; U.S. Public Health Service, *Public Health Survey*, pp. 50–51.

57. Henderson, *Maury Maverick*, p. 178.
58. Federal Security Agency, U.S. Public Health Service, "Public Health Reports" 9, no. 5 (1945): 1, quoted in Pauline R. Kibbe, *Latin Americans in Texas*, pp. 127–28.

59. Federal Writers Project, *San Antonio*, p. 62.
60. For the relationship between the conditions of poverty and the culture of poverty, see Oscar Lewis, "The Culture of Poverty," *Scientific American* 215, no. 4 (October, 1966); San Antonio Public Service Company, *Economic and Industrial Survey*, 1942, pp. 33, 122–24.

61. Wayne Moquin and Charles Van Doren, eds., *A Documentary History*

of the Mexican-Americans, p. 342. For an interesting discussion on ethnicity, see Robert Park (*Race and Culture*), Stephen Steinberg (*The Ethnic Myth: Race, Ethnicity, and Class in America*), Orlando Patterson (*Ethnic Chauvinism: The Reactionary Impulse*), and Thomas Sowell (*Ethnic America*).

62. Woods, *Mexican Ethnic Leadership*, p. 21.

63. Manuel Gamio, *The Life Story of the Mexican Immigrant*, p. 243.

64. San Antonio Chamber of Commerce, *You Can Manufacture for Less*, p. 3.

65. Interview with Rubén Mungía, June 8, 1978; interview with a real estate agent (who did not want his name disclosed), October 4, 1977.

66. Robert Redfield, "The Folk Society," *American Journal of Sociology* 52 (1940): 300–308; Ruth A. Allen, "Mexican Peon Women in Texas," *Texas Sociology and Social Research* 3 (1931): 131–42; Lyle Saunders, "The Spanish-speaking People of the Southwest," paper presented at 4th Annual Workshop in Cultural Relations, Denver, May 5, 1958, p. 7. For a discussion of the continuity and change issue in immigration, see Herbert G. Gutman, "Work, Culture, and Society in Industrializing America, 1815–1919," *American Historical Review* 3 (1973): 556; and Emilio Willems, "Peasantry and City: Cultural Persistence and Change in Historical Perspective," *American Anthropologist* 72 (1970): 542.

67. See Park, *Race and Culture*, p. 5; idem, "Racial Assimilation in Secondary Groups," *American Journal of Sociology* (1914): 607; and idem, "Human Migration and the Marginal Man," *American Journal of Sociology* 23 (1928): 890. In addition, see Milton Gordon, *Assimilation in American Life: The Role of Race, Religion, and National Origins;* John Higham, *Ethnic Leadership in America;* Allen, "Mexican Peon Women."

68. American G.I. Forum, *What Price Wetbacks?* p. 31. For further insight into this process of de facto segregation, see Mario T. Garcia, "Obreros: The Mexican Workers of El Paso 1890–1920," diss., University of California, San Diego, 1975; idem, *Desert Immigrants;* interview with the manager of Bell Furniture Store, June 4, 1978. For a discussion of the concept of consciousness of historical collectivity, see the work of Emile Durkheim, William Graham Sumner, and the cultural anthropological school of Franz Boas, Margaret Mead, and Ruth Benedict. For a specific use of this concept, see Richard A. Garcia, "Creating a Consciousness, Memories, and Expectations: The Burden of Octavio Romano," paper presented at National Association for Chicano Studies Meetings, Salt Lake City, Utah, 1987.

69. Federal Writers Project, *San Antonio*, p. 62.

70. Max S. Handman, "San Antonio: The Old Capital City of Mexican Life and Influence," *Survey Graphic* 66 (1931): 163.

71. Julia Kirk Blackwelder, *Women of the Depression: Caste and Culture in San Antonio, 1929–1939*, p. 4.

72. Handman, "San Antonio," p. 164.

73. Richard Vásquez, *Chicano*, p. 53.

74. Read F. Scott Fitzgerald's classic *The Great Gatsby* within a philosophical and historical context that emphasizes the American individualistic self merging with the materialism of the 1920s. Also look at it within the tension and loss of the nineteenth-century world of Ferdinand Tönnies' gemeinschaft (community) with the United States' twentieth-century developing gesellschaft (society).

It was within this context that Mexican immigrants arrived and were becoming part of U.S. life and culture.

75. Handman, "San Antonio," p. 165.

76. Gamio, *The Life Story*, p. 149.

77. William O. Altus, "The American Mexican: The Survival of a Culture," *Journal of Social Psychology* 29 (1949): 218. I have paraphrased E. P. Thompson, who is quoted in Gutman, "Work, Culture, and Society," p. 556: "We should not assume any automatic, or overdirect correspondence between the dynamic of eco-

Our Fathers.

80. Bogardus, "Attitudes and the Mexican Immigrant," pp. 310, 312. For the development of a theory from which to understand the changing consciousness of the family, see Mark S. Poster, *Critical Theory of the Family;* and Griswold del Castillo, *La Familia*, which incorporates Poster's theoretical concepts.

81. Gamio, *The Life Story*, p. 252.

82. Ibid., p. 151.

83. Peña, *The Texas-Mexican Conjunto;* p. 5. Peña's study of the interrelated dynamics of music, culture, society, and consciousness is excellent. For an excellent discussion of acculturation and assimilation, see Michael Parenti, "Ethnic Politics and Ethnic Identification," *American Political Science Review* 61 (1967): 718; Joan Moore, "Social Class Assimilation and Acculturation," in *Proceedings of the 1968 Annual Spring Meeting of the American Ethnological Society*, ed. June Helm; Erick Rosenthal, "Acculturation without Assimilation?" *American Journal of Sociology* 88 (1960): 275–88; and Gamio, *The Life Story*, p. 151.

84. Gamio, *The Life Story*, pp. 178–79.

85. For an interesting discussion of the question of marginality, see Park, "Human Migration," p. 893; the works of Frantz Fanon; Gamio, *The Life Story*, pp. 178–79; and Gutman, "Work, Culture, and Society," p. 565. There have been some mobility studies by Chicano scholars such as Romo, *East Los Angeles*. Romo's work has been highly influenced by Stephen Thernstrom's mobility studies. Also see Richard Griswold del Castillo, "Myth and Reality: Chicano Economic Mobility in Los Angeles, 1850–1880," *Aztlán* 6 (1975): 153–54, and idem, *The Los Angeles Barrio, 1850–1890: A Social History*.

86. Interview with Rubén Mungía, January 4, 1976. For a beginning discussion of the rising middle class, see Woods, *Mexican Ethnic Leadership;* Paul S. Taylor, *An American-Mexican Frontier: Nueces County, Texas;* O. Douglas Weeks, "The League of United Latin American Citizens: A Texas-Mexican Civic Organization," *South Western Political and Social Science Quarterly* 10 (1929): 257–

78; idem, "The Texas-Mexican and the Politics of South Texas," *American Political Science Review* 24 (1930): 606–27; Julie Leininger Pycior, "La Raza Organizes: Mexican-American Life in San Antonio, 1915–1930"; diss., University of Notre Dame, 1979; Richard A. Garcia, "Class, Consciousness, and Ideology: The Mexican Community of San Antonio, Texas, 1930–1945," *Aztlán* 9 (Fall, 1978): 23–69; and idem, "The Mexican-American Mind: A Product of the 1930s," in *History, Culture, and Society: Chicano Studies in the 1930s*, ed. Mario T. Garcia et al.

87. For labor activities in San Antonio, see Zamora, "Mexican Labor Activity"; Blackwelder, *Women of the Depression*; Harold A. Shapiro, "The Workers of San Antonio,Texas, 1900–1940," diss., University of Texas, Austin, 1952; Landolt, "The Mexican Workers of San Antonio, Texas." For information on the Mexican exiles, see Michael C. Meyer, *Huerta: A Political Portrait*; W. Dirk Raat, *Los Revoltosos: Mexico's Rebels in the United States, 1903–1923*.

2. Mexican Labor and the Depression

1. Gamio quoted in James H. Botten, "New Features of Mexican Immigration: The Case against Further Restrictive Legislation," *Pacific Affairs* 3 (October, 1930): 961. See also Landolt, "Mexican-American Workers," p. 266.

2. Gamio, *The Life Story*, pp. 69–79; Bogardus, "Attitudes and the Mexican Immigrant," p. 320; John Bodnar, "Symbols and Servants: Immigrant Americans and the Limits of Public History," *Journal of American History* 73 (June, 1986): 144.

3. Landolt, "Mexican-American Workers," p. 26; Harold A. Shapiro, "The Pecan Shellers of San Antonio, Texas," *Southwestern Social Science Quarterly* 32 (March, 1952): 230–33; Seldon Menefee and C. C. Cassmore, *The Pecan Shellers of San Antonio*, p. 23.

4. Shapiro, "Pecan Shellers" p. 233; Landolt, "Mexican-American Workers," p. 26; Menefee and Cassmore, *Pecan Shellers*, p. 23.

5. *San Antonio Express*, April 6, 1941, pp. 12c, 21c.

6. *The Weekly Dispatch*, January 15, 1937, p. 4.

7. *La Prensa*, March 3, 1930, p. 9; *La Prensa*, April 2, 1932, p. 6; Landolt, "Mexican-American Workers," pp. 153–215.

8. Landolt, "Mexican-American Workers," pp. 215, 61; Mario T. Garcia, "Racial Dualism, pp. 198–200.

9. Knox, *Economic Status of the Mexican*, pp. 1–12; Chambers, "San Antonio," p. 294.

10. San Antonio Public Service Company, *Economic and Industrial Survey*, pp. 6, 31, 32; *San Antonio Light* (January 4, 1931), p. 1; San Antonio Chamber of Commerce, *You Can Manufacture for Less*, 1942, p. 11.

11. San Antonio Public Service Company, *Economic and Industrial Survey*, 1942, p. 314; San Antonio Chamber of Commerce, *You Can Manufacture for Less*, p. 4; Federal Writers Project, *San Antonio*, p. 42.

12. Landolt, "Mexican-American Workers," pp. 170–74; McWilliams, *North from Mexico*, pp. 170–74.

13. *La Prensa*, December 3, 1934, pp. 1, 2.

14. *La Prensa*, December 3, 1934, pp. 1, 2; *Weekly Dispatch*, January 8, 1937, pp. 1, 2.

Notes to Pages 61–74

15. *La Prensa*, December 23, 1934, p. 1; Landolt, "Mexican-American Workers," p. 173.

16. *La Prensa*, April 7, 1937, p. 5.

17. *La Prensa*, April 7, 1937, p. 5; *La Prensa*, April 4, p. 5.

18. Landolt, "Mexican-American Workers," p. 176.

19. Green, *San Antonio*, pp. 168–77; interview with Rubén Mungía, January 4, 1976; Landolt, "Mexican-American Workers," pp. 231–32; Blackwelder, *Women of the Depression*, pp. 141–45, 147–49.

20. *San Antonio Express*, May 11, 1938, p. 1; *Weekly Dispatch*, May 4, 1938,

27. Harry L. Hopkins, *Federal Emergency Relief Administration: Unemployment Relief Census*, p. 104; American Public Welfare Association, *Public Welfare Survey*, p. 28; San Antonio Public Service Company, *Economic and Industrial Survey*, 1942, p. 131.

28. Hopkins, *Unemployment Relief Census*, p. 104; American Public Welfare Association, *Public Welfare Survey*, p. 28; San Antonio Public Service Company, *Economic and Industrial Survey*, 1942, pp. 171–77.

29. Bodnar, "Symbols and Servants," p. 144; *Weekly Dispatch* (May 4, 1938), p. 1.

3. Culture and Society

1. Archbishop Drossaert, letter to the American Board of Catholic Missions, (ABCM), in ABCM Report, 1936, Drossaert Papers.

2. Carmelo Tranchese, "Housing Problems in Relation to Labor," n.d., Tranchese Papers.

3. Ibid.; Nathan Straus, administrator, Department of Interior, United States Housing Authority, letter to Eleanor Roosevelt, April 11, 1939, Tranchese Papers; *San Antonio Express*, September 3, 1936, p. 1.

4. *San Antonio Express*, September 3, 1936, p. 1; interview with Oscar Elizondo, October 28, 1977; 1939 report cited in "Public Housing Day Comes to San Antonio," *America* 2 (August 31, 1940): 570; *San Antonio Express*, August 20, 1948, p. 26.

5. Frances Parkinson Keyes, letters to Eleanor Roosevelt, May 30, June 2, 1941, Tranchese Papers; *La Voz de la Parroquia* (April 9, 1939): 4.

6. Bernard A. Tonman, S.J., "He Made a Date with a Dream," *The Savior's Call: A Catholic Family Magazine* 24, no. 4 (1946), p. 101; Shapiro, "Pecan Shellers," p. 232.

7. American Public Welfare Association, *Public Welfare Survey*, pp. 449–

50; Granneberg, "Maury Maverick's San Antonio," p. 424; Fred R. Crawford, *The Forgotten Egg: An Exploration into Mental Health Problems among Mexican-American Families and Their Children*, pp. 3–4.

8. Tranchese quoted in Tonman, "He Made a Date with a Dream," p. 110.

9. *San Antonio Express*, September 3, 1936, p. 3; Tranchese letter to Senator David I. Walsh, February 16, 1935, Tranchese Papers; interviews with Dora Elizondo Guerra, October 27, 1977; Rubén Mungía, June 1–21, 1978. I approximated these figures on the basis of conversations with Mungía, census records, and figures from "N.C.C.C. Report at New Orleans," November 12, 1929, San Antonio Catholic Chancery Archives. We can estimate that the middle class was composed of four thousand to five thousand individuals. There were approximately five children in each family. Although the numerical estimates are approximate, the percentage within each class is roughly accurate.

10. Carmelo Tranchese, "Memorandum," n.d., Tranchese Papers. For a discussion of the relationship between poverty and culture, see Lewis, "The Culture of Poverty," pp. 19–25; Charles Valentine, *Culture and Poverty*; Nathan Glazer, "Slums and Ethnicity," in *Social Welfare and Urban Problems*, ed. Thomas D. Sherrard; Thomas Sowell, *Race and Economics*; Nathan Glazer and Daniel Patrick Moynihan, *Beyond the Melting Pot*; Eleanor Burke Leacock, *The Culture of Poverty: A Critique*; and Steinberg, *The Ethnic Myth*.

11. Pearl Wright, "Religious Fiestas in San Antonio," p. 11.

12. Ibid.

13. Archbishop Drossaert, "Memorandum: Our Negro and Indian Missions." pp. 111–24. January, 1934, Josephite Papers. While this report focused on the Indians and the blacks, the same approach and conclusions applied to the Mexicans.

14. Wright, "Religious Fiestas in San Antonio," pp. 12, 13; Rebecca N. Porter. "Three Days of Romance," *Survey* 3 (1931): 424. See Octavio Paz, *The Labyrinth of Solitude*, for an excellent insight into the relationship among society, history, psychology, and religion in the making of the Mexican mentality.

15. George Sessions Perry, "The González Family: How Our People Live." *Saturday Evening Post*, October 2, 1948, pp. 51–53, 56; *La Prensa*, January 20, 1930, p. 10; *La Voz*, April 9, 1939, p. 2; Julia Kirk Blackwelder, "Women in the Work Force: Atlanta, New Orleans, and San Antonio, 1930–1940," *Journal of Urban History* 4 (1978): 344–51; "N.C.C.C. Report at New Orleans," November 12, 1929.

16. Wright, "Religious Fiestas in San Antonio," p. 7.

17. This description of the plazas was drawn from the following material: Bushick, *Glamorous Days*, p. 953; Pearson Newcomb, *The Alamo City*; Handman, "San Antonio."

18. *La Prensa*, January 12, 1930, p. 3; *San Antonio Express*, December 16, 1934, p. 7, April 2, 1936, p. 3, May 9, 1937; interviews with Dora Elizondo Guerra, October 27, 1977; Oscar Elizondo, October 28, 1977; Rubén Mungía, June 12, 1978; manager, Bell Furniture Company, June 9, 1978.

19. Bodnar, "Symbols and Servants," p. 146. See also idem, *The Transplanted: A History of Immigrants in Urban America*. A "social" directory of the red light district was available beginning in the 1920s. It contained a listing of the differ-

ent houses and a rating of the prostitutes. Few of the rated prostitutes were Mexican (University of Texas at San Antonio, Special Collections Archives). I selected the names of the Mexicans and their occupations from the 1929–39 *San Antonio City Directory*, pp. 337, 338, 390, 406, 407, 452, 505, 638, 760, 870, 955, 970, 971, 1062, 1135.

20. "N.C.C.C. Report at New Orleans," November 12, 1929; Archbishop Drossaert, letter to ABCM, 1932, Drossaert Papers.

21. Archbishop Drossaert, letters to ABCM, 1931, 1933, Drossaert Papers.

22. Drossaert, letter to ABCM, 1933, Drossaert Papers.

26. Ibid. Ruben Mungia of San Antonio has a copy of a *corrido* dedicated to Magdaleno Rodríguez, which was written during the 1930s when Rodríguez was a leader of the pecan shellers' strike.

27. City directories for the 1930s; "N.C.C.C. Report at New Orleans," November 12, 1929.

28. The idea that a small group can extend its influence well beyond its numbers, politically, socially, and culturally is commonly accepted and used as an intellectual hypothesis by both Marxists and non-Marxists. See the work of C. Wright Mills, William Domhoff, Parrato, Gramsci, Lenin, or even V. O. Key and de Tocqueville. Above all, in relation to this study, see Robert Wiebe, *A Search for Order, 1877–1920*.

29. "N.C.C.C. Report at New Orleans," November 12, 1929.

30. Gamio, *The Life Story*, p. 232.

31. Arnold, "Folklore, Manners, and Customs," p. 19.

32. Ibid., p. 21.

33. Ibid., pp. 20–22.

34. Ibid., pp. 21–22; interview with Carmen Perry, November 3, 1977. For excellent discussions on the major themes influencing southwestern, U.S., and Mexican thought and culture, see Stanley Coben and Lormon Ratner, *The Development of an American Culture*; Henry Steele Commager, *The American Mind*; Louis Hartz, *The Liberal Tradition in America*; Patricia Nelson Limerick, *The Legacy of Conquest: The Unbroken Past of the American West*; Schmidt, *The Roots of Lo Mexicano*; Henry Nash Smith, *Virgin Land: The American West as Symbol and Myth*; and Barrera, *Race and Class*. Also see the excellent interpretive work by John P. Diggins, *The Lost Soul of American Politics: Virtue, Self-Interest, and the Foundations of Liberalism*.

35. Knox, *Economic Status of the Mexican*, pp. 10, 11.

36. Interviews with Dora Elizondo Guerra, October 27, 1977; manager of Bell Furniture Company, June 4, 1978.

37. Knox, *Economic Status of the Mexican*, pp. 11–12; Bodnar, "Symbols and Servants," p. 144.

38. Knox, *Economic Status of the Mexican*, pp. 16–19.

39. Interviews with Rubén Mungía, January 4, 1976, and June 9, 1978; Mario T. Garcia, "Obreros," chap. 5. For a view of a similar process in the black community, see Kusmer, *A Ghetto Takes Shape;* chap. 5. For a brief discussion of the theme of *gente decente* versus *gente corriente*, which emanated from European society and was taken up with variations in Mexico, see Colin M. Maclachlan and Jaime E. Rodríguez Q., *The Forging of the Cosmic Race: A Reinterpretation of Colonial Mexico*, chap. 7; and for a general cultural understanding of why there could be such distinctions as elite and commoner/Indians see Mariano Picón-Salas, *A Cultural History of Spanish America: From Conquest to Independence*.

40. *San Antonio City Directory*, 1929–30, under "Mexican Business"; *La Prensa*, January 1, 1930, p. 1.

41. *La Prensa*, February 27, 1930, p. 8; Gamio, *The Life Story*, pp. 131–34.

42. *La Prensa*, January 31, 1930, p. 7, February 21, 1930, p. 6, June 29, 1930, p. 7, April 3, 1932, p. 7, December 3, 1934, p. 5.

43. *La Prensa*, February 2, 1930, pp. 7, 9, February 7, 1930, p. 7, February 9, 1930, p. 7, February 19, 1930, p. 7, June 19, 1930, p. 7.

44. *La Prensa*, February 7, 1930, p. 7.

45. Ibid.

46. *La Prensa*, February 1, 1930, pp. 7, 8, February 8, 1930, p. 7, February 16, 1930, p. 7, February 26, 1930, pp. 1, 7.

47. *La Prensa*, February 5, 1930, pp. 8, 10.

48. Ibid.

49. *La Prensa*, February 12, 1930, p. 7.

50. *La Prensa*, February 17, 1930, p. 7.

51. *La Prensa*, February 13, 1930, p. 10.

52. *La Prensa*, January 1, 1930, pp. 1, 7, February 13, 1930, p. 10; Woods, *Mexican Ethnic Leadership*, pp. 20–21; interview with Carmen Perry, November 3, 1977. I located the names and percentages of the *ricos* by meticulously combing the editorial and society pages of *La Prensa*, Woods, *Mexican Ethnic Leadership* (and a conversation with her), Taylor, *An American-Mexican Frontier*, having conversations with Carmen Perry, R. Mungía, D. Elizondo, and countless others, and then matching their information with works on Mexican exiles by Michael C. Meyer, William L. Sherman, W. Dirk Raat, and others.

53. For a discussion of the exiles, see W. Dirk Raat, "The Diplomacy of Suppression: Los Revoltosos, Mexico, and the United States, 1906–1911," *Hispanic American Historical Review* 56 (November, 1976): 529–50; Michael C. Meyer and William L. Sherman, *The Course of Mexican History*, chaps. 7, 8, and 9; and Meyer, *Huerta*. For a discussion of the ideology of the Porfiriato, see W. Dirk Raat, "Ideas and Society in Don Porfirio's Mexico," *The Americas* 30 (July, 1973): 32–53; idem, "Auguste Comte, Gabino Barreda, and Positivism in Mexico"; *Aztlán* 14 (1984): 235–51; Jacqueline Rice, "Beyond the Científicos: The Educational Background of the Porfirian Political Elite," *Aztlán* 14 (1984): 289–305; John Skirius, "Barreda, Vasconcelos, and the Mexican Educational Reforms," *Aztlán* 14 (1984): 307–41; David Maciel, "Nacionalismo cultural y política liberal en la

República restaurada, 1867–1876," *Aztlán* 14 (1984): 267–87; Anthony Byron, *The Politics of the Porfiriato* (Bloomington: Indiana University Press, 1973); Carlos B. Gil, ed., *The Age of Porfirio Díaz*; Schmidt, *The Root of Lo Mexicano.*

54. Meyer, *Huerta*, pp. 214, 215.

55. Ibid., pp. 197–98, 217–20.

56. Ibid., pp. 203, 214, 220–21, 226–27; Francine Medeiros, "*La Opinión*, a Mexican Exile Newspaper: A Content Analysis of Its First Years, 1926–1929." *Aztlán* 11 (Spring, 1980): 67–85.

57. Meyer. *Huerta*. pp. 176–77, 219–20, 231.

63. Ibid.

64. Ibid.

65. Interview with Manuel C. González, June 10, 1978; Alonzo S. Perales, *En defensa de mi raza*, p. 1.

66. *La Prensa*, February 23, 1930, p. 9.

67. *La Prensa*, February 18, 1930, p. 7.

68. Raymond Williams, *The Sociology of Culture*, p. 13.

69. *La Prensa*, February 23, 1930, p. 9.

70. *La Prensa*, February 4, 1930, p. 7.

71. *La Prensa*, January 5, 1930, p. 1; January 23, 1930, p. 7; October 2, 1931, p. 5.

72. *La Prensa*, January 21, 1930, pp. 1, 7, January 22, 1930, p. 10, March 2, 1930, p. 8.

73. *La Prensa*, January 22, 1930, p. 10, March 2, 1930, p. 8.

74. *La Prensa*, January 8, 1930, p. 7, February 5, 1930, p. 7, June 5, 1930, p. 7.

75. Quoted in Zamora, "Mexican Labor Activity," pp. 90, 91, 163–65.

76. *La Prensa*, January 29, 1930, p. 10, January 31, 1930, p. 7, February 23, 1930, p. 6, April 7, 1932, pp. 7, 9; *San Antonio Express*, July 4, 1936, p. 4; Meyer and Sherman, *The Course of Mexican History*, p. 588.

77. *La Prensa*, January 5, 1930, p. 10, January 27, 1930, p. 1, February 12, 1930, p. 7; interview with Rubén Mungía, January 4, 1976.

78. *La Prensa*, June 22, 1930, p. 5; *San Antonio Light* quoted in *La Prensa*, January 27, 1930, p. 1.

79. *La Prensa*, January 12, 1930, p. 7, January 26, 1930, pp. 3, 6, February 10, 1930, p. 3.

80. Interview with Oscar Elizondo, October 28, 1977; Landolt, "Mexican-American Workers," p. 173; Blackwelder, *Women of the Depression*, p. 148.

81. Sisters of Charity, "Santa Rosa Hospital Report," pp. 84, 164. See also Hopkins, *Federal Emergency Relief*, p. 104; *La Prensa*, February 16, 1930, p. 1.

82. *Revista* story reported in *La Prensa,* February 13, 1930, p. 10; *La Prensa,* June 20, 1930, p. 1.

83. *La Prensa,* January 31, 1930, p. 10.

84. *La Prensa,* January 27, 1930, p. 1.

85. *San Antonio Express,* April 1, 1935, p. 2.

86. *San Antonio Express,* January 7, 1931, p. 5.

87. *La Prensa,* June 9, 1930, p. 1.

88. *La Prensa,* February 13, 1930, p. 4.

89. *La Prensa,* June 30, 1930, pp. 1, 6.

90. *La Prensa,* January 26, 1930, p. 1, February 12, 1930, pp. 1, 5, February 21, 1930, pp. 1, 5, February 23, 1930, p. 1; interview with Rubén Mungía, January 4, 1976; Mario T. Garcia, "Obreros," pp. 212–60.

91. *La Prensa,* January 19, 1930, p. 7, February 12, 1930, p. 1, February 19, 1930, p. 7, June 1, 1930, p. 7, February 2, 1930, pp. 1, 7, February 2, 1932, pp. 1, 6.

92. *La Prensa,* February 23, 1930, p. 3.

93. *La Prensa,* February 29, 1930, p. 1.

94. Meyer and Sherman, *The Course of Mexican History,* p. 530. For a discussion of Gabino Barreda and positivism, see the fall, 1983, issue of *Aztlán* (vol. 14, no. 2), completely devoted to Barreda.

95. Perales, *En defensa de mi raza,* p. 1; Gonzales quoted in Dickens, "The Political Role," p. 136. For a discussion of John Dewey's life, ideas, and philosophy, see H. S. Thayer, "John Dewey, 1859–1952," in *American Philosophy,* ed. Marcus G. Singer. Dewey's view was that societies maintain themselves through education, and education permeates all of a person's feelings, habits, and actions. Consequently, the educational system is part of and integral to society and not an isolated insitution dispersing classical education (see Dewey, *Democracy and Education, Middle Works*). For an interesting discussion that is opposed to Dewey's theory, see Frank Lentricchia, *Criticism and Social Change.* Lentricchia discusses the role of intellectuals, their writing, social criticism, and place in education. On the whole, it is a critique of pragmatic education.

96. *La Prensa,* February 5, 1930, p. 7, February 19, 1930, p. 7, February 23, 1930, p. 9; *San Antonio Express,* October 13, 1939, p. 12; interview with Rubén Mungía, June 8, 1978.

97. *La Prensa,* January 23, 1930, p. 1, January 30, 1930, pp. 1, 6, June 8, 1930, p. 1. Also see Hoffman's *Unwanted Mexican-Americans,* and Francisco E. Balderama, *In Defense of La Raza: The Los Angeles Mexican Consulate and the Mexican Community, 1929–1936.* Also see the excellent discussion in McWilliams, *North from Mexico.* McWilliams's book contains most of the historical and political themes accepted by the majority of Chicano academics.

98. Meyer and Sherman, *The Course of Mexican History,* p. 628.

99. *La Prensa,* June 8, 1930, p. 1.

100. *La Prensa,* January 2, 1930, p. 3, January 10, 1930, p. 3, January 23, 1930, p. 1, January 30, 1930, pp. 1, 6, June 3, 1930, p. 5.

101. *La Prensa,* January 25, 1930, p. 1, February 3, 1930, pp. 1, 10, June 6, 1930, p. 5.

102. *La Prensa,* January 31, 1930, p. 10.

103. *La Prensa*, January 30, 1930, p. 10, January 31, 1930, p. 7.

104. *La Prensa*, January 30, 1930, p. 10. See Alexis de Tocqueville, *Democracy in America*, for the role of associations and pluralist theory. Also see Michel Foucault, *The Archaeology of Knowledge and the Discourse of Language;* idem, *Power/Knowledge: Selected Interviews and Other Writings.* Also see Mark S. Poster, *Foucault, Marxism, and History: Mode of Production versus Mode of Information.*

105. See the concept of hegemony in Carl Boggs, *Gramsci's Marxism*, pp. 36–55; and Antonio Gramsci, *The Modern Prince and Other Writings.*

110. *La Prensa*, June 1, 1930, p. 7.

4. The Family

1. Tamara K. Hareven, "The History of the Family as an Interdisciplinary Field," *Journal of Interdisciplinary History* 2 (1971): 55. Also see Poster, *Critical Theory of the Family.* This chapter draws its theoretical underpinnings from Mark Poster's work. Mark Poster was one of my teachers, and his book on the family as well as countless discussions on family theory, theory in general, and European intellectual thought have, I am sure, worked their way into my formulations. I have adapted many of his concepts without, however, following them exactly.

2. Emory Bogardus, "Current Problems of Mexican Immigrants," *Social Research* 25 (1940): 165–74; San Antonio Public Service Company, *Economic and Industrial Survey*, pp. 306–11; interview with Oscar Elizondo, October 28, 1977.

3. Landolt, "The Mexican-American Workers," p. 215; Blackwelder, "Women in the Work Force," pp. 336, 345–47, 351, 354. This is a cultural pattern brought from Mexico. It dictated that the wives do housework or work in cottage industries, although the children, female or male, were available for work outside the home. See Mario T. Garcia, "The Mexican Family, 1900–1930," in *Work, Family, Sex Roles and Language*, ed. Mario Barrera et al. (1980). This was also a pattern in Italian families; see Virginia Yans-McLaughlin, *Family and Community: Italian Immigrants in Buffalo, 1880–1930.*

4. Blackwelder, "Women in the Work Force," pp. 339, 344, 345, 355.

5. Ibid., pp. 337–51.

6. Knox, *Economic Status of the Mexican*, p. 22.

7. Ibid., pp. 13, 15–19, 22; Handman, "San Antonio," p. 165; Shapiro, "Pecan Shellers," p. 25; Menefee, *Pecan Shellers*, p. 5; Henderson, *Maury Maverick*, p. 146; Hopkins, *Federal Emergency Relief*, pp. 23, 79, 84.

8. Griswold del Castillo, *La Familia*, pp. 8–9. Griswold del Castillo's book is an excellent study that also draws from Poster's work and, in addition, from Barbara Laslett's work on the family. See Laslett's "Production, Reproduction, and Social Change: The Family in Historical Perspective," in *The State of Sociology: Problems and Prospects*, ed. James F. Short, Jr. (Beverly Hills: Sage Publications, 1981).

9. Handman, "San Antonio," p. 165; *San Antonio Express*, January 9, 1931, p. 1; *La Voz*, April 9, 1937, p. 2.

10. Griswold del Castillo, *La Familia*, p. 9; Laslett, "Production, Reproduction, and Social Change"; *La Prensa*, January 7, 1930, p. 7; *La Voz*, May 17, 1936, p. 5; Kathleen May González, *The Mexican Family in San Antonio, Texas*, pp. 20–21.

11. González, *The Mexican Family*, pp. 20–21.

12. Ibid.

13. Genevieve Smith, "The Mexican Element in Texas," *Banker's Monthly* 2 (1930): 118. This was a photocopy of the article found at the Daughters of the Texas Revolution Library at the Alamo, San Antonio; González, *The Mexican Family*, pp. 21–22.

14. *La Voz*, January 9, 1937, p. 2, April 29, 1939, p. 7.

15. Interview with manager of Bell Furniture Company, June 9, 1978. Poster in *Critical Theory of the Family* argues that the very size, arrangement, and location of the house are factors to consider in examining the change in people's consciousness.

16. Quoted in Mary John Murry, *A Socio-Cultural Study: 118 Mexican Families Living in a Low-Rent Public Housing Project in San Antonio*, p. 139; Frances Parkinson Keyes to Eleanor Roosevelt, May 30, 1941, Tranchese Papers.

17. Frances Parkinson Keyes to Eleanor Roosevelt, May 30, 1941, Tranchese Papers; Shapiro, "Pecan Shellers," pp. 230, 232, 233.

18. Frances Parkinson Keyes to Eleanor Roosevelt, May 30, 1941, Tranchese Papers; Shapiro, "Pecan Shellers," p. 231; pecan sheller's quote in Juan Gilberto Quezada, "Father Carmelo Antonio Tranchese S.J.: A Pioneer Social Worker in San Antonio, 1932–1953," Master's thesis, St. Mary's University, 1972, p. 55.

19. Menefee, *Pecan Shellers*, p. 37.

20. Ibid.; Archbishop Drossaert, American Board of Catholic Missions (ABCM) Report no. 1, 1933, Drossaert Papers. See the work of Robert Coles.

21. Thomas G. Rogers, "The Housing Situation of the Mexicans in San Antonio, Texas," Master's thesis, University of Texas, Austin, 1927, quoted in Henrietta A. Castillo, "Educational Handicaps of Latin American Children in the American Schools," Master's thesis, St. Mary's University, 1941, pp. 10, 67; *San Antonio Express*, September 3, 1936, p. 1.

22. Castillo, "Educational Handicaps," p. 67; Handman, "San Antonio," p. 165; *Weekly Dispatch*, March 5, 1937, p. 4; Max Handman, "Economic Reason for the Coming of the Mexican Immigrant," *American Journal of Sociology* 25 (January, 1930): 601–11.

23. Guadalupe Mission Parish Report, 1925, Our Lady of Guadalupe Papers, San Antonio Catholic Chancery Archives.

24. Carmen Carrillo-Barón, "Traditional Family Ideology in Relation to Lo-

cus and Control: A Comparison of Chicano and Anglo Women," Master's thesis, St. Mary's University, 1954, pp. 4, 5; interview with Oscar Elizondo, October 28, 1977; interview with Dora Elizondo Guerra, October 27, 1977; interview with Rubén Mungía, June 8, 1978.

25. Jet C. Winters, *A Report on the Health of Mexicans Living in Texas*, University of Texas Bulletin no. 3127, July 15, 1931, pp. 21, 31–35, 51, 52, 67, 68.

26. Ibid.

27. Ibid., pp. 21, 31–35, 51; Gamio, *Life of the Immigrants*, p. 231.

28. Winters, *Report on the Health of Mexicans*, pp. 51–52, 67–68.

33. Arnold, *Folklore, Manners, and Customs*, pp. 43–44. This acculturation process does not necessarily employ assimilation, which depends on full acceptance by the outside community. In San Antonio, this was almost impossible because of racial prejudice, de facto segregation, social discrimination, and poverty. For a discussion of acculturation with assimilation, see Rosenthal, "Acculturation without Assimilation?"; Park, "Racial Assimilation."

34. Arnold, *Folklore, Manners, and Customs*, pp. 6, 11.

35. González, *The Mexican Family*, p. 4.

36. Ibid., p. 5; interviews with Oscar Elizondo, October 28, 1977; Dora Elizondo Guerra, October 27, 1977.

37. González, *The Mexican Family*, p. 5; interviews with Oscar Elizondo, October 28, 1977; Dora Elizondo Guerra, October 27, 1977.

38. González, *The Mexican Family*, p. 12.

39. Interview with manager, Bell Furniture Company, June 4, 1978.

40. Interview with M. C. González, June 3, 1978; González, *The Mexican Family*, p. 13.

41. González, *The Mexican Family*, p. 12; Arnold, *Folklore, Manners, and Customs*, pp. 44.

42. Knox, *Economic Status of the Mexican*, p. 38; Arnold, *Folklore, Manners, and Customs*, pp. 11–13.

43. Interview with Dora Elizondo Guerra, October 27, 1977; Gamio, *Life of the Immigrants*, p. 226.

44. González, *The Mexican Family*, pp. 11–13.

45. Gamio, *Life of the Immigrants*, pp. 232–37.

46. Ibid.

47. Ibid., pp. 217–18.

48. Mario T. Garcia, "Americanization and the San Antonio Immigrant, 1880–1930," *Journal of Ethnic Studies* 6 (1975): 28.

49. González, *The Mexican Family*, p. 15.

50. Ibid., pp. 17-18.

51. Ibid., p. 18. For an interesting discussion of the attitudes of the family members see Bogardus, "Attitudes and the Mexican Immigrant," pp. 291-327. For a discussion of Mexican family patterns in the 1940s, see Robert C. Jones, "Ethnic Family Patterns: The Mexican Family in the United States," *American Journal of Sociology* 53 (1948): 450-53.

52. *La Voz*, May 3, 1936, p. 5.

53. Handman, "San Antonio," p. 164; Jones, "Ethnic Family Patterns," p. 451; Arnold, *Folklore, Manners, and Customs*, p. 5; González, *The Mexican Family*, p. 38.

54. González, *The Mexican Family*, pp. 38, 39.

55. Ibid., pp. 22, 32.

56. Ibid., pp. 22, 39; Arnold, *Folklore, Manners, and Customs*, p. 6.

57. *La Voz*, April 9, 1939, p. 2. For a discussion of the transference of family responsibilities to outside institutions throughout the United States, see Christopher Lasch, *Haven in a Heartless World: The Family Besieged*.

58. *La Prensa*, June 10, 1930, p. 10.

59. González, *The Mexican Family*, p. 34.

60. Tranchese, "Guadalupe Parish Report," ca. 1941, San Antonio Catholic Chancery Archives.

61. *La Prensa*, February 11, 1930, p. 10; González, *The Mexican Family*, p. 27.

62. Arnold, *Folklore, Manners, and Customs*, p. 36.

63. Interview with Rubén Mungía, June 12, 1978; *La Voz*, May 17, 1935, p. 5.

64. *La Prensa*, February 9, 1930, p. 7.

65. *La Prensa*, February 20, 1930, p. 7; *La Voz*, April 10, 1938, p. 3.

66. González, *The Mexican Family*, p. 40.

5. THE CATHOLIC CHURCH

1. Randall M. Miller and Thomas D. Marzik, eds., *Immigrants and Religion in Urban America*, pp. xiv-xv. This book contains a good discussion of the church's effect on different immigrant groups. In addition, there is an excellent discussion of the different groups' responses to religion and their use of religion in everyday life. The Mexicans in San Antonio, for the most part, responded in similar ways.

2. Ibid., pp. xiv-xv, xvi-xviii.

3. Archbishop Drossaert, "Speech at N.C.C.C. at New Orleans," November, 1929, Drossaert Papers.

4. Ibid. For a sketch of the growth of one parish in San Antonio, see José Antonio Navarro, "History of the School and the Church of Our Lady of Guadalupe"; Catholic Chancery Archives. Also see the Rev. Msgr. Alexander C. Wangler, ed., *Archdiocese of San Antonio, 1874-1974*.

5. *San Antonio Express*, January 13, 1935, p. 10; Murry, *A Socio-Cultural Study*, pp. 16-17; "Guadalupe Mission, Parish Report," ca. 1925, Drossaert Papers.

6. Archbishop Drossaert, *ABCM Report*, 1936, Drossaert Papers. There are constant references to Mexicans in church documents during the 1930s as "child-like, humble, and swarthy." The attitude and tone of the church toward the

working-class Mexican was always patronizing and racist. This tone was set by Archbishop Drossaert, who constantly referred to his Mexican parishioners in a loving but demeaning manner. See Albert Memmi, *The Colonizer and the Colonized*, for a discussion of this kind of attitude. It was not that Drossaert was consciously racist, but that the situation in San Antonio brought out this kind of attitude.

7. "Guadalupe Mission Parish Report," ca. 1925, Drossaert Papers.

8. Guadalupe Church, Archdiocese of San Antonio, Annual Report, 1933, 1937, San Antonio Catholic Chancery Archives

11. *La Prensa*, January 24, 1930, p. 1.

12. James Curtis Masdorff, "The Southern Messenger and the Mexican Church-State Controversy, 1917–1941," Master's thesis, St. Mary's University, 1968, pp. 141–44; *San Antonio Express*, November 13, 1934, p. 6; Drossaert, *ABCM Report*, 1930, Drossaert Papers; J. C. M. Gorde, S.J., vicar, general pastor, letter to Carmelo Tranchese, S.J., May 2, 1934, Jesuit Papers; Drossaert, *ABCM Report*, 1931, Drossaert Papers, p. 2; *La Voz*, February 27, 1938, p. 3. Drossaert as the archbishop set the ideological and philosophical tone for the diocese. Traditionally, the views of the archbishop within his archdiocese are unquestioned. He is in many respects the personification of his archdiocese and is viewed as the church in his locality. He sets church policy in his district and establishes the racial tone and the attitudinal approach toward the church's everyday responses in the community. However, at times this creates friction between the parish priests and the archbishop. In the 1940s, for example, there was a conflict between Archbishop Lucy and Father Luther over the approach to labor. In the 1930s the parish priests, without regard to the church's policy on communism, in the West Side were active in helping the striking workers. See the Lucy Papers for the Luther controversy and the Drossaert Papers for Drossaert's views on the conflict over *La Voz* and the parish priests. Also see the Drossaert and Lucy papers for the difference in the tone and the approach of the church during the "reigns" of these two archbishops.

13. Masdorff, "The Southern Messenger," pp. 141–44; *San Antonio Express*, November 13, 1934, p. 6; Archbishop Drossaert, ABCM Report, 1930, Drossaert Papers; L. C. M. Gorde, letter to Carmelo Tranchese S.J., May 2, 1934, Jesuit Papers; Drossaert, ABCM Report, Drossaert Papers; 1931, p. 2, *La Voz*, February 27, 1938, p. 3.

14. *San Antonio Express*, November 4, 1934, p. 12; Masdorff, "The Southern Messenger," p. 144.

15. Drossaert, Speech to NCCC, Drossaert Papers.

16. Guadalupe Mission, Parish Report, ca. 1925, Drossaert Papers; Drossaert, *ABCM Report*, 1933, Drossaert Papers.

17. Drossaert, ABCM Report, 1933, Drossaert Papers.

18. C. J. Massey, letter to J. Marshall Butz, July 12, 1951, cited in J. Marshall Butz, "A Brief History of the Church of Christ in San Antonio, Texas, 1876–1951," Master's thesis, St. Mary's University, 1951. Jacobo Rodríguez was a Protestant before he joined the Church of Christ: interview with Mrs. Jacobo Rodríguez, June 14, 1978.

19. *La Prensa*, January 21, 1930, p. 7, February 26, 1930, p. 7, June 1, 1930, p. 9; Drossaert, speech to NCCC, 1929, Drossaert Papers.

20. Drossaert, "Mission Work among the Negros and the Indians," January, 1924, pp. 14–40, Josephite Papers; idem, *ABCM Report*, 1932, Drossaert Papers; Guadalupe Mission, *Parish Report*, ca. 1925, pp. 4–5.

21. Guadalupe Mission, *Parish Report*, ca. 1925, pp. 4–5.

22. Carmelo Tranchese, "Guadalupe Parish, an Account for His Excellency Robert E. Lucy D.D., Archbishop of San Antonio, 1941," Our Lady of Guadalupe Papers.

23. American Public Welfare Association, *Public Welfare Survey*, p. 119; Angela María Chappelle, "Local Welfare of Religious Organizations in San Antonio, Texas," Master's thesis, St. Mary's University, 1939, pp. 116–31; George Sessions Perry, "Rumpled Angel of the Slums," *Saturday Evening Post*, August 21, 1948, p. 3; Maury Maverick, *A Maverick American*, p. 51; *San Antonio Express*, January 6, 1931, p. 8.

24. Tranchese, "Guadalupe Parish, an Account."

25. *Southern Messenger*, April 7, 1938, pp. 1, 5; *La Voz*, April 10, 1938, p. 1.

26. *Southern Messenger*, January 23, 1936, p. 1; *La Voz*, May 3, 1936, pp. 8–9, 10; San Fernando Cathedral Annual Reports: 1927, 1929, 1931, 1934, 1937, 1939, San Antonio Catholic Chancery Archives.

27. San Fernando Cathedral Annual Reports, 1927, 1929, 1931, 1934, 1937; San Fernando School Annual Report, 1939; *La Voz*, May 3, 1936, p. 10; Guadalupe Mission, Parish Report, ca. 1925; Navarro, "History of the School," p. 4.

28. *San Antonio Express*, January 10, 1931, p. 7; Perry, "Rumpled Angel," p. 47; *La Voz*, March 1, 1936, p. 6; *La Voz*, May 3, 1936, p. 6, May 17, 1936, p. 8.

29. *Southern Messenger*, July 8, 1937, p. 6; Quezada, "Father Carmelo Antonio Tranchese," p. 49; Shapiro, "Pecan Shellers," pp. 32–42.

30. Drossaert, draft of article to *Catholic Extension Magazine*, ca. 1936, p. 2, Drossaert Papers; *San Antonio Express*, January 25, 1931, p. 1a. For a discussion of liberation theology, see Phillip Berryman, *Liberation Theology: The Essential Facts about the Revolutionary Movement in Latin America and Beyond*.

31. *San Antonio Express*, January 25, 1931, p. 1a; *Southern Messenger*, November 28, 1929, p. 6; *La Voz*, November 10, 1946, p. 4.

32. For a discussion of the Americanization of the Catholic Church through the efforts of Francis Cardinal Spellman, see John Cooney, *The American Pope: The Life and Times of Francis Cardinal Spellman*. For a discussion of language, power, and ideology, see Poster, *Foucault*, pp. 129–31; and Foucault, *The Archaeology of Knowledge*, pp. 111–13. "Loci of power" is Poster's term (p. 131).

33. *Southern Messenger,* November 28, 1929, p. 6; *La Voz,* March 29, 1939, p. 9, November 10, 1946, p. 4. "Pioneer social worker" is used by Juan Quezada in "Father Carmelo Antonio Tranchese." Quezada's manuscript is more a description of Tranchese's parish work than an analysis of his social philosophy. Perry referred to Tranchese as a "rumpled angel" in "Rumpled Angel." Quotes are from transcript of Coca-Cola radio tribute to C. Tranchese, ca. 1946, Tranchese Papers; Tranchese, "The Housing Problem"; John MaCarmady, letter to Eleanor Roosevelt, October 6, 1941, Tranchese Papers; idem, memorandum to Nathan Strauss, September 26, 1941, Tranchese Papers.

pers; Minutes of Consultors' Meeting, November 11, 1931, San Antonio Catholic Chancery Archives (this document contains excerpts from letters regarding the transfer of the Guadalupe Church from the Claretians to the Jesuits in the early 1930s); Carmelo Tranchese, letter to Archbishop Drossaert, March 7, 1931, Jesuit Papers; interview with Father Barnabas Diekemper, O.S.M., archivist, San Antonio Catholic Chancery Archives, June 9, 1978.

37. Archbishop Drossaert, letter to Tranchese, March 9, 1940, Drossaert Papers; Minutes of Consultors' Meeting, November 11, 1931; interview with Father Barnabus, June 9, 1978.

38. Estella Brown et al., West End Baptist Church, letter to Carmelo Tranchese, March 9, 1940, Tranchese Papers; José Oliveras, president, Comité Latino Americano, American Red Cross chapter, letter to Carmelo Tranchese, April 29, 1944, Tranchese Papers.

39. Leo V. Murphy, S.J., letter to Rev. Carmelo Tranchese, S.J., September 30, 1954, Tranchese Papers.

40. Carmelo Tranchese, letter to A. J. Drossaert, May 31, 1935, Drossaert Papers.

41. *La Voz,* September 29, 1935, p. 1, February 16, 1936, p. 3, February 1, 1939, p. 1.

42. *La Voz,* September 29, 1935, pp. 1, 3.

43. *La Voz,* February 16, 1936, p. 4.

44. *La Voz,* March 1, 1936, p. 3, March 2, 1936, p. 8.

45. *La Voz,* April 26, 1936, p. 5, May 3, 1936, p. 5, May 17, 1936, p. 3.

46. *La Voz,* March 1, 1936, p. 1, October 11, 1937, pp. 1, 3, 4, April 2, 1938, p. 2.

47. *La Voz,* October 11, 1937, pp. 1, 2, 4, December 12, 1937, p. 4.

48. *La Voz,* October 11, 1937, pp. 1, 2, 4, December 12, 1937, p. 4.

49. *La Voz,* October 11, 1937, p. 3, December 26, 1937, p. 1.

50. *La Voz,* October 11, 1937, pp. 1, 3, December 26, 1937, p. 1.

51. Ibid.

52. *La Voz*, October 17, 1937, p. 1, January 31, 1938, p. 1, February 6, 1938, p. 2.

53. *La Voz*, February 6, 1938, p. 2, February 20, 1938, p. 2. See Joseph Wood Krutch, *The Modern Temper: A Study and a Confession*, for a critique of modernity that is still pertinent.

54. *La Voz*, March 6, 1938, p. 2, March 20, 1938, p. 2, April 3, 1938, p. 3, April 10, 1938, p. 1, May 1, 1938, p. 3, June 3, 1938, p. 1, January 8, 1939, p. 2, July 2, 1939, p. 2.

55. *La Voz*, March 6, 1938, p. 2, March 20, 1938, p. 2, April 3, 1938, p. 3, April 10, 1938, p. 1, May 1, 1938, p. 3, January 8, 1939, p. 2, July 2, 1939, p. 2.

56. Drossaert, "Our Negro and Indian Missions," pp. 11-24, Drossaert Papers; idem, *ABCM Report, 1929, 1930*, Drossaert Papers.

57. Drossaert, *ABCM Report, 1930*, Drossaert Papers. During the 1930s Drossaert did nothing to stop social segregation in the Catholic churches and schools or the social and racial prejudice of some of the parish priests. The racial discrimination in the Catholic Church of San Antonio was not ordered stopped until Archbishop Lucy ordered it in the 1950s. See *Alamo Messenger, Special Supplement*, May 6, 1966, p. 29.

6. EDUCATION

1. Gilbert González, "Crisis of Urbanization: Racism, Education, and the Mexican Community in Los Angeles, 1920-1930," p. 5. See also J. F. Bobbit, *The San Antonio Public School System: A Survey*, pp. 8, 9, 25, 191. The School Board saw the educational system as tied directly to the economic growth of the city. It was aware, reports indicated, that the Mexicans were an important part of the city's development. Therefore, it adopted Dewey's philosophy because it stressed the integration of all working people into the economy and society. Dewey's theories on education stressed the relationship between personal and industrial growth through the process of education. San Antonio was one of the first cities in the Southwest to understand the advantage of utilizing the Mexican population on a level higher than as unskilled labor or agricultural workers. Above all, the educational system wanted a return on its money: skilled workers for school board monies.

2. John Dewey, *Education Today*, p. 349, quoted in González, "Crisis of Urbanization," pp. 1, 5.

3. Bobbit, *San Antonio Public School System*, p. 16.

4. Ibid. In a vocational distribution survey of 1,000 men employed in San Antonio, 336 were in manufacturing and mechanical industries, 226 in trade, 129 in transportation, 120 in domestic and personal service, 69 in clinical occupations, 56 in professional service, 32 in agriculture and gardening, 28 in public service, and 4 in the extraction of minerals (ibid., p. 17). Because of this skewed labor market, the San Antonio School Board accepted the progressive philosophy of education. According to González, "Vocational courses were selected into the curriculum on the basis of the labor needs of business, industry, and the adapta-

bility of students for their occupations. This was also true in the city of San Antonio" ("Crisis of Urbanization," p. 14).

5. González, "Crisis of Urbanization," p. 14. For a discussion of Americanization, philosophy, and progressive education, see Clarence J. Karier, Paul C. Violas, and Joel Spring, *Roots of Crisis: American Education in the Twentieth Century*.

6. Bobbit, *San Antonio Public School System*, p. 26. Progressive educational philosophy had advantages and disadvantages for Mexicans. On the negative side, l...ti... w... t. b. a training for work, that is, vocationally oriented and seg-

also saw German as a living language, but according to the 1914 report, the German children of "the second and third generation . . . are more proficient in English . . . [than the Mexican children] and German is not needed as a commercial language" (Bobbit, *San Antonio Public School System*, p. 25).

8. Bobbit, *San Antonio Public School System*, pp. 159–62, 164–65, 191, 194–95.

9. Ibid., pp. 191, 192.

10. Kimball Young, "Immigrant Groups in California," quoted in González, "Crisis of Urbanization," pp. 9–10. For a discussion of these studies from the perception of the Chicano radicalism of the sixties, see the articles by Nick Vaca in the early 1970 issues of *El Grito* (University of California, Berkeley).

11. San Antonio Public Service Company, *Economic and Industrial Survey*, 1942, pp. 277–305; *San Antonio City Directory*, 1929–39, pp. 1591–97.

12. U.S. Bureau of the Census, "Financial Statistics for the City Government of San Antonio," pp. 1, 2; idem, *Financial Statistics of Cities, 1938*, p. 68; Castillo, "Educational Handicaps," p. 10.

13. Handman, "San Antonio," p. 164; Charles H. Hufford, *The Social and Economic Effects of the Mexican Migration into Texas*, p. 20; T. H. Shelby and J. O. Marberry, *A Study of the Building Needs of San Antonio Senior High Schools*, pp. 9–11.

14. Castillo, "Educational Handicaps," pp. 28–29.

15. San Antonio Municipal Commission, *1940 Social Welfare Report*, p. 91.

16. Hufford, *Social and Economic Effects*, p. 23; H. T. Manuel, "The Education of Mexican and Spanish-speaking Children in Texas," in *Education and the Mexican American*, ed. Carlos Cortez, p. 89; Franklin J. Keller, *The Double-Purpose High School: Closing the Gap between Vocational and Academic Preparation*, pp. 110–11.

17. Manuel, "Education of Mexican and Spanish-speaking Children," pp.

346   NOTES TO PAGES 182-192

72–78, 155, 139–44; George T. Sánchez, *Concerning Segregation of Spanish-speaking Children in Public Schools*, p. 40; Michel Foucault, *Language, Counter-Memory, Practice*.

18. Hufford, *Social and Economic Effects*, pp. 21–22.

19. Castillo, "Educational Handicaps," p. 28; R. de la Garza, "Our School Children," quoted in Guadalupe San Miguel, Jr., *"Let All of Them Take Heed": Mexican-Americans and the Campaign for Educational Equality in Texas, 1910–1981*, p. 76.

20. *San Antonio Express*, October 13, 1939, p. 12.

21. Ibid.

22. Hufford, "Social and Economic Effects," pp. 24–25; Manuel, "Education of Mexican and Spanish-speaking Children," p. 36; Castillo, "Educational Handicaps," p. 30.

23. Castillo, "Educational Handicaps," p. 54.

24. *San Antonio Express*, June 19, 1930, pp. 1a, 2a, May 26, 1935, p. 1a; Hufford, "Social and Economic Effects," p. 23.

25. U.S. Department of Commerce, Bureau of the Census, *Fifteenth Census of the United States, 1930, Population*, III, pt. 2, pp. 945–1009; Shapiro, "Pecan Shellers," p. 47.

26. Shapiro, "Pecan Shellers," pp. 47, 48.

27. Carleton Beals, "Mexican Intelligence," *Southwest Review* 11 (1931): 23–31; Manuel, "Education of Mexican and Spanish-speaking Children," p. 93.

28. Manuel, "Education of Mexican and Spanish-speaking Children," pp. 73, 154.

29. James K. Harris, "A Sociological Study of a Mexican School in San Antonio, Texas," quoted in Manuel, "Education of Mexican and Spanish-speaking Children," p. 17.

30. Castillo, "Educational Handicaps," pp. 32–33.

31. Handman, "San Antonio," p. 165.

32. Castillo, "Educational Handicaps," pp. 35, 88–90.

33. Thelma Fuller, "A Survey of Art Education," Master's thesis, St. Mary's University, 1939, p. 3.

34. Manuel, "Education of Mexican and Spanish-speaking Children," p. 117.

35. Knox quoted in Manuel, "Education of Mexican and Spanish-speaking Children," pp. 116–17.

36. Moquin and Van Doren, *Documentary History of the Mexican-Americans*, pp. 190–91.

37. Willie Leanzo Brown, "Knowledge of Social Standards among Mexican and Non-Mexican Children," Master's thesis, University of Texas, Austin, 1934, pp. 5, 6; Aurora M. González, "A Study of Intelligence of Mexican Children in Relation to Their Socio-Economic Status," Master's thesis, University of Texas, 1932, p. 5.

38. Katherine H. Mequire, *Educating the Mexican Child in the Elementary School*, pp. 36–41. Mequire was a teacher from San Antonio and used San Antonio as the basis of her study.

39. *La Prensa*, December 4, 1934, p. 4, December 23, 1934, p. 1.

40. Parr, *A Comparative Study*, pp. 2, 12, 13–15, 18.

41. Mequire, *Educating the Mexican Child*, p. 6; Parr, *A Comparative Study*, p. 46.

42. Mequire, *Educating the Mexican Child*, pp. 15, 58, 60.

43. Ibid., pp. 64, 65.

44. Manuel, "Education of Mexican and Spanish-speaking Children," p. 139; Mequire, *Educating the Mexican Child*, p. 13.

45. *San Antonio Express*, May 26, 1935, pp. 1a, 2a, May 16, 1937, p. 2a; *La Prensa*, February 11, 1930, p. 6.

46. *La Prensa*, January 22, 1930, p. 6, June 1, 1930, p. 9; *San Antonio Ex-*

52. *Josephite Report on Mission Work among the Negros and the Indians in San Antonio*, p. 4, Josephite Papers; *Southern Messenger*, September 18, 1930, p. 9. The church in San Antonio was following Pope Pius's new encyclical on Christian education. It stated that maintaining the education of the young was the first responsibility of the church. The second responsibility was the family, and finally the state. See *San Antonio Express*, January 12, 1930, p. 3; *Guadalupe Mission Report*, ca. 1925, Drossaert Papers; Drossaert, *ABCM Report*, 1930, 1936, Drossaert Papers.

53. *La Prensa*, June 1, 1930, p. 9.

54. Drossaert, speech at NCCC, 1929, Drossaert Papers; idem, draft of article for the *Catholic Church Extension Magazine*, Drossaert Papers; *La Voz*, February 3, 1946, pp. 2, 8.

55. *Alamo Messenger*, Special Supplement, May 6, 1966. The Catholic schools were finally integrated in 1954 by Bishop Lucy, who stated, "I have urged the clergy and the county, in reason and out of reason, to stop this sin of racial segregation and to treat all human beings as children of God. . . . Henceforth, no Catholic child may be refused admittance to any school maintained by the Archdiocese for reasons of color, race, or paricity."

56. *La Prensa*, June 8, 1930, p. 4; *La Voz*, April 5, 1936, p. 9; Castillo, "Educational Handicaps," p. 69; Perry, "Rumpled Angel," p. 47.

57. José Antonio Navarro, *History of the School*; *La Voz*, June 5, 1938, p. 5; interview with Dora Elizondo Guerra, October 27, 1978.

58. Guadalupe Church, *Annual Reports*, 1934–39, San Antonio Catholic Chancery Archives; Immaculate Heart of Mary, *Church Reports*, 1932, 1940, San Antonio Catholic Chancery Archives.

59. *La Prensa*, January 2, 1930, p. 5, January 3, 1930, p. 10.

60. Federal Writers Project, *San Antonio*, p. 24; *La Voz*, April 10, 1938, p. 4; Altus, "The American Mexican," p. 218.

61. *San Antonio Express*, October 1, 1939, p. 2a.

62. L. O. Moore, *Education in the Community: San Antonio Public Affairs Forum Report*, p. 41.

63. Kibbe, *Latin Americans in Texas*, p. 138a.

64. Ibid., pp. 85, 88; Manuel, "Education of Mexican and Spanish-speaking Children," p. 19; San Antonio Chamber of Commerce, *San Antonian* 14, no. 40 (October 11, 1946): 1. By 1946 there were 12,000 Mexican children in the Catholic schools, and 60,489 students all told in San Antonio, *San Antonio Express*, October 13, 1946, p. 1a; Castillo, "Educational Handicaps," p. 1a.

65. San Miguel, "*Let All of Them Take Heed*," p. 117.

66. Kibbe, *Latin Americans in Texas*, pp. 91, 102, 118, 234.

67. Ibid., pp. 91, 118.

68. San Antonio Municipal Commission, *1940 Social Welfare Report*, p. 96.

7. SAN ANTONIO POLITICS AND THE MEXICAN COMMUNITY

1. Menefee and Cassmore, *Pecan Shellers*, pp. 49–51.

2. Granneberg, "Maury Maverick's San Antonio," p. 423.

3. Quoted in Menefee and Cassmore, *Pecan Shellers*, p. 49.

4. Ibid., p. 51.

5. *San Antonio Express*, September 3, 1936, p. 1; Castillo, "Educational Handicaps," p. 127 (Castillo also refers to Tranchese's high estimate of Mexicans as U.S. citizens); Carmelo Tranchese, letter to Senator David I. Walsh, February 3, 1935, Tranchese Papers.

6. Green Peyton, *San Antonio: City in the Sun*, pp. 180–86; O. P. White, "Machine Mode," *Collier's*, September 18, 1937; Menefee and Cassmore, *Pecan Shellers*, p. 50; Granneberg, "Maury Maverick's San Antonio," p. 425; Henderson, *Maury Maverick*, pp. 176, 178, 184 (quote on political machine from p. 47); Arthur Simpson, *Southwest Texas Business and Professional Directory*, p. 94; interview with Rubén Mungía, June 8, 1978.

7. U.S. House of Representatives, *Immigration from Countries of the Western Hemisphere, Hearings before the Committee on Immigration and Naturalization*, p. 598, quoted in Menefee and Cassmore, *Pecan Shellers*, p. 50.

8. John Garrett, *The Citizens' Revolt*, pp. 10, 12.

9. *San Antonio Express*, July 8, 1938, p. 20.

10. *Weekly Dispatch*, April 30, 1937, p. 1.

11. Stuart Jamieson, *Labor Unionism in American Agriculture*, p. 279.

12. Ibid. See also *San Antonio Express*, January 22, 1931, p. 61, February 11, 1931, pp. 1, 5; *Weekly Dispatch*, July 2, 1937, p. 1.

13. Granneberg, "Maury Maverick's San Antonio," p. 426.

14. Archbishop Robert E. Lucy, D.D., letter to the Rev. Joseph A. Luther, July 24, 1946, Jesuit Papers.

15. *San Antonio Express*, January 11, 1930, p. 22, January 25, 1930, p. 3.

16. *La Prensa*, June 12, 1930, pp. 1, 2; *San Antonio Express*, January 11, 1930, p. 22.

17. *La Prensa*, June 12, 1930, pp. 1, 2; *San Antonio Express*, January 11, 1930, p. 22.

18. *San Antonio Express*, February 6, 1931, p. 22, May 22, 1935, p. 16, April 21, 1936, p. 16, July 20, 1936, p. 10a; San Antonio Chamber of Commerce, *San Antonian*, 3, no. 7 (June, 1935), p. 7; *La Prensa*, June 11, 1930, p. 1.

19. Granneberg, "Maury Maverick's San Antonio," p. 425; Peyton, *San Antonio*, pp. 185–86; San Antonio Public Service Company, *Economic and Industrial Survey*, 1942, p. 33.

20. Robert C. Brook, "One of the Four Hundred and Thirty-Four: Maury Maverick of Texas," in *The American Politician*, ed. J. T. Salter, p. 160; Ronnie C. Davis, "Maury Maverick Sr.: The Rise and Fall of a National Congress-

ber 19, 1937, p. 1a.

24. *San Antonio Express*, May 5, 1939, p. 9, May 6, 1939, pp. 7, 10a, May 9, 1939, p. 4; interview with Rubén Mungía, June 12, 1978.

25. *San Antonio Express*, December 31, 1938, pp. 1–2, May 10, 1939, p. 1.

26. Henderson, *Maury Maverick*, pp. 198–99.

27. *San Antonio Express*, July 2, 1938, p. 8.

28. Henderson, *Maury Maverick*, pp. 199–201.

29. Social Welfare Commission, *1940 Social Welfare Report*, p. 25.

8. The Exiled *Ricos*

1. Woods, *Mexican Ethnic Leadership*, pp. 20–21.

2. These general themes have been derived from the following: Meyer, *Huerta*, pp. 156–77, 213–27; Maciel, "Nacionalismo cultural," pp. 267–87; W. Dirk Raat, "Auguste Comte, the Positive Philosophy," in *The Age of Porfirio Díaz: Selected Readings* (Albuquerque: University of New Mexico Press, 1977) pp. 45–47; idem, "Auguste Comte, Gabino Barreda and Positivism," pp. 241–50; idem, *Los Revoltosos*; idem, "Ideas and Society," pp. 35–53; Rice, "Beyond the Científicos," pp. 289–305; Medeiros, "La Opinión," pp. 67–85; Meyer and Sherman, *The Course of Mexican History*, pp. 433–36, 439–51, 453–64, 483–97, 498–502, 543, 560, 592–93, 628, 645.

3. *La Prensa*, January 29, 1930, pp. 1, 5, January 30, 1930, p. 10.

4. *La Prensa*, April 6, 1937, p. 1.

5. For information on this group of Mexicans see Nancie C. González, *The Spanish Americans of New Mexico*. Exiles in El Paso also called themselves Spanish rather than Mexican: interview with Alma Garcia, November 13, 1979; *La Prensa*, April 6, 1937, p. 1.

6. Medeiros, "*La Opinión*," pp. 67–68.

7. Ibid., pp. 76, 79, 80, 82. Also see E. C. E. Evans-Pritchard, *The Sociology of Comte: An Appreciation; La Opinión*, April 8, 1926, p. 3, November 24, 1929, p. 3.

8. Medeiros, "*La Opinión*," pp. 75, 77, 78.

9. Ibid., pp. 78, 79, 80.

10. Ibid., pp. 76, 77, 78.

11. *La Prensa*, September 27, 1929, p. 3.

12. *La Prensa*, September 21, 1929, p. 3, January 14, 1930, p. 7.

13. *La Prensa*, January 31, 1930, p. 3.

14. *La Prensa*, January 2, 1930, p. 3, January 10, 1930, p. 3, January 12, 1930, p. 1, March 1, 1930, p. 3.

15. *La Prensa*, January 2, 1930, p. 3.

16. *La Prensa*, January 2, 1930, p. 3, January 10, 1930, p. 3.

17. Nemesio García Naranjo, *Porfirio Díaz*, pp. 314, 315.

18. *La Prensa*, January 10, 1930, p. 3.

19. *La Prensa*, September 15, 1929, p. 7.

20. García Naranjo, *Porfirio Díaz*, pp. 311–14.

21. *La Prensa*, September 17, 1929, p. 10; Arthur F. Corwin, ed., *Immigrants and Immigrants: Perspectives on Mexico's Labor Migration to the United States*, p. 117.

22. *La Prensa*, August 15, 1929, p. 3, January 23, 1930, p. 1.

23. *La Prensa*, August 15, 1929, p. 3, January 2, 1930, p. 3, January 10, 1930, p. 3, January 12, 1930, p. 1, January 23, 1930, p. 1; *La Prensa*, March 1, 1930, p. 3.

24. Wuthnow et al., *Cultural Analysis*, pp. 24–67; Peter Berger and Thomas Luckmann, *The Social Construction of Reality: A Treatise in the Sociology of Knowledge*, chaps. 1, 2, esp. pp. 174–76; interview with Ignacio Lozano, Jr., August 3, 1978. *La Prensa* editorials throughout the 1930s reflected this constant tension between the *ricos*' role in Mexico and their role as the *gente decente* in the United States. The *ricos*, regardless of changes, tried to remain *Mexicanos de afuera*.

25. *La Prensa*, January 1, 1939, p. 3.

26. *La Prensa*, January 9, 1939, pp. 1, 10; Meyer and Sherman, *Course of Mexican History*, p. 530.

27. *La Prensa*, January 2, 1930, p. 3, January 9, 1930, pp. 1, 10, January 10, 1930, p. 3, January 12, 1930, March, 1930, p. 3; Medeiros, "*La Opinión*," pp. 76, 77, 78.

28. *La Prensa*, February 2, 1930, p. 8.

29. *La Prensa*, February 16, 1930, p. 3, February 23, 1930, p. 8, June 6, 1930, p. 7, June 13, 1930, p. 7.

30. *La Prensa*, June 1, 1930, p. 3, June 5, 1930, p. 10.

31. *La Prensa*, June 1, 1930, pp. 3–4; Medeiros, "*La Opinión*," pp. 75, 78, 82.

32. *La Prensa*, January 29, 1930, p. 10, January 31, 1930, p. 7, February 23, 1930, p. 6.

33. *La Prensa*, January 16, 1930, p. 4, January 25, 1930, January 27, 1930, pp. 1, 4, February 2, 1930, p. 9.

34. *La Prensa*, February 16, 1930, p. 3.

35. *La Prensa*, June 1, 1930, p. 7.

36. *La Prensa*, February 11, 1930, p. 7, June 3, 1930, p. 7.

37. *La Prensa*, September 23, 1929, pp. 3, 7, September 27, 1929, p. 1, November 19, 1933, p. 5.

38. *La Prensa*, January 9, 1930, pp. 1, 10, January 13, 1930, p. 8, February 11, 1930, p. 7, February 22, 1930, p. 7, February 23, 1930, November 26, 1933, p. 3, January 4, 1941, p. 1.

39. *La Prensa*, January 30, 1930, p. 10.

40. *La Prensa*, January 8, 1930, p. 5, June 2, 1930, p. 4. For further information on the Alianza Hispano Americana, see Kaye Lynn Briegel, "Alianza Hispano-

44. *La Prensa*, February 17, 1930, pp. 3, 7, February 24, 1930, p. 3.

45. *La Prensa*, February 20, 1930, p. 7, March 1, 1941, p. 3.

46. *La Prensa*, September 2, 1929, p. 3. Moheno, like Huerta, formed a policy of nationalization that in some ways anticipated the reforms of the 1930s. The *ricos* in San Antonio were extremely nationalistic, as Moheno's ideas indicated, not only culturally, but politically and economically (Meyer, *Huerta*, pp. 170–72).

47. *La Prensa*, August 23, 1929, p. 3.

48. Meyer and Sherman, *Course of Mexican History*, pp. 630–34.

49. *La Prensa*, February 20, 1930, p. 7, March 1, 1941, p. 3.

50. *La Prensa*, January 25, 1930, p. 3.

51. *La Prensa*, January 25, 1929, p. 4.

52. *La Prensa*, January 1, 1930, p. 3.

53. *La Prensa*, September 19, 1929, p. 7, September 20, 1929, p. 7.

54. *La Prensa*, October 2, 1931, p. 3, June 25, 1939, p. 3.

55. *La Prensa*, January 26, 1930, p. 3. See Krutch, *The Modern Temper*, for an excellent analysis of the relationship between humankind and modernity. Many of the *ricos* would have agreed with Krutch's criticism of science, progress, and secularism.

56. *La Prensa*, January 26, 1930, p. 3.

57. *La Prensa*, January 26, 1930, p. 3.

58. *La Prensa*, February 5, 1930, p. 1.

59. *La Prensa*, January 18, 1930, p. 3, August 16, 1939, p. 3.

60. *La Prensa*, August 15, 1929, p. 3, January 8, 1930, p. 3, January 16, 1930, p. 3, January 18, 1930, p. 3, January 21, 1930, p. 3, February 6, 1930, p. 3, August 16, 1930, p. 3, November 23, 1933, p. 3, November 24, 1933, p. 1, January 2, 1941, p. 2.

61. *La Prensa*, January 14, 1930, pp. 1, 5.

62. *La Prensa*, February 5, 1930, p. 1.

63. *La Prensa*, April 6, 1937, p. 1.

64. *La Prensa*, February 15, 1930, p. 3.

65. *La Prensa*, February 26, 1930, p. 3.

66. This is Wuthnow et al.'s paraphrase of Berger's idea on culture, in *Cultural Analysis*, p. 71.

67. *La Prensa*, February 6, 1930, p. 3, March 1, 1941, p. 3.

68. Meyer and Sherman, *Course of Mexican History*, pp. 630–31.

69. *La Prensa*, March 1, 1941, p. 3.

9. The Emerging Middle Class and LULAC

1. "A History of LULAC, Part I," *LULAC News* 36 (January, 1974): 10.

2. J. Montiel Olivera, ed., *Latin American Yearbook*, p. 9.

3. J. C. Sologaist, *Guía general directorio mexicano*, 1924, pp. 211–22.

4. Weeks, "The League of United Latin American Citizens," p. 258.

5. Taylor, *An American-Mexican Frontier*, pp. 242, 247.

6. Taylor, *An American-Mexican Frontier*, p. 245.

7. M. C. González quoted in Dickens, "The Political Role," p. 134.

8. J. Luz Saenz, *Los mexicano-americanos en la gran guerra y su contingente en pro de la democracia, la humanidad y la justicia*, pp. 8, 18, 292.

9. Olivera, *Latin American Yearbook*, pp. 6, 7. For an examination of the Mexicans' plight, see Theodore N. Picnot, "Address on the Socio-Economic Status of Low Income Groups of San Antonio."

10. "Richard Erickson Interview with John Solís," *South Side Sun*, July 7, 1976, John Solís Papers.

11. *LULAC News*, 1974, p. 11.

12. Quoted in Taylor, *An American-Mexican Frontier*, p. 245.

13. Edward D. Garza, "LULAC: League of United Latin American Citizens," Master's thesis, Southwest Texas State Teachers College, 1951, pp. 3, 4.

14. *La Prensa*, February 9, 1960, p. 1; interview with John Solís, June 3, 1978. Regrettably, most of Solís's papers, according to him, were lost or accidentally destroyed over the years.

15. Quoted in Taylor, *An American-Mexican Frontier*, p. 246; *La Prensa*, February 9, 1960, p. 1.

16. Garza, "LULAC," pp. 1–11; *LULAC News*, 1974, p. 11.

17. San Miguel, *"Let All of Them Take Heed,"* p. 69.

18. Ibid., pp. 71–74.

19. Ibid., pp. 7, 70, 71.

20. Garza, "LULAC," pp. 10, 15, 24; *La Prensa*, February 10, 1960, pp. 1, 4; interview with Rubén Mungía, June 8, 1978.

21. Olivera, *Latin American Yearbook*, p. 6.

22. Interview with M. C. González, June 10, 1978.

23. Quoted in Olivera, *Latin American Yearbook*, p. 6.

24. Ibid.

25. San Miguel, *"Let All of Them Take Heed,"* p. 70.

26. Weeks, "LULAC," pp. 264, 265.

27. Ibid., p. 259.

28. Ibid., pp. 259, 260.

29. Ibid.

30. Interview with Rubén Mungía, January 4, 1976.

31. Rubén Mungía, "Prospect Hill—Then, Now, and Tomorrow," p. 1. Rubén Mungía is the son of Rómulo Mungía, the printer-editor of *La Voz* in the 1930s. Rubén Mungía was an important figure in a circle of LULAC and other Mexican American activists who discussed and inspired many political activities and campaigns in the late 1940s and 1950s in San Antonio.

32. Ibid., pp. 7, 8.

39. Ibid., p. 249.

40. Ibid. Dickens suggests this idea of "tenacity" in his study of politics in the San Antonio community by quoting Robert Dahl, *Who Governs?*, p. 59: "In spite of growing assimilation, ethnic factors continue to make themselves felt with astonishing tenacity."

41. Weeks, "LULAC," pp. 264, 265.

42. *La Prensa*, September 7, 1929, pp. 1, 5.

43. *San Antonio Express*, June 25, 1936, p. 9, August 7, 1936, p. 11, January 19, 1937, p. 16, July 14, 1937, p. 20.

44. Dickens, "The Political Role," p. 136.

45. J. Luz Saenz in *El Paladín*, Corpus Christi, Texas (May 17, 1929), quoted in Weeks, "LULAC," p. 274.

46. Garza, "LULAC," pp. 10, 15, 24.

47. *La Voz*, March 29, 1936, p. 7, February 20, 1938, p. 1, January 8, 1939, p. 1.

48. *El Pueblo: El Peridico Hispano Americano de Texas*, July 22, 1939, p. 1.

49. *LULAC News*, November, 1940, p. 2.

50. George J. Garza, "Along the Trail with Council #12," pp. 9, 14, quoted in Edward D. Garza, "LULAC," pp. 38, 39. Scout work was instrumental in LULAC youth activities beginning in 1929. See A. de Luna, "Minutes of Regular Meetings of LULAC, Record Book of the League of United Latin American Citizens," May 20, 1929, footnoted in Garza, "LULAC," p. 40.

51. Garza, "LULAC," pp. 32, 33.

52. *LULAC News*, November, 1940, p. 2.

53. "LULAC Code," *LULAC News*, November 1940, p. 3.

54. Interview with Lalo Solís, June 2, 1978. Although not a member in the 1930s, he generally approved of LULAC and its activities.

55. Interview with John Solís, May 24, 1978.

56. George J. Garza, "Back to School," pp. 14, 17, in Garza, "LULAC," p. 34;

Garza, "LULAC," p. 12; Dennis Chávez, "LULAC through the Eyes of Senator Chávez," *LULAC News*, 7, No. 3 (March, 1940): 6.

57. San Miguel, "*Let All of Them Take Heed*," p. 70.

58. H. T. Manual, "Education, the Guardian of Democracy and the Hope of Youth," *LULAC News* (November, 1940): 3.

59. Ibid.

60. George I. Sánchez, "Americanism," *LULAC News* 7 (November, 1940): 4.

61. Ibid.

62. Ibid.

63. Carlos E. Castañeda, "Trained Leadership," *LULAC News* 7 (November, 1940): 5.

64. F. T. Martínez, "Harmony and Unity: The Means to Solidify Our League," *LULAC News* 7 (November, 1940): 6.

65. Interviews with George de la Garza, May 25, 1978; M. C. González, June 10, 1978; John Solís, May 24, 1978; Lalo Solís, June 2, 1978.

66. *LULAC News*, November, 1940, p. 2; interview with George de la Garza, May 25, 1978; interview with John Solís, May 24, 1978.

67. Alonzo S. Perales, *Are We Good Nieghbors?* p. 5; Adela Sloss-Vento, *Alonzo S. Perales: His Struggle for the Rights of Mexican-Americans*, p. 6.

68. Ibid., pp. 6, 10; Perales, *Neighbors*, p. 5.

69. Interview with John Solís, May 24, 1978; Sloss-Vento, *Alonzo S. Perales*, pp. 6, 7, 9.

70. Carlos Castaéda, foreword, in Perales, *En defensa de mi raza*, quoted in Sloss-Vento, *Alonzo S. Perales*, p. 11.

71. Sloss-Vento, *Alonzo S. Perales*, p. 14.

72. Ibid., pp. 15, 16.

73. Sloss-Vento, *Alonzo S. Perales*, p. 10.

74. Marcus G. Singer, ed., *American Philosophy*, p. 261.

75. Sloss-Vento, *Alonzo S. Perales*, p. 22; Perales, *Neighbors*, p. 9.

76. Perales, *Neighbors*, p. 9; *La Prensa*, September 6, 1929, cited in Weeks, "LULAC," p. 273.

77. Quoted in Weeks, "LULAC," p. 273.

78. *San Antonio Light*, September 11, 1977, p. 1.

79. Alonzo S. Perales, *El Mexicano-Americano y la Politica del Sur de Texas*, pp. 3, 6.

80. Ibid., pp. 7, 10, 11.

81. Ibid., p. 11.

82. Ibid., p. 13.

83. Alonzo S. Perales, "Nuestra actual forma de gobierno y nuestra lucha en pro de justicia social," *El Pueblo*, March 24, 1938, p. 3; idem, *El Pueblo*, March 27, 1939, p. 3, April 3, 1938, p. 3. These three issues of *El Pueblo* are in Rubén Mungía's files.

84. *La Prensa*, February 4, 1939, pp. 1, 6.

85. "Un joven mexicano-texano que ha sabido triunfar honrando a su estado natal," M. C. González Papers.

86. Ibid.; M. C. González's curriculum vitae, M. C. González Papers.

87. "Twenty-Four Years on the Board," *The Fourth Write* (Spring, 1978): 24. This is a San Antonio Public School Board publication.

88. "Un joven mexicano-texano."

89. Ibid.

90. Ibid.

91. Ibid.; *San Antonio Express*, January 25, 1964, p. 8a; "Bexar Facts" column, clipping dated June 6, 1930, M. C. González Papers.

92. Newspaper clipping dated September 21, 1924, in M. C. González Papers. Article is in Spanish, so is probably from *La Prensa*.

98. In several interviews I conducted, González's contemporaries seemed to feel that González tended to be more aloof because of these actions. However, they would not expound on their resentment. It seems to me that the differences between González and Perales were accentuated by life-style, personal idiosyncrasies, and Perales's emphasis on his Mexicanness as opposed to González's emphasis on his Americanness.

99. Interview with Rubén Mungía, January 4, 1976; M. C. González, "What Is LULAC?," *Alma Latina* 1 (March, 1932): 1, M. C. González Papers.

100. Ibid.

101. M. C. González, "LULAC Prepares for Battle: The Social Evolution of the Texas Mexican," M. C. González Papers. This article was written many years after 1929. According to González, it was an attempt to convey the drama of the founding of LULAC as being comparable to the U.S. Constitutional Convention.

102. Ibid.

103. M. C. González, special notes, n.d., M. C. González Papers.

104. M. C. González, speech notes; idem, "LULAC through the Years," *LULAC News*, n.d., n.p., M. C. González Papers; idem, "What Is LULAC?," p. 1.

105. *El Pueblo*, November 9, 1931, pp. 1, 3, June 20, 1934, p. 1; *San Antonio Light*, October 3, 1930, p. 1; "Court Upholds Pool in Bar on Latins," February 2, 1937 (clipping), M. C. González Papers; unidentified clipping announcing González's legislative candidacy, M. C. González Papers; interview with M. C. González, June 10, 1978.

106. González, *Vita*, M. C. González Papers; M. C. González, "Brief History of the Camara Mexicana de Commercio," February 27, 1975; González Papers; idem, speech notes for banquet honoring the secretary of the treasury, Mrs. Banuelos, ca. 1977, González Papers; interview with M. C. González, June 10, 1978.

107. Interview with M. C. González, June 10, 1978.

108. Ibid.

109. Ibid.

110. M. C. González, draft of graduation speech, ca. 1941–42, González Papers.

EPILOGUE

1. Roth, pp. 82–134; Levine, "Progress and Nostalgia," pp. 195, 196, 200; Ralph Waldo Emerson, "Lecture on the Times," quoted in Arthur M. Schlesinger, *The American as Reformer*, p. 65.

2. See James MacGregor Burns, *Roosevelt: The Lion and the Fox;* Arthur Schlesinger, *The Crisis of the Old Order: The Coming of the New Deal,* and *The Politics of Upheaval;* Mario Einaudi, *The Roosevelt Revolution;* William E. Leuchtenburg, *Franklin Roosevelt and the New Deal;* and Alonzo L. Hanby, *The New Deal: Analysis and Interpretation.*

3. Montejano, *Anglos and Mexicans,* pp. 262–87. See also John R. Martinez, "Leadership and Politics"; Paul M. Sheldon, "Community Participation and the Emerging Middle Class"; Donald N. Barrett, "Demographic Characteristics"; all in Julián Samora, ed. *La Raza: Forgotten Americans;* Montejano's data clearly show the importance of the middle class since World War II; however, he de-emphasizes this by suggesting that the Texas elites allowed this growth because the middle class was simply a new power broker that could be used by them.

4. Kibbe, *Latin Americans in Texas.*

5. Castañeda quoted in Montejano, *Anglos and Mexicans,* p. 269.

6. Castañeda's article quoted in San Miguel, *"Let All of Them Take Heed,"* p. 114.

7. Romo, *East Los Angeles,* pp. 167–68.

8. For information on the rise of the middle class in the 1940s and 1950s, see ibid.; Sheldon, "Community Participation," pp. 125–27; Montejano, *Anglos and Mexicans,* pp. 257–308; Rodolfo Acuña, *Occupied America: A History of Chicanos,* pp. 251–306; San Miguel, *"Let All of Them Take Heed";* John R. Chavez, *The Lost Land: The Chicano Image of the Southwest,* pp. 107–27. Also see Mario T. Garcia, *Mexican Americans: Identity, Ideology, and Leadership,* on the Mexican American generation of the 1940s and 1950s. Each of these books has a different interpretation of the Mexican American era, but the evidence is overwhelming that the Mexican American mentality and ideology permeated the Mexican communities. However, class, geographical area, and generation affected which aspect of the Mexican American mind a given individual would adopt.

9. Montejano, *Anglos and Mexicans,* p. 280.

10. Ibid.

11. Ibid. See also Acuña, *Occupied America,* pp. 279–99.

12. For a discussion of Eisenhower, see Charles C. Alexander, *Holding the Line: The Eisenhower Era, 1952–1961;* Stephen E. Ambrose, *Eisenhower: The President.* Also see Arthur M. Schlesinger, Jr., *The Vital Center,* for an interesting discussion on liberalism's impact on the Left. For a good discussion on consensus, see Godfrey Hodgson, *America in Our Time: From World War II to*

Nixon – What Happened and Why. For a discussion of LULAC's political ideology within the themes of social integration and political accommodation, see Benjamin Márquez, "The Politics of Race and Class: The League of United Latin American Citizens in the Post World War II Period," *Social Science Quarterly* 68 (1987).

13. Acuña, *Occupied America,* pp. 279–99. See also John R. Martinez, "Leadership and Politics," pp. 47–62; Sheldon, "Community Participation," pp. 125–59; Manuel P. Servín, *The Mexican-Americans: An Awakening Minority,* pp. 142 79

Mario T. Garcia, *Desert Immigrants;* Oscar Martínez, *Border Boom Town: Ciudad Juárez since 1948;* Benjamin Márquez, *Power and Politics in a Chicano Barrio: A Study of Mobilization Efforts and Community Power in El Paso, Texas (1960–1981).* For information on acculturation, mobility, intermarriage, and family conditions during the 1950s and 1960s, see Leo Grebler et al., *The Mexican-American People: The Nation's Second Largest Minority.*

17. George Sánchez, "History, Culture, and Education," in Samora, *La Raza,* pp. 9, 10, 11, 13, 23.

18. Sánchez in Samora, *La Raza,* pp. 1–26. Also see the rest of the articles in Samora, *La Raza;* Montejano, *Anglos and Mexicans,* pp. 259–87, for information that underscores the Americanization of the Mexican American middle class, although Montejano gives it a different interpretation. Also see George Sánchez, "The American of Mexican Descent," *Chicago Jewish Forum* 20 (Winter, 1961–1962); Chavez, *The Lost Land,* pp. 112–15.

19. Acuña, *Occupied America,* pp. 294–95; Montejano, *Anglos and Mexicans,* pp. 279–81. For three good accounts of McCarthyism and its impact on American society, see Richard H. Rovere, *Senator Joe McCarthy;* I. F. Stone, *The Truman Era;* Richard Hofstadter, *The Paranoid Style in American Politics;* Samora, *La Raza,* p. 55.

20. Galarza, "Mexicans in the Southwest," pp. 265–66.

21. Ibid., p. 266. See also Acuña, *Occupied America,* pp. 294, 295; Chavez, *The Lost Land,* pp. 124–26.

22. Galarza, "Mexicans in the Southwest," pp. 261–97; idem, *Barrio Boy.*

23. Montejano, *Anglos and Mexicans,* pp. 277–91. Montejano's brief comments indicate Henry B. González's strength of character, use of power, and the respect shown him by people like Mario Cuomo of New York.

24. See David Potter, *People of Plenty: Economic Abundance and the American Character;* Daniel J. Boorstin, *The Americans: The Democratic Experience;* and Werner Sombart, *Why Is There No Socialism in the United States,* for in-

terpretations that treat the effect of abundance on the American people. Statistics come from Donald N. Barrett, "Demographic Characteristics," in Samora, *La Raza*, pp. 159–99. For the effect of racism in the United States, see Gunnar Myrdal, *An American Dilemma: The Negro Problem and Modern Democracy*; Barrett, "Demographic Characteristics"; Grebler et al., *The Mexican-American People*, pp. 101–442.

25. Samora, *La Raza*, pp. 201, 199, xi–xvii, 201–11.

26. Acuña, *Occupied America*, pp. 283, 285, 281, 287–88; Grebler et al., *The Mexican-American People*, pp. 189–203.

27. Woods, *Mexican Ethnic Leadership*, p. 107; Chávez, *The Lost Land*, p. 116; Kibbe, *Latin Americans in Texas*, p. 264.

28. Woods, *Mexican Ethnic Leadership*, pp. 106–109; conversations with Mario T. Garcia; see also his *Mexican Americans*. All the information on PAPA is drawn from Woods.

29. Woods, *Mexican Ethnic Leadership*, p. 110

30. For a discussion of the relationship between modernization, consciousness, and the concept of the "homeless mind," see Peter L. Berger, *The Homeless Mind: Modernization and Consciousness*. For an interesting discussion of the relationship between environment, pragmatism, individuals, and ideology in the formation of a consciousness of modernization, see Eugene Rachberg-Halton, *Meaning and Modernity: Social Theory in the Pragmatic Attitude*.

31. Woods, *Mexican Ethnic Leadership*, p. 107.

32. Ibid., pp. 4, 6, 54, 56–57, 64, 66.

33. Acuña, *Occupied America*, pp. 282–84; Mario T. Garcia, *Mexican Americans*. For a comparison of the social worlds of San Antonio and Los Angeles in the 1950s, see Grebler et al., *The Mexican-American People*, pp. 297–316. In 1962 the middle class, through a coalition of organizations, elected Henry B. González to the House of Representatives, and in 1964 it elected Kika de la Garza.

34. There are many studies for this period, although none are critical or analytical. See Richard A. García, "The Chicano Movement and The Mexican-American Community, 1972–1978: An Interpretive Essay," *Socialist Review* 8 (1978).

35. Acuña, *Occupied America*, pp. 259, 334, 338–39, 367, 376, 448, 449; Larralde, *Mexican-American Movements*, pp. 212–15; Richard A. Garcia, "The Chicano Movement"; José Angel Gutiérrez, "La Raza and Revolution: The Empirical Conditions of Revolution in Four South Texas Counties," Master's thesis, St. Mary's University, 1968

36. Acuña, *Occupied America*, pp. 419, 420–22, 449; speech by Henry Cisneros, Santa Monica College, spring, 1986.

37. Alonso S. Perales quoted in San Miguel, "*Let All of Them Take Heed*," p. 72; M. C. González quoted in Olivera, *Latin American Yearbook*, p. 6.

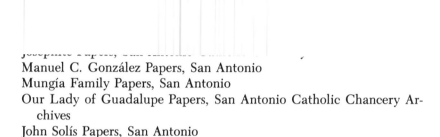

Josephine Papers, San Antonio...

Manuel C. González Papers, San Antonio
Mungía Family Papers, San Antonio
Our Lady of Guadalupe Papers, San Antonio Catholic Chancery Archives
John Solís Papers, San Antonio
Tranchese Papers, St. Mary's University, San Antonio

INTERVIEWS

Barnabus, Father, June 5, 1978
De la Garza, George, May 25, 1978
Elizondo, Oscar, October 28, 1977
Garcia, Alma A., November 13, 1979
Gonzales, Manuel C., June 10, 1978
González Espinoza, Epigminio, May 22, 1978
Guerra, Dora Elizondo, October 27, 1977·
Lozano, Ignacio, Jr., August 3, 1978
Manager, Bell Furniture Company, San Antonio, June 4, 1978
Mungía, Rubén, January 4, 1976, June 1–21, 1978
Perry, Carmen, November 3, 1977
Real estate agent, San Antonio, October 4, 1977
Rodríguez, Mrs. Jacobo, June 14, 1978
Solís, John, May 24, 1978
Solís, Lalo, June 2, 1978

PUBLIC DOCUMENTS

American Public Welfare Association. *Public Welfare Survey of San Antonio, Texas: A Study of a Local Community, 1940.* Chicago: American Public Welfare Association, 1940.

Bobbit, J. F. *The San Antonio Public School System: A Survey.* San Antonio: San Antonio School Board, 1914.

Hopkins, Harry L. *Federal Emergency Relief Administration: Unemployment Relief Census.* October, 1933. Washington, D.C.: GPO, 1934.

Menefee, Seldon C., and Orin C. Cassmore. *Pecan Shellers: The Problem of Underpaid and Unemployed Mexican Labor.* Washington, D.C.: GPO, 1940.

San Antonio City Directory, 1911, 1921–22, 1937.

San Antonio Municipal Commission. *1940 Social Welfare Report.* San Antonio: Municipal Government, 1940.

San Antonio Municipal Government. *Business Interest in Decent Standards,* 1930.

———. *The Industries of San Antonio.* Reprint, San Antonio: Norman Brock, 1977.

———. *San Antonio: Where Life Is Different.* Municipal Information Bureau, ca. 1930.

———. *San Antonio Sets the Stage for Industry.* Ca. 1910.

———. *San Antonio, Texas, through a Cameraman's Club.* Ca. 1950.

San Antonio Public Service Company. *Economic and Industrial Survey.* Municipal Reports, 1940, 1942.

San Antonio Social Directory, 1937.

Sisters of Charity. "Santa Rosa Hospital Report." Typescript, ca. 1930. San Antonio Public Library.

Texas State Employment Service Division. *Origins and Problems of Texas Migratory Farm Labor.* Austin: Texas State Employment Bulletin, 1940.

United States Presidential Report of the Commission on Migratory Labor: Migratory Labor in American Agriculture. Washington, D.C.: GPO, 1950.

U.S. Bureau of the Census. *15th Census of the United States: 1930, Population.* Vol. III, Part 2. Washington, D.C.: GPO, 1932.

———. *Financial Statistics for the City Government of San Antonio.* Washington, D.C.: GPO, 1931.

———. *Financial Statistics of Cities, 1938.* Washington, D.C.: GPO, 1940.

U.S. House of Representatives. *Immigration from Countries of the Western Hemisphere: Hearings before the Committee on Immigration and Naturalization.* 71st Congress, 2d Session, March 14, 1930.

U.S. Public Health Service. *Public Health Survey of San Antonio,* Washington, D.C.: GPO, 1935.

UNPUBLISHED PAPERS, THESES, AND DISSERTATIONS

Arnold, Charles. "The Folklore, Manners, and Customs of the Mexicans in San Antonio." Master's thesis, St. Mary's University, 1928.

Briegel, Kaye Lynn. "Alianza Hispano-Americana, 1894–1965: A Mexican-American Fraternal Insurance Society." Ph.D. dissertation, University of Southern California, 1974.

Brown, Willie L. "The Knowledge of Social Standards among Mexican  dren in the American Schools." Master's thesis, St. Mary's University, 1941.

Chapelle, Angela María. "Local Welfare of Religious Organizations in San Antonio, Texas." Master's thesis, University of Texas, 1939.

Davis, Ronnie C. "Maury Maverick Sr.: The Rise and Fall of a National Congressman." Master's thesis, St. Mary's University, 1966.

Dickens, Edwin Larry. "The Political Role of the Mexican-Americans in San Antonio, Texas." Ph.D. dissertation, Texas Technological College, 1969.

Fuller, Thelma. "A Survey of Art Education." Master's thesis, St. Mary's University, 1939.

Garcia, Mario T. "Obreros: The Mexican Workers of El Paso, 1890–1920." Ph.D. dissertation, University of California, San Diego, 1975.

Garcia, Richard A. "Creating a Consciousness, Memories, and Expectations: The Burden of Octavio Romano." Paper delivered at the National Association for Chicano Studies Meetings, Salt Lake City, Utah, April, 1987.

Garza, Edward D. "LULAC: League of United Latin American Citizens." Master's thesis, Southwest Texas State Teachers College, 1951.

González, Aurora M. "A Study of Intelligence of Mexican Children in Relation to Their Socio-Economic Status." Master's thesis, University of Texas, Austin, 1932.

González, Gilbert. "Crisis of Urbanization: Racism, Education, and the Mexican Community in Los Angeles, 1920–1930." School of Social Science, University of California, Irvine, 1976.

González, M. C. "LULAC Prepares for Battle: The Evolution of the Texas Mexican." M. C. González Papers.

Gutiérrez, José Angel. "La Raza and Revolution: The Empirical Conditions of Revolution in Four South Texas Counties." Master's thesis, St. Mary's University, 1968.

Harris, James K. "A Sociological Study of a Mexican School in San Antonio, Texas." Master's thesis, University of Texas, Austin, 1927.

Laird, Judith F. "Argentine, Kansas: The Evolution of a Mexican-American Community, 1905–1940." Ph.D. dissertion. University of Kansas, 1975.

Landolt, Robert Garland. "The Mexican-American Workers of San Antonio, Texas." Ph.D. dissertation. University of Texas, Austin, 1965.

Masdorff, James Curtis. "The Southern Messenger and the Mexican Church-State Controversy, 1917–1941." Master's thesis, St. Mary's University, 1968.

Mequire, Katherine H. "Educating the Mexican Child in the Elementary School." Master's thesis, University of Southern California, 1938.

Mungía, Rubén. "Prospect Hill—Then, Now, and Tomorrow." Essay, ca. 1960. Mungía Papers, San Antonio.

Paulus, Marjorie. "Fifteen Years in Old San Antonio, 1850–1865." Master's thesis, St. Mary's University, 1939.

Picnot, Theodore N. "Address on the Socio-Economic Status of Low Income Groups of San Antonio." Address, ca. 1942. San Antonio Public Library.

———. "The Businessman's Interest in Decent Standards of Living." Speech to Catholic Conference on Industrial Problems in San Antonio, Texas, 1942. San Antonio Public Library.

Pycior, Julie Leininger. "La Raza Organizes: Mexican-American Life in San Antonio, 1915–1930." Ph.D. dissertation, University of Notre Dame, 1979.

Quezada, Juan Gilberto. "Father Carmelo Antonio Tranchese S.J.: A Pioneer Social Worker in San Antonio, 1932–1953." Master's thesis, St. Mary's University, 1972.

Rogers, Thomas G. "The Housing Situation of the Mexicans in San Antonio, Texas." Master's thesis, St. Mary's University, 1927.

Romo, Richard. "Mexican Workers in the City: Los Angeles, 1915–1930." Ph.D. dissertation, University of California, San Diego, 1975.

Saragoza, Alex M. "The Formation of a Mexican Elite: The Industrialization of Monterrey, Nuevo Leon, 1880–1920." Ph.D. dissertation, University of California at San Diego, 1978.

Saunders, Lyle. "The Spanish-speaking People of the Southwest." Paper presented at the 4th Annual Workshop in Cultural Relations, Denver, Colorado, May 5, 1958.

Shapiro, Harold A. "The Workers of San Antonio, Texas, 1900–1940." Ph.D. dissertation, University of Texas, Austin, 1952.

Wright, Pearl. "Religious Fiestas in San Antonio." Master's thesis, St. Mary's University, 1946.

Zamora, Emilio. "Mexican Labor Activity in South Texas, 1900–1920." Ph.D. dissertation, University of Texas, Austin, 1983.

ARTICLES

ten Americans, ed. Julián Samora, pp. 159–99. Notre Dame, Ind.: University of Notre Dame, 1966.

Beals, Carleton. "Mexican Intelligence." *Southwest Review* 11 (1927): 23–31.

Blackwelder, Julia Kirk. "Women in the Work Force: Atlanta, New Orleans, and San Antonio, 1930–1940." *Journal of Urban History* 4, no. 3 (1978): 330–60.

Bodnar, John. "Symbols and Servants: Immigrant Americans and the Limits of Public History." *Journal of Urban History* 4, no. 3 (1978): 330–60.

Bogardus, Emory S. "Attitudes and the Mexican Immigrant." In *Social Attitudes*, ed. Kimball Young, pp. 291–327. New York: Henry Holt, 1931.

———. "Current Problems of Mexican Immigrants." *Social Research* 25 (1940): 165–74.

Botten, James H. "New Features of Mexican Immigration: The Case against Further Restrictive Legislation." *Pacific Affairs* 3 (October, 1930): 10–20.

Brook, Robert C. "One of the Four Hundred and Thirty-Four: Maury Maverick of Texas." In *The American Politician*, ed. J. T. Salter, pp. 150–74. Raleigh: University of North Carolina Press, 1938.

Cardenas, Gilbert. "United States Immigration Policy toward Mexico: An Historical Perspective." *Chicano Law Review* 2 (1975): 66–80.

Castañeda, Carlos E. "Trained Leadership." *LULAC News* 7, no. 3 (November, 1940): 5–6.

Chambers, William T. "San Antonio, Texas." *Economic Geography* 16, no. 3 (1940): 293–305.

Chávez, Dennis. "LULAC through the Eyes of Senator Chávez." *LULAC News* 7, no. 3 (March, 1940): 6–7.

Corwin, Arthur. "Mexican-American History: An Assessment." *Pacific Historical Review* 42, no. 3 (1973): 30–45.

De la Garza, R. "Our School Children." *LULAC News* (November, 1932): 4–5.

Galarza, Ernesto. "Mexicans in the Southwest." In *Plural Society in the Southwest*, ed. Edward H. Spicer and Raymond H. Thompson, pp. 261–97. New York: Interbank, 1972.

Garcia, Mario T. "Americanization and the Mexican Immigrant, 1880–1930." *Journal of Ethnic Studies* 6 (1975): 28–40.

———. "The Mexican Family, 1900–1930." In *Work, Family, Sex Roles and Language*, ed. Mario Barrera, Alberto Camarillo, and Francisco Hernandez. Berkeley: Tonatiuh-Quinto Sol International, 1980.

———. "Racial Dualism in the El Paso Labor Market, 1880–1920." *Aztlán* 6 (Summer, 1975): 197–218.

Garcia, Richard A. "The Chicano Movement and the Mexican-American Community, 1972–1978: An Interpretive Essay." *Socialist Review* 8, nos. 4–5 (July, 1978): 117–36.

———. "Class, Consciousness, and Ideology: The Mexican Community of San Antonio, Texas, 1930–1945." *Aztlán* 9 (Fall, 1978): 23–69.

———. "The Mexican-American Mind: A Product of the 1930s." In *History, Culture, and Society: Chicano Studies in the 1930s*, ed. Mario T. Garcia et al., pp. 67–93. Ypsilanti: Michigan Bilingual Press, 1983.

Glazer, Nathan. "Slums and Ethnicity." In *Social Welfare and Urban Problems*, ed. Thomas D. Sherrard, pp. 80–110. New York: Columbia University Press, 1968.

González, M. C. "What Is LULAC?" *Alma Latina* 1 (March, 1932): 3–4.

Granneberg, Audrey. "Maury Maverick's San Antonio." *Survey Graphic* 1, no. 28 (1939): 423–30.

Griswold del Castillo, Richard. "Myth and Reality: Chicano Economic Mobility in Los Angeles, 1850–1880." *Aztlán* 6 (1975): 153–54.

Gutman, Herbert G. "Work: Culture, and Society in Industrializing America, 1815–1919." *American Historical Review* 3 (1973): 550–75.

Handlin, Oscar, and Mary Handlin. "The New History and Ethnic Factor in American Life." *Perspectives on American History* 4 (1970): 5–24.

Handman, Max S. "San Antonio: The Old Capital City of Mexican Life and Influence." *Survey Graphic* 66 (1931): 160–68.

———. "Economic Reason for the Coming of the Mexican Immigrant." *American Journal of Sociology* 25 (January, 1930): 601–11.

Hareven, Tamara K. "The History of the Family as an Interdisciplinary Field." *Journal of Interdisciplinary History* 2 (1971): 25–40.

"A History of LULAC, Part I." *LULAC News* 36 (1974): 10.

Jones, Robert C. "Ethnic Family Patterns: The Mexican Family in the United States," *American Journal of Sociology* 53 (1948): 450–53.

Laslett, Barbara. "Production, Reproduction and Social Change: The Family in Historical Perspective." In *The State of Sociology: Problems and Prospects*, ed. James F. Short, Jr., Beverly Hills, Calif.: Sage Pub-

restaurada, 1867–1876." *Aztlán* 14, no. 2 (1984): 267–87.

Maitlan, Ralph. "San Antonio, the Shame of Texas." *Forum and Century* 102 (1939): 50–54.

Manuel, H. T. "Education of Mexican and Spanish-speaking Children in Texas." In *Education and the Mexican American*, ed. Carlos Cortez. New York: Arno Press, 1974.

———. "Education, the Guardian of Democracy and the Hope of Youth." *LULAC News* 7, no. 3 (November, 1940): 1.

———. "The Mexican Population of Texas." *Southwestern Social Science Quarterly* 15 (1934): 29–51.

Márquez, Benjamin. "The Politics of Race and Class: The League of Latin American Citizens in the Post World War II Period." *Social Science Quarterly* 68, no. 1 (March, 1987): 84–101.

Martínez, F. T. "Harmony and Unity: The Means to Solidify Our Leagues." *LULAC News* 7, no. 3 (November, 1940): 3.

Martinez, John R. "Leadership and Politics." In *La Raza: Forgotten Americans*, ed. Julián Samora, pp. 47–62. Notre Dame, Ind.: University of Notre Dame Press, 1966.

Medeiros, Francine. "*La Opinión*, a Mexican Exile Newspaper: A Content Analysis of Its First Years, 1926–1929." *Aztlán* 11 (Spring, 1980): 67–85.

Moore, Joan. "Social Class Assimilation and Acculturation." In *Proceedings of the 1968 Annual Spring Meeting of the American Ethnological Society*, ed. June Helm. Seattle: University of Washington Press, 1968.

Parenti, Michael. "Ethnic Politics and Ethnic Identification." *American Political Science Review* 61 (1967): 718–25.

Park, Robert E. "Human Migration and the Marginal Man." *American Journal of Sociology* 23 (1928): 890–900.

———. "Racial Assimilation in Secondary Groups" *American Journal of Sociology* (1914).

Perales, Alonzo S. "Nuestra actuel forma de gobierno y nuestra lucha en prode justicia social," *El Pueblo: Periodico Nacionalista*, March 24, 1938.

Perry, George Sessions. "The González Family: How Our People Live." *Saturday Evening Post*, October 20, 1948, pp. 50–60.

———. "Rumpled Angel of the Slums." *Saturday Evening Post*, August 21, 1948, pp. 47–55.

Porter, Rebecca N. "Three Days of Romance." *Survey* 3 (1931): 420–26.

"Public Housing Day Comes to San Antonio." *America* 2 (August 31, 1940): 570.

Raat, W. Dirk. "Auguste Comte, Gabino Barreda, and Positivism in Mexico." *Aztlán* 14 (1984): 235–51.

———. "Auguste Comte, the Positive Philosophy," in *The Age of Porfirio Diaz: Selected Readings*, ed. Carlos B. Gil. Albuquerque: University of New Mexico Press, 1977.

———. "Ideas and Society in Don Porfirio's Mexico." *The Americas* 30 (July, 1973): 32–53.

———. "The Diplomacy of Suppression: Los Revoltosos: Mexico, and the United States, 1906–1911." *Hispanic American Historical Review* 56 (November, 1976): 529–50.

Redfield, Robert. "The Folk Society." *American Journal of Sociology* 52 (1940): 300–308.

Rice, Jacqueline. "Beyond the Científicos: The Educational Background of the Porfirian Political Elite." *Aztlán* 14, no. 2 (1984): 289–305.

Romo, Ricardo. "The Urbanization of Southwestern Chicanos in the Early 20th Century." In *New Directions in Chicano Scholarship*, ed. Ricardo Romo and Raymund Paredes, pp. 183–207. La Jolla: University of California, San Diego, 1978.

Rosenthal, Erick. "Acculturation without Assimilation?" *American Journal of Sociology* 88 (1960): 275–88.

Sabin, E. L. "Cow Capital." *Saturday Review of Literature* 29 (1946): 15–20.

Sánchez, George I. "Americanism." *LULAC News* 7, no. 3 (November, 1940): 3–4.

———. "The American of Mexican Descent." *Chicago Jewish Forum* 20, no. 2 (Winter, 1961–62): 42–45.

Shapiro, Harold A. "The Pecan Shellers of San Antonio, Texas." *Southwestern Social Science Quarterly* 32, no. 4 (1952): 230–33.

Sheldon, Paul M. "Community Participation and the Emerging Middle Class." In *La Raza: Forgotten Americans*, ed. Julián Samora, pp. 125–57. Notre Dame, Ind.: University of Notre Dame Press, 1966.

Simpson, Lewis. "The Southern Recovery of Memory and History." *Sewanee Review* 82 (1974): 1–32.

Skirius, John. "Barreda, Vasconcelos, and the Mexican Educational Re-

A *Catholic Family Magazine* 24, no. 4 (1946): 100–107.

Weeks, O. Douglas. "The League of United Latin American Citizens: A Texas-Mexican Civic Organization." *Political and Social Science Quarterly* 10 (1929): 257–78.

———. "The Texas-Mexican and the Politics of South Texas." *American Political Science Review* 24 (August, 1930): 606–27.

White, O. P. "Machine Mode." *Collier's*, September 18, 1937.

Willems, Emilio. "Peasantry and City: Cultural Persistence and Change in Historical Perspective. *American Anthropologist* 72 (1970): 540–60.

Young, Kimball. "Immigrant Groups in California." *University of Oregon Publications* 1, no. 11 (July, 1922).

BOOKS

Acuña, Rodolfo. *Occupied America: A History of Chicanos*, 3d ed. New York: Harper & Row, 1988.

Alexander, Charles C. *Holding the Line: The Eisenhower Era, 1952–1961*. Bloomington: Indiana University Press, 1975.

Allen, Frederick Lewis. *The Big Change: America Transforms Itself, 1900–1950*. New York: Harper, 1952.

Ambrose, Stephen E. *Eisenhower*. New York: Simon & Schuster, 1983.

American G. I. Forum of Texas and Texas State Federation of Labor. *What Price Wetbacks?* Austin, 1955.

Aniol, Claude B. *San Antonio: City of Missions*. San Antonio: Naylor Company, 1942.

Arenas, Reinaldo. *Farewell to the Sea.* New York: Penguin Books, 1986.

Arnold, Charles August. *The Folklore, Manners, and Customs of the Mexicans in San Antonio, Texas.* 1928. Reprint, San Francisco: R&E Research Associates, 1971.

Babbit, J. F. *The San Antonio Public School System: A Survey.* San Antonio: School Board, 1914.

Balderama, Francisco E. *In Defense of la Raza: The Los Angeles Mexican Consulate and the Mexican Community, 1929–1936.* Tucson: University of Arizona Press, 1982.

Barrera, Mario. *Race and Class in the Southwest: A Theory of Racial Inequality.* Notre Dame, Ind.: University of Notre Dame Press, 1979.

Berger, Peter L. *The Homeless Mind: Modernization and Consciousness.* New York: Random House, 1974.

Berger, Peter, and Thomas Luckmann. *The Social Construction of Reality: A Treatise in the Sociology of Knowledge.* N.p., 1966.

Berryman, Phillip. *Liberation Theology: The Essential Facts about the Revolutionary Movement in Latin America and Beyond.* New York: Pantheon Books, 1987.

Blackwelder, Julia Kirk. *Women of the Depression: Caste and Culture in San Antonio, 1929–1939.* College Station: Texas A&M University Press, 1984.

Bodnar, John. *The Transplanted: A History of Immigrants in Urban America.* Bloomington: University of Indiana Press, 1985.

Boggs, Carl. *Gramsci's Marxism.* London: Pluto Press, 1976.

Boorstin, Daniel J. *The Americans: The Democratic Experience.* New York: Random House, 1973.

Bradbury, Malcolm, ed. *The American Novel and the 1920's.* London: Arnold Press, 1971.

Burns, James MacGregor. *Roosevelt: The Lion and the Fox.* New York: Harcourt, Brace, 1965.

Bushick, F. H. *Glamorous Days.* San Antonio: Naylor Company, 1934.

Business Men's Club. *San Antonio, Texas through a Camera.* San Antonio, n.p., ca. 1905.

Byron, Anthony. *The Politics of the Porfiriato.* Bloomington: Indiana University Press, 1973.

Camarillo, Alberto. *Chicanos in a Changing Society: From Mexican Pueblos to American Barrios in Santa Barbara and Southern California, 1848–1930.* Cambridge: Harvard University Press, 1979.

Carranza, Eliu. *Pensamientos on los Chicanos: A Cultural Revolution.* Berkeley: California Book Co., 1969.

Chabot, Frederick Charles. *Genealogies of the Early Latin, Anglo-American, and German Families.* San Antonio: Naylor, 1937.

———. *San Antonio and Its Beginnings.* San Antonio: Artes Gráficas, 1936.

———. *With the Makers of San Antonio: Genealogies of the Early Latin, Anglo-American and German Families.* San Antonio: Artes Gráficas, 1937.

Chavez, John R. *The Lost Land: The Chicano Image of the Southwest.* Albuquerque: University of New Mexico Press, 1984.

Clecak, Peter. *America's Quest for the Ideal Self: Dissent and Fulfillment*

Corwin, Arthur F., ed. *Immigrants and Immigrants: Perspectives on Mexico's Labor Migration to the United States.* Westport, Conn.: Greenwood Press, 1979.

Crawford, Fred R. *The Forgotten Egg: An Exploration into Mental Health Problems among Mexican-American Families and Their Children.* Austin: Texas State Department of Public Health, 1961.

Croly, Herbert. *The Promise of American Life.* Princeton, N.J.: Princeton University Press, 1985.

Curtis, Albert. *Fabulous San Antonio.* San Antonio: Naylor Company, 1955.

Dahl, Robert. *Who Governs?* New Haven: Yale University Press, 1961.

Davis, Edward. *The White Scourge.* San Antonio: Naylor Company, 1940.

De la Cuevo, Mario, et al. *Major Trends in Mexican Philosophy.* Notre Dame, Ind.: University of Notre Dame Press, 1966.

De León, Arnoldo. *The Tejano Community, 1836–1900.* Albuquerque: University of New Mexico Press, 1982.

———. *They Called Them Greasers: Anglo Attitudes toward Mexicans in Texas, 1821–1900.* Austin: University of Texas Press, 1983.

Dewey, John. *Democracy and Education, Middle Works.* New York: Free Press, 1966.

———. *Education Today.* New York: G. P. Putnam & Sons, 1940.

Diggins, John P. *The Lost Soul of American Politics: Virtue, Self-Interest, and the Foundations of Liberalism.* New York: Basic Books, 1984.

Durkheim, Emile. *Essays on Sociology and Philosophy.* D. R. Pocock, trans. Glencoe, Ill.: Free Press, 1953.

Einaudi, Mario. *The Roosevelt Revolution*. New York: Harcourt, Brace, 1959.

Evans-Pritchard, E. C. E. *The Sociology of Comte: An Appreciation.* Manchester: Manchester University Press, 1970.

Everett, Donald E. *San Antonio: The Flavor of Its Past, 1845–1898.* San Antonio: Trinity University Press, 1975.

Febvre, Lucien. A New Kind of History and Other Essays. New York: Harper Torch Books, 1973.

Federal Writers Project. *San Antonio: An Authoritative Guide to the City and Its Environs.* American Guide Series. San Antonio: Clegg Company, 1941.

———. *Texas: A Guide to the Lone Star State.* New York: Hastings House, 1940.

Fitzgerald, F. Scott. *The Great Gatsby.* New York: Charles Scribner's Sons, 1953.

Forcey, Charles. *The Crossroads of Liberalism: Croly, Weyl, Lippmann, and the Progressive Era, 1900–1925.* New York: Oxford University Press, 1961.

Foucault, Michel. *The Archaeology of Knowledge and the Discourse of Language.* New York: Pantheon Books, 1972.

———. *Language, Counter-Memory, Practice.* Donald F. Bouchard and Sherry Simon, trans. Ithaca, N.Y.: Cornell University Press, 1977.

———. *Power/Knowledge: Selected Interviews and Other Writings.* Colin Gordon, ed. New York: Pantheon, 1980.

Galarza, Ernesto. *Barrio Boy.* New York: Ballantine Books, 1971.

Gallegly, Joseph. *From Alamo Plaza to Jack Harris Saloon: O. Henry and the Southwest He Knew.* The Hague: Mouton, 1970.

Gamio, Manuel. *The Life Story of the Mexican Immigrant.* New York: Dover Publications, 1971.

———. *Mexican Immigration to the United States: A Study of Human Migration and Adaptation.* New York: Dover, 1971.

García, Jorge J. E., ed. *Latin American Philosophy in the Twentieth Century: Money, Values, and the Search for Philosophical Identity.* New York: Prometheus Books, 1986.

Garcia, Mario T. *Desert Immigrants: The Mexicans of El Paso, 1880–1920.* New Haven: Yale University Press, 1981.

Garcia, Mario T., et al., eds. *History, Culture, and Society in the 1930's.* Ypsilanti: Michigan Bilingual Press, 1983.

———. *Mexican Americans: Identity, Ideology, and Leadership.* New Haven: Yale University Press, 1989.

Garcia, Richard A. *Political Ideology: A Comparative Study of Three Chicano Youth Organizations.* San Francisco: R&E Research Associates, 1977.

García Naranjo, Nemesio. *Porfirio Díaz*. Mexico City: Editorial Letras, 1970.

Garrett, John. *The Citizens' Revolt*. San Antonio: Standard Printing Company, 1930.

Genovese, Eugene. *Roll Jordan Roll: The World the Slaves Made*. New York: Pantheon Books, 1975.

Gibson, Etienne. *The Philosophy of Saint Thomas Aquinas*. New York: Dorset Press, 1929.

que: University of New Mexico Press, 1967.

Gordon, Milton. *Assimilation in American Life: The Role of Race, Religion, and National Origins*. New York: Oxford University Press, 1964.

Gramsci, Antonio. *The Modern Prince and Other Writings*. New York: International Publishers, 1968.

Grebler, Leo, et al. *The Mexican-American People: The Nation's Second Largest Minority*. New York: Free Press, 1970.

Green, Peyton. *San Antonio: City in the Sun*. New York: McGraw-Hill.

Grimes, Alan Pendleton. *American Political Thought*. New York: Holt, Rinehart & Winston, 1960.

Griswold del Castillo, Richard. *La Familia: Chicano Families in the Urban Southwest, 1848 to the Present*. Notre Dame, Ind.: University of Notre Dame Press, 1984.

――――. *The Los Angeles Barrio, 1850–1890: A Social History*. Berkeley & Los Angeles: University of California Press, 1979.

Gutman, Herbert G. *Work, Culture, and Society in Industrializing America*. New York: Vintage Books, 1976.

Hanby, Alonzo L. *The New Deal: Analysis and Interpretation*. 1946.

Handlin, Oscar. *The Uprooted: The Epic Story of the Great Migrations That Made the American People*. New York: Little, Brown & Company, 1951.

Hansen, Harry, ed. *Texas: A Guide to the Lone Star State*. New York: Hastings House, 1969.

Hartz, Louis. *The Liberal Tradition in America*. New York: Harcourt, Brace, Jovanovich, 1955.

Helm, June, ed. *Proceedings of the 1968 Annual Spring Meeting of the American Ethnological Society*. Seattle: University of Washington Press, 1968.

Henderson, Richard B. *Maury Maverick: A Political Biography*. Austin: University of Texas Press, 1970.

Heusinger, Edward W. *San Antonio: A Chronology of Events*. San Antonio: Naylor Company, 1951.

Higham, John, ed. *Ethnic Leadership in America*. Baltimore: Johns Hopkins University Press, 1978.

Hodgson, Godfrey. *America in Our Time: From World War II to Nixon — What Happened and Why*. Garden City, N.Y.: Doubleday, 1976.

Hoffman, Abraham. *Unwanted Mexican-Americans in the Great Depression: Repatriation Pressures, 1929–1939*. Tucson: University of Arizona Press, 1974.

Hofstadter, Richard. *The Paranoid Style in American Politics*. New York: Knopf, 1966.

House, Boyce. *City of Flaming Adventure*. San Antonio: Naylor Company, 1949.

Howe, Irving. *World of Our Fathers: The Journey of the East European Jews*. New York: Harcourt, Brace, Jovanovich, 1976.

Hufford, Charles H. *The Social and Economic Effects of the Mexican Migration into Texas*. 1929. Reprint, San Francisco: R&E Research Associates, 1971.

Hundley, Morris, Jr., ed. *The Chicano*. Pacific Historical Review Series. Los Angeles: Clio Books, 1975.

Jamieson, Stuart. *Labor Unionism in American Agriculture*. Washington, D.C.: USGPO, 1945.

Jones, Lamar B. *Mexican-American Labor Problems in Texas*. 1963. Reprint, San Francisco: R&E Research Associates, 1965.

Jones, Robert, and Gustav L. Seligmann, Jr. *The Sweep of American History*. New York: John Wiley & Sons, 1981.

Karier, Clarence J., Paul C. Violas, and Joel Spring. *Roots of Crisis: American Education in the Twentieth Century*. Chicago: Rand McNally, 1973.

Kazin, Alfred. *An American Procession*. New York: Alfred A. Knopf, 1984.

Keller, Franklin J. *The Double-Purpose High School: Closing the Gap between Vocational and Academic Preparation*. New York: Harper & Brothers, 1953.

Kessner, Thomas. *The Golden Door: Italian and Jewish Immigrant Mobility in New York City, 1880–1915*. New York: Oxford University Press, 1977.

Kibbe, Pauline R. *Latin Americans in Texas*. Albuquerque: University of New Mexico Press, 1946.

Knox, William J. *The Economic Status of the Mexican Immigrant in San Antonio, Texas*. 1927. Reprint, San Francisco: R&E Research Associates, 1971.

Krieger, Murry. *The Aims of Representation: Subject/Text/History*. New York: Columbia University Press, 1987.

Krutch, Joseph Wood. *The Modern Temper: A Study and a Confession*. New York: Harcourt, Brace, Jovanovich, 1929.

Kusmer, Kenneth L. *A Ghetto Takes Shape: Black Cleveland, 1870–1930*.

Simon & Schuster, 1971.

Lentricchia, Frank. *Criticism and Social Change*. Chicago: University of Chicago Press, 1983.

Leuchtenburg, William E. *Franklin Roosevelt and the New Deal: 1932–1940*. New York: Harper & Row, 1963.

Levine, Lawrence, *Black Culture and Black Consciousness: Afro-American Folk Thought from Slavery to Freedom*. New York: Oxford University Press, 1977.

Levy, David W. *Herbert Croly of the New Republic: The Life and Thought of an American Progressive*. Princeton, N.J.: Princeton University Press, 1985.

Limerick, Patricia Nelson. *The Legacy of Conquest: The Unbroken Past of the American West*. New York: W. W. Norton, 1987.

Lowrie, Samuel H. *Cultural Conflict in Texas, 1821–1835*. New York: Columbia University Press, 1932.

Lukacs, Georg. *History and Class Consciousness: Studies in Marxist Dialectics*. Cambridge: MIT Press, 1971.

MacLachlan, Colin M., and Jaime E. Rodríguez. *The Forging of the Cosmic Race: A Reinterpretation of Colonial Mexico*. Berkeley & Los Angeles: University of California Press, 1980.

McWilliams, Carey. *North from Mexico: The Spanish-Speaking People of the United States*. New York: Greenwood Press, 1968.

Martínez, Oscar. *Border Boom Town: Ciudad Juárez since 1848*. Austin: University of Texas Press, 1978.

Márquez, Benjamin. *Power and Politics in a Chicano Barrio: A Study of Mobilization Effects and Community Power in El Paso, Texas (1960–1981)*. Lanham, Md.: University Press of America, 1985.

Maverick, Maury. *A Maverick America*. New York: Covici Priede, 1937.

Mazón, Mauricio. *The Zoot-Suit Riots: The Psychology of Symbolic Annihilation*. Austin: University of Texas Press, 1984.

Meinig, D. W. *Imperial Texas: An Interpretive Essay in Cultural Geography*. Austin: University of Texas Press, 1969.

————. *Southwest: Three Peoples in Geographical Change, 1600–1970*. New York: Oxford University Press, 1971.

Memmi, Albert. *The Colonizer and the Colonized*. Boston: Beacon Press, 1965.

Menefee, Seldon, and C. C. Cassmore. *The Pecan Shellers of San Antonio*. Washington, D.C.: GPO, 1940.

Mequire, Katherine H. *Educating the Mexican Child in the Elementary School*. 1938. Reprint, San Francisco: R&E Research Associates, 1973.

Meyer, Michael C. *Huerta: A Political Portrait*. Lincoln: University of Nebraska Press, 1972.

Meyer, Michael C., and William L. Sherman. *The Course of Mexican History*. 2d ed. New York: Oxford University Press, 1983.

Miller, Randall M., and Thomas D. Marzik, eds. *Immigrants and Religion in Urban America*. Philadelphia: Temple University Press, 1977.

Montejano, David. *Anglos and Mexicans in the Making of Texas, 1836–1986*. Austin: University of Texas Press, 1987.

Moore, L. O. *Education in the Community: San Antonio Public Affairs Forum Report*. San Antonio: San Antonio Public Schools, 1938.

Moquin, Wayne, and Charles Van Doren, eds. *A Documentary History of the Mexican-Americans*. New York: Bantam Books, 1971.

Morrison, Andrew, comp. *The City of San Antonio*. The Engelhardt Series: American Cities. San Antonio: Norman Brock Reprint, 1977.

Murry, Mary John. *A Socio-Cultural Study: 118 Mexican Families Living in a Low-Rent Public Housing Project in San Antonio*. Washington, D.C.: Catholic University Press, 1954.

Myrdal, Gunnar. *An American Dilemma: The Negro Problem and Modern Democracy*. New York: Pantheon, 1975.

Nelli, Humbert S. *The Italians in Chicago, 1880–1930*. New York: Oxford University Press, 1970.

Newcomb, Pearson. *The Alamo City*. San Antonio: Naylor, 1950.

Nixon, P. I. *A Century of Medicine in San Antonio*. San Antonio: Naylor Company, 1936.

Olvera, J. Montiel, ed. *Latin American Yearbook*. San Antonio: n.p., 1939.

Osofsky, Gilbert. *Harlem: The Making of a Negro Ghetto, 1890–1930*. New York: Harper & Row, 1963.

Pancost, Clara C., ed. *San Antonio, 1937 Social Directory*. San Antonio: Cless, 1937.

Park, Robert. *Race and Culture.* Glencoe, Ill.: Free Press, 1950.

Parr, Eunice Elvira. *A Comparative Study of Mexican and American Children.* 1926. Reprint, San Francisco: R&E Research Associates, 1971.

Patterson, Orlando. *Ethnic Chauvinism: The Reactionary Impulse.* New York: Stein & Day, 1977.

Paz, Octavio. *The Labyrinth of Solitude,* trans. Lysander Kemp. New York: Grove Press, 1961.

Pells, Richard H. *Radical Visions and American Dreams.* New York:

Perrett, Geoffrey. *America in the Twenties: A History.* stone, 1982.

Peyton, Green. *San Antonio: City in the Sun.* New York: McGraw Hill, 1946.

Picón-Salas, Mariano. *A Cultural History of Spanish America: From Conquest to Independence.* Irving A. Leonard, trans. Berkeley & Los Angeles: University of California Press, 1962.

Pitt, Leonard. *The Decline of the Californios: A Social History of the Spanish-speaking Californians, 1846–1890.* Berkeley & Los Angeles: University of California Press, 1966.

Poster, Mark S. *Critical Theory of the Family.* New York: Seabury Press, 1978.

———. *Foucault, Marxism, and History: Mode of Production versus Mode of Information.* Cambridge: Polity Press, 1984.

Potter, David. *People of Plenty: Economic Abundance and the American Character.* Chicago: University of Chicago Press, 1954.

Raat, W. Dirk. *Los Revoltosos: Mexico's Rebels in the United States, 1903–1923.* College Station: Texas A&M University Press, 1981.

Rachberg-Halton, Eugene. *Meaning and Modernity: Social Theory in the Pragmatic Attitude.* Chicago: University of Chicago Press, 1986.

Rischin, Moses. *The Promised City: New York's Jews, 1870–1914.* New York: Harper & Row, 1962.

Rodríguez, Jaime E., and Colin M. MacLachlan. *The Forging of the Cosmic Race: A Reinterpretation of Colonial Mexico.* Berkeley & Los Angeles: University of California Press, 1980.

Romano, Octavio. *Voices: Readings from El Grito.* Berkeley: Quinto Sol Books, 1973.

Romo, Ricardo. *East Los Angeles: History of a Barrio*. Austin: University of Texas Press, 1983.

Romo, Ricardo, and Raymond Paredes, eds. *New Directions in Chicano Scholarship*. La Jolla: University of California at San Diego, 1978.

Roth, Jack J., ed. *World War I: A Turning Point in Modern History*. New York: Alfred A. Knopf, 1967.

Rovere, Richard H. *Senator Joe McCarthy*. New York: Harcourt-Brace, 1959.

Saenz, J. Luz. *Los Mexicano-americanos en la gran guerra y su contingente en pro de la democracia, la humanidad y la justicia*. San Antonio: Artes Gráficas, 1933.

Salter, J. T., ed. *The American Politician*. Chapel Hill: University of North Carolina Press, 1938.

Samora, Julián. *La Raza: Forgotten Americans*. Notre Dame, Ind.: University of Notre Dame Press, 1966.

San Antonio Chamber of Commerce. *You Can Manufacture for Less in San Antonio*. San Antonio, 1934.

San Antonio Express. *San Antonio Express: 100 Years of Progress in South Texas*. 1965.

Sánchez, George T. *Concerning Segregation of Spanish-speaking Children in Public Schools*. Austin: University of Texas Press, 1951.

San Miguel, Guadalupe, Jr. *"Let All of Them Take Heed": Mexican-Americans and the Campaign for Educational Equality in Texas, 1910–1981*. Austin: University of Texas Press, 1987.

Saragoza, Alex M. *The Monterrey Elite and the Mexican State, 1880–1940*. Austin: University of Texas Press, 1988.

Sartre, Jean-Paul. *Anti-Semite and Jew*, trans. George J. Becker. New York: Schocken Books, 1965.

Schlesinger, Arthur M. *The American as Reformer*. New York: Atheneum, 1968.

———. *The Crisis of the Old Order: The Coming of the New Deal*. American Heritage Library, 1988.

———. *The Politics of Upheaval*. American Heritage Library, 1988.

———. *The Vital Center*. Da Capo, 1986.

Schmidt, Henry C. *The Roots of Lo Mexicano: Self and Society in Mexican Thought, 1900–1934*. College Station: Texas A&M University Press, 1978.

Servín, Manuel P. *The Mexican-Americans: An Awakening Minority*. Beverly Hills: Glencoe Press, 1970.

Shelby, T. H., and J. O. Marberry. *A Study of the Building Needs of San Antonio Senior High Schools*. Austin: University of Texas Bulletin, no. 2845, 1928.

Sherrard, Thomas D., ed. *Social Welfare and Urban Problems*. New York: Columbia University Press, 1968.

Simpson, Arthur J. *Southwest Texas Business and Professional Directory*. San Antonio: Southwest Publishing Company, 1941.

Singer, Marcus G. *American Philosophy*. Cambridge: Cambridge University Press, 1985.

Sloss-Vento, Adela. *Alonzo S. Perales: His Struggle for the Rights of Mexican-Americans*. San Antonio: Artes Gráficas, 1977.

Sonnichsen, Philip, ed. *Texas-Mexican Border Music, 1930-1960*. N.p., n.d.

Sowell, Thomas. *Ethnic America*. New York: Basic Books, 1981.

———. *Race and Economics*. New York: McKay, 1975.

Spicer, Edward H., and Raymond H. Thompson, eds. *Plural Society in the Southwest*. New York: Interbank, 1972.

Steinberg, Stephen. *The Ethnic Myth: Race, Ethnicity, and Class in America*. Boston: Beacon Press, 1981.

Steiner, Stan. *La Raza: The Mexican-Americans*. New York: Harper & Row, 1970.

Stone, I. F. *The Truman Era*. New York: Vintage Books, 1973.

Stumpf, Samuel E. *Socrates to Sartre: A History of Philosophy*. 2d ed. New York: McGraw-Hill, 1975.

Sturmberg, Robert. *History of San Antonio and the Early Days in Texas*. San Antonio: St. Joseph's Society, 1920.

Susman, Warren, ed. *Culture and Commitment: 1929-1945*. New York: George Braziller, 1973.

———, ed. *Culture as History: The Transformation of American Society in the Twentieth Century*. New York: Pantheon Books, 1984.

Taylor, Paul Schuster. *An American-Mexican Frontier, Nueces County, Texas*. New York: Russell & Russell, 1934.

Thompson, E. P. *The Making of the English Working Class*. New York: Vintage Books, 1963.

Tocqueville, Alexis de. *Democracy in America*. George Lawrence, trans., J. P. Mayer, ed. Garden City, N.Y.: Doubleday, 1969.

Trilling, Lionel. *Sincerity and Authenticity*. Cambridge: Harvard University Press, 1972.

Urrutia, Francisco. *Pinacoteca del Dr. Aureliano Urrutia.* San Antonio: Artes Gráficas, 1940.

Valentine, Charles. *Culture and Poverty.* Chicago: University of Chicago Press, 1968.

Vásquez, Richard. *Chicano.* Garden City, N.Y.: Doubleday, 1970.

Wangler, Alexander C., ed. *Archdiocese of San Antonio, 1874–1974.* San Antonio: Catholic Diocese, 1974.

Wiebe, Robert. *A Search for Order, 1877–1920.* New York: Hill & Wang, 1967.

Williams, Raymond. *The Sociology of Culture.* New York: Schocken Books, 1982.

Winters, Jet C. *A Report on the Health of Mexicans Living in Texas.* Austin: University of Texas Bulletin, no. 3127, July 15, 1931.

Woods, Frances Jerome. *Mexican Ethnic Leadership in San Antonio, Texas.* Washington, D.C.: Catholic University of America Press, 1949.

Woolford, Sam. *San Antonio: A History of Tomorrow.* San Antonio: Naylor Company, 1963.

Wright, S. J. *San Antonio de Bexar: Historical, Traditional, Legendary.* Austin: Morgan Printing Company, 1916.

Wuthnow, Robert, et al. *Cultural Analysis: The Work of Peter L. Berger, Mary Douglas, Michel Foucault, and Jürgen Habermas.* London: Routledge & Kegan Paul, 1984.

Yans-McLaughlin, Virginia. *Family and Community: Italian Immigrants in Buffalo, 1880–1930.* Ithaca, N.Y.: Cornell University Press, 1977.

Young, Kimball, ed. *Social Attitudes.* New York: Henry Holt, 1931.